The Trail
of
the Loup

The Trail
of
the Loup

Being a History of the
Loup River Region with
Some Chapters on the State

H.W. Foght

Introduction by William Beachly

Hastings College Press | Hastings, Nebraska

Introduction © 2016 by Hastings College Press

Text © 1906 by H.W. Foght and W.W. Haskell. This book has fallen into the public domain and is no longer subject to copyright protection.

All rights reserved. No part of this book may be used or reproduced in any manner whatsoever without permission from the publisher, except in the case of brief quotations embodied in critical articles and reviews.

Production Staff
Emilie Barnes
Megan Beirow
Jordan Brown
Natalee Hanway
Nicole Havlik
Alexandria Kreikemeier
Gabrielle Rodgers
Makenzie Shofner
Carly Spotts-Falzone
Jeri Thompson
Anna Weber

ISBN-10: 1942885296
ISBN-13: 978-1-942885-29-0

Dedication
To all those early "trailers of the Loup," living and dead, who by their indomitable courage and energy overcame all obstacles of nature and redeemed for civilization and enlightenment the beautiful Valley of the Loup, in order that we, their children, might reap in fullest measure the fruits of their sowing, this book, is affectionately dedicated. By the author.

Note on the text: This edition has been reset from the first (1906) edition. The text has been edited for accuracy and consistency, and some images have been moved from their original locations. Punctuation has been modernized.

Manufactured in the United States of America.

Text is printed on acid-free, chlorine-free paper with 30% postconsumer recycled content. Cover is printed on 100% recycled paper.

Contents

Introduction vii

Introductory xix

    I Some Physical Features of Nebraska 1

   II The Aborigines. 17

  III Glimpses of State History 31

  IV Glimpses of the North Loup Valley 49

   V Cowboy Regime and Forerunners of
      Civilization 63

  VI Coming of the Pioneers 79

 VII Organization of Valley County—
      Early Politics. 101

VIII The Memorable Year 1873. 113

  IX Indians and Grasshoppers 129

   X Fort Hartsuff, Its Rise and Fall 137

  XI Village Organization. 143

 XII The Middle Loup and Arcadia 159

XIII The Further History of Garfield County 169

XIV Loup County and Its Possibilities 191

 XV Scotia and Her Builders 199

XVI Harrowing Tales of a Third of a Century. . . .209

XVII Changes Down Through the Years 229

XVIII The Newspaper and the Valley 239

XIX	The Critical Period in Loup Valley History	.247
XX	The Brave Men and Women Who Opened the "Trail of the Loup"	.261
XXI	The Men and Women Who Are Making the History of the Loup Valley	.307

About the Author. 353

Introduction

William Beachly

Wallace Stegner once called the West "the native home of hope," by which he was referring to the resiliency of intentions, if not outcomes. The settlement of the Middle and North Loup Valleys is a microcosm of the wanderlust that infected Euro-Americans of the nineteenth century but in the realization of dreams, details matter. We are offered here a detailed view of one drop in a much larger pond, where the causes and consequences are intimately shaped by the landscape, climate, and soils but tethered to policies and politics from afar. The 98th Meridian, where the Loup forks conjoin, marks the western edge of tallgrass prairie and the eastern range limit of prairie dogs. Stegner's West is entered here and his summary of its optimism rings true here as well: "When [the West] fully learns that cooperation, not rugged individualism, is the quality that most characterizes and preserves it, then it will have achieved itself and outlived its origins. Then it has a chance to create a society to match its scenery" (38). One could well argue that Pawnee had already done so in the 1800s; they had found a way to live here with a sense of belonging without the taint of ambition to always have more, the very ambition which would press upon their margins and ultimately rout them. But if there were a singular purpose to the usurpers, we would miss the mark by focusing on doctrines and destinies, however manifest, without recalling the simple act that Mari Sandoz described so well:

> Somewhere, some evening, the homeseeker would drop the wagon tongue with finality, water and hobble his team while his wife bent over the supper fire of dead wood or buffalo chips. Afterward they might lean against a wagon wheel, the baby at the woman's breast, and look out over the prairie gilded by a sky that blazed beyond anything they ever saw in the country left behind them, almost any country. The man might test the grass with his teeth, consider last year's sunflower stalks to gauge the earth's fertility, the height he would expect his corn to grow. Perhaps he dragged a spade from the wagon, struck it deep into the ground, shook out a sod to examine the root system, tried

a ball of soil in his hand and nodded to himself. This was the place. (120)

Harold W. Foght (1869–1954) published this historical trove on the Loup lands in 1906, recalling his own time here as a cowhand and rural school teacher. It is a sweeping history of a region very close to his heart: the Loup Rivers region of central Nebraska, particularly the North and Middle Loup Rivers, which have their origins in the Nebraska Sand Hills. The Sand Hills had belatedly been recognized as excellent grazing country, but in this time of transition, settlers were attempting to crop the river bottoms in a region that averages only 18 inches of rainfall during a growing season. Of course, averages mean little in this region of extremes: blizzards in late spring, drought in midsummer, ice storms in autumn, and cattle-entombing drifts in winter. Foght collected oral histories from early settlers, combed newspaper and county records, photographed historic buildings, and summarized other sources to get a holistic view of this area's history. Even if you've never thought about or visited central Nebraska, this book will make you want to. Central Nebraska is a true gem of unique and inspiring landscapes.

Educator and Scholar

Born in Norway in 1869, Foght emigrated with his family from Fredrickshall, Norway, to join his father, Emil, at Fort Niobrara in the Dakota Territory in 1881. Then frightened by the Spotted Tail-Crow Dog incident, the family moved to Ord when Harold was 11 years old (as described in Emil John Foght's biography, pp. 272–73 of this book). In his Introductory to this book, he describes himself as "then a little chap herding cattle in the valley above Ord," who "according to his daily wont, reclined one day in his retreat in a shaded nook on the banks of the river, while his charges were left to shift for themselves; and well they might, for was not the prairie theirs for miles around! He dreamed all enrapt in the charm of the virgin prairie, dreamed of things yet to be" (50).

After the publication of *The Trail of the Loup*, Foght went on to write articles and books on rural education as a professor of sociology at the State Normal School in Kirksville, Missouri, and as president of the Northern Normal and Industrial School at Aberdeen, South Dakota (Ohles 113). His dual focus on education and settlement of the land emphasized the increasing importance of agricultural education in the early twentieth century, as established by the 1862 Morrill Act, which allowed states to set aside public land for land-grant colleges; the 1872 Hatch Act, which established experiment stations for original agricultural research; and the 1914 Smith-Lever Act, which bridged the gap between researchers and farmers.

In a 1912 article called "The Country School," Foght links the dual phenomena of increased industrialization in agriculture and the exodus of people from farms to the city, prophesizing, "Those who have been exploiting the soil must give way before the husbandman farmer. He is soon to possess the land. When this comes to pass, the desertion of the rural community by the people who should furnish it both intelligence and vigorous life will end" (149). I cannot but compare his prophecy to that presented by Wendell Berry in *The Unsettling of America* sixty-five years later: "The standard of the exploiter is efficiency, the standard of the nurturer is care… Whereas the exploiter asks of a piece of land only how much and how quickly can it be made to produce, the nurturer asks a question that is much more complex and difficult: What is its carrying capacity?" (7). Foght had argued the "city school" in which most educators receive their credentials is more of the former than the latter. Education is not the handmaiden of industry, and efficiency for the sake of one cog is the ruin of all.

Foght served seven years (1927–1933) as president of the financially troubled Municipal University of Wichita (Ohles 114). With its aeronautics and oil wells, Wichita was already poised to become a part of the military-industrial complex. In 1927 Foght and his wife were invited to tour schools in Japan and occupied Formosa. Impressed by the modernization of Formosa's agricultural and educational institutions under Japanese rule, they wrote a book ironically titled *Unfathomed Japan* in which Foght seems oblivious to signs that imperialist Japanese expansion could ultimately draw the United States into WWII: "The changes that have come about on the Island within the thirty-three years of Japanese possession speak well for Japan's greatness as a colonizing people" (341).

The *Wichita Beacon* of June 1 and 2, 1933, reported that Foght was embroiled in a conflict with the Board of Directors at Wichita over the hiring of athletic coaches (by his predecessor), and in spite of student protests to retain him, Foght resigned his presidency and moved to California. Subsequently, he became a director of a Navajo Agency school, a superintendent of education of the Cherokee Tribe, and in 1934 administrator of FDR's New Deal policies in the Bureau of Indian Affairs. As John R. Finger describes in *Cherokee Americans*, in many ways this marked a reversal of our government's pogroms against Indian cultural expression. Fought encouraged traditional basketry, wood carving, and pottery as sources of tourist income, while also emphasizing modern vocational and agricultural skills in the curriculum. The Cherokee tradition of communal tribal ownership and Foght's inclusion of traditional culture and crafts in their education would soon encounter resistance from an emerging anti-communist hysteria in Congress and, curiously, among other tribal representatives. After a series of accusations against his educational initiatives as "atheism, communism, and un-Americanism" Foght responded, "The only astonishing thing to me is that the propaganda used could so utterly mislead people who ordinarily do their own thinking" (Finger 91).

The Trail of the Loup

Foght was both impressed by the pace of settlement in this former wilderness and concerned prophetically with the post-settlement isolation of rural educators from productive collaborations. It was a time of "progressive" transition from education for its own sake to vocational training for an increasingly industrialized country. While educational theory would embrace the ideas of Pavlov and Thorndike, Foght urged rural schools to practice nature study by exploration, tree-planting, and gardening. For instance, he reiterated Theodore Roosevelt's injunction to school children to celebrate Arbor Day: "So any nation which in its youth lives only for the day, reaps without sowing, and consumes without husbanding, must expect the penalty of the prodigal… A people without children would face a hopeless future; a country without trees is almost as hopeless" (*The American Rural School* 178–79).

In his appendices to *The American Rural School*, Foght also outlines specific curricular topics and activities to engage students at each grade in nature study of a nearby brook or interpretation of the landscape around them. He encourages journaling about the seasonal events in wildlife events, local agriculture, and meteorology. For example,

> The spring shower comes up suddenly; the room darkens and the children cannot see to work. This is the time to have them feel the part that the rain storm takes in their lives. It will be restful

> to lay all books aside, clear the desks, and study the shower.
> Can the rain be heard on the roof? How cheery it sounds! With
> closed eyes you know the drops are coming down thick and fast.
> Let us go to the windows. It is interesting to watch the water
> dash against the panes and roll down; to see it falling on the trees
> and flowers; to think what it means to the fields. (341)

And I particularly like this next bit, after the shower…

> The wise teacher will go out with the children to see the results
> of the storm … she may take this opportunity for teaching some
> of the land and water forms, for after a shower these are present
> in miniature and best taught afield… Who will be the first to
> find an island, a peninsula, a lake, a mountain, a valley, a delta, a
> mountain range? (342)

He advocates for art in the schools, particularly modeling of landforms in clay or sand, and further exercises in crafts, textiles, and woodworking. His idea of industry always includes ecology, the understanding of interrelations among what we bring and what was here before us.

This emphasis on hands-on ecological education certainly has an influence on Foght's gem, *The Trail of the Loup*, which documents the effects of industrialization, agriculture, and settlers' culture on the ecology of the Loup country in the late nineteenth century. Take his account of the felling of sheltered, "centuries old" stands of eastern red cedar and ponderosa pine, for instance. Early settlements and railroads demanded lumber, but in particular he bemoans the cost of Fort Hartsuff, quoting Truman Freeland: "The Jones Canyon, which is now a dreary waste of broken cliffs and naked ravines with scarcely a bush ten feet high, was then heavily timbered, the tall graceful pines stood by the thousands on the hillsides … this evergreen forest was the haunt of thousands of bright-plumaged birds … and bore not the mark of a single woodsman's axe in 1871" (139). I've found a few old Ponderosas clinging precariously to cliff sides or perched on a knife-edge ridge in the isolated reaches of Jones Canyon, and some stands remain in the rough canyons of Custer county, while the high ridges of Valley county still have a few ancient groves of bur oak tucked into their folds. For the most part, however, these centuries-old stands never recovered from the destruction described by Foght, and the bison, elk, and wolf—the Loup was named for the wolf—disappeared with the trees.

His stage-setting chapter, accurate in its time, outlines the geologic history of the region; its description of soils and drainages is based largely on Samuel Aughey's summary in Andreas' *History of the State of Nebraska* (1882) and other research from the geologic surveys of the University of Nebraska. On the whole his geologic picture is accurate up to Cenozoic times. The main inaccuracy is the interpretation (probably originated by Ferdinand V. Hayden in the 1850s) of the stream-borne outwash of the Rockies as lake deposits, which in Foght's time were attributed to the Pliocene Epoch. We now know these range (from West to East) in age from Oligocene to Miocene, capped by the widespread Ogallala Group limestones that underlie the soft deposits of the region. Pliocene streams reworked many of these sediments and cast gravel beds that groundwater streams follow to this day. The erroneous interpretation of the loess and sands as being part of a giant lake bed (covering most of Nebraska, in Foght's account) has been supplanted by more recent origins of these soils. While there are some interesting prehistoric lake deposits, revealed along parts of the upper Niobrara and in the Chalk Mines of Scotia, we now know wind was the agent that brought the loess deposits and sand hills here during the Pleistocene and Holocene. In fact, central Nebraska has some of the thickest and most widespread loess deposits, and certainly the Sand Hills are the largest dune field in this hemisphere. Only China has comparable loess deposits. Foght's book has important photographs of curious landforms in the Loess Canyons of the region and Toadstool Park (in Nebraska's Northwest corner).

Of Toadstool Foght writes,

> The writer has personally inspected these regions, and nowhere is the story of the past told in more forcible language than in this vast graveyard. Banks full of fossil bones, baccolites, huge petrified tortoises and fossil leaves tell the story of how Nebraska looked in those times ... Indeed, a semi tropical vegetation stretched far away towards the Poles. Droves of Miocene horses frequented the lake shores, the ancestral hog wallowed in the bogs, flockes of monkeys chattered in the treetops, and plain and forest were the haunt and breeding ground of droves of huge mastadons [*sic*] and wicked-eyed rhinoceroces and tapirs. Such then were the Ma-koo-si-teka, or hard-lands to travel over, as the Sioux nomad has seen fit to describe these regions. (9)

Well, maybe not monkeys, but who's to fault Foght when the famous nineteenth-century paleontologist E. D. Cope thought they might be here and H. F. Osborne later identified a peccary tooth as belonging to an archaic hominid he called "Nebraska Man"? This very same quote (minus the first clause) is repeated in Dale P. Stough's 1921 *Histories of Hamilton, York and Clay Counties* (with attribution in the preface to Foght and Aughey). There were tarsier-sized primates here during the Eocene Thermal Maximum, which ended in a big chill around 34 million years ago, but not since. Across the river from Ord he describes a former lake bed of "Miocene" age (now limited to 23–5.3 million years ago), and even a waterfall on the North Loup with a 12-foot drop and 50-foot breadth as "the second largest in the state," which now may have retreated deep into the Sand Hills. (Horseshoe Falls and Big Falls in Cherry county are the only named waterfalls on the North Loup, but neither is the size described by Foght.)

Foght wouldn't have known about the Valley County Woodland site, excavated in the 1930s, but does provide an account of the movements and conflicts of "the aborigines"—who lived here before the trappers, cavalry dragoons, Civil War veterans, European refugees, and the Kinkaiders. Subsequent chapters offer a nice summary of the history of plains exploration from the Spaniards to Major Long and the early history of Nebraska Territory. He is particularly sympathetic to the plight of the once-mighty Pawnee who were decimated by smallpox and cholera. They were incessantly at war with their erstwhile foes, the Sioux, and were both feared and pitied by immigrant families. Indeed, part of the mission of Fort Hartsuff was to protect Pawnee who were relocated downstream along the Loup Forks where the Skidi band had historic villages.

Following these the focus is on the Middle and North Loup Valleys in fine detail: the lives of colorful figures like Happy Jack Swearingen, Conrad Wentworth, and many others. Excellent photographs accompany stories from the diaries of Danes, Seventh-Day Baptists, and a host of others whose firsthand accounts are lively. Foght attended high school in Ord and probably knew many of these settlers' families. When he would later write a thesis for Augustana University, it would be about the Norse explorers who set the first European footprints on this continent and the mystery of how far they wandered inland.

Whatever those Norsemen encountered in the New World, they were alone, unlike the early settlers of Loup country who hailed from Denmark and many other European nations and had to be interdependent to survive. Willa Cather's writings help us to understand the language barriers they faced, but most of them were farmers or direct descendants of farmers, which was then like a common language. Some were part of a second-generation diaspora, whose parents may have settled in Wisconsin or Ohio but could not resist the lure of open country. One wonders if they saw this as destiny, or if each just saw opportunity for their material needs. But dreams of what a new land can bring are often flawed, and many could not survive the hardships without a determination that, it seems, went well beyond their personal desires. But Foght does not go there: as far as motives go, his is not a postmodern analysis, but neither is it romanticized. He sticks to plain accounts from the diaries that are not very introspective. Yet the power of these stories, as retold by Foght, remains.

East of Cotesfield, across the North Loup River, is a rugged line of loess bluffs and canyons where one little tragedy unfolded in the Easter Blizzard of '73. It is the story of Emma Cooper. Emma's father and brother had been away to town and as the blizzard raged outside the fuel ran out so Emma and her sister left their aging mother alone in search of firewood. They were soon lost and sheltered in a canyon as snow covered their refuge under a bank. Emma shivered in total darkness as her sister's embrace grew cold. The next day she wandered out in the blowing snow and was spotted, miraculously, by a neighbor. Their mother had gone outside in search of the girls and a trail of clothing led to her frozen body. Emma led a sad and lonely life after the tragedy. Being alone would be the specter that haunted so many in the territories.

The darkness of winter brought scavenging bands of Sioux into conflict with the settlers. You can still visit the site of the Pebble Creek "battle," one of the last conflicts in the area, but the settlers had no weapons against the plague of grasshoppers that descended on their crops the following summer. Just consider this scene: "At first some of the settlers made vain attempts to scare the pests from their fields, but this was usually rewarded by having the clothes eaten literally from off their limbs... In places branches of trees are said to have been bent almost to the ground under their living burden" (136). Nor were they prepared for that blizzard of April 1873, the night after a mild spring Easter shower blessed already planted fields, that "filled canyons forty feet deep to the very top, and it became hard enough for a man to walk across on the crust" (125). Many livestock sheds were filled to the rafters, and a number of settlers, like poor Emma's mother, wandered desperately to their doom. One family was survived only by a six-month-old infant, found clutching to her mother's cold breast. Natural tragedies would continue with the prairie fires of '78, the hail of '85, the blizzard of '88, and the drought of '90. Add to this the bank failures, misrepresentations by Eastern land investors, cattle barons harassing sodbusters—the tale of Print Olive is recounted in some detail—and the speculations about rail access, and settlers must have felt like rats in an operant box, not knowing when the next shock will come.

But Foght recounts the lighter moments as well, such as the fevered anticipation of many settlers that a railroad would eventually favor their location. When the City of Ord made elaborate plans for the first Union Pacific train in 1886 it didn't come, but a year later an extension of the Burlington and Missouri railroad came by surprise. Only later, when railroads refused to pay property taxes, did these communities actually "look the gift horse in the mouth." Foght recounts the comical misappropriations of the ballot box to decide the Garfield county seat between the contenders of Burwell and Willow Springs. Then there was the high-spirited competition between rival Republican and Populist Democratic newspapers in Ord of the 1880s and other upstarts like the *Quiz*, the *Prohibition Star*, and the *Blizzard*. One paper, the *Loyalist*, apparently died with panache: a scathing editorial that accused North Loupers of "things that would look anything but complementary [*sic*] should they be repeated here" (243).

Loup county is interesting in its dual geographic character: bisected by the North Loup River, with loess canyons to the south and sand hills to the north. A close call (merely two votes) resulted in Taylor becoming the county seat over Almeria. I personally own land near Almeria and visit this area often to kayak on the North Loup or simply enjoy the peaceful landscape around the river. I agree with Foght's assessment that "to have land holdings in Loup county is now to be fortunate" but not for the reasons he cites. He extolled the value of introduced brome grass and bluegrass and its apple orchards. But its enduring wealth is in the native grasslands, and scarcely a better example can be seen than to travel up Pleasant Valley Road, which begins northwest of Almeria. Meanwhile the loess canyons are losing valuable forage every year to the eastern red cedar invasion. In 2000, Myrtle Hall and her brothers bequeathed nearly two thousand acres of these canyons cut into the high divide between the North and Middle Loup to the Nebraska Game and Parks Commission, which is now restoring their native character with cedar removal and prescribed burning. Exploration of these secluded hollows is not easy, as the loess holds in nearly vertical slopes studded with yucca and cacti. One is amazed that a prairie can grow at such a steep pitch in soils that absorb moisture poorly even when level.

These little gems prompt me to begin a quest, to find the remnant stand of ancient trees in some shadowed, deep loess gorge, or perhaps the waterfall that may or may not still exist. It is my hope that bringing this book to your hands will encourage you to visit this beautiful area and seek to learn more of its wildlife, natural resources, and history. Perhaps you have already met some of its interesting people, including the "quiet folk" of Taylor, painted as one artist's passion in black and white on plywood cutouts, or visited bustling Burwell during the rowdy rodeo. You can take a lazy float down the Calamus River in a cattle tank, or rise before dawn on a chilly spring day to watch prairie chickens dance at a lek. Once, camping in autumn on the Calamus Reservoir, I was treated to the sight of six whooping cranes wading along the sandy shoreline along with dozens of sandhill cranes and pelicans. A visit to Fort Hartsuff and the Dowse Sod House may prompt you to reflect on the loneliness of frontier life. Maybe you will try popped blue corn from North Loup, or a Danish pizza in Dannebrog, or just wonder at the strange hills you pass through south of Ord. On a tour you might learn the Chalk Mines of Scotia were formed as diatoms settled in a Miocene lake bed or you might trudge up the many steps to peer out over the North Loup Valley from Happy Jack Hill. From this eagle's vantage point, time's long workings of the river and its sandbars can be seen for miles, the "cat steps" formed in the steep loess slopes are evident, and in the canyons, centuries-old oak trees and linden betray a relict of wetter times. I can almost picture how it looked when the bison and the Pawnee played hide and seek in these hills. Or one can imagine the view from here two millennia ago when people of the Early Woodland Culture had circular lodges in Valley county, hunting bison and a variety of smaller game with spear and atlatl.

I recall a magical day at Myrtle Hall in winter when, upon cresting one of the sharp ridges, I saw each surrounding canyon enshrouded in fog. Out of this fog arose a clamor and then, oblivious to me, a flock of cedar waxwings arose to alight on a weather-beaten, grotesque skeleton of an elm. I was stunned by a transcendental moment of elegance, endurance, and mystery. But I've also witnessed moments when the fabric of nature seemed torn. I had just kayaked part of the river with a German exchange student and we were puzzled by the many dead deer lying on sandbars. The explanation came to us dramatically as we heard a crashing sound in the thick heath of false indigo bush. Out came a deer, grunting and clearly in distress. It approached us boldly, wading across the pond, and we froze where we stood, not knowing what would happen next. Desperation showed in that odd horizontal pupil. Just yards before us, it threw its head back, emitting a wretched cry, and fell dead in the water. It was burning inside with a hemorrhagic fever, the deer equivalent of Ebola, that had been spread that summer through tiny biting midges. As Thoreau's Walden Pond was an eye of Nature with many moods, so I have seen the passing tantrums along with the embracing peace in the happenings around this pond.

Foght, too, is a romantic, often quoting poetry of John Greenleaf Whittier and extolling the beauty of the country and its simple pleasures. It is the personal observations that bring you back to his time there in an intimate way. He had an innocent vision of progress out there and was a bit too optimistic about what cultivation the upland soils could support, but would be amazed today to see the pivot-irrigated cornfields in the river valley. He would be sad, I think, to see the empty shells of so many rural schools and the rather sterile lawns of their consolidated replacements, or the complete takeover of many riverside bluffs by eastern red cedar. But he would wholeheartedly agree with Theodore Roosevelt when he said,

> Here is your country. Cherish these natural wonders, cherish the natural resources, cherish the history and romance as a sacred heritage, for your children and your children's children. Do not let selfish men or greedy interests skin your country of its beauty, its riches or its romance.*

Works Cited

Berry, Wendell. *The Unsettling of America: Culture and Agriculture.* San Francisco: Sierra Club Books, 1977.

---

* Attributed to Roosevelt's speech at the rim of the Grand Canyon, May 6, 1903. However, this version is not in the official record and may have been popularized by magazine editor Charles F. Lummis, who was present at the speech. (Thompson 237; Roosevelt 370–71.)

Finger, John R. *Cherokee Americans: The Eastern Band of Cherokees in the Twentieth Century.* Lincoln: University of Nebraska Press, 1991.

Foght, Harold W. *The American Rural School, Its Characteristics, Its Future, and Its Problems.* New York: The MacMillan Co., 1918.

———. "The Country School." *Annals of the American Academy of Political and Social Science.* 40 Country Life (Mar. 1912). 149–157.

———. *The Norse Discovery of America with Some Reference to Its True Significance. An Historical Thesis.* Blair, NE.: Danish Lutheran Publishing House, 1901.

Foght, H.W. and A. Foght. *Unfathomed Japan: A Travel Tale in the Highways and Byways of Japan and Formosa.* New York: The MacMillan Co., 1928.

Ohles, F., S.M, Ohles and J.G. Ramsay. *Biographical Dictionary of Modern American Educators.* Westport: Greenwood Publishing Group, 1997.

Roosevelt, Theodore. *The Works of Theodore Roosevelt: Presidential Addresses and State Papers.* Part 1. New York: P. Collier & Sons, 1889.

Sandoz, Mari. *Love Song to the Plains.* Lincoln: University of Nebraska Press, 1961.

Stegner, Wallace. *The Sound of Mountain Water.* New York: Penguin Paperback, 1946.

Thompson, Mark. *American Character: The Curious Life of Charles Fletcher Lummis and the Rediscovery of the Southwest.* New York: Arcade Publishing, 2001.

....

William Beachly is a Nebraska Native and professor of biology at Hastings College. His favorite class to teach is The Natural History of the Nebraska Sand Hills and Pine Ridge, which includes a week-long camping trip and many adventures in this fascinating region. He frequently guides tours and gives public programs about the Platte River during the great Sandhills Crane Migration. He also has taught geology trainings at many different localities for the Nebraska Master Naturalist program. His essays about unique places have appeared in *Nebraskaland Magazine, Prairie Fire Newspaper,* and *Humanimalia.* In developing a better sense of place, he attempts to relate its biodiversity and subtle landscape features to its long history and engender a new perspective on our place here.

Introductory
(Original Introduction)

Years ago—a quarter century past—the author, then a little chap herding cattle in the valley above Ord, according to his daily wont, reclined one day in his retreat in a shaded nook on the banks of the river, while his charges were left to shift for themselves; and well they might, for was not the prairie theirs for miles around! He dreamed all enrapt in the charm of the virgin prairie, dreamed of things yet to be. As he lay there, listening to the gurgling, eddying water swishing by, he saw visions and heard

> ... the tread of pioneers
>   Of nations yet to be,
> The first low wash of waves where soon
>   Shall roll a human sea.*

And they came, those pioneers, and they are as silently leaving us again, passing away to the mysterious realm beyond; while the great human sea, wave upon wave, rolls over the prairies first trodden by them, obliterating their very footprints, making this a new land, almost beyond the recognition of the old-timers.

They endured much, those pathfinders, for us their children, that we might reap the fruits of their industry and toil. And shall we then repay them thus, leaving the history they made, unchronicled, unsung? No! a thousand times no! Let it be taken down, that the generations yet unborn may know at what a cost "The Trail of the Loup" was blazed, and how the fathers suffered and toiled, and even died, that the trail might remain open.

To write an old settlers' chronicle is at best difficult; and when, as in the instance of the North and Middle Loup valleys, no systematic efforts have been made to collect and save historic data or to spare from untimely destruction historic structures, the task becomes almost impossible. In the following pages the author has had to depend, in great part, upon the memory of the first settlers. When more than one

---

* Editor's note: From John Greenleaf Whittier's "On Receiving an Eagle Quill from Lake Superior."

version of an episode or event was offered, the materials were carefully sifted, and the version which seemed the most likely made use of.

I lay no claims to have exhausted this interesting field of investigation, but I do claim that I have, in the work as far as it has been carried, stated the facts just as I found them, without fear or favor. This is not a partisan history, but the story of a limited section of our commonwealth, and, as such, the individual has in every instance been accorded a space in the narrative in due proportion to the part played by him.

Finally, I wish to make grateful acknowledgment to the men and women who have assisted in the work by valuable information, freely given, and by furnishing photographs and other materials for the illumination of the text. Special obligation is due Hon. Peter Mortensen, Elder Oscar Babcock, Messrs. George McAnulty, David Gard, George Miller, Truman Freeland, James Barr, G. J. Rood, W. G. Rood, John Kellogg, W. B. Weekes, Jorgen Miller, Tom Hemmett, Will Johns, William S. Mattley, Melville Goodenow, W. H. Rood, Mansell Davis, Miss Ina Draver, Mrs. George McAnulty, Mrs. A. M. Robbins and Mrs. Emma Haskell.

Harold W. Foght

I

Some Physical Features of Nebraska

> To me it seems, that to look on the first land that was ever lifted above the wasted waters, to follow the shore where the earliest animals and plants were created when the thought of God first expressed itself in organic forms, to hold in one's hand a bit of stone from an old sea-beach, hardened into rock thousands of centuries ago, and studded with the beings that once crept upon its surface or were stranded there by some retreating wave, is even of deeper interest to man, than the relics of their own race, for these things tell more directly of the thought and creative acts of God.
> —Jean Louis Agassiz, "The Silurian Beach"*

It does not come within the scope of this work to dwell at any length upon the evolution of our state from the primal rock. Such a discussion, while interesting in the extreme, belongs rather to the field of science than to that of history; the space herein allotted it is therefore necessarily somewhat limited. Particularly is this true since the bulk of the text is intended to narrate the story not so much of Nebraska as a whole, as the living, throbbing history of a limited section of the state—the Loup Valley. However, a passing glance at the geological structure of Nebraska may not be altogether out of place.

In the aeons of time since Creation, our planet, the Earth, has passed through many marvelous changes. At first a companion star to the Sun, blazing a path through the universe, cooling gradually, its enshrouding mantle of vapors condensing to water, the Earth became involved in a universal, shoreless ocean. Then countless ages slowly slipped away; the first folds of contracting firerock-crust of the earth appeared, and we had the first dry land. In the Western World the wedge-shaped Laurentian Highlands, approaching the shores of Hudson Bay, had appeared, and strips of land were slowly emerging to the east of the present Appalachians, and in the western part of the

---

* Editor's note: Published in *The Atlantic Monthly*, Vol. XI, No. LXVI (April 1863), pp. 460–471.

Chapter I

United States stretching from Colorado to California. This was during the so-called Archian Time—the dawn of earth-building. And all through this immense age, as far as we know, Nebraska formed a part of the bed of a turbulent ocean.

Now followed the Paleozoic (Ancient Life) Time during which the land areas were gradually enlarged, and myriad forms of strange organisms appeared. Geologists usually divide this aeon into three distinct ages: The Age of Invertebrates—subdivided into the Upper and Lower Silurian Eras—when numberless Sponges, Corals, Starfishes, Molluska and other strange animal types dominated the ocean depths, and a few terrestrial plants appeared; the Age of Fishes, or Devonian Era, when the ocean swarmed with sharks, gar-pikes and turtlelike placoderms of huge size; and the Carboniferous Age—subdivided into Subcarboniferous, Carboniferous and Permian Eras—when coal plants grew and the coal measures were formed.

During neither the Age of Invertebrates nor the succeeding age of Fishes did dry land appear in Nebraska. Vast land stretches had however been added to the Archian backbone and numerous islands dotted the present states of Illinois, Kentucky, Missouri and Iowa.

The Subcarboniferous Era, too, must be passed over as unproductive so far as Nebraska is concerned. But we now approach the Carboniferous Age proper, of absorbing interest because then did the first dry land appear in Nebraska, and because during its progress were the greatest and most valuable coal measures formed.

That the Era was of great duration there cannot be the slightest doubt. "A murky, cloudy atmosphere, surcharged with carbon-dioxide gas, enveloped the earth and gave it a uniform hothouse temperature. A vegetation remarkable in its luxuriance sprang up. Conifers much akin to the Araucanian pines of present day equatorial regions flourished and ferns of surpassing grace and beauty grew to the size of mighty trees." The American Continent over its broad surface was now just balancing itself near the water's edge, part of the time bathing in it and then out in the free air. From Pennsylvania to eastern Nebraska and central Kansas, it presented a changing view "of vast jungles, lakes with floating grove islands, and some dry-land forests." Vast amounts of vegetable debris accumulated, forming peat beds of varying depths.

The era of verdure then gradually drew to a close. A general settling of vast land areas took place and salt water by degrees submerged the low lands, destroying every vestige of the late prolific vegetation. Thus, we may picture the old peat-marsh, with its bottom

Toadstool Park, Nebraska Bad Lands.

4   Chapter I

full of stumps and roots in position as they grew, with its surface covered over with heaps of leaves, branches and prostrate tree trunks, to have been overwhelmed and buried. Subjected to enormous pressure from accumulating top sediment and slow chemical change, it, in time, became one of the several coal measures. Alternate submergence and emergence of the surface crust readily explains the alternation, in these rockbeds, of coal seams with layers of sandstones, conglomerate, shales, clays and limestones. The second and largest coal measures of this age extends from Texas and Arkansas northward through Kansas and Missouri, Nebraska and Iowa. The westward boundary is near the central part of Kansas, and crosses the state line into Nebraska near the banks of the Blue River, whence it takes a northeasterly trend, leaving the state in southern Washington county. It will thus be seen that part or the whole of some twelve counties in our state overlie these interesting beds. In Richardson county a workable stratum has been encountered, though borings at Lincoln and other places seem to indicate that profitable mines should not be looked for in Nebraska.

The closing period of the Paleozoic aeon was the Permian Age, in which the ocean once more prevailed, though with gradually contracting limits. The greater part of Nebraska was yet a part of the ocean bed, covered by turbulent waters. On stormy days the breakers must have roared along the shore and hurled their spray against the limestone cliffs now marked by a line drawn from Beatrice in Gage county to Blair in Washington county. Some fifteen of our present-day counties in southeast Nebraska had by this time lifted their surface above the waters; all else were engulfed in the briny deep.

The Permian Age is in reality a transition period which ushers in the next great aeon of time, the *Mesozoic* or Middle Life. This is also called the *Era of Reptiles* "for never in the history of the

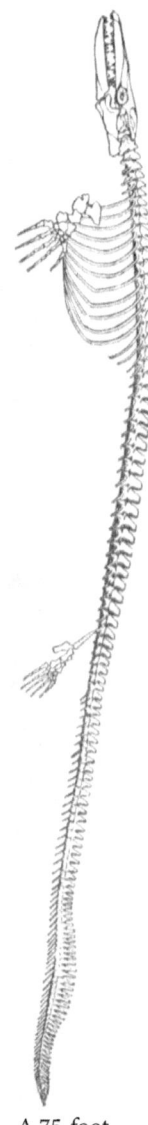

A 75-foot Mosasaurus from the Cretaceous beds of Kansas.

earth were reptiles so abundant, of such size and variety, or so highly organized as then." The era includes three periods: 1. The *Triassic*, so named for the triple rockbeds in Germany; 2. The *Jurassic*, named after the Jura Mountains in France; 3. The *Cretaceous*, from the Latin *creta, chalk*, referring to the formation of large chalk beds in England and continental Europe.

Careful examination of the rock strata of our state fails to disclose the least trace of a Juro-Triassic deposit. The probable explanation of this fact seems to be that this region had now, all of it, by some upward movement of the earth, become dry land. The continental sea had retired to Kansas on the south and Colorado on the west. The indications are that Nebraska then drained westward, emptying her surface water into Colorado, where flood-time deposits of Triassic and Jurassic land fossils are now to be sought. If the above supposition is correct, it stands to reason that the deposits of the age, which were all of them submarine, could not have been formed in Nebraska, hence we find our Permian rocks directly overlaid by rocks of the Cretaceous period.

During these numberless centuries of dry land existence in Nebraska,

> ...on either side
> Is level fen, a prospect wild and wide,
> With dykes on either hand by ocean's self supplied:
> For on the right the distant sea is seen,
> And salt the springs that feed the marsh between.*

And yet the marsh was slowly becoming upland, though the climate was still moist and warm. A tropical vegetation of myriad species of giant ferns and noble cycads again clad the land with brilliant hues. These immense thickets and forests teemed with animal life. Most striking were the giant Brontosaurus of the Wyoming fossil beds, often measuring 60 feet in length; the Atlantosaurus, which reached the phenomenal length of 80 feet; and the lately dicovered gigantic Stegosaurus, remarkable for a series of huge bony plates mounted along the back. As if these curious creatures were not enough to give character to the time we find uncanny, birdlike reptiles, pterosaurs,

---

* Editor's note: From George Crabbe's "Tale X."

Chapter I

Nebraska forest of late Cretaceous times.

swarming the upper air and adding much to this the strangest and most interesting of faunas.

The Cretaceous period marks the beginning of the end of the Mesozoic Era. A general subsidence now set in which seems to have embraced even the Rocky Mountain region. The latter, together with the eastward-lying plain, was once more brought to the water level. A marine bay broke northward from the Gulf of Mexico and, before the middle of the period, covered Texas, Indian Territory, part of Kansas, the western half of Nebraska, and much territory lying northwestward.

Thus the Rocky Mountain nucleus was again reduced to groups of islands, as in Paleozoic times, and all western Nebraska was once more, though now for the last time, a part of the ocean bed. Toward the later part of the period the continent slowly rose again and the great western internal sea was narrowed and made shallow, the connection between the Gulf and the Arctic Seas was interrupted, lakes of fresh water, bays and swamps with brackish water, took the place of the ocean, and vast quantities of vegetable matter were formed in the marshes of this closing epoch.' But this was more than a period of emergence; indeed a great geologic revolution was preparing. From the plains on the east to the Wasatch, the entire Rocky Mountain region was thrown into a series of earth folds; the crust was bent and the mountain system, as we have it today, was lifted up, getting a drainage seaward. Nebraska now faced eastward, a part of the continental plain.

The Cretaceous deposits in Nebraska are of vast extent and importance. For convenience the strata have been classified into the following groups: The *Dakota*, extending from near Dakota City, where many outcroppings are to be found, in a southwesterly direction, underlying practically every part of the state; the *Fort Benton Group*, lying conformably on the *Dakota Group* in the eastern part of the state; the *Niobrara Group*, extending from the mouth of the Niobrara River, dipping under the central portion of the state and reappearing again in the southwest in Harlan county; the *Fort Pierre Group*, lying above the Niobrara deposits, cropping out in Knox

Tusks of mammoth excavated in Gosper county, and now in the Museum of the University of Nebraska at Lincoln.

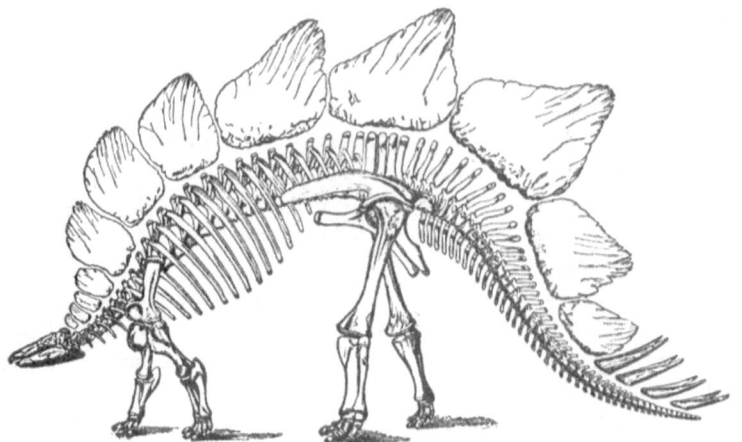

Jurassic Stegosaurus, which flourished in Wyoming and Colorado while Nebraska was an inland sea. It measured from 25 to 30 feet in length.

county and other places; the *Laramie Group*, exposed in southwestern counties.

These beds comprise various clays, chalks and sandstones, and are rich in finds of fossil leaves and remains of animal life. Thus several hundred species of ferns, cycads and conifers have been counted, and some hundred or more reptile forms, ranging in size from twelve to seventy-five feet, are known to have existed.

The last great aeon in geological history is now at hand. This is the *Cenozoic Time*, or *Era of Modern Life*. A higher vegetation makes its appearance and the great reptiles are rapidly giving way to higher species of animal life—the mammals. For convenience this aeon is divided into two ages, the *Tertiary* and the *Quaternary*.

The *Tertiary Age* embraces three epochs, the *Eocene*, the *Miocene* and the *Pliocene*. Of these only the latter two are represented in Nebraska. From our discussion above it will be borne in mind that over the western part of the continent the region of marine waters was past. The Rocky Mountain revolution had left the Great Plains a part of the continent. But this plain was yet very near the sea level, the proof of which is found in the existence of vast lakes of fresh water both east and west of the Rocky Mountain range. These were not, however, contemporaneous, but succeeded one another as the age proceeded. Thus, in Nebraska we find no trace of Eocene lake beds. Conditions were on the other hand quite changed during Miocene

Some Physical Features of Nebraska 9

times; for then a freshwater lake covered much of the western part of the state, receiving the drainage of the rivers that now have their outlet in the Missouri. Into this lake bed were carried broken-down materials from the Rocky Mountain axis and the Black Hills, and from the higher lying Juro-Triassic and Cretaceous deposits. Hither, too, were gathered, as in an immense cemetery, remnants of all the vegetable and animal life of the epoch A gradual uplifting of strata has left these lake bottoms high and dry. Erosion too has changed their contour much, cutting valleys, leaving cliffs and buttes in endless variety.

These *Mauvais Terres* of the French trapper, or "Bad Lands," are today clearly defined in the White River Country of northwestern Nebraska, and covers hundreds of square miles in southwestern South Dakota and northeastern Wyoming. The writer has personally inspected these regions, and nowhere is the story of the past told in more forcible language than in this vast graveyard. Banks full of fossil bones, baccolites, huge petrified tortoises, and fossil leaves tell the story of how Nebraska looked in those times. Magnolias, oaks, palms, figs, maples, lindens and pines grew in wild luxuriance, and the giant sequoias of California grew on every hill. Indeed, a semi-tropical vegetation stretched far away towards the Pole. Droves of Miocene horses frequented the lake shores, the ancestral hog wallowed in the bogs, flocks of monkeys chattered in the treetops, and plain and forest were the haunt and breeding ground of droves of huge mastadons and wicked-eyed rhinoceroces and tapirs. Such were then the *Ma-koo-si-tcha*, or hard-lands-to-travel-over, as the Sioux nomad has seen fit to designate these reigons.

The Pliocene Epoch of the Tertiary Age is marked by a general enlargement of the old Miocene lake bed, particularly eastward and southwestward. The Pliocene strata in Nebraska far outreach the Miocene and are, on this account, found to overlie the Cretacious from the central counties east. These beds were of considerable thickness but thin out eastward since the bulk of the materials forming them came from the mountains. Much of the Pliocene material is exceedingly coarse. Beds of conglomerate rock, made up "of waterworn pebbles, feldspar and quartz in masses, and some small pieces or chips of all the Archian rocks," overlie beds of much worn sandstones and clays.

Along the *Loup Forks*, and in other localities, the upper beds have become decomposed and an immense amount of fine sand of a more or less stable nature has heaped up to form the famous "sand hills." Beneath lie strata of compacted gravel; then come limestone formations, yellow grits and layers of many colored sands and clays. In many places on the North Loup River calcarious outcroppings are seen. Such are the bottom rocks forming the "Falls of the Loup," the sandstones and limestones forming the channel bottom near old Willow Springs in Garfield county, and again near Scotia in Greeley county.

With the close of the Tertiary Age and the opening of the *Quaternary Age* a great change came over the earth. In Nebraska the lake beds gradually drained out, and there is evidence to show that the semi-tropical conditions which had so long existed were now undergoing changes. Arctic conditions began to prevail at the north, gradually extending into what is now the North Temperate zone, pushing, as it were, both fauna and flora equatorward. Much of the old life was exterminated or forced to give way before the rigors of the *Glacial Period* which was now preparing.

For reasons which it does not come within our province to discuss here the temperature of North America gradually fell so low that the snows of winter accumulated too rapidly for the summer's warmth to remove. The result was a glaciation of vast land areas. A great ice sheet, forced by its own weight, slowly moved southward, enfolding the earth in its embrace. In the west we know that it extended almost to the 36th degree north latitude. Traces of the ice movement in Nebraska are abundant. Along the Missouri wherever the superficial deposits are removed the underlying limestone beds are worn smooth as glass and are full of glacial scratches and flutings. Indications are that the drift covered at least the eastern one third of the state. Here are found the beds of blue clay so characteristic of this period; and in strata above these, drift gravel and clay, and next above gravel and water worn boulders of various size.

After countless ages of polar winter an era of general subsidence took place in the glaciated regions; a great increase in humidity resulted and the ice mantle began to melt and recede. Immense floods were raging in the valleys and the continent from glacier edge to the gulf was converted into an inland sea, full of floating icebergs, which drifting aimlessly about, when they melted, dropped their immense loads of sand gravel and boulders to the lake bottom. These floods covered all of Nebraska with the exception of the Miocene beds of the White River region and the western uplands and a few of the highest crests of the Pliocene deposits which lay too high to be reached by the

Some Physical Features of Nebraska 11

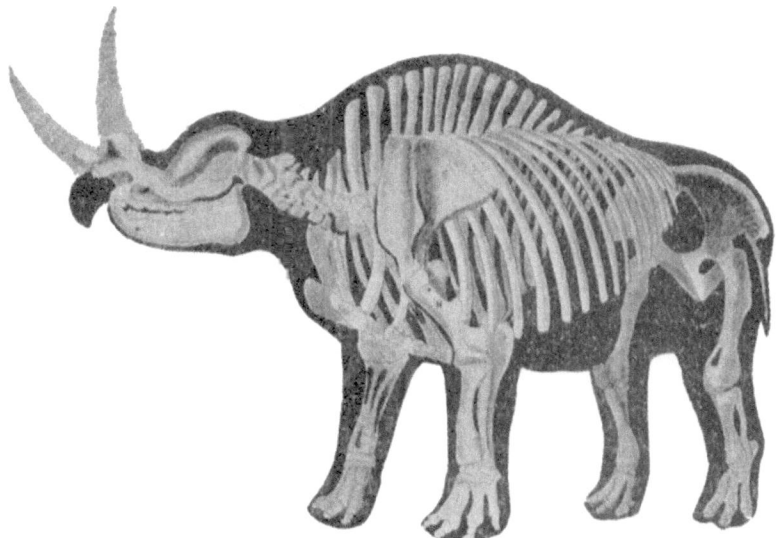

Titanotherium Robustum from the Sioux county Bad Lands. When full grown it measured 14 feet in length and 8 feet in height at the shoulders.

engulfing waters. The Miocene or Pliocene formations, known to us by such names as Scott's Bluffs and Chimney Rock, must, in those times, have been so many islands set in a turbulent sea. The entire Loup region was submerged throughout this period, receiving then those loess-clay deposits which have made it one of the most fertile regions in the state. A change in level now set in. "The farther retreat of the glaciers and the elevation of eastern Iowa reduced the area of this great lake. What had been a great interior sea of turbulent waters now became a system of placid lakes that extended from Nebraska and Western Iowa at intervals to the Gulf." The Missouri, Platte and other well-known streams of today drained through them, carrying immense loads of ground-up Pliocene and Cretacious materials suspended in the muddy water. In the course of vast ages the lake beds became filled with this mud (loess) and, after passing through the stage of bog and marsh, became dry land. Vegetation soon covered the virgin earth; and this from its annual decay and accumulation of debris gave us the rich surface loam so characteristic to Nebraska.

The chains of river bluffs familiar to every Nebraskan were heaped up while the river yet filled the whole trough from bluff to bluff, and, in fact, while these bluffs themselves were under water. They were in a way piled up on the flanks of the raging, mud-carrying flood current; as the glacial flood declined, the waters gradually fell below the top of the bluff formation, and the first terrace or upper bench of the valley flood plain appeared. The waters continued falling and the river dwindled down to a mere run, leaving the valley terrace above terrace, bench above bench. Thus in Nebraska river basins there are often found three and even four such "bottoms." The terrace building at an end, recent time is well along and geological history need be pursued no further. The earth, topographically speaking, must

Fine loess formation in Garfield county.

have had practically its present day appearance; vegetation covered hill and valley; the highest orders of mammalia roamed over it and man took possession of it. In Nebraska, indeed, we find traces of a pre-glacial race of man. Discoveries of stone implements, and then chiefly flint arrow heads and spear-heads, have been made deep in undisturbed loess beds, side by side with bones of the mastodon and huge elk of this period. We may thus with some reason presume that man roamed the Nebraska plains ages before the advent of the long glacial winter.

From the foregoing pages it may be noted that in Nebraska formations older than the Pliocene are nowhere exposed excepting the Miocene deposits in the "Bad Lands" of the northwest. The former, indeed, are represented only in a few isolated neighborhoods in the western part, where lofty "buttes" of Pliocene formation tower high above the flood plain. The remainder of the state is covered with glacial drift and loess, the drift being confined to the eastern third. The loess clay forms a soil of inexhaustible fertility, and ranges in thickness from 5 to 200 feet.

Nebraska, the Land of Shallow Water, lies at the geographical center of the United States, and is bounded by parallels 40°43' North and longitude 95°20' and 104° West. The extreme length of the state from east to west is 420 miles, and its breadth from north to south is 208.5 miles. In area it comprises 77,510 square miles, or 49,606,400 acres, of which nearly 500,000 acres represent water.

The state stretches from the foothills of the Rockies to the Missouri, having a gentle eastward slope. The western half averages more than 2500 feet above the sea, to only 1200 feet for the eastern half. Scott's Bluffs reach the height of fully 6000 feet, while Richardson county is only 878 feet above the sea. Nebraska is drained entirely by the Missouri and its tributaries. Of the latter the most important are the Platte and the Niobrara, which flow through valleys extending the length of the state from west to east. The Republican comes from western Kansas and, after draining much of the "South Platte Country," returns again to that state. The Elkhorn and, farther west, the Loup are the only important northern tributaries of the Platte. The latter, with its three forks, the North, Middle and South Loup, flows from an interesting lake region in Cherry county and empties into the Platte just above Columbus. This river system will presently be treated more in full.

Chapter I

The climate of Nebraska is dry and exhilarating. It is subject to sudden changes in temperature, the thermometer being known to have varied from 114° to 42°. The mean temperature for January is, however, 19.7°, for July 74.8°. The nights are for the most part cool and refreshing. Nebraska autumns are delightful, the period from early frost till well toward Christmas is peculiar for its mellow, hazy atmosphere—crisp and bracing—this is the well known "Indian Summer Time." The annual rainfall is 23 inches, most of it falling east of the 100th meridian. The moisture is indeed very unevenly distributed. In the eastern half it averages 30 inches and locally it has gauged as high as 50 inches. In the western half it averages a little more than 19 inches, though on the extreme western border it scarcely reaches 10 inches. Most of the rainfall occurs between April and September, the greatest amount falling in May and June.

As is peculiar to the great continental plain, the weather is very changeable. Snow storms, or "blizzards," may in winter burst with scarcely any warning, and rage with sudden fury over the prairie which but a few moments before lay bathed in brightest sunshine. Occasional hot winds have in summer repeatedly injured the growing crops. It is only justice, however, to add that Nebraska, east of the 99th meridian, is as "safe" for agricultural purposes as any state in the union. West of this line it is better adapted for grazing purposes, where not irrigated. Nebraska climate is extremely healthful. "The stranger settling within the state cannot help noticing a general quickening of spirit and a strange increase of vitality. His appetite becomes voracious, and he sleeps as never before. The dry, continental climate is surcharged with an invigorating ozone which acts as a new life vigor to him who comes into it from the malaria and ague ridden districts of other states."

To the travelling public not intimately acquainted with its topography Nebraska is a part of the Great Plains—this, and no more. Tourists have passed through the state from east to west and pronounced it a monotonous, tiresome prairie. But such impressions are at best faulty and do our great commonwealth injustice. A birdseye view would disclose a varied scene of rich valley and grassy upland, of broad basin and rolling watershed.

The surface is indeed varied. The river valley, ranging in width from a few hundred yards to miles, is usually wooded along the river bank. Beyond the rich alluvial or sometimes sandy bottom lands lie the chain of border bluffs, steep or rounded and often of considerable height. These once passed, a gently undulating watershed meets the eye, stretching perhaps for scores of miles, or again may be for but a very brief distance, to be cut by a second bluff chain, the border of another water course.

The northwest is wild and broken but extremely picturesque—this is the Bad Lands. The Niobrara basin is in great part gently undulating; along the river are many almost romantic spots. Here limestone outcroppings and pine-growths make one forget that this is a prairie state. To the south of the Niobrara are the "sandhills," which are mostly great dunes of Pliocene sands fantastically heaped up. This great region, which, by the way, affords excellent range for cattle-grazing, is gradually being covered with grasses and shrubs, and will no doubt in time become fit for agriculture. These hills with their grasses and wild flowers, occasional "blowouts" and reed-grown lakes give one an impression of a country yet in the making.

The valley of the Platte is of a sandy nature near the river bed, but, as it recedes, is transformed into a fertile, rising plain north and south, losing itself in wavy undulating farmlands, as rich as found anywhere in the country. Westward the state changes from rich prairie, so well adapted to agriculture, to dry plains and sage-covered foothills, the typical range country of the west. Toward the southeast are excellent farm lands, beautiful water courses and wooded lowlands. On the eastern border winds the "Big Muddy" through its great flood plain, with chains of towering bluffs on either side—bluffs remarkable for their changeful beauty. "Occasionally," says Professor Aughey, "an elevation is encountered from whose summit there are such magnificent views of river, bottom, forest and winding bluffs as to produce all the emotions of the sublime."

"There are many landscapes everywhere of wonderful beauty along all the principal rivers. The bluffs are sometimes precipitous, but generally they round off and melt into gently rolling plains. They constantly vary, and in following them you come now into a beautiful cove, now to a curious headland, then to terraces, and however far you travel you can look in vain for a picture like the one just passed."

Pawnee village.

II

The Aborigines

> The land was ours—this glorious land—
>   With all its wealth of wood and streams;
> Our warriors strong of heart and hand.
>   Our daughters beautiful as dreams—
> When wearied at the thirsty noon,
>   We knelt us where the spring gushed up,
> To take our Father's blessed boon—
>   Unlike the white man's poison cup.
> —John Greenleaf Whittier, "The Indian's Tale"

The first mention of Nebraska Indians by white explorers comes from the pen of Father Jaques Marquette. In June 1673, that devout Christian worker and missionary, accompanied by Louis Joliet, embarked upon his great exploring trip of the "Father of Waters." Fired by a religious enthusiasm and by a determination to convert the Algonquin tribes roaming its banks, he made the perilous descent as far south as the Red River. From his account of this momentous expedition we draw many a thrilling picture of hair breadth escapes and dramatic scenes. Interesting to our narrative is Marquette's description of the hitherto unknown Missouri country. The voyagers were rapidly approaching the mouth of the great western tributary, when, to quote from that Reverend Father's account, "we heard a great rushing and bubbling of waters, and soon beheld small islands of floating trees coming from the mouth of the Pekitanoni (the Missouri) with such rapidity that we could not trust ourselves to go near it. The waters of this river are so muddy that we could not drink it. It so discolors the Mississippi as to make the navigation of it dangerous. This river comes from the northwest and on its banks are situated a number of Indian villages."

In a most interesting chart of the expedition, now in the archives at Montreal, Marquette locates, in what is now Kansas and Nebraska, the following Indian villages: The Ouemessouriet (Missouri), the Kenza (Kansas), the Ouchage (Osage), the Paneassa (Pawnee), and the Maha (Omaha). That his information was indeed surprisingly accurate is seen from this that French explorers found these very tribes in relatively the same position as indicated in the chart nearly 200 years later.

Lewis and Clark, in the expedition of 1804, found Pawnees, Missouris and Otoes in possession of the Platte, the Poncas near the mouth of the Niobrara and the Omahas in the northeastern part of the state, centering around what is now Sioux City. The Pawnees were then the dominant tribe of the western prairie, the others here mentioned being treated as wards and dependents.

Their original home seems to have been somewhere in the lower Red River Valley in Louisiana, where they formed the chief tribe of the important Caddoan stock. At an early date several of these tribes migrated northward. Thus the Arikari moved by way of the Missouri, penetrating far into North Dakota. Sometime later the Skidi (Wolves) advanced northward and halted at the Platte, there to be overtaken by the Pawnees proper.

The Pawnees called themselves Skihiksihiks, or "men par excellence." The popular name, and the one most in vogue, is Wolf People. They were a warlike and powerful nation, claiming the whole region watered by the Platte from the Rocky Mountains to its mouth. They held in check the powerful Kiowas of the Black Hills and waged successful war against the Comanches of the Arkansas.

From an early day we find them divided into four grand divisions, or clans, having distinct government though with language in common. There were the Shani, or Grand Pawnees, with villages on the south bank of the Platte, opposite the present Grand Island; the Kitkehaki, or Republican Pawnees, on the Republican in northern Kansas; the Pitahauerat, or Noisy Pawnees, also on the Platte; and the Skidi, or Loup (Wolf) Pawnees, on the Loup Fork of the Platte. Here they lived in well built log houses, covered with turf and earth, preferring these to the movable tepee, which was only used when the bands were on an extended hunt. They depended more on horticulture, the raising of corn and pumpkins, than upon the buffalo hunt. In this manner they never outgrew the sedentary and agricultural habits peculiar to all southern tribes.

Lieutenant Zebulon Pike's exploring expedition, when on its way to the mountains in 1806, encountered the Republican Pawnees in northern Kansas. This was a few years before they moved north to join their brothers already established on the Loup Forks. Lieut. Pike and his aide Lieut. Wilkinson held a grand council with the chiefs of that nation on the 29th of September, which is interesting to us, as it gives an idea of the northward limit of Spanish activity at that time. The council is described in the following language: "The council was held at the Pawnee Republic village (near the present site of Scandia in Republic county) and was attended by 400 warriors. When the parties assembled for their council, Lieut. Pike found that the Pawnees had unfurled a Spanish flag at the door of the chief, one which had lately been presented by that government, through the hands of Lieut. Malgoras. To the request of Lieut. Pike that the flag should be delivered to him, and one of the United States hoisted in its place, they at first made no response; but, upon his repeating his demand, with the emphatic declaration that they must choose between Americans and Spaniards and that it was impossible for the nation to have two fathers, they decided to put themselves, for the time, at last, under American protection. An old man accordingly rose, went to the door, took down the Spanish flag and laid it at the feet of Lieut. Pike, and in its stead elevated the stars and the stripes."

Another expedition was sent out by the War Department in 1819, for the purpose of gaining a more thorough topographical knowledge of the central region of the great Louisiana purchase. This was the Long Expedition. Leaving "Engineer Cantonment" just below Council Bluffs on the 10th of June, it crossed the Missouri near the site of Omaha and struck boldly across the "Indian Country." And indeed there was nothing just then to fear from the Indians, as treaties of amity had lately been entered into by government agents and the leading tribes along the route.

One was ratified with the Pawnees as early as January 5, 1812, one with the Mahas, December 26, 1815, and one with the Otoes, December 26, 1817. Major Long's instructions read to see that the treaties were strictly lived up to by redskin and white man alike. In the course of his westward advance he made it a point to visit the Pawnee villages. His account has it that after crossing the Elkhorn he trailed along the north bank of the Platte till the confluence of the Loup was reached. At sunset, June 10th, the expedition went into camp at a small creek about eleven miles distant from the village of the Grand Pawnees. Then in Major Long's account of the visit we read:

"On the following morning, having arranged the party according to rank, and given the necessary instructions for the preservation of order, we proceeded forward, and in a short time came in sight of the first of the Pawnee villages. The trail on which we had travelled since leaving the Missouri had the appearance of being more and more frequented as we approached the Pawnee towns; and here, instead of a single footway, it consisted of more than twenty parallel paths, of similar size and appearance; at a few miles distance from the village, we met a party of eight or ten squaws, with hoes and other implements of agriculture, on their way to the corn plantations. They were accompanied by one young Indian, but in what capacity—whether as assistant, protector or taskmaster, we were not informed. After a ride of about three hours we arrived before the village, and dispatched a messenger to inform the chief of our approach.

"Answer was returned that he was engaged with his chiefs and warriors at a medicine feast, and could not, therefore, come out and meet us. We were soon surrounded by a crowd of women and children, who gazed at us with some expressions of astonishment; but as no one appeared to welcome us to the village, arrangments were made for sending on the horses and baggage to a suitable place for encampment while Major Long with several gentlemen who wished to accompany him, entered the village. The party, after groping about for some time and traversing a considerable part of the village, arrived at the lodge of the principal chief. Here we were again informed that Tarrarecawaho, with all the principal men of the village, was engaged at a medicine feast. Notwithstanding his absence, some mats were spread for us upon the ground in the back part of the lodge. Upon them we sat down, and, after waiting some time, were presented with a large wooden dish of hominy or boiled corn. In this was a single spoon of the horn of a buffalo, large enough to hold a pint, which, being used alternately by each of the party, soon emptied the dish of its contents."

After this strange reception and feast the expedition visited in turn the villages of the Republican and Loup (Wolf) Pawnees, lying a few miles apart, an hour's ride above the village of the Pawnee Grand. Major Long was especially struck with the thrift of these villages. For miles up and down the river large droves of horses were grazing; fields of maize and patches of tomatoes, pumpkins and squashes were seen in many places and added much to the apparent wealth of the community. This was before misfortune overtook the nation.

The expedition spent the night of June 12 on the banks of the river, within a stone's throw of the Loup village. This was, as far as we know, the first organized party of white men to slumber on the banks of this beautiful stream.

Roam Chief (Pawnee) and Yellow Hair (Sioux) agree to "bury the hatchet."

The Pawnee nation formerly numbered some 25,000 souls and in the day of its prime was the terror alike of trapper and trader and bands from other tribes which by chance ventured too far into the hunting grounds of these fierce fighting foes. But calamity was at hand. In 1831, a terrible smallpox epidemic carried off several thousand of their number, leaving the nation in a pitiable condition. Their agent, John Dougherty, in making his report to the government, says: "Their misery defies all description. I am fully persuaded that one-half the whole number will be carried off by this frightful distemper. They told me that not one under thirty years of age escaped, it having been that length of time since it visited them before. They were dying so fast, and taken down at once in such large numbers that they had ceased to bury their dead, whose bodies were to be seen in every direction—lying in the river, lodged on the sandbars, in the weeds around the villages and in their corn cashes."

On the 9th of October 1834, a treaty was made between the Pawnees and the United States government whereby the former agreed to vacate all their lands south of the Platte. All the plague-stricken southern villages were abandoned and the miserable remnant of a once proud tribe reassembled on the Loup and westward along the Platte.

But scarcely had the enfeebled nation had time to set up their tepees and break soil in their new home, when the Sioux, made bold by their hereditary foes' apparent weakness, swept down the North Loup and the Cedar and began a war of extermination. Villages and fields were abandoned to the revengeful foe and safety sought in flight. The Pawnee found every man's hand against him. Even the government was indifferent and did little to check the depredations of the Sioux. To make matters still worse, other enemies on the south, the Cheyennes and the Arapahoes, infested the Pawnees' old Kansas hunting grounds, eager to strike the final blow. But this was not to come by the hand of red men. In 1849, gold seekers on their way to California brought the cholera to the Pawnee camps. Again several thousand died and the handful of survivors, reduced to beggary, besought the government for protection, which was granted. By the treaty of September 4, 1857, they ceded all their original territory except a strip 30 miles long by 15 wide upon the lower Loup river. This was the old Nance county Reservation, whence they were finally removed to their present abode in Oklahoma. During the Indian troubles of 1862–65 the Pawnees furnished scouts to the government and proved a valuable aid against the crafty Sioux. The latter, however, reaped sweet revenge after the war closed. The Pawnees were never safe if they ventured away from the reservation. Red Cloud's bands might at any moment sweep down upon them to kill and plunder. As if the loss of their hunting grounds were not enough to fill the cup of troubles, the grasshoppers, in 1872, devoured their corn crop. This meant starvation. Congressional appropriation through land sales kept

The Aborigines   23

them alive till 1874, when, as stated above, the Pawnees set their faces southward, forever to leave the Loup and the Platte.

The story of their rapid decay is read in the following figures: In 1835, according to the missionaries Dunbar and Allis, they numbered 10,000. In 1840 disease and war had reduced them to 7500. In 1849 cholera had reduced them to 5000. Later official reports give 4686 in 1856; 3416 in 1861; 2376 in 1874; 1440 in 1879; 824 in 1889; 629 in 1901.

Thus passed the Pawnees, the Wolf People of the North, while their arch enemy, the Sioux, still roamed the plains.

The latter belonged to one of the most widely extended and important Indian families in North America. Prior to the advent of white man to this country they appear to have held sway of the Atlantic seaboard of Virginia and the Carolinas, outlying tribes even penetrating south to the Gulf. In those days the Sioux were sedentary and inclined to horticulture. They lived in well built lodges and tilled the soil. Within the recent historic period they set their faces westward and removed to the banks of the Ohio. The cause of this migration can only be surmised. In all probability it was the outcome of an undue pressure by Maskoki tribes living in the South Atlantic states, coupled with a like Algonquin or Iroquoian movement from the north.

From their own traditions we learn that at some point on the Ohio, probably near the mouth of the Wabash, the Sioux and Winnebago parted company with the rest of the tribes and took a

Pawnee ceremonial lodge. Now abandoned by the dying tribe.

northwesterly trail across Illinois, the former taking possession of the headwaters of the Mississippi, the latter pitching their lodges around the lake that bears their name in Wisconsin. Meanwhile other tribes of the great family had reached the mouth of the Ohio and descended the Mississippi till the Missouri was reached. Here the tribes further separated. The "Quapas"—"the people who went down stream"—penetrated the wilds southward and possessed themselves of Arkansas; the "Omahas"—"the people who went up the stream"—ascended the Missouri and made their home in eastern Nebraska. The Poncas and Iowas are usually classed as belonging to this tribe. The Otoes, Peorias and Missouris, who we will recall were first mentioned by Father Marquette in 1673, also belonged to the Siouan family. They all took up abodes along the Missouri and drifted westward up the Kaw and the Platte. At this juncture the Pawnees swarmed in from the south and by sheer force of numbers overcame the smaller Siouan tribes and reduced them to a state of vassalage. This was, however, of so mild and paternal a nature that the vanquished appear to have been quite content with the new condition of things. Indeed when in later times the Pawnees became weak and dependent, the wards took the part of the taskmaster against their own kinsmen, the Dakotahs.

The Sioux are the most important of the Siouan stock. Numerically they are the largest in the United States with the possible exception of the Ojibwas. The Sioux call themselves Dakotah, Nakotah, or Lakotah, according to the respective dialect, the name signifying "allies." The popular name by which we know them is a corruption of the old Ojibwa "Nadawesiwug," meaning "enemies." The early French pronounced this as "Nadaousioux," which by shortening became modern "Sioux." This warlike tribe had at an early date forgotten their sedentary habits and become a nation of roaming buffalo hunters. From the headwaters of the Mississippi they gradually moved westward, pressed upon the east by the fierce Ojibwas who were aided by the French. Crossing the Missouri they invaded the hunting grounds of the Kiowas, Cheyennes and Crows, whom they crowded beyond the Black Hills. For many years the Niobrara River in Nebraska formed the line of demarcation between the Sioux and Pawnees. When the Sioux finally extended their hunts and forays beyond this stream a relentless war commenced, which ended only with the utter annihilation of the valient foe from the southland. In 1837 the Sioux sold to the government all their claims to lands east of the Mississippi. In 1851 they surrendered the greater part of Minnesota and removed to the plains of Dakotah. But a general dissatisfaction with the manner in which the government fulfilled the terms of the treaty led to the massacre of white settlers at Spirit Lake, Iowa, in 1857. A few years later, in 1862, the shrewd chieftain, Little Crow, still chafing under real and imaginary wrongs, took advantage of the national government's embarassment consequent upon the Civil War and with his bands fell upon the outlying settlements in Minnesota, massacring fully 1000 of the settlers. This inaugurated a bitter war which lasted until 1869. The Indians were speedily driven out of Minnesota by General Sibley. Little Crow and his bands escaped to Canada, while the remainder, under command of Red Cloud and other noted chiefs, sought refuge in Nebraska, where they continued the contest for seven years. Those were bloody days upon the plains. The valley of the Platte was then the great thoroughfare to California. Along a line hundreds of miles in length the plainsmen were exposed to attack. To hazard crossing the plains in small companies was now to invite sure destruction. The pioneers were forced therefore to organize in strong caravans or trains, armed to the teeth. Even then they were not always successful in making their way to the mountains. The trail from the Missouri to the Rockies became marked with bleaching bones, burnt wagons and rotting harness.

The military had its hands full and indeed on occasion suffered severely. Thus, in 1866, Colonel Fetterman's entire command of 165 men was massacred near Fort Phillip Kearney. The frontiers and outlying ranches were panic stricken and at one time in 1864 many were entirely abandoned. The Sioux were aided by the Cheyennes in these raids or, more correctly, the latter headed the first Platte River attack, after which the Brules and other Sioux joined in the fray, soon becoming the leaders. The Cheyennes were by this time closely allied to the Sioux through intermarriage of the tribes, and trouble with the one nation was sure to mean war with both. The Cheyennes had long been dissatisfied with the way the whites treated them and especially did they hate the soldiers at the army posts along the route. These seem to have been unnecessarily harsh in their treatment of the Indians, and at times to have brutally misused them.

Let us here note the magnitude of the traffic by the great overland route of the Platte. It was not unusual, says an old rancher, to stand at one's cabin door and count from 1000 to 1500 wagons passing in a single day. Or to take an example more to the point: One St. Louis firm, Russell, Majors, Waddell & Co., operated no less than

Rosebud Sioux group.

6250 wagons, requiring a team force of 70,000 oxen, and representing an investment of nearly $2,000,000, When it is borne in mind that this firm was only one of the many doing business between the river and the mountains, we shall readily comprehend the enormous proportions of the traffic.

The first outbreak of the war occurred at Plum Creek in Dawson county on the 17th day of August 1864. This point was at that time the most important stage and telegraph station between Fort Kearney and Fort McPherson. After leaving the station and the broad valley the route led to a point where steep bluffs and wood-covered canyons afforded excellent concealment to a prowling foe. In this death trap the Indians planned their ambuscade, and fell upon an unsuspecting wagon train, killing the entire party of eleven, plundering the wagons and then setting fire to them. Fortunately the Indians had neglected to cut the telegraphic communication eastward, and this alone prevented the general massacre, long planned. Settlers and ranchmen received timely warning and generally succeeded in reaching some point of refuge. For weeks all was panic and confusion. However, with the aid of the military, some degree of reassurance was established and many of the fugitives returned to their homes. For almost five years did the war drag on, involving terrible loss in life and property. During these years numerous pitched battles were fought between the government regulars and the Sioux. The last and decisive fight took place at Summit Springs, Sunday, July 11, 1869.

The Sioux, under command of the vile chief, Tall Bull, had for some time made life unsafe along the Republican, when Gen. Carr of Fort McPherson started in pursuit with several companies of U.S. Troops and Major Frank North's band of 300 Pawnee scouts and fighters. William Cody, better known as "Buffalo Bill," acted as guide. July 5, Cody and six Pawnee scouts discovered the Sioux in the sand hills south of the Platte, whither they had retreated in haste upon hearing of the pursuit. When the attack was made the Sioux broke up into small bands and escaped under cover of darkness. Three days later, however, 600 Sioux were discovered in the act of fording the river and a sharp fight ensued. The Indians suffered heavy loss among others the famous chief, Tall Bull, falling a victim to Cody's unerring aim. On the following Sunday General Carr, who had followed the main trail, overtook the reunited bands at Summit Springs. The Sioux held their ground and a day-break battle ensued. It was short but decisive. Many soldiers and Pawnee scouts were slain, and at least 700 of the

28 Chapter II

Sioux mother and babe: early trailers of the Loup.

Sioux, including many chiefs and sub-chiefs. The handful who escaped the carnage sought safety in headlong flight. Considerable booty was made. Herds of ponies, the entire camp outfit and 300 squaws fell into the victors' hands. This battle practically ended the war. The Indians' power of resistance was broken and while a few depredations were committed after this time, they were limited to the stealing and running off of stock in the border settlements.

The same year a treaty of peace was made which remained unbroken until the invasion of the Black Hills by miners, consequent upon the discovery of gold, led to another war in 1875–77. Nebraska fortunately was spared the brunt of this outbreak, the main actions taking place in Montana. The chief event of the war was the surprise and massacre of the intrepid Gen. George A. Custer and his entire command of nearly 300 regular troops in the bluffs of the Little Big Horn country. Sitting Bull is credited with being the leader of the hordes who on that memorable occasion overwhelmed one of the most daring and idolized Indian fighters of his century. Four days later Gen. Crook arrived upon the battlefield and in a series of fights took summary revenge upon the Indians. Of these Sitting Bull with several thousand followers escaped to Canada where he remained till 1881, when he returned on promise of amnesty.

In 1889 another treaty was made by which the Sioux surrendered the richest lands of the "Great Sioux reservation," embracing all of South Dakota west of the Missouri. In lieu for this they were given five small, distinct reservations and certain annuities. The new arrangements were exceedingly distasteful to a powerful minority, and this, together with an Indian "Messiah Craze" led to a new outbreak in the fall of 1890. At Wounded Knee, on the White River, one of the bands, which had voluntarily surrendered, attempted a treacherous surprise of the troops which all but succeeded. The trick was, however, discovered in the nick of time, and what had at first promised the annihilation of the unsuspecting regulars, was turned into a terrible massacre of the red men. When the affray was ended fully 300 Indian dead covered the field.

A blot upon our escutcheon in this war was the slaying of old Sitting Bull and members of his family December 15, 1890, by a troop of soldiers sent to arrest him at his lodge. The old chieftain made but little show of resistance and his death was entirely unwarranted.

The Sioux were typical nomad hunters and warriors. Numerically and physically strong, they made themselves masters of the buffalo plains, no other tribes being able to make a successful stand against them. In their skin tepees they dwelt where the buffalo was plentiful. They had their horses, dogs and weapons of war and were content As warriors they were ruthless and unforgiving. No more striking example of these traits is found than in the vengeful spirit with which they hunted down and hounded the Pawnees to utter annihilation.

The census of 1900 places the nation at fully 24,000, distributed as follows: Canada (refugees from the U.S.), 600; Minnesota, 930; Montana (Port Peck Agency), 1180; Nebraska (Santee Agency), 1310; North Dakota (Devil's Lake and Standing Rock Agencies), 4630; South Dakota (Cheyenne River, Crow Creek, Lower Brule, Pine Ridge and Rosebud Agencies), 15,480.

III

Glimpses of State History

> Now let us climb Nebraska's loftiest mount.
> And from its summit view the scene below.
> The moon comes like an angel down from heaven;
> Its radiant face in the unclouded sun;
> Its outspread wings the over-arching sky;
> Its voice the charming minstrels of the air;
> Its breath the fragrance of the brightest wild-flowers.
> Behold the prairie, broad and grand and free—
> 'Tis God's own garden unprofaned by man!
>
> —*Nebraska—A Poem**

One is accustomed to think of Nebraska as a state with but a brief history. And when we consider her history in relation to her forty-four sister states this is perfectly true. In another sense, however, the state has a history surprisingly old. Fully sixty years before the founding of Jamestown in Virginia, and three quarters of a century prior to the coming of the Pilgrim Fathers to New England shores, did white men travel over the great plains of which Nebraska forms a part, and write narratives minutely describing the fauna and flora of those parts. Not from the east but from the far southland, Mexico, came the adventurers who were first to gaze upon her virgin beauty of plain and hill. It fell to the lot of the romantic Spaniard to shed poetic glamour over the first pages of Nebraska history. And it came with the far famed expedition of Cavalier Francisco Vasquez de Coronado, which left Compostela, Mexico, February 23, 1540.

From an early date wild stories had been afloat in New Spain (Mexico), telling about a marvelous province, Cibola, in which were said to be seven magnificent cities, far surpassing the city of

---

* Editor's Note: *Nebraska—A Poem*, which was published anonymously in 1854 by John P. Jewett and Company (Boston), addressed contemporary debates on slavery and the Kansas-Nebraska Act of 1854. The author is believed to be abolitionist and journalist George Washington Bungay. Excerpts of the poem were republished in a variety of Nebraska publications, including the 1902 Bulletin of the Nebraska Bureau of Labor and Industrial Statistics (p. 5).

Chapter III

One of the "Seven Cities of Cibola."

the Montezuma in riches and splendor. Several expeditions were dispatched to find the much coveted prize, but all these, daunted by the terrible journey across mountain and through desert waste, despairing of success, returned empty-handed. It was not till the year 1536 that the government determined to make a concerted effort to reach Cibola. In that year Cabeza de Vaca and three companions—the only survivors of the Narvaez Expedition, which had been shipwrecked at the mouth of the Mississippi—arrived at San Miguel on the Gulf of California. These men told marvellous tales of their tramp from gulf to gulf. Of how their Indian captors had carried them from tribe to tribe and how in course of these wanderings they had at one time come to mavellous cities, built of stone and brick and surpassingly rich in gold and silver. These tales gave new life to the "Cibola" stories, and stirred the covetous Spaniards to immediate action. The friar Marcos de Niza was accordingly sent forward on a preliminary expedition. This was in 1539. Marcos, who evidently did discover one of the Zuni or Moqui pueblos in upper Arizona or New Mexico, brought back glowing reports to Coronado, the governor of New Gallicia. He had, said he, not alone found fair Cibola, but the half had not been told about its marvels.

An expedition was now organized which had for its avowed purpose the conquest and Christianization of this fairy realm. And accordingly the governor in own person set forth with a large force of horsemen, infantry and native allies, supplied with artillery and large stores of ammunition and foodstuffs. With much difficulty he made his way across the mountains and into eastern Arizona, and there stormed the strongly built stone pueblo of Hawiku, which may yet be seen in its ruined state. This was, no doubt, one of friar Marcos' "Seven Cities." Not finding the fabled riches here, Coronado sent out expeditions to the west and north, which explored the country as far as the mud pueblos of Tusayan and the Grand Canyon of the Colorado. But as these expeditions were equally unsuccessful, the small army was ordered eastward and wintered on the banks of the Rio Grande in New Mexico.

During the winter of 1540–41 the river tribes were subjugated after fierce resistance. Such shocking cruelty did the Spaniards display in their fights with the tribes that these in a dire extremity preferred death by fire to the small mercy of their Christian conquerors. At this juncture an Indian warrior appeared before Coronado with a strange story about "the great kingdom of Quivera" lying many leagues to the northeast. A wonderful land indeed was this, "with its river seven miles wide, in which fishes large as horses were found; its immense canoes; its trees hung with golden bells, and dishes of solid gold." This remarkable tale had all the effect that could have been intended for it. The credulous Spaniards took the bait and one self-sacrificing red man, thinking more of ravaged kin than life, led the way into the Stalked Plains of Texas, drawing the hated white man as far as possible from the poor, tortured, peace-loving tribes at home.

After 700 miles of weary plodding across "mighty plains and sandy heaths" the explorers reached the banks of a great river which they called "St. Peter or St. Paul," and which from all reports must have been the Arkansas. Prior to leaving this stream the leader ordered the main body of his soldiers back to the old camp on the Rio Grande; with only 30 picked and mounted men did he then continue the search for Quivera. Northward, day after day, till 48 had sped by, did they continue—not always in a straight line, but searching out the country as they advanced.

And here let us pause long enough in our search for the promised land to peruse a quaint but graphic description of early day life on the great buffalo plain, as it comes from the pen of the Spanish chronicler, the first civilized man to see such wonders: "The men," he says, "clothe and shoe themselves with lether, and the women which are esteemed for their long lockes, cover their heads...with the same. They have no bread of any kinds of graine, as they say, which I account a very great matter. Their chiefest foode is flesh, and that oftentimes they eate raw, either of custome or for lacke of wood. They eate the fatts as they take it out of the oxe, and drinke the bloode hotte, and die not therewithall, though the ancient writers say that it killeth, as Empedochs and others affirmed. They drinke it also colde dissolved in water. They seeth not the flesh for lack of pots, but rost it, or so to say more properly, warme it at a fire of Oxe-dung; when they eat, they chaw their meate but little, and raven up much, and holding the flesh with their teeth, they cut it with rasors of stone which seemeth to be great beastialitie; but such is their manner of living and fashion. They goe together in companies, and moove from one place to another as the wild Moores of Barbarie, called Alarbes doe, following the seasons and the pasture after their oxen.

"These Oxen are of the bignesse and color of our Bulles, but their homes are not so great. They have a great bunch upon their fore shouldres, and more haire on their fore part than on their hinder part, and it is like wool. They have as it were an horse-manne upon their backe bone, and much haire and very long from their knees downward. They have great tuftes of haire hanging downe at their chinnes and throates. The males have very long tailes and a great knobbe and pocke at the end: so that in some respect they resemble the lion, and in some other the camel. They push with their hornes, they runne, they overtake and kill an horse, when they are in their rage and anger. Finally it is a foule and fierce beast of countenance and form of bodie. The horses fledde from them, either because of their deformitie, or because theye had never seene them."

In July the expedition reached a group of tepee villages somewhere near the borderline between Kansas and Nebraska. Coronado, at last satisfied that he had been duped by his crafty guide, straightway hanged that unfortunate to a tree on the banks of a stream which may have been the Republican or the Blue, in Nebraska. Farther to the north, he was told, was another large stream, presumably the Platte. No records are left to show that he approached this river any nearer.

This we know, however, that he now turned eastward, marching till he reached the banks of a "large tributary of the Mississippi," no doubt the Missouri. And there he set up a cross with the inscription: "Thus far came Francisco de Coronado, General of an Expedition."

Upon returning home to his province our explorer wrote a letter to the Viceroy of New Spain, in which he states that, "the province of

Quivera is 950 leagues (3.230 miles) from Mexico. The place I have reached is 40° in latitude. The earth is the best possible for all kinds of productions of Spain, for while it is very strong and black, it is very well watered by brooks, springs and rivers. I found prunes like those of Spain, some of which were black, also some excellent grapes and mulberries."

Much good ink has been wasted in efforts to determine the exact northward limits of Coronado's march. One of the most learned of the scholars writing upon this subject is Judge Jas. W. Savage, whose interesting paper is found in the Nebraska State Historical Society's report for the year 1880. The gist of this gentleman's argument is that Coronado simply could not have failed to have reached the Platte or at least the Republican in Nebraska. He says that "from the point where he left his army, Coronado must have proceeded in a direction west of north, 'They had diverged too much toward Florida,' says Castanada. The time occupied in the march by the detachment is uncertain; Castanada gives it as 'forty-eight days,' while Coronado says in one place that it was forty, and in another forty-two days. Taking the lowest of these numbers, and conceding that it includes also the twenty-five days spent by the general in exploring Quivera, and there was ample time to reach the Platte or the Republican River." Now here we have it, "there was ample time," but have we the proof? Everything being equal, as we say, he should have reached both the Republican and the Platte, but, alas! what does this prove? Such hypotheses are dangerous to say the least, and we must not in our enthusiasm run away from the hard, cold fact. To the writer it does not appear that the evidence in the case is sufficient to substantiate the allegation; he prefers, therefore, to let the case rest upon Coronado's own statement that he reached 40 north latitude. And this may mean that he never set foot on Nebraska soil, and again, that he advanced some distance into the state.

"In the twenty-five years since Judge Savage presented his paper a great deal of new light has been shed on the subject. The route of Coronado has been minutely studied. It has been established beyond question that the Quivera Indians were the Wichitas,—they being the only Indians in all that region who built grass houses. A great river which Coronado crossed on his way to Quivera has been very closely identified as the Arkansas. With these two points conceded it is not hard to fix the valley of the Kansas river in the vicinity of Fort Rily as the true site of Quivera. Here are the remains of a vast former Indian

Chapter III

population,—acres of rough flint axes, knives and arrow heads, and at a distance of a few miles other remains of a finer flint workmanship mixed with thousands of fragments of pottery. Exploration begun in 1896 on this site by Mr. J. V. Brower of Minnesota, culiminated in the declaration by him that he had rediscovered Quivera."— A. E. Sheldon in Semi-Centennial History of Nebraska, Lincoln 1904.

It is surprising how often even really great scholars will overreach themselves in their zealous endeavors to substantiate their claims and to prove their contentions. Much eager credulity is too often displayed in attempts to prove one's pet theory. And in this respect it seems to me, our esteemed friend, Judge Savage, was no exception. He states in

Quierva Monument, Junction City, Kansas.

a note to his paper "that the engineer of the new branch of the Union Pacific Railway, now building northward along one of the forks of the Loup, report numerous ancient mounds along their route, and many evidences of once populous cities. Specimens of the ancient pottery, with the shards of which the ground is thickly strewn, are almost identical with those still to be found at Pecos and other cities in New Mexico. This fact is peculiarly interesting in view of one of the statements of the Turk, just before his execution, to the exasperated Spaniards, that the cities to which he was conducting them were still beyond."

The "new branch of the Union Pacific Railway" here spoken of is none other than the Republican Valley (Union Pacific) Railway between Grand Island and Ord, and then refers more particularly to that section of the road which lies between St. Paul and Ord. To think that the railway engineers should have found "evidences of once populous cities" on the beautiful Loup will certainly come as a surprise to the many old settlers of the Valley who as early as 1872 became familiar with almost every foot of ground between "Athens," and "The Forks" of the Loup and the Calamus, but who never dreamt of any such great past for their beloved valley. Many of them were good old plainsmen, too, and well versed in Indian lore. They were not ignorant of the fact that theirs was an "Indian country," and that it had for years been the stamping ground of two great, contending Indian nations the Pawnees and the Sioux. Almost any pioneer from the early seventies can show a goodly collection of chipped arrows spearheads, war clubs and specimens of pottery. They were acquainted, and well acquainted with the so-called mounds, but never had cause to disassociate them with the Indians of their time. Even now the zealous collector may when the ground is burned over chance upon chipped flints and shards of broken pottery in great abundance. The author, who has been identified with the valley for almost 25 years and who knows by sight the outline contour of almost every hill bordering the valley for 50 miles or more, has spent much time in excavating the "mounds" and has been well repaid for his efforts with a store of wampum, flints and pottery. But that these "mounds" and deserted camps bore "evidences" of some great and buried civilization certainly never occurred to him. Indeed, his knowledge of Indian lore, limited as it is, has but a very prosaic explanation for the "evidences," and forces him thus, at one fell stroke, to rob the valley of the distinction of having been the wonderful province of Quivera, the realm of

Tartarrax, "the long-bearded, gray-haired and rich, who took his noon day sleep in a garden of roses, under a huge, spreading tree, to the branches of which were suspended innumerable gold balls, which sounded in exquisite harmony when shaken by the wind."

The "once populous cities," we do not hesitate to state, were *chateaux en Espagne* in the minds of men more at home in engineering than in ethnology. Old, deserted Pawnee and Sioux camps took on marvelous shapes in their imagination and the hilltop burial grounds became, by some strange mind contortion, mounds of unknown wealth and antiquity. No, let us stick to the fact. The North Loup Valley was at no time the home of the semi-civilized Indian. But up and down its whole length the barbarous plains Indians, for untold ages, lived and fought and died. His bones lie buried there and the Manitou still guards the sacred places of the departed.

When Coronado, discouraged and heartsore, forever turned his back upon Nebraska, the darkness of barbarism again settled down over the plains, not to be dispelled for another 200 years. Not till after the acquisition of the Louisiana Territory in 1803 did men's minds turn to the possibilities of the great unknown West. The Lewis and Clark Expedition left St. Louis on the 14th of May 1804, and spent two whole years exploring the great purchase. The reports brought back tended to familiarize the east with this vast region and its unlimited resources, and paved the way to the first commercial enterprise between the two sections of our country. Even before Lewis and Clark skirted the state had enterprising Frenchmen crossed the Missouri in quest of pelts. Pierre and August Choteau, brothers engaged in the fur trade, are known to have passed beyond the forks of the Platte away back in 1762. They may at that early date have trailed along the Loup, fully a hundred years in advance of the first settlers.

Traders, hunters and explorers soon began to pour into the "Indian country," beyond the Missouri. The first known settlement on Nebraska soil was a trading post founded at Bellevue by a wealthy Spaniard, Manuel Lisa, in 1805. The American Fur Company organized by that early captain of industry, John Jacob Aster, established its Missouri headquarters at Bellevue in 1810. This post became the center of a monster traffic with the Indian tribes as far westward as the mountains. Other posts were established for like purposes at Omaha, in 1825, and at Nebraska City, in 1826.

Lack of space forbids a detailed account of the men, the first to blaze the way for later comers to the territory. A bare list of names and dates of a few must suffice. Lieutenant Zebulon Pike travelled through southern Nebraska on his way to the Rockies in the fall of 1806. Thos. Nutell and John Bradbury spent a part of 1808 in the territory botanizing. Major Stephen Long crossed the Missouri into Nebraska on the 10th day of June 1819, and traversed the state from east to west. William Asheley, the head of the Rocky Mountain Fur Company of St. Louis, ascended the Missouri in boats, to the mouth of the Yellowstone. This was in 1822. Colonel John C. Fremont left St. Louis in May 1842, bound upon his important trip across the purchase to the mountains. He spent part of the summer in Nebraska.

At this juncture an event of much interest occurred. It was the advent of Mormons to Nebraska soil. This religious sect had been driven from its home at Nauvoo, Illinois, and was now, after much buffeting around, massing on the banks of the Missouri, preparatory to crossing the "Great Desert" to the Promised Land beyond the reach of law. Immediately above Omaha, where the present town of Florence lies, some 15,000 Mormons established a camp, spoken of as "Winter Quarters." Here they remained through 1845–46, and to all intents began permanent settlement. Such inroads did they make however on the timber up and down the valley that the Indians, angered at what they considered wanton devastation of their lands, sent a bitter complaint to the government. This resulted in a peremptory order for the Mormons to move on. The terrible journey to the Great Salt Lake was thus begun. Months of toil and hardship, of suffering and death, amidst the burning desert sands and at the hands of hostile Indian bands finally brought the wearied advance guard into the beautiful Jordan Valley. But at what a cost! The trail from "Winter Quarters" to Salt Lake City was indelibly marked but for later comers. Castaway garments, broken and burned vehicles, bleaching bones of cattle and horses fallen by the wayside, and graves of weary pilgrims scattered along the route of a thousand miles told the cost.

Many a disheartened wanderer shrank from facing these hardships and preferred to settle along the route of progress in the fertile valleys of Nebraska. In this way numerous small Mormon settlements sprang up along the Platte and its forks. The most interesting of these, in many respects, was the Genoa settlement in Nance county. Here a large tract of land was enclosed and divided

Chapter III

among a hundred families comprising the original settlers and foundations for solid prosperity were laid. Unfortunately for them this land was part of the tract set aside by the government for the Pawnee Indians, under the treaty of 1857. On account of this circumstance they could not obtain title to the lands. In addition to this trouble frequent raids upon their cattle and horses by Sioux and Pawnees alike made life precarious. It thus came about that the settlement was abandoned and today only a few low, crumbling earthworks mark the spot.

Then came the gold fever. This most seductive of metals was discovered in 1848, and by the following year thousands were already moving through the Platte Valley on their way to California. This event was of much importance to the future history of the state. "The moving host left here and there a permanent impress upon the land nor was this all; the land in turn so charmed the eye, and created so abiding an impression on the mind of many a beholder, that wearied with the unequal contest of the camp, they abandoned the pick and spade for the surer implements of husbandry; remembering the beautiful valley of the Platte, they sought its peaceful hills and plains wherein to erect homes for their declining years." In 1851 one William D. Brown established a ferry on the Missouri River between the trading post of "Lone Tree," or Omaha, founded back in 1825, and the present Council Bluffs. The effect was to divert a measure of the traffic held by "Winter Quarters" and Bellevue and to lay the foundations for the growth of Nebraska's future metropolis. Furthermore the discovery of gold and the consequent growth of empire on the Pacific led to the erection of the trans-continental railway lines. Thus originated the Union Pacific, hugging close the old overland trail, and other trunk lines which together have been the means of throwing open wide the vast resources of the state.

Indeed did the opening of the great Overland route work wonders in the development in the future state. Favorable reports were by the thousands flocking to the gold coast or returning home, carried to all parts of the country. The exceptional advantages held out to all turned the tide of immigration into the Nebraska valleys, and prosperous communities sprang up along the many rivers. Politicians, too, casting about for more territory to erect into slave states early took a hand in the making of the new commonwealth. But, first, let us pause for a moment.

In 1803 the most important real estate transaction in American history was consummated. On the 30th of April of that year, Napoleon Bonaparte, acting for France, ceded to the United States that vast region lying between the Mississippi and the Rockies, popularly known as the Louisiana Purchase. Thus, for the paltry sum of $15,000,000—less than four cents an acre—were 1182.752 square miles of the richest lands in the world added to our domain, and at the same fortunate stroke was the future mastery of the Western Hemisphere by the United States made an assured fact. On the 20th of December the Stars and Stripes were raised in New Orleans "amidst the acclamations of the inhabitants," and the purchase became American soil.

Prior to the purchase of Louisiana the Ohio river was considered the line of demarcation between the free north and slave south. About year 1820 the slavery agitation began to take on a new and dangerous face. The struggle had by this time come to center in the national congress. Southern politicians feared to lose the balance of power in Congress and persistently held out for more slave territory, which would mean more representatives in Congress favorable to the perpetuation of their system.

The province of Maine asked for admission as a state in 1819 and the House of Representatives promptly passed the bill; but when it came before the Senate, a clause providing for Missouri as a slave state was tacked on by the way of amendment. After much heated debate the matter was compromised. The contesting factions accepted an amendment proposed by Jess B. Thomas of Illinois, which provided, "that in all that territory ceded by France to the United States under the name of Louisiana, which lies north of thirty-six degrees, thirty minutes north latitude, not included within the limits of the state contemplated by this act, slavery...shall be and is hereby forever prohibited." In plain language, Missouri became a slave state and slavery was forbidden in the remainder of the Louisiana territory north of Arkansas. In this way it came about that slavery could never be lawfully carried on within the bounds of the future state of Nebraska.

When Missouri was admitted to statehood the territory yet unorganized became grossly neglected. Finally in 1834, the jurisdiction of the United States District Court of Missouri was extended over part of it; another portion was annexed to Michigan Territory, and the remainder became a part of Arkansas Territory. A

42   Chapter III

Nebraska Territory in 1854.

natural consequence of this arrangement was the great laxity in law and order on the frontier. Almost the only protection against the lawless element in certain parts infesting the territory, was the few military posts scattered here and there at long intervals.

Naturally enough the settlers began to long for a more stable form of government.

Meanwhile the slavery question would not down. The California problem had opened again partially healed sectional wounds. That rich territory, it will be remembered, lies partly north and partly south of the old line of demarcation—latitude 36°30'. Naturally enough this led the pro-slavery people to hope for the erection of a slave state on the Pacific. In this they were however destined to sore disappointment as California, in December 1849, asked for admission as a free state. The south felt outraged.

Have we not, exclaimed southern men, been robbed of the richest region acquired from Mexico—the region of the war acquisition best suited to the furtherance of our system! Just so, and hadn't California and extension of slavery to the Pacific been one of the most potent causes of the war? Exactly. Little wonder the contest grew exceedingly bitter, and engendered a dangerous spirit on both sides of the Mason and Dixon line. Again was balm poured upon sectional feeling and the inevitable breach postponed for a few years longer. This came about through the Compromise of 1850. But the remedy proved in time almost as bad as the disease and early proved a disappointment to friends of peace in both sections of the country. Out of it came, in 1857, the Dred Scott Decision by the United States Supreme Court, which to all intents opened all northern territory to the nefarious traffic. A northern Democrat who held that the Compromise of 1850 had nullified the Missouri Compromise was Stephen Arnold Douglas, United States Senator from Illinois. For many years this gentleman had been anxious to organize the vast territory lying west of Missouri and Iowa. In January 1854, Douglas introduced a bill to provide for the organization of all this tract as the territory of Nebraska. The bill provided "that this territory should be admitted to the Union at some future time as one state or as several states, with or without slavery as their constitution may prescribe at this time." Douglas was an ardent advocate of "Popular Sovereignty" and desired to leave the question of slavery or no slavery to the vote of the people of the proposed states. Before its final passage the bill was changed to provide for the organization of two territories, Kansas and Nebraska, instead of just Nebraska. Of these, the latter was to include all that part of the region lying between 40 and 49° north latitude, and extending from the Missouri and the White Earth River to the mountains. The bill finally passed both houses and was signed by President Pierce on the 30th of May.

The limits of the new territory were greatly reduced in 1861, when all the region north of the 43d parallel became a part of Dakota Territory. The same year a part of the southwest corner was added to Colorado and the western limit definitely settled on the 110th meridian. This left Nebraska in the shape of a rectangle some 700 miles long and fully 200 miles wide. A further carving down occurred in 1863. Then the portion to the west of the 104th meridian was added to Idaho Territory. This reduced Nebraska to the present limits, if we except a very small strip in the northwest, added to the state in 1882.

As a first step in the organization of Nebraska Territory, the president, Franklin Pierce, appointed Francis Burt of South Carolina, governor, and Thomas B. Cuming of Iowa, secretary. The governor reached Bellevue October 7, 1854, and took up his abode with Rev. William Hamilton, in charge of the Presbyterian Mission House there. No sooner had the new head of the government arrived than sickness forced him to take to his bed; from this he was destined never again to rise.

In spite of sickness the oath of office was administered to him by Chief Justice Ferguson. This took place on the 16th of October and two days later the governor was dead. Thus the very first act in the history of the new territory became a sad and tragic one.

Secretary Cuming immediately took up the reins of government and first of all ordered a census taken. To this end the territory was divided into six counting districts. By November 20th the table of returns from all districts was completed, and showed a population of 2732, which, no doubt, consisted in a great part of "floaters" on their way through the counting districts. The population ascertained, the acting governor next apportioned the 13 councilmen and 26 representatives provided for in the Organic Act among eight voting districts. The first general election ever held in Nebraska occurred on the 12th day of December 1854, at which time not only were the 39 legislators elected but also a representative to Congress.

The machinery of government was now set in motion in all its departments. The first Territorial Legislature convened, in obedience to gubernatorial proclamation, at Omaha City, January 16, 1855, and the bitter contest for the location of the territorial capital was on. Governor Burt had intended to make Bellevue the seat of government; but his early demise gave the acting governor an opportunity to decide in favor of his personal choice, Omaha. For days after the opening of the session crowds of armed men paraded the streets of Omaha and vowed that no session should be held there. Fortunately these hot headed pioneers did not go beyond threats, and our new territorial escutcheon was spared the stains of early, needless bloodshed. Florence, Nebraska City, Plattsmouth, and several towns farther inland, were all eager to capture the plum, and now for twelve years was the fight waged with unceasing bitterness, at one time indeed causing the secession of a part of the Territorial Legislature in favor of Florence. The struggle developed into a fight for sectional supremacy—it became the North Platte country against the South Platte country. At last when Nebraska in 1867 was admitted to the union, Lincoln, in Lancaster county, became the permanent capital.

It is not our purpose in these pages to attempt a portrayal of the state history of our noble commonwealth. In the passage from this part of the work to the story of the North Loup Valley let it here suffice that the statehood question came up at a very early date.

The first dwelling in Lincoln, 1867.

In 1860 the people voted down a proposal to call a constitutional convention. Congress passed an Enabling Act four years later, and in 1866 a constitution was adopted by the state. Congress immediately ratified this action by passing the "Admission Act" of July 18, 1866. This act was however pocket-vetoed by President Johnson. Next February he again vetoed a similar bill; but this was passed over his veto and Nebraska became a state upon the first day of March 1867.

Thirty-seven years of peaceful development have changed the state from the wild "Indian Country" that it was to one of the richest agricultural states in the Union. This evolution, indeed, albeit surprisingly rapid, was not brought about but at some cost. Our fathers, who first broke the virgin prairie, suffered all the hardships consequent upon the settlement of a new country, before we their children could enjoy the fruits of their labor. There were the Indian uprisings, with sad stories of settlements destroyed and families broken up, repeated destruction of crops by swarms of locusts, destructive windstorms in summer and blizzards in winter, hail storms and droughts, in a word, all the evils and hardships that go hand in hand with blazing a trail in the unknown.

In education, Nebraska bears the proud distinction of having the lowest percent of illiteracy in the United States. The public school system has reached a degree of excellence attained by but few of the older states. 250 public high schools with almost 16,000 scholars, 19 private high schools and academies with 700 students, an excellent state university with 2500 students, and a dozen flourishing denominational and private schools for higher education are all doing their share in the great work of maintaining for the state the high intellectual rank already attained.

The increase in population, too, has been remarkable. The census of 1854 showed only 2732. Since that time, by decades, the census shows the following figures: In 1860, 28,841; 1870, 122,993; 1880, 452,402; 1890, 1,058,910; 1900, 1,066,300. In the decade 1890–1900 the population remained almost stationary. This is accounted for by the serious droughts which were especially severe in the early nineties. A number of the western counties actually decreased in population on this account at that time. Since 1900 there has been a steady and even rapid influx in population, and every county in the state has showed a marked increase.

Nebraska is chiefly an agricultural state. All the cereals are raised, though corn is the most important crop. Up to 1880 the acreage of wheat was almost as great as that of corn, but since that time the acreage of the former decreased more than 2–5 of the entire area devoted to it. Since 1890, however, wheat culture has again forged to the fore to such a marked extent indeed that the acreage which in 1890 amounted to 798,855, was ten years later, 2,538,949. The corn crop acreage increased during the same decade from 5,480,279 to 7,335.187, and the hay and forage crop from 2,462,245 to 2,823,652.

The census of 1900 further shows that for the census year $4,137,000 was realized from the sale of dairy products, while an equally great amount was consumed by the farm population. This is remarkable in the face of the fact that a few years ago dairying as we now understand it was of but little importance. Then cattle were raised chiefly for the packing trade. The beef raising industry is nevertheless on the increase. In 1900 there were in the state 2,663,699 head of cattle. In the same year only three states exceeded Nebraska in the number of swine.

Politically, Nebraska is ranked as a Republican state. In every national election save one, that of 1896, when a favorite son, William Jennings Bryan, carried the state, has it cast its electoral vote for the Republican candidate. In state politics, as will appear from the appended list of territorial and state governors, the elections have by no means been so uniformly Republican:

Territorial

Francis Burt, 1854
T. B. Cuming (acting), 1854–55
Mark W. Izard, 1855–57
T. B. Cuming (acting), 1857–58
Alvin Saunders, 1861–67

Wm. A. Richardson, 1858
J. S. Morton (acting), 1858–59
S. W. Black, 1859–61
A. S. Paddock (acting), 1861

State

David Butler, Rep., 1867–71
W. H. James (acting), 1871–73
R. W. Furnas, Rep., 1873–75
Silas Graber, 1875–79
Albinus Nance, 1879–83
Jas. W. Dawes, 1883–87
Jobn M. Thayer, 1887–91
James E. Boyd, Dem., 1891

John M. Thayer, Rep., 1891–92
James E. Boyd, Dem., 1892–93
Lorenzo Crounse, Rep., 1893–95
Silas A. Holcomb, Fusion, 1895–99
Wm. A. Poynter, 1899–01
Chas. H. Dietrich, Rep., 1901
Ezra P. Savage, 1901–03
John H. Mickey, 1903–

IV

Glimpses of the North Loup Valley

> The land lies open and warm in the sun.
> Anvils clamor and mill wheels run,—
> Flocks on the hillsides, herds on the plain,
> The wilderness gladdened with fruit and grain!
> — John Greenleaf Whittier, "The Preacher"

It was midsummer in the year 1904. The author found himself aboard an "accommodation" train on the Burlington running between Palmer and Burwell. For hours had the puffing engine been jerking and jolting the creaking cars through deep cuts in the grotesque hills of Greeley county. A thunder-storm was passing overhead. This was the last cut; then came the down-grade. And that meant that we were about to enter the North Loup Valley. A sudden careening around a steep curve—and the first glimpse of the Valley is caught. Wonderful! Beautiful! The angry thunder-cloud has passed by and only scattered drops are falling, glistening in the sudden burst of sunlight. A few puffs of cloud by contrast give life to the deep blue afternoon sky. Right before us the bluff chain is broken, and we gaze through the beautiful natural gap to the far-stretching panorama beyond. Through a fringe of gnarled, dark green scrub-oak the eye seeks the landscape just beyond—a vista of river valley, reaching out some four or five miles in width. Through it winds, like a silver chord, the clear, low-banked North Loup river. Broad acres of waving corn, just bursting into tassle; golden squares of wheat and oats in shock, and stack. Well-built farm houses, surrounded by orchards and groves of shade-tree, stud the beautiful expanse everywhere. On all sides are manifest signs of thrift. Ah! this is indeed "God's Country." The magic wand of enterprise has already outstripped the words of the poet who sings:

> The rudiments of empire here
>   Are plastic yet and warm:

Chapter IV

> The chaos of a mighty world
>   Is rounding into form!*

Indeed it has been shaping swiftly. Thirty-three years ago saw the first furrow broken, and now this thronging humanity, this throbbing life and thrift!

Years ago—a quarter century past—the author, then a little chap, herding cattle in the valley above Ord, according to his daily wont, had retreated to a shady nook on the bank of the river, while his charges were left to shift for themselves. And well they might, for was not the prairies theirs for miles around! He was dreaming all enrapt in the charm of the virgin prairie—dreaming of things yet to be. As he lay there seeing visions and listening to the gurgling eddying waters swishing by he could almost

> —Hear the tread of pioneers
>   Of nations yet to be
> The first low wash of waves where soon
>   Shall roll a human sea.†

And they came, these pioneers, and they are silently leaving us again passing away to the realm beyond. And the great human sea is rolling, wave upon wave, over the prairie, first trodden by them, obliterating their footprints, making this a new land, almost strange to the first comer. They endured much, those pathfinders, for us their children, that we might reap the fruits of their industry and toil. And shall we thus repay them by leaving the history they made unsaid, unsung? No! a thousand times no! Let it be taken down that the generations yet unborn may know at what a cost the way was paved. How they suffered and toiled and even died that the trail of the Loup might be opened. And now where and what is the North Loup Valley—this much praised garden spot of Nebraska! Let us answer this query at once. By the North Loup Valley or region, as here understood, is meant all that portion of this drainage system included in Loup, Garfield, Valley, Greeley and Howard counties, linked into one commonality by one common history, by mutual ties

---

* Editor's note: From John Greenleaf Whittier's "On Receiving an Eagle's Quill from Lake Superior."
† Editor's note: From John Greenleaf Whittier's "I Hear the Tread of Pioneers."

of friendship and good will, cemented at the time of first settlement, which have drawn these political communities into a bonded union strong enough to disregard mere artificial boundary lines set up by law of government. It includes, on the rough, the Taylor-Kent district in Loup county, the Burwell-Willow Springs lowland in Garfield county, all of Valley county, the Scotia district of Greeley county, and the Cotesfield district in Howard county. In other words it includes not merely those communities which have a history in common but virtually all the really fertile, valuable lands drained by the North Loup river and sections from the Middle Loup as well.

The most important of all this region is the river valley. Here we find a fine alluvial floodplain, usually marked by two terraces, the upper bench so well adapted to all agricultural purposes, and the "bottoms" chiefly important for their rank growth of forage grasses. The valley, in places, reaches a width of almost six miles, and then again, in its upper course, dwindles down to a few yards. Geologically almost the entire region belongs to the Champlain Period of the Quaternary Age. The mighty rolling or abruptly jutting hills, everywhere flanking the river basin, are composed almost exclusively of the wonderfully loess clays characteristic of that period. As this clay is inexhaustible in its fertility, even the steepest hills may be cultivated year after year without the aid of artificial fertilizers. The upper part of the region only belongs to another and more ancient period—the Pliocene. Portions of Loup and Garfield counties and a few square miles in northeastern Valley county are encroached upon by the great Pliocene Sand Hills. This part of our Valley is therefore more properly a grazing district. To get a more definite idea of its topography, let the reader study carefully the maps of Loup and Garfield counties given elsewhere in the book. The North Loup river rises among a cluster of small lakes in western Cherry county, just east of the 101st meridian and about 50 miles from the north line of the state. Some twenty or more lakes comprise this group. And a more beautiful region can hardly be imagined. Some of the lakes are crystal clear, with pebbly bottoms. All nestle in the sandhills, but they are immediately surrounded by grass plots of remarkable richness. Out of them flows the river at first a mere silver thread, making its way by tortuous windings through the hills, which in the upper course approach almost to the river brink. After it enters Loup county the valley becomes well defined, though at first narrow and of a sandy consistency. By degrees, however, an alluvial soil appears, which becomes deeper and richer

52   Chapter IV

A view taken in Olsen's Canyon.

as Garfield county is approached. The stream itself is shallow and bounded by low, usually treeless banks. Small islands, often covered with a dense growth of cotton wood, box-elders, ash, and thickets of wild plums and choke cherries, dot the rippling, eddying stream, and add much to a scenery which might otherwise become a little monotonous. The river bottom is, for the most part, fine shifting sand, but compact enough to make fording by heavy wagons perfectly safe. The river sands are, as far as we can ascertain, of Pliocene origin. It should be added, though, that in places these beds have been worn through and the underlying Miocene sand-stones laid bare. A most remarkable instance of this water activity is seen in the falls of the North Loup in the sand hill region. Here the river suddenly tumbles over a sandstone ledge 12 feet high and almost 50 feet wide, forming quite a romantic fall, and indeed the second largest in the state. At Burwell, in Garfield county the North Loup receives its only important tributary, the Calamus. This beautiful, clear stream drains a large section of the sand hills and is remarkable for the numberless springs that everywhere well up from its bottom.

The sand hills cover hundreds of miles lying north of the Loup and even encroach greatly upon its upper drainage. They must have originated, as pointed out in Chapter I, from a disintegration of young and poorly consolidated Miocene and, more particularly, Pliocene rocks.

Before the advent of white man the hills were not so stable as now. The vast herds of buffalo which used to roam here trampled the grasses and loosened the sand exposing it to wind and weather, thereby causing a perpetual shifting in surface. Then too, the great prairie fires, which in bygone years annually laid the surface bare and destroyed a very important fertilizing debris, are now much more infrequent and may soon be a thing of the past. Within the memory of the oldest settler important changes have taken place in the once decried sand hills. Now they are completely grassed over and are coming to be recognized as some of the most important grazing and alfalfa lands in the state.

An impetus was given to the settlement of the sand hills when in the summer of 1904, the so-called Kinkaid Law went into effect. Under this act any bona fide settler in this region may homestead as many as four quarter sections of land where previously one quarter section was the limit allowed any one homesteader. The wisdom of the law is already manifest in the great increase in actual settlers during the first year after its passage.

A typical "Blowout."

Chapter IV

To the northeast of the river, covering a few square miles in Valley county and extending into Garfield county, lie the "Sand Flats." This weird tract has always been of absorbing interest to the writer. As one drives along over its undulating surface, abrupt bluffs rise out of the distance, encompassing the whole area. It appears for everything in the world like an immense amphitheatre. The bluffs along the horizon, many of them, rise in steps much like the tiered Roman theatres. There cannot be the least doubt as to the origin of this strange land formation. It represents the bottom of a lake, drained out almost within historic times. Drifting sands have then blown over the lake bed and given to it the present undulating surface.

South of the sand hills Valley county is a mighty, wavy loess plain pierced diagonally by the flood trough of the North Loup River, which divides the county into two unequal triangles. The hill lands to the northeast have a southward trend and drain through a series of small creeks into the river. The Middle Loup River cuts across the southwest corner of the county, whence it runs parallel with the north fork till the two unite in Howard county. The uplands between the

Road in Olsen's Canyon.

two streams in Valley county form a rolling plateau and drain partly into the North Loup, partly into the Middle Loup. The soil is highly fertile and almost every foot of ground may be tilled.

It is interesting to note that the three forks of the Loup, which, after uniting to form one stream, meander along for a hundred miles parallel to the Platte before pouring their waters into the latter, flowed at one time as three separate streams and emptied as such into the Platte. "Later, the stronger Platte, while building up a bed some 300 feet thick, obstructed the flow of the Loup by throwing sandbars across their mouths, and thus forced them to shift their courses eastward or down the Platte valley to find a new and united outlet over the steadily rising barrier of sand."

The following description of Valley county townships is taken from the Bulletin of the Bureau of Labor, Lincoln, 1902, and gives in the main a fair estimate of our soil:

Range 13

T. 17. Rolling, fertile; North Loup valley.
T. 18. Northeast half: in North Loup valley; fertile; rest rolling; fertile.
T. 19. Southwest half North Loup valley; rest gently rolling; fertile.
T. 20. Northeast quarter mostly sand flats, fertile; rest rolling, one-half tillable.

Range 14

T. 17. All quite rolling, fertile; about two thirds tillable.
T. 18. Northeast part quite hilly, fertile; rest Mira valley, gently undulating, very fertile.
T. 19. Southwest third quite rolling, about one-half tillable; rest North Loup valley, fertile.
T. 20. North Loup valley; rest pretty rough, but one-half tillable.

Range 15

T. 17. Rolling; fertile; good farm land.
T. 18. All very fertile, mostly in Mira valley; little of it quite rolling.
T. 19. Mira valley, very fertile; rest rolling, fertile, one half tillable.

Section of Jones' Canyon.

T. 20. North Loup valley, fertile; northeast sixth rough, fertile, southwest half quite rolling, but fertile.

Range 16

T. 17. Middle Loup valley, sandy, fertile; balance rolling, fertile.
T. 18. East two-thirds rolling, fertile, about one-half tillable; rest sandy and rough.
T. 19. Mira valley in middle east; portions in north and south rough; balance rolling, fertile.
T. 20. South half quite rolling, about one-half tillable; north half very rough, good pasture.

By far the larger fraction of lands in the Loup Valley is fertile though here and there right in the heart of the best loess and alluvial soils are found unproductive alkali spots. These are, it is true, less frequent and smaller in our part of the state than in many other localities. They appear usually in tablelands and lowlands having poor drainage. The standing water escapes by evaporation and the saline compounds, found in all water, are left behind. An analysis of the white, brinelike substance gathered on the surface of such spots will usually contain a large proportion of soda compounds, with an occasional excess of lime, potash or magnesia. Alkali lands should be kept well plowed, and be given artificial drainage if at all possible. Careful tests have proven that wheat rapidly consumes the alkali. A few crops of this cereal on alkali grounds is known to have made the latter well adapted for other grains.

Thirty-five years ago the Valley was preparing for the advent of the pioneer. Before this an occasional pathfinder had hunted and trapped along its water courses; but the Sioux war which dragged along and hardly came to an end before the close of the sixties made such expeditions extremely hazardous, and kept all but the most foolhardy away. Now, however, the war was closed and the trapper set his face in earnest northward, intent on making the beautiful valley his home. And close upon his trail followed the pioneer farmer, the maker of the valley. But here let us pause again to picture the virgin soil as it must have appeared to the first comer, with its flora and fauna.

A luxuriant growth of wild grasses covered hill and valley, all untouched by the plow. Myriad wild flowers in their season helped to give color to the landscape. A heavy growth of hard and soft wood trees then covered the river islands much the same as in our day. The really important forest growth of those times was the cedar canyons, now long ago despoiled of their giant cedars and pines. The most extensive of these were found on the north side of the river between Fort Hartsuff and Willow Springs, although well-timbered canyons were found on both sides of the river as far up as Taylor, in Loup county. East of the Perks of the Loup and Calamus grew an abundance of the Western Yellow Pine (Pinus Ponderosa), a remnant of the great fir forests which at one time covered much of the sandhill region, and which may again under government care be made to flourish there. The cedar canyon especially celebrated was "Jones Canyon" in the immediate vicinity of Willow Springs, known to settlers for many miles up and down the valley. The canyons were usually deep rifts in the hills, running more or less at right angles to the river plain, with sides so steep and broken as to form an adequate protection against the annually recurring prairie fires. Here a splendid growth of evergreens flourished. The red cedar (Juniperus Virginianus) was the most important for all purposes. Out of them the best dwellings in the settlements were erected; and so sought after were they that settlers would come from two and three days' journey to get the coveted timber. During the early days, when the grasshoppers ravaged the crops, leaving the settlers to stare starvation in the face, this logging industry became their salvation. Great oxloads of cedars were carted all the way to Grand Island, a distance of fully eighty miles, and sold to the Union Pacific Railway Company.

Three of the most valuable native grasses, growing on the Loup in the early days, were the sorghum grass (Surghum nutans), the blue joint (Andropogon furcatus), and the buffalo grass (Buchlae dactyloides). Of these all but the latter yet flourish and form the bulk of all our wild forage grasses. The sorghum grass is by many experts picked as Nebraska's most nutritious native grass. In early springtime it is not easy to distinguish it from bluejoint; when, however, its russet like spikelets in a compact panicle make their appearance, all danger of such mistakes disappears. It is very hardy and if cut just before frost, makes splendid hay. Blue joint grows ranker than the foregoing; the stem when full grown is from four to five feet high and is surmounted by a cluster of four to six straight, rigid and hairy spikes, from three to five inches long, and of a purple color.

The famous buffalo grass once grew over the whole region between the Missouri and the mountains. It formed the chief food of the buffalo and has ever been favorite with all kinds of domestic stock. This nutritious grass, too well known to need description, is curiously enough rapidly disappearing from the plains, and is in our state threatened with total extinction. In the Loup valley where it used to be so abundant now only isolated patches are found, and these in depressions and alkali spots. Many theories have been advanced to explain this disappearance, occurring as it did contemporaneously with that of the buffalo. The most common sense explanation seems to be "that change of climate, especially increase of rainfall, had most to do with this phenomenon."

The Loup was formerly a veritable paradise for game and carnivorous beasts. The monarch of all the game roaming here was the bison (Bos Americanus), popularly known as the buffalo. Almost

The last buffalo on the Loup. (From a photograph taken some years ago at the county fair held at Ord.)

incredible stories are told by early settlers and freighters across the plains about the size of herds they so often encountered. Thus we hear of "Buffalo Bill" estimating a certain herd at 500,000. By 1872 the large herds had already left the valley of the Loup. Bands from half a dozen to a score continued to roam in Garfield and Loup counties for several years longer. As late as the summer of 1874 Charles Post and his brothers killed some fine specimens on Pebble Creek, and even in 1875 James Barr found a last straggler, dead in a wallow near "The Forks." They had for some time been drifting over onto the Middle Loup, soon to disappear altogether. For years skulls, with fairly well preserved horns, could be found on the prairie and in many an old time home may they yet be seen, adorning some mantel piece or wall.

Great herds of elk (Cervus canadensis) frequented the Loup for years after its settlement and were a source of much highly valued food. They usually kept to the hills, but would occasionally enter the valley. Mira valley, with its surrounding hills, seemed to be their most favorite haunt. Two old-timers, Truman Freeland and A. R. Harper, state that on one occasion they counted fully 500 in one herd grazing in that valley, with many smaller bands scattered over the hillsides.

Again we are told that while Fort Hartsuff was being erected away back in 1875, one day a fine herd estimated at least 300 poured out of the hills on the opposite side of the river, near where Elyria now stands, and sought the bottoms at the water's edge. All work on the fortifications immediately ceased, as the workers to the last man threw down pick and shovel to seize the rifle instead. In the pine groves at "The Forks" the elk held out the longest, Alex Draver slaying the last one there in the winter of 1882. It was not an uncommon thing in those days to see tame elk and deer grazing peacefully about the dooryard of some homestead.

The pronghorn antelope (Antilocapera Americana) was very common. Herds of from 20 to 100 of these graceful animals were common sights along the hill ranges. Their natural curiosity made them an easy prey for the early hunter and they passed from the valley about the same time that did the elk. Three species of deer were formerly found here. These were the common red deer (Cervus virginianus), the white tailed deer (C. leucrus), and the black tailed deer (C. columbianus). 1885 saw the last deer in the valley proper. At that time they sought the less frequented sand hills to the north, where they were hunted for some years. Even in our day an occasional deer may be shot on the Calamus or in the lake country. The writer had the good fortune to see several excellent specimens on the reed grown banks of Dad's Lake as late as 1893.

Bears were never plentiful in our state, the Niobrara country alone being their natural haunt. In 1875, however, it appears that one had wandered far to the south of his native wilds, for in that year William Pierson killed a large silvertipped bear (Ursus Americanus) between the North Loup River and Brush Lake.

Of carnivorous beasts several species of timber wolves skulked about in the wooded canyons, and the night on the prairie was often made hideous with the yelp of the prairie wolf, or coyote. A few lynxes and wild cats were shot in the timber lands. Such valuable fur bearing animals as the beaver, otter, mink and marten were numerous. Raccoons and badgers yet survive. Opossums, while more at home farther south, have been found on the Calamus and the upper Loup. Polecats and skunks, prairie dogs and ground squirrels of many species have always been with us. Gallinacious birds were represented by four species, and of those only three now remain. Of these the wild turkey has been seen only a few times in our section, and that long ago. The sharp tailed grouse were very numerous at one time but are now

Elk at play: an old-time winter scene from "The Forks."

62 Chapter IV

In his native wilds.

much reduced in numbers. The prairie chicken and quail arrived in the settlements with the first crops and have been with us in goodly numbers ever since. The enforcement of stringent game laws has made both of these birds, and especially the industrious and useful little quail or "Bob White," very plentiful.

Anserine birds are represented in many species of ducks, geese and brants. Wading birds, such as the king plover, the piper and the gray snipe, are abundant in the lowlands while the shrill call of the long billed curlew is still heard in the sand hills. Numerous songsters, piscarian birds, and birds of prey of many species make the valley their home in season. Of reptiles and saurians various turtles and lizards are represented. Of snakes, the black snake, the garter snake, the bull snake and the prairie rattlesnake have been common. Of these the latter has now fortunately become practically extinct. Many species of edible fish have ever been abundant in our water courses. Much other animal life, altogether too numerous to dwell upon here, filled land and water and air when the first settler arrived.

Hill and valley were inviting and rich with an almost profligate abundance of natural wealth. Nature awaited only the hand of civilized man to turn it all to practical uses. And he was coming. The forerunners were already in the Valley.

V

Cowboy Regime and Forerunners of Civilization

> Your creeds and dogmas of a learned church
> May build a fabric, fair with moral beauty;
> But it would seem that the strong hand of God
> Can, only, 'rase the devil from the heart.
>
> —Duo*

The early pages of frontier history are usually written in blood. There are the harrowing tales of massacre by prowling and vengeful Indians, or if these are wanting, then desperate encounters with the lawless element incident to life beyond the reach of the arm of law and justice—the confidence man and gambler, preying upon every newcomer; the old time cowboy element, "shooting up" the town or embroiled in desperate feuds with the homesteader; fugitives from justice, lawbreakers of all kinds escaped from the older states "back East." The North Loup Valley settlements were in most respects no exception to this rule. They experienced their share of Indian scares, and can record some thrilling encounters with the red men. The desperado and gambler too appeared on the borders after the first waves of settlement had subsided. But they did not long remain. The atmosphere was not congenial and the field anything but profitable. The character of the pioneer fathers was of too sterling a makeup to long countenance outlawry and all that it begets. So this scum of all new civilizations passed away, no more to show its face. Yes, the settlements did not escape these experiences, but this was to be expected. They might have fared much worse. Indeed, should we compare our early days with the pioneer history of, say, the Middle Loup settlements, our immediate neighbors on the west, we might consider ourselves very fortunate indeed.

In the evolution of the virgin prairie to settled homestead, our valley by its fortunate location escaped such harrowing incidents of

---

* Editor's note: James Fenimore Cooper uses the same epigraph for Chapter XII of his novel *The Pioneers*.

border feud and bloodshed between cowboy occupant and pioneer homesteader as fell to the lot of Custer and other counties west of us.

At the time when our narrative opens, the cattle industry on the Great Plains had taken on vast proportions. Great herds of cattle from Texas and the "Pan Handle" were in full possession of "No Man's Land" and western Kansas, and great tracts in southern and western Nebraska were swarming with thousands of "rangers." The cattle kings seized upon all the good herding grounds and built their home ranch on every available watercourse, to the exclusion of actual settlers. Once in possession the cattlemen proposed to hold the range in spite of herd law and homestead law, by force if necessary. To the good fortune of the North Loup country, when the cattle kings first began to invade our state settlers were already in full possession of the Platte valley as far west as Dawson county. This circumstance checked a direct northward movement and forced the oncoming tide to turn to the northwest, thereby sparing our part of the state for a few years, long enough for the first settlers to take possession. So by the time the cattle movement could outflank the Platte settlements and again swing eastward, gradually to spread over the unorganized territory embraced in the South and Middle Loup valleys, the North Loup was absolutely safe against encroachment.

The unorganized territory immediately west of Valley county was, at an early date, attached to that county for judicial purposes. And its history in a way becomes our history. To properly understand all the details surrounding our own development, therefore, it becomes necessary to give some attention in the passing, to the lawlessness and bitter strife and bloodshed which for some years possessed our Custer county border. The natural fertility of the soil in the unorganized territory early attracted the attention of landseekers. But to actually homestead the land occupied by the cattlemen was a serious matter. The latter considered all such attempts as encroachments upon their personal rights, and the settlers as so many intruders. The first homesteaders accordingly lived precarious lives. Thousands of cattle ranged at will over the country and necessitated a constant watch over the fields by night and by day. To fence one's fields was to invite a raid from cowboys who made short work of all such protections. And to resist force with force meant the loss of house and home and sometimes life to boot. In those days discretion became the better part of valor.

The years 1877 and '78 witnessed a great influx of settlers to Custer county. The fine bottom lands along the water courses became settled and it really began to look as though the great herds of cattle would be entirely excluded from their old watering places. This to them seeming gross injustice angered the cattlemen, especially as it was the general opinion then that only the bottom lands were fit for agriculture; these occupied by farmers would render practically valueless for grazing the thousands of acres of unwatered hill country. Custer county, they argued, was a natural grazing country, and should be maintained as such. Another, and the immediate cause of many deeds of violence, was the prevalence of "cattle rustling." It will be borne in mind that the cattlemen allowed their stock to roam at will over the range. This meant that for months at a time perhaps they would be beyond their owner's reach, who saw them usually but once a year at the annual "round up." The straying cattle thus fell an easy prey to unscrupulous characters, who would coolly shoot them down, slaughter them, and haul them by the wagon load to the nearest railroad station for shipment. This traffic took on vast proportions before the cattlemen could notice their losses. When finally they woke to a realization of what was happening their rage knew no limits, and death by lynching would have been considered almost too good for a culprit caught in the act. The real thieves were and remained unknown. The cowboys, already prejudiced against the settlers, naturally enough charged these crimes to the latter. That the settlers did occasionally shoot and slaughter a beef or two there can be little doubt—nor was it more than fair recompense for ruined crops—but that they were guilty of this wholesale slaughter and exportation no one believes for a moment. This crime must be laid at the door of cattle thieves from the state at large.

Matters went from bad to worse till the cattlemen in their desperation resolved to drive the settlers to a man from the country. This initiated a state of lawlessness very seldom equalled in border feuds. Cold blooded murder, in its most cruel form, was repeatedly committed, and no man's life or property was deemed safe. The climax of all this misery was the murder and burning of Luther Mitchell and Ami Ketchum—one of the most dastardly crimes ever chronicled in the criminal history of any nation. So gruesome are the details of this heartrending tragedy that we almost rebel against repeating them in this narrative. But it is deemed advisable to do so in order better

Chapter V

Old Mitchell Ranch House, Custer county.

to impress our readers with the true significance of the North Loup Valley's escape from cowboy regime:

"One of the most wealthy of the cattle-owners of Nebraska, was I. P. Olive, who owned many thousand head of stock that found pasturage in Custer county. He had, from time to time, lost a great many animals, some of them undoubtedly stolen by cattle thieves. For this reason he became the prime mover in the attempt to expel the settlers from Custer county. His headquarters were in this county, although he resided in Plum Creek, Dawson county. He had come to Nebraska from Texas on account of having been concerned in the killing of several men while there, and it is said that he had been guilty of other murders. Fearing both legal and personal vengeance, he fled to Nebraska. He was accompanied by his brother Robert Olive, who had, to prevent all knowledge of his whereabouts, assumed the name of Stevens.

"Luther M. Mitchell and Ami Ketchum were homesteaders, living on Clear Creek, where they had made a settlement some time previous. Mitchell was an old man, sixty three years of age, a farmer, who had removed here from Merrick county. Ketchum had resided in the state for some years and had worked at his trade, that of a blacksmith, in several towns, but, having decided to go to farming, he entered a homestead here.

"For some time there had been trouble between the Olives and Ketchum. In the attempt to frighten or drive the settlers from the county, they found Ketchum too courageous to be frightened, and too quick and accurate in the use of firearms to be driven successfully. Between Stevens, or Bob Olive, and Ketchum, there had been a great deal of difficulty. Stevens, as he was then known, had on several occasions threatened to kill Ketchum and had also accused him of stealing cattle.

"Some days previous to the trouble that resulted in the death of Stevens, one Manley Capel had been arrested on the charge of stealing cattle in Custer county, and in his confession, seemed to implicate Ami Ketchum.

"Stevens, or Bob Olive, was well known as a desperado, and it was also known that he and Ketchum were enemies. Yet, Sheriff David Anderson, of Buffalo county, made him deputy for the occasion, and gave him a warrant for the arrest of Ketchum. This warrant was sworn out by some members of the Olive gang, and it has been a question whether this warrant was gotten out in good faith, believing Ketchum to be a cattle thief, or merely as a pretext to get him into the custody of the Olives. It is now generally thought that Ketchum was innocent of any crime, that he was merely a peaceable settler, whom Stevens was anxious to kill on account of the old enmity, and because he could not be driven from the country by threats. It is also generally believed that had he fallen into Stevens' hands, he would have been killed on some pretext or other; that there are reasons to believe these opinions to be correct, as the following sketch of the ensuing tragedy will show.

"Stevens engaged three others to accompany him, all rough and desperate men among whom was Barney Armstrong, and proceeded to the home of Ketchum, arriving here on Wednesday morning, November 27, 1878. Mitchell and Ketchum were getting ready on that morning to go to a neighbor's to return a bull they had been keeping. Mrs. Mitchell was preparing to go with them to visit the family of this neighbor—one Mr. Dows—during the day. When they were nearly ready to start, a stranger rode up and asked Ketchum, who was a blacksmith, to shoe his horse. Ketchum told him that he could not on that day, and asked him to return the next morning, which he promised to do and rode off. It has since been supposed that he came there in the interests of the Olives, to see if the intended victims were there. Mitchell and Ketchum had put their rifles in the wagon, hoping to see some same on their journey. Ketchum also took his pistol, which he always carried, from the fact of Stevens having threatened his life.

"While the men were taking care of the animal, Mrs. Mitchell took her place on the seat to hold the team. While Mitchell and Ketchum were tying the bull to the axle of the wagon and gathering in the long lariat rope by which it was tied, Mrs. Mitchell observed a party of men riding toward them, but it attracted no particular attention, as they were frequently visited by hunters and land seekers. As these men came up, they dashed along, four abreast, and, when they came near, began shooting. Stevens, or Bob Olive, was the first to fire, and as he did so, he called to Ketchum to throw up his hands. For reply, Ketchum drew his pistol, and, at his first shot, Stevens fell forward in his saddle, mortally wounded. Meanwhile, the other men kept up the shooting, and Ketchum was wounded in the arm. The children came running out of the house, when one of the men began firing at them but without effect. Mitchell reached into the wagon, secured his rifle and began firing, but Stevens now turned and rode off, and he was soon followed by the remaining cowboys. There were from twenty-five to thirty shots fired, but only with the effect stated. As soon as the cowboys had ridden away, Mitchell and Ketchum packed up a few of their household goods and started to go to Merrick county, where Mitchell had formerly lived. They did this as they feared violence from the now enraged cowboys. Arriving in Merrick county, they went directly to the residence of Dr. Barnes to attend to Ketchum's wounds. The next morning, acting upon the advice of their friends, the men, Mitchell and Ketchum, having secured a place of safety for Mrs. Mitchell and the children, started for Custer county, to give themselves up and stand a trial for the killing of Stevens. On their way, when they reached Loup City, they visited Judge Wall for legal advice. Judge Wall advised them to go no farther, as the cowboys were waiting for them, prepared to lynch them. They remained here two or three days, and then went to the house of John R. Baker, on Oak Creek, in Howard county, where they were arrested by Sheriff William Letcher, of Merrick county, and Sheriff F. W. Crew, of Howard county, giving themselves readily into custody.

"I. P. Olive had offered a reward of $700 for the arrest of Mitchell and Ketchum, and several sheriffs, among whom were Crew, of Howard; Gillan, of Keith; Anderson, of Buffalo; and Letcher, of Merrick, were anxious to capture them that they might secure the reward. But after they were captured and in the hands of Crew and

Letcher, these officers were unwilling to incur the responsibility of taking them to Custer county, and turning them over to the blood-thirsty cowboys; therefore, they were finally taken to the Buffalo county jail, in Kearney, and placed in charge of Capt. David Anderson, the sheriff of that county, for safe keeping. The prisoners were first held without any legal authority, as I. P. Olive had given the warrant for their arrest, issued in Custer county, into the hands of Harney Gillan, Sheriff of Keith county to serve. The prisoners had engaged T. Darnall, of St. Paul, Neb., and E. C. Calkins of Kearney, as their attorneys. The attorneys endeavord to keep the prisoners in the jail at Kearney, fearing that violence might be done them. The feeling in Kearney at that time was against Mitchell and Ketchum, who were represented as having killed Stevens while he was fulfilling his duty as an officer of the law. A question arose among the sheriffs as to the division of the money offered as a reward for Mitchell and Ketchum, which Olive had declined paying until they were delivered in Custer county. A proposition was finally made to Sheriff Anderson to take them to that place, and $50 was offered him for his services. This he declined to do, however, unless he was paid enough to enable him to employ a sufficient number of men to guard the prisoners. It was finally arranged that Gillan, since he held the warrant for their arrest, should take the prisoners to Custer county, and he promised to notify their attorneys, Calkins and Darnall, so that they could accompany them. As Gillan was a sheriff, and his desperate character was not then known, even these attorneys did not anticipate any serious difficulty. They, however, kept close watch lest the prisoners should be stolen away.

"On the forenoon of the 10th day of December, Darnall, fearing that the prisoners were about to be taken away, was keeping close watch until after the emigrant train came in. This train was late, but Darnall remained at the depot until he thought it was about time for it to leave, when he started away. In the meantime, Gillan had taken the prisoners from the jail, and at just the last moment hustled them on the cars Darnall, then fearing trouble, telegraphed to Gillan, at Elm Creek, first station west of Kearney, asking him if he would hold the prisoners at Plum Creek until the arrival of the next train from the East. Gillan replied that he would do so. To still further secure their safety he also telegraphed to Capt. C. W. McNamar, an attorney at Plum Creek, asking him to keep close watch, to see what was done with the prisoners on their arrival at that town. Plum Creek was the home of I. P. Olive, and here he was surrounded by many friends and employees. They, with wagons, met the party as they got off the train, and, putting the prisoners into a wagon, started at once for Custer county. This was about 3 o'clock in the afternoon. Capt. McNamar being unable to prevail on them to remain, and believing that it was the intention to murder the prisoners, followed them for some distance, when the party separated, some going in one direction and some in another. He followed after the prisoners, however, until after dark, when he lost their trail. The Olive party kept on, all coming together on the Loup River, about five miles from Olive's ranch, where they went through the process of transferring the prisoners from Gillan to Olive. Among those who took the prisoners were Bion Brown, Pedro Dominicus and Dennis Gartrell, Gillan and Dufran walked up the road for a short distance, while the remainder of the party started on for Devil's Canyon, Olive riding ahead and Gartrell driving the wagon. Olive stopped under a large elm tree. Two ropes were thrown over a branch and Gartrell tied one around Ketchum's neck and Pedro Dorninicus tied the other around Mitchell's neck. The ropes were not prepared with slip nooses, however, but were simply tied that their agony might be prolonged. The prisoners were handcuffed together. Ketchum was first drawn up. Olive caught up a rifle and shot Mitchell. Olive and Gartrell then caught hold of the rope and drew Mitchell up. Fisher and Brown pulled on Ketchum's rope. A fire was then kindled under them. Accounts differ as to whether this was done purposely or not. The party had been indulging freely in whisky, and some of them claim that this fire was started accidentally. However this may be, the bodies were frightfully burned. Then next day, when the bodies were found, about three o'clock in the afternoon, Ketchum was still hanging, with his legs burned nearly to a crumbling condition. Mitchell's rope had either burned off or had broken, and he was lying on the ground, one arm drawn up to Ketchum by the handcuffs, while the other was burned off up to the shoulder.

"As soon as the bodies were found, Capt. McNamar returned to Plum Creek and reported the fact. I. P. Olive lived here and also several of the men who participated in the murder. They were well known as dangerous characters, and no one cared to attempt to arrest them. Indeed returning at once to Plum Creek, Olive and his men had threatened to kill any one who should attempt to molest them.

"After a few days, a conference was held at the office of E. C. Calkins, at Kearney, to see what could be done. Sheriff James of Plum Creek, Dawson county; Sheriff Anderson, of Buffalo; Judge Gaslin, E. C. Calkins and others were present. The Judge expressed a willingness to issue a warrant, but the question was who should serve it. Sheriff James refused to do so, fearing that the murderers could not be captured, and even if they could, that he would soon be hunted down by their confederates. Sheriff Anderson objected to going into another county to make an arrest attended with so much danger, but said that if the murderers came into Buffalo county, he would not hesitate to attempt their arrest. Two warrants were then made out for the citizens of Kearney and the law abiding portion of the inhabitants of Plum Creek had resolved that the capture should be made Atty. Gen. C. J. Dilworth, who resided on his farm in Phelps county, near Plum Creek, had for some time, with the assistance of others, been working up a plan for the capture of the gang. On Saturday, January 5, 1879, he telegraphed to Kearney Junction that arrangements had been made to take the murderers, and that the citizens of Plum Creek only awaited assistance. At the former place, a well armed and determined party had been organized under the leadership of Lawrence Ketchum, a brother of one of the murdered men. This party had been anxious to attempt the capture of Olive, but had hitherto been held back by the wiser counsels of Dilworth, who sought by the use of a little strategy to surprise the criminals, and thus save the loss of life that would necessarily result from an open attack.

"On receipt of the message above referred to, the Kearney party took the first train bound west and arrived at Plum Creek after dark. Here they were met by some of the citizens, who took them to a place of concealment, and, upon reconnoitering, it was decided to wait until the next morning, when there would be no suspicion, and they could be captured one at a time. On Sunday morning, Baldwin was seized at break of day at his hotel while starting a fire. A number of the party were concealed in the postoffice where Olive and a number of others were captured, one at a time, as they came for their mail. Fisher and others were arrested singly on the street. There was no bloodshed, and but little show of resistance. The prisoners were then taken to Kearney on a special train. On their arrival, Olive, Green and some of the others, fearing that they were to be lynched, turned pale and showed the most craven fear. They were all confined in the Kearney jail at first, but subsequently were distributed to jails in different parts of the state.

Chapter V

On Monday morning, after the capture of Olive, the Mexican Pedro Dominicus, Barney Gillan, Sheriff of Keith county, and Phil Dufran were captured and brought in to Kearney.

"The time appointed for the trial was the next spring. The place selected by the presiding judge, William Gaslin, was at Hastings. An indictment was found against I. P. Olive, John Baldwin. William H. Green, Fred Fisher, Barney Gillan, Pedro Dominicus, Bion Brown, Phil Dufran, Dennis Gartrell, Barney Armstrong, Peter Bielec and a man called McInduffer, for the murder of Mitchell and Ketchum.

"The trial of I. P. Olive and Fred Fisher began at once and lasted for some time. Brown and Dufran turned State's evidence, and the evidence showed the murder to have been committed in the manner above stated. But Olive and his relatives were wealthy, and no expense was spared in conducting the case in their behalf. During the trial, which attracted the attention of the entire state, hundreds of indignant citizens of various parts of the state went to Hastings, hoping to see justice done. Judge Gaslin was scrupulously honorable, and the murderers had a fair trial. It was known, however, that money was spent freely in behalf of the prisoners and at one time it became so apparent that the end of justice would be thwarted that the people talked of lynching the prisoners, but as a company of soldiers guarded them this was not attempted. Although the evidence was strong against the prisoners, showing that they had deliberately planned and executed a most foul and cowardly murder, the jury went out and returned with a verdict of guilty of murder in the second degree. Judge Gaslin then sentenced I. P. Olive and Fred Fisher to imprisonment for life in the state penitentiary to which place they were taken.

"Immediately after the sentence of Olive and Fisher, their friends began to try to devise plans to secure their release, and the trial of their associates in crime was postponed. The following year, these efforts were successful, and the convicts were released from the penitentiary upon a decision of the Supreme Court of the state ordering them to be set free on account of technical irregularities in the proceeding of their trial. Let it here be stated that Custer county had recently been formed from territory that had before the county organization been in two judicial districts but now was understood to be attached to the western district. The Supreme Court held that the prisoners must be tried within the limits of Custer county and at the same time held that this county 'was in no judicial district,' and hence, that the murderers could be tried before no district judge in the state.

This was the decision of two of the judges of the Supreme Court, but Judge Samuel Maxwell, all honor to him, dissented in one of the ablest legal documents ever prepared in that court.

"The decision of the court of course practically released the convicts and put an end to the prosecution of their associates, nearly all of whom, however, had been allowed to escape from the county jails in which they were confined."

The closing scene in this terrible drama of blood was enacted in Colorado whither I. P. Clive had sought refuge with his son William. For four years, so the story goes, had the released murderer been shadowed by some vengeful enemy, who had gone so far as to bring his son up to share this hatred. The two, father and son, never let the Olives get a moment's respite, but pursued them with the bitterness of death. Finally in 1884 the stroke falls. The son of the unknown avenger shoots young Olive dead in a billiard room; the next day, at a cattle round-up, the crime hardened father falls before the unerring shot of the avenger in person.

It is now time to return to the North Loup, grateful that Providence has shielded the Valley from all such horrible tragedies as the one just narrated, proud in the knowledge that lynchings, and violence of a similar nature against man and law, have never tarnished our fair coat of arms.

But more, turn back in time—back to the years 1868, and for the last time see the Valley preparing for the settler. The surveyor was then busy running township lines and preparing the way for the homesteaders. Nicholas J. Paul, well known as one of the founders of St. Paul in Howard county, had charge of this work. Records show that he completed his task in September 1868. One William Hardin ran all subdivisions between 1868 and '70. The lands were now ready for filing.

We have already learned that the first white custodians of the Loup were trappers and scouts. Several of these strange dwellers on the outskirts of civilization played important roles in the making of the Valley and should be introduced without further delay.

When the first settlers reached the "Big Bend" in 1872 they encountered there an odd character, living in a habitation, half dugout, half log hut, perched on the side of a prominent bluff. Standing seventy inches in his moccasined feet, erect, muscular, with keen blue eyes, blonde hair, falling in waves over his broad shoulders and massive chest—such was Jack Swearengen, popularly known for miles around as "Happy Jack." A more upright frontiersman can not be imagined. Always cheerful, willing and ready to tramp for days to guide strangers in the Valley. Giving was almost a weakness with him. Many a time is he known to have gone hungry that some poor fellowman in want might be fed. "Happy Jack" has with justice been termed the "Pathfinder of the Loup." When the first settlers arrived he became their guide and adviser. Later, when the first settlement was assured, he again took up the trail and became their outpost on the Calamus. It was while here that Sioux Indians almost put an end to his eventful career. They took him captive and proceeded to kindle the fire for a slow roasting alive, when wiser council prevailed and he escaped with his life, on promise never again to be seen in the "Indian country." In 1872 he filed upon a claim almost opposite from the site of the future Fort Hartsuff. Here he lived for years in a dugout on the edge of the picturesque canyon which to this day goes by the name of "Jack's Gulch," or "Happy Jack's Canyon." As a government scout Jack won an enviable reputation. He alone should be given the credit for running to earth the notorious horsethief "Doc" Middleton, a feat which many had attempted but failed.

Jack was by nature a recluse, and in time melancholia began to cloud his old time "happy" countenance. He became distrustful of his fellow-men, and immured himself in the old dugout, where no one cared to approach him save his old friends and neighbors, the Goodenows. In 1879 he was removed by a brother to the old family home in Ohio; here, we are told, his malady, pronounced by physicians as "tobacco tremens," yielded to expert treatment, and Jack soon regained much of his old vigor and cheerfulness. Soon after this his father died, leaving an estate worth fully $40,000. Thus was the old trapper and scout at a stroke placed in easy circumstances for the rest of his days. And thereon the old homestead he now dwells, no doubt living over again the many stirring events of his life on the plains.

It is deemed advisable to close this chapter on beginnings with the life story of another great pathfinder in the Valley, that of Conrad Wentworth. The very graphic sketch herewith given was prepared at the author's request by one who knew "Little Buckshot" as intimately as a brother—George McAnulty of Scotia, himself no mean Indian fighter and soldier, and honored as one of our most substantial pioneers. He writes:—

"Among the many scouts, trappers, hunters, and all around plainsmen who have figured in the early history of the North Loup

Conrad Wentworth, or "Little Buckshot," Government scout, Indian hunter and friend of the pioneers.

Valley, the most picturesque personality was Conrad Wentworth, known at that time from the Missouri river to the Rockies as 'Little Buckshot,' government scout and Indian trailer and fighter. His splendid courage and daring and countless deeds of heroism and self sacrifice have long been celebrated in romance and song. To this great scout's tireless energy and constant watchfulness the early settlers

Chapter V

Garfield county hunters: Alec Draver and Jim Barr.

on the Loup no doubt often owed their so safety from attack by the savage Sioux. Wentworth came from a fine old southern family, but a natural love of adventure early led him to seek life in the West.

"While yet a mere boy he was employed to carry the United States mail from Independence, Missouri, to Santa Fe, New Mexico. Here he saw his first Indian-fighting and developed the natural instincts of the scout and guide, always watching, guarding. Later he went to Salt Lake City and took part in Gen. Johnson's campaign against the Mormons. At this period he performed some excellent work as a scout and gained the lifelong friendship and gratitude of the officers with whom he served. During the Civil War Wentworth acted as scout for Generals Sheridan, Hancock and Merritt; his work was ever of the most perilous nature and full of the greatest service to the government. After the war 'Buckshot' returned to the plains to renew his acquaintance with the Indian and the buffalo, and for the twelve years next following he was employed as government scout and in that capacity came to the Loup Valley in 1871, as chief of scouts for the troops sent to guard the first settlers' homes. He was at that time an ideal trailer. He was well at home in all the western Indian tongues and dialects and his knowledge of the different tribes and their customs was simply wonderful. In stature he was rather below medium height. As he appeared in those early days dressed in his handsome suit of buckskin, with long curly hair with braided scalp-lock or riding the prairie mounted on his famous pony, 'Billy,' he presented a picture never to be forgotten.

"The settlers had, one and all, the utmost confidence in his judgment in all affairs pertaining to Indian craft, and felt perfectly secure when he was known to be in the vicinity. Reticent and modest, he seldom referred in anyway to the adventures which had made his name a household word. A man of great natural refinement, he led a life above all reproach. His domestic life was particularly happy, and his devotion to his charming young wife and children was touching to behold. Mrs. Wentworth was born and reared in Washington D.C. but the brave little woman that she was, she soon adapted herself to her husband's life and spent many happy years with him on the frontier. After passing through scenes of adventure such as falls to the lot of but few, the Wentworths settled in beautiful San Antonio, Texas, surrounded by their children and grandchildren. 'Little Buckshot' has lived to see the trackless prairie over which he helped guide the vanguard of civilization transformed to a great and prosperous section of our common country—the great American Republic."

VI

Coming of the Pioneers

> Center of equal daughters, equal sons,
> All, all alike endear'd, grown, ungrown, young or old,
> Strong, ample, fair, enduring, capable, rich.
> Perennial with the Earth, with Freedom, Law and Love,
> A grand, sane, towering, seated Mother,
> Chair'd in the adamant of Time.
> —Walt Whitman, "America"

The popular highway by which a majority of the early settlers made their way into the upper North Loup Valley had its southern terminus at Grand Island on the Union Pacific railway; thence it extended northward, by devious windings, through the sand range south of the Middle Loup, crossing that river near St. Paul. From this place the trail continued its northward trend, entering the North Loup Valley almost due north of the above mentioned town, and continuing thereafter up the south bank of the river. When the tide of immigration began to turn into the upper North Loup country two important settlements were already in progress in Howard county— the settlement of the Paul Brothers and associates at "Athens," or St. Paul, and that of "The Danish Land and Homestead Colony" at Dannebrog. As the history of the upper settlements, especially during the early years, is more or less intimately linked with the colonization of Howard county it becomes necessary to pause and note the circumstances of its origin.

A cold winter night in December 1870 saw Nicholas Paul, one of the well known Paul Brothers—surveyors and colonizers, and a Mr. Moeller, Vice Consul from Denmark to Milwaukee, camped in the protecting underbrush on the South Loup, not far from where Dannebrog now is. These two gentlemen, huddled under the bank of the river for protection, almost perishing with cold, represented interests which culminated in locating the first colonies in the county. Not in the least dismayed by such unpropitious a beginning, they weathered the wintery blasts and explored the South Loup as far as Sweet Creek before returning to the settlements. Acting upon N. J. Paul's favorable report a locating committee, consisting of N. J. Paul,

Chapter VI

Major Frank North, A. J. Hoge, Ira Mullen, Joseph Tiffany, Luther H. North, J. E. North, Enos Johnson, S. W. Smith, Gus Cox and Charles Morse, ascended the Loup from the Pawnee reservation in Nance county and carefully explored sections of all three forks of the river. The committee eventually concluded to stake their town near the Middle Loup, just midway between the other two forks. This important event occurred about the middle of January 1871. A couple of months later N. J. Paul arrived on the ground with thirty-one colonists and in a short time houses were springing up in and about the new town. This, by the way, was first called "Athens," later changed to St. Paul, in honor of its founders, since there was already one town of the former name in the state.

Meanwhile vice-consul Moeller returned to Milwaukee and organized "The Danish Land and Homestead Colony." This organization also selected a locating committee to come west to further examine the land and determine upon the most practical place for settlement. The men chosen for this task were Lars Hannibal, John Seehusen, L. M. Petersen, and Paul Hansen. A search of several weeks ended in the selection of lands on picturesque Oak Creek, southwestward from St. Paul. When the colonists arrived they founded here a town and named it Dannebrog to commemorate the cross-banner of Denmark, their old homeland.

Both of the settlements had a normal growth and time and, circumstance considered, prospered. The men who built them did not long remain strangers to the upper settlements. Our fathers found it very convenient to stop over at St. Paul or Dannebrog on their periodic trips to and from the "Island." Those were the days of open hearts and hearths. The best the household could afford was none too good for the weary wayfarers. Ties of friendship were formed then between our fathers and the Howard county colonists that neither time nor changing circumstances have been able to sunder. Our hearts go out to those sturdy old pioneers "down the river" who were ever ready to extend a helping hand to the travel-worn trailers of the Loup. Long will their memory be cherished by the sons of these fathers.

It is a well recognized fact in American history that the Church was ever a leader in the colonization of our country in the day of its making. And when it was ripe for a westward growth the various church denominations were among the first to lead their flocks into the wilds. The consecrated man of God has been the most important factor upon the frontier. He became a pathfinder in a double sense.

Historic map: The Trail of the Loup.

Chapter VI

Not alone did he blaze a trail for the later comers, but he also fought to give the settlements the Word of God, which meant to establish law and order where chaos might otherwise have reigned. He saved the settlements from years of disregard for law and usurpation of the rights of the individual. He made it possible that right and not might ruled the wilds.

The North Loup Valley was fortunate in this respect. The first comers were all earnest church men, seeking here an asylum where to worship God according to their own dictates, and untrammeled by other denominations; or they were other honest folk of several nationalities, intent upon making permanent homes for themselves and their families. The very first to consider the possibility of a colony here were Seventh Day Baptists in Wisconsin. A community of these people, in casting about for homes in the new west, were attracted by the general press to the great possibilities of Central Nebraska and the Loup river country then in the course of exploitation. They lost no time in sending out a committee to investigate the practicability of settlement in those much vaunted sections.

Accordingly, C. P. Rood, N. B. Prentice, Amos Travis, and C. H. Wellman arrived in the North Loup Valley in June 1871. They explored the river northward as far as the chalk hills opposite Scotia, but determined to go no farther, as the majority of the committee were not very favorably impressed with the country. Especially did it seem to them to be too far removed from the railway and ready facilities for transportation.

At least one man of the four, however, was not disposed to turn back, and that was C. P. Rood. As he stood on the lofty bluffs looking north up the valley, this must have appeared to him a veritable promised land, if we are to judge of the enthusiastic minority report he made after the committee returned to Wisconsin. The majority report was adopted and for a time the

C. P. Rood, member of first and second locating committees of the Seventh-Day Baptists.

matter was held in abeyance. Fortunately, this was not to be the end of it. For shortly we hear that young men in the Waushara county community had decided to seek homes in the Loup Valley. And for this decision no one is to receive more credit than C. P. Rood. When the boys had finally determined to look up cheap lands in the west, his earnest pleadings and offers of financial assistance had the desired effect. What was more, Mr. Rood in person for a second time that year made the trip from Wisconsin to Nebraska. And be it remembered, such a trip was no laughing matter in those days. It meant weeks of weary journeying overland by team, over roads oftentimes almost impassable or through wilds where the only paths were Indian trails. This second "voluntary committee" kept a diary of their journey from the hour of leaving till the hour of return and from it are drawn the following data, which will not alone illustrate the difficulties to be surmounted in reaching the Loup, but will also tell the story of the first men to actually select claims in the Valley. The writer is W. H. Rood, who still resides at North Loup. He says:

"September 28, 1871, in company with my father C. P. Rood, my brother-in-law Mansell Davis and John Sheldon a neighbor of my boyhood days, I left Dakota, Wisconsin, to view the Loup Valley country in Nebraska. My father who had been one of a committee of four sent out by a colony with headquarters at Dakota, Wis., had in the latter part of June and early July visited the North Loup Valley. When a majority report of the committee was against the advisability of settling in that part of the country, my father in a minority report strongly favored the Loup, declaring it extremely well adapted for just such a colony. Mansell Davis, John Sheldon and myself, having decided to go somewhere to look for a home, received the proposition from my father, that if we would go to the Loup country in Nebraska he was willing to furnish the outfit for travelling (horses and wagons) and would stand an equal share of the expenses. It was to make this journey that we left Dakota on Sept. 28th 1871. Our first day's journey was naturally a heavy-hearted one knowing as we did, that it was to be a long one and likely to keep us from home for some time, since our intention was to remain in Nebraska through the winter. We found some very sandy roads today. We passed through Monticco and camped for the night at Fort Hope on the Fox River."

With this introduction let us leave our trailers to find their own way across the states of Illinois and Iowa, as nothing of an unusual nature occurred during twenty-four days required for that part of the trip.

As they are about to enter upon Nebraska soil Mr. Davis writes further: "Sunday, October 22. Was on the road by four o'clock this morning. Reached a point opposite Nebraska City by sunrise. Crossed the Missouri River on a steam ferry, and soon were on a rough and hilly road in Nebraska Thursday, Oct. 26. Were later than usual getting started this morning. Faced a hard cold wind, with lots of dust from burned-off prairie. Our road look us up Lincoln Creek to Hamilton Center where we camped for the night. The town consisted of one stone building and a dwelling house. The inhabitants were excited over the prospect of a rumored railroad. Friday, Oct. 27. was cold this morning and rather tough getting breakfast. Were on the road again at sunrise. Left the creek soon after leaving Hamilton and took across the prairie to Grand Island. The prairie had recently been burned off, so it was very nasty travelling in such a high wind. John and I chased some antelope but failed to bag any. Crossed the Platte river ford but found little running water. Arrived at Grand Island at about noon. Letters from home. Saturday Oct. 28. As this was Saturday we remained in camp all day. Saw our first Indians. The "Island" is a lively little place. Provisions are getting high. We begin to realize that we are getting a long way from home.

"Sunday, Oct. 29. A terrible wind came up in the night. As we were in an exposed place we thought best to hitch up and get on the road again. So between two and three o'clock in the morning we were on our way across the sand hills to the Loup River. We reached the river at an early hour and camped on an island, where we cooked breakfast. In crossing over the bluffs between the South Loup and the North Loup we rested for a little while at the home of a Mr. Ward (A. Ward of Mira Creek) and camped for the night at a sod house where dwelt Andrew J. Gillespie (near where Cotesfield now is). This has been our hardest day's travel yet. Monday, Oct. 30th. After getting a good breakfast we set our faces toward the bluffs (chalk hills below Scotia Junction). Camped for dinner before crossing the bluffs. We boys followed the river while father crossed the hills with the team to the valley above. Went into camp all tired out at some willows on the river near where Mansell Davis's farm now is. Are now near our journey's end; indeed, we feel as though this is "out West" for all settlers are now below us. The day has been fine. Antelope are plentiful but there is no time to hunt them.

Tuesday, Oct. 31. Father and I went down the river and looked at some heavy timber before breakfast. On the way back we went up stream some distance, and then took across the prairie to reach the wagon, but encountered instead a beautiful little creek which I followed for some distance. Here I shot a coon. After breakfast I followed a large herd of antelope but again failed to bag any. About noon I saw some elk and wolves. After some further exploring we returned to the Gillespie home for the night. Wednesday, Nov. 11. This morning we started early to see what the country was like away from the river. Followed a canyon for some distance, and about noon reached a fair sized creek (Davis Creek) on what is now the Scott place south of North Loup. After dinner we followed the creek for some distance. Father now doubled on the trail with the team. We missed one another that night, and we boys got neither supper nor bed that night… Friday, Nov. 3. Wanted to go hunting today but were obliged to give it up as we had some surveying to do to find the lines of the boys' (Mansell and John's) claims. Went up Mira Creek this afternoon with Will West, a young man who had been with us for a few days. Again we saw game in plenty but failed to kill any. The boys have settled upon what claims to take at last, so we are now ready to return to Grand Island…"

This is as far as we need pursue the reading of Mr. Rood's diary. It should be added that the committee retraced their long journey to Wisconsin that same fall. Here they spent a busy winter talking up the new enterprise and making actual preparations to settle the Loup Valley the succeeding spring.

From the foregoing narrative it appears that the Wisconsin colony were the first to look over lands of the upper Valley and the first to select claims in what had just been organized under the name of Greeley county; but when it comes to first actual settlement, then the palm must be given to a handful of men coming out of old Denmark.* And the facts in the case are as here set forth: Between

---

* Our attention has just been called to the fact that A. M. Stewart, now residing across the line in Greeley county, actually settled on a claim in Valley county five months before the Danish colony entered the county. He picked his quarter in September 1871, and filed on it January 1, 1872. Likewise, A. P. Fish was the very first to move onto a farm in Greeley county. This he did in September 1872. He therefore appears to be the very first actual settler in the entire valley above Howard county.

Chapter VI

George Miller.

1869 and '71 five enterprising young Danes had arrived in the United States, hoping here to win the way for themselves which economic circumstances in the old homeland forbade. In the spring of 1872 we find them all in Missouri where George Moller (George Miller) was engaged in the Iron Works of Crawford county, while Niels Andersen (Nels Andersen) toiled in the Warrensburg coal mines. Peter Mortensen, Christian Frey and Jeppe Smith, the other members of the little band, took any work which promised to turn an honest penny. It early dawned upon the friends that Missouri was not the place for them; indeed they longed for a chance to become their own masters, a chance to show their abilities in the line of "nation-building." Thus it came about that they formed a "partnership for weal and woe" and cast their lot with the North Loup Valley. This was no sooner said than done. All but Christian Prey immediately took ticket for Grand Island and arrived there April 10, 1872. The former was obliged to await the arrival of a sum of money from Denmark. He is nevertheless to be considered as one of the original five, and as one of them he owned his share in the partnership outfit.

At Grand Island all preparations were made for the proposed settlement. There was the outfit to be procured and the thousand and one things so essential in a new country, miles from nearest trading depot. Peter Mortensen says that "jointly we purchased two ox teams for which we paid nearly $400.00, one wagon which cost us an even $100.00, two breaking plows and some few other farm and household utensils, for which we paid proportionately high prices." When all was ready for the start the cattle were "inspanned" and our four adventurers faced north for the conquest of the Loup. George Miller, by right of seniority and because of much experience gained in

Australian wilds and mining camps, was recognized as "lead trecker" and headed the train.

Behold them then good reader, honest men as you know them today—Hon. Peter Mortensen, State Treasurer of our great Commonwealth, Nebraska, and the others, thrifty men all, gee-ing and haw-ing, perspiring and "cussing," as they endeavored to keep the stubborn oxen in the trail of those tiresome sandhills south of the Middle Loup! Little did they then realize what the future had in store for them, either of hardship and tribulation or of wealth and honor! The Middle Loup was forded between Dannebrog and St. Paul. The latter town was then just one year old and boasted four houses all told. On up the valley the journey continued. At Cotesfield our travellers found a handful of settlers and a company of soldiers on scouting duty. "Happy Jack's" quarters were next reached and passed. They were now on the frontier—the very outpost of civilization. The many hues of early springtime were beginning to tint hill and vale as the two creaking ox-carts crossed the southern line to the confines of Valley county. And there was springtime in the pioneers' hearts too; for here at last was their land of promise; of these beautiful river bottoms, of these gently rolling hills—the very pick was theirs. The first camp was pitched on Raccoon Creek, now known as Myra or Mira Creek, near the site of the present day North Loup. Claims were located and all preparations made for permanent settlement. It soon became apparent, however, that the quarters chosen would logically belong to the Seventh-Day Baptist Colony already projected. Accordingly stakes were again pulled and our little band continued up the valley and for a second time camp was pitched, but now immediately above Dane Creek and not far from its confluence with the river.

The farm lands in the river valley at this point are not excelled for beauty

Peter Mortensen.

of location or fertility of soil by any in our section of the state. Here, then, in the very heart of the valley, our pioneers selected for permanent settlement, section eight of the present Ord Township. The very first thing done was to plow a furrow around the entire section—this, by the way, was done by Nels Andersen, who on this account, and justly, claims to have been the first to turn the virgin glebe in the Valley—and then to cast lots for choice of quarters. These fell out as follows: Jeppe Smith, N. W.1/4; Peter Mortensen, N. E. 1/4; George Miller, S. E. 1/4; and Nels Andersen, S. W. 1/4. When Christian Frey, the fifth member, arrived a few weeks later, he selected the S. E. 1/4 of Section six, cornering with the other section on the northwest.

For economy's sake the newcomers deemed it advisable to spend the first year in a "joint habitation," as Mr. Mortensen puts it. This was a part dugout and part log-house, set in the sunny bank of a low sink in the latter's claim. Not alone did this humble abode answer as a home for the owners, but it became also a sort of hostelry—no pay being taken, let it be known—from later comers. Its hospitable roof sheltered many a weary wayfarer in the early days. Furthermore, in these unpretentious quarters was tried the first criminal suit in the annals of the new county; here was held the first school for the upper half of the county; and here for several years, was the county treasurer's office located. We cannot but regret that this modest, though historic landmark should have been demolished, not even a photograph remaining. The cut here inserted is drawn as faithfully as possible from memory and is, at least, in main features, true to the original.

Jeppe Smith.

The first summer was a busy one for the newcomers. Prairie had to be broken for a first crop of sod corn; trees must be felled on the river islands and logs hauled out for buildings to be erected. Then there was the all important culinary department. This was George

Miller's forte. He had, as remarked above, spent some years in the gold fields of Australia, and there proved himself much more successful as a plain cook than as a prospector after the delusive gold. Such early experiences stood him well in stead now. His "boarders" never grew weary boasting of "Uncle" George's culinary skill and of his warm-hearted hospitality to the hungry wayfarer. Mr. Mortensen avers that "Uncle George, in addition to being a good cook, had considerable luck with his hooks and lines, and often

Christian Frey.

surprised his boarders with a fine mess of well baked catfish—a rare change from the usual meal of fat bacon." As a single instance of the open-handed hospitality common to all settlers of the early years, let us relate the first experiences of Melville Goodenow in the county. "Mell" Goodenow, as will be shown elsewhere in these pages, first beheld the valley from the hilltops east of the river. In scanning the beautiful, peaceful landscape lying immediately below him, where he had scarcely expected to find trace of white men, he was, to again quote Mr. Mortensen, "happily surprised in finding evidence of civilization, and was not slow in wading the river. In a weak and nearly starved condition he arrived at our dugout. Mr. Miller received him in true Danish hospitality, and while he was sipping a cup of George's extra strong coffee, the latter soon had a catfish and a pan of hot biscuit ready, and soon our friend sat down to his first—and probably the best relished meal eaten in the Loup Valley." But let us leave the dugout hostelry and trace out the fortunes of Christian Frey.

When the long awaited money from Denmark finally made its appearance, Mr. Frey lost no time in shaking the dust of old Missouri from his feet and setting out for Grand Island. This thriving little burg he reached without any adventures, and was there lucky enough to make the acquaintance of a Paul Andersen from Dannebrog, who gave

Chapter VI

A poor reproduction of Hon. Peter Mortensen's first dugout.

him a lift as far as that place. From Dannebrog the journey was more difficult. It meant a fifty mile tramp across the hills, with knapsack on back.

"Happy Jack's" cabin was the only oasis on this part of the trip, and there Mr. Frey rested for the night. Bright and early the next morning, he was again upon the road, ever northward along the river. By noon he climbed the hills south of where Ord now stands and had little difficulty to locate the white tent of his comrades, some two or three miles up the valley. Footsore and hungry he reached the camp, which to his disgust he found deserted and the tent closed. However, feeling morally sure that he was in the right camp and his companions not far away, he made the most of a bad case by forcing his way into the tent, where after some foraging he succeeded in finding cold victuals enough to satisfy a voracious appetite. Then with a sigh of the well filled he threw himself upon a handy bunk, and was all but drifting into dreamland when, hark! muffled hoof beats in the distance! With a leap he is on his feet and outside the tent, where a hasty survey of the field lends a vision of several Indian warriors on horseback, dashing furiously toward the tent, arms waving and well burnished rifle-barrels brandished on high. This was a moment to try men at home on the plains, to say nothing of a weary stranger in a strange land, suddenly roused from sweet dreams of home across the sea! But if these were savage red skins on murder intent, our camp defender certainly made ready to sell his life as dearly as possible. His old navy pistol, of 50 bore, could surely be relied on to dispatch at least one of the foe and then the Lord would preserve the just! A handy wagon box made an excellent barricade. Back of this protection, then, Mr. Frey crouched, frantically signalling to the oncoming horsemen to halt. Then as bad luck would have it, his ancient weapon exploded, all unpremeditated on his part, and sent its missile whistling dangerously close to the foe.

Here was indeed a predicament! The only weapon of defense suddenly made useless, for we can scarcely count the folding knife which never had seen more serious service than to carve tobacco! And right here the Indians make a diversion. They dash apart to take him on the flanks. They are almost upon him now. The horses' labored breath is audible above the din. The empty pistol may yet make an excellent weapon in a hand-to-hand struggle; so, calmly bracing himself for the final, inevitable crash, when—what means this? Panting horses suddenly reined to their haunches, two astonished pale faces, two pairs of staring blue eyes, such as are found only close up under the Aurora Borealis of old Scandinavia, and—"Det var da som Pokker!" from the one, and "Nu bar jeg aldrig seet Magen!" from the other. Was he dreaming, or was that the tongue he had learned to lisp across the sea! There could be no doubt about it. Here was a case of mistaken identity—a case of Dane meet Dane! Mutual handshakings and explanations revealed the fact that the horsemen were Danish trappers, Dahl and Andersen, who had for some time made their camp with the colonists. They knew that their hosts were away from camp, not to return till night. It was therefore very natural that they should mistake the lone defender of the barricade as an invader and enemy, especially as he fired the first shot. Some of our early fathers have claimed that Frey got rattled and lost his nerve. But, tell me, what tenderfoot in a like predicament could have improved upon our little melodrama? But, as the author is no Irving and this is no Knickerbocker History, we must be done. Only, in passing, let it be said that never for one moment should Christian Frey's courage be questioned. A man who is willing and eager to hunt Indians on no better steed than a mule and who slept week after week all alone in his little ten by twelve log house when many of his neighbors had retired to Cotesfield for fear of Indians is no craven!

The small Danish colony had hardly more than broken ground on their claims before the advance guard of the above-mentioned Seventh-Day Baptists reached the deserted first camp on Raccoon

Creek. The story of their advent is well told by Walter Rood in the North Loup Loyalist which runs as follows:

"Inspired by the glowing accounts of Nebraska as given by the second party that had gone to spy out the land, a number decided to emigrate in the spring to this land—the west. On April 1, 1872, the first party consisting of John Sheldon and wife, Mrs. S. M. Janes and family, Mansell Davis and wife, and Mrs. Bartow, started on their long overland journey. Mrs. Bartow did not reach the place for which she started as she met and loved a man in Iowa; they were married and went to Kansas. On April 3 of the same year Charlie Wellman and wife, George Rood and wife and Charlie Rood took their departure. It was expected that the latter party would overtake the former but for some reason failed to do so, tho' Mansell was overtaken before the end of the journey was reached. The journey at that season of the year was not an easy one to make and was full of incidents and mishaps which are laughable now, but which at that time were rather serious. At a place where a stop was made one night in the Platte Valley they first met and became acquainted with a family that soon followed them up into the Loup country—the family was that of Alonzo Shepard. When Grand Island was reached George and Charlie Rood waited a day or two for Elder Oscar Babcock who was coming by rail and who was to join them there and to go up with them. Thus they did not reach their journey's end till the 13th of May.

"Thru letters written to the Sabbath Recorder, the denominational organ of the Seventh Day Baptists, others of like faith in Iowa, Wisconsin, Missouri, and at Hurnbolt, Nebraska, had learned of the new country and many had decided to cast their lot in the new land, so the parties from Dakota found others had preceded them. There had come from Humbolt, L. S. Davis, A. H. Terry, John Furrow, A. H. Davis and others; from other places H. A. Babcock, George Larkin, G. H. Johnson, N. W. Babcock and others whose names are familiar. Those coming first had camped near the river on Will Negley's place opposite 'Shepard's Grove;' the other party camped near the river and across the creek opposite where N. W. Babcock now lives. The days of the first week were spent in getting acquainted and in looking over the country; and when the Sabbath came, May 18, all gathered at the upper camp where religious services, the first ever held in all this Loup Country, were conducted by Elder Babcock, who had been ordained to the ministry but a few years before this time. The services were conducted in the open air, not even a tent being available for shelter. In lieu of a better thing for a pulpit, or something behind which he might stand, the Elder used an old rocking chair. The singing was led by Charley Rood who was at that time a beardless boy. Thus the beginning of their life here, and the foundation upon which they hoped to build their homes, was a recognition of God's power and an acknowledgment of their faith and trust in Him.

"The week following this service was spent by the men in locating claims and by the women in discussing those questions which are dear to every woman's heart—babies, dress, cooking and their neighbors. The first one to take out homestead papers was Garrett Maxson who filed on the farm now owned and occupied by A. S. Cleary. The original dugout built by Mr. Maxson is still in existance, and is used by Mr. Cleary as a summer kitchen. It, with the house on what is known as the Billins farm, built by John Sheldon, is the only original house that is in use at this time. It is part dugout and part cottonwood logs cut from what used to be an island in the river south of the R. R. bridge at Scotia.

"Among those who filed on land at this time we mention Elder Babcock who homesteaded a part of what is now the townsite of North Loup; Amos Burdick, the farm just west of the 42 schoolhouse; Col. Davis, the farm occupied by Charley Rich; H. A. Babcock, the farm where Claud Hill lives; Bert Davis, Burgess' place; Charley Wellman, the place the family still owns; A. H. Terry, O. S. Potter's farm where Ed. Brace lives; Dr. Badger, McClelan's farm. Nearly all the land taken was in the valley and near to North Loup. But few of these who homesteaded first now own the land then taken; and Mansell Davis is the only one who still owns his farm intact and who has resided continuously upon his land.

"By the time the second sabbath had come several of the new settlers

Hon. Oscar Babcock: first preacher in the valley.

Chapter VI

Marilla (Frederick) Flynn: First white woman on the Upper Loup.

were on their farms, living yet in their wagons, so it was decided to meet at the home—wagon—of Charley Wellman for worship on the second sabbath, and again Elder Babcock preached for the little band who gathered at the appointed place. During the week following this second sabbath service the Elder departed for his home in Wisconsin, thus no preaching services were held, yet the colonists continued to meet for worship during the summer though somewhat irregularly.

"By the 28th all had broken camp and were located on their claims, and had begun in real earnest the work of developing the country. The summer was spent in breaking prairie, putting up hay, trying to raise a little sod corn, building some sort of shelter for the winter and by some of the men in working in the Platte Valley to earn a little money with which to purchase their few necessities. As nearly all who came here were poor and not at all provided with ready cash, not very many luxuries were indulged during this period. And the sod house and dugout made were not the finest in the world, nor were they as well furnished as one might wish them to be, yet all were happy and contented with their lot.[*] Did a plow need sharpening, or were some groceries needed a trip to Grand Island was necessary. In order that letters from home might be received or letters sent to friends, a trip of from thirty to fifty miles

---

[*] Elder Oscar Babcock in speaking of the dugout says: "It required but little money to build one of these houses and to finish it in all its parts. I herewith produce a duplicate of an itemized account of money actually expended in building one of the structures 14 × 14 feet on the ground and one story high: 1 window, 8 × 10 glass $1.25: 18 feet lumber for front door .54; 1 latch and hinge, no lock, .50; 1 joint pipe to go through roof .30; 3 lbs. nails to make door, etc. .19. Total $2.78."

must be made. However, as these were to be a part of their daily life the hardy settlers made the best of them and they but little realized the hardships they were passing through. During the summer other settlers continued to arrive from various parts of the country and by fall quite a respectable settlement was formed."

While the Seventh-Day Baptist colony was thus rapidly getting on its feet, the upper colony was by no means lagging. In June a second contingent arrived. These were Fred Dowhower with family, and a brother, John Dowhower, who filed respectively on the northwest quarter and the southwest quarter of section six, Ord township, and Falle Moller with family, who homesteaded the northeast quarter of the same section. In this way it came that by the middle of July the settlement comprised eight farmsteads contiguous to one another. Fred Dowhower was from the first an eccentric and excitable character, but withal a good neighbor, and honest and upright in all his dealings. It is with many regrets that his many friends, yet living, contemplate his sad end in an asylum for the insane, after having weathered all the storms incident to the early seventies and laid the foundations to the substantial prosperity which his family now enjoys. The old homestead settled in '72 has never been allowed to pass out of the family being at the present farmed by a son, Fred Dowhower, Jr. The brother John early tired of the strenuous frontier life and abandoned his claim, soon after filed on by "Harve" C. Potter.

Falle Moller arrived with his family direct from Hadersley, Denmark. He reached Grand Island on the 14th of September and there left the family in comfortable quarters, while he, with true Danish grit, tramped the entire distance from the "Island" to the Dane Creek settlement, a distance of between 60 and 70 miles, "without feeling," as he puts it, "one bit the worse for the trip." After selecting his

Falle Moller.

Chapter VI

claim Mr. Moller retraced the journey to Grand Island, and purchased there a team of horses, wagon, two cows and all necessary household utensils.

Thus equipped he set out for the Loup Valley, reaching the Mortensen dugout late in the day of July 28. While buildings were being erected on their homestead the Mollers found shelter under the hospitable roof of our bachelors. Quite an addition indeed was this to the dugout family of five—parents, the son Jorgen, and three daughters, Marie, Elizabeth and Laura. But those were the days when to incommode oneself was a duty and to suffer inconvenience a rule. The Mollers, too, have religiously guarded the old homestead and never allowed it to pass out of the family. It now belongs to the son, Jorgen, who through industry and exceptional ability has not alone become one of the largest land owners and stock raisers in the Valley, having at the present under cultivation fully 2000 acres, but he is also prominent in public life, having filled several places of trust in his county, such as chairman of the Board of Supervisors for fourteen years.

Shortly after the arrival of the Dowhowers and the Mollers, a second large contingent arrived in search of new homes. They were A. G. Post and his son, Frank; William E. Post and his four sons, David, Charles, Calvin and Louis; John Case, a brother-in-law of the Posts; Doctor E. D. McKenney, and Frank E. Curtis, William E. Post, or "Uncle Billy" as he was familiarly called, made the original entry on the farm now owned by J. W. Gregory; A. G. Post on the Dick Rea farm now owned by the Garrisons; David Post on the Tully farm; Charles on the Elyria townsite; Calvin on the farm just west of the Gregory place; "Uncle" John on a tract across the river and in the same section with the Gregory place; Frank E. Curtis on the Ervin Dodge farm; Doctor McKenney on part of section 22, just above Elyria. "The Post clan," says Mr. Mortensen, "were regular frontiersmen, having been in the advance guard of civilization in Illinois, Missouri, Kansas, Iowa and Minnesota. They came to Valley county, I believe, from near Logan, Harrison county, Iowa, brought and with them a large number of horses, mules, oxen, cattle, utensils and machinery, and very soon had a considerable portion of their claim broken, and substantial cedar log houses and stables erected.

"A. G. Post constructed buildings of his own, and with his young wife and son Frank, lived at some distance from the others, on the Garrison farm: but Uncle Billy with his wife and sons, who were all single men, Doctor McKenney and wife, and Uncle John Case, all lived with Mr. Curtis on the Dodge farm, where they occupied a large two room combination log house and dugout, with large corrals, sheds and stables for their horses and cattle. From these quarters the men would scatter in the morning for their several occupations, improving their homesteads or jointly getting out the heavy cedar logs from the cedar canyons near by, while Mrs. Post and Mrs. McKenney remained at home to prepare the roast venison and cornbread, which comprised the bill of fare for our table at that time. After their day's work the whole company would gather around a common table and enjoy the frugal meal prepared by these good ladies; and later the men would circle around the fire place with its blazing cedar log fire, on their three-legged stools, to talk over their past experiences of frontier life and to lay plans for the development and upbuilding of the new country and to consider plans of defense in case of sudden attack by the Indians who at that time were roaming over the entire state. They were a brave and light-hearted set, these men, generous and accommodating and would divide their last morsel with anyone in need."

Here let us leave them, pathfinders that they were, to further trace out the fortunes of Melville Goodenow, whom we left, some pages above, in the hospitable care of George Miller at the dugout hostelry. "Mell" had left his family and most of his worldly goods near Sioux City, Iowa, and in his covered wagon, with an extra saddle-horse, "Billy," tied behind, struck out westward to find a home for his family. Failing to find what he was seeking in the Elkhorn Valley, he left his heavily loaded wagon there, saddled "Billy" and boldly struck out westward. In this way it came about that he came to Valley county and found the Danish colony in possession. After but little delay he selected a claim some miles beyond the first colony, near what was later called "Happy Jack's Gulch" and now in his turn became the extreme outpost to the north. Mr. Goodenow's privations and hardships, endured this summer, picture in a graphic way what so many of the first settlers had to go through. He broke his first twenty acres of prairie, carrying an old army musket; for Indians were getting troublesome, and the only safety lay in eternal vigilance.

During this period of preparatory toil his chief diet was mush and milk, the latter coming from a cow borrowed from Nels Anderson. But he was in a worse plight when we come to consider wearing apparel. He tells us that in the course of some months his clothes became entirely worn out, and in lieu of anything better he braided a hat out of grass, and fashioned pads of the same material, which he lined with soft buffalo grass and tied with buckskin thongs to the swollen and festering feet. Grain sacks patterned into trousers then completed this grotesque toilet. He must have presented a startling appearance indeed when, in the early fall, he appeared at the Mortensen dugout, on his way home to Iowa after his family.

Before being allowed to continue on his way Mr. Mortensen thrust upon this Nebraska Robinson Crusoe a ten dollar bill from his own scant store, with which to procure civilized garb before leaving Grand Island.

It is interesting to remember that this kindly act was never lost upon the receiver. When in the spring of '73 he returned from the East with his entire household, including family, cattle, horses and smaller stock, he proceeded straightway to even up scores. Mr. Mortensen tells us that among Mr. Goodenow's provisions was a large barrel of pork, which Mrs. Goodenow divided evenly among all present.

"But, better still, he brought me," continues Mr. Mortensen, "a young Chester White pig which was intended as a starter, or a foundation…for building a fortune. Having no pen, I lariated the animal close to my dugout, but fate was against me. Either the grass was too rich a diet for the animal or the sun too hot on the open prairie. In a few weeks the pig died and it took years before I was able to get another start in the industry which has done so much to develop our country and state."

In order to complete our list of settlers of '72 we must not forget to count the families who during the summer and fall took possession of land east of the river, immediately across from and below the Danish settlement. At Springdale "Doc" Elias S. Harter opened a small general store which sold among many other commodities medicines, tinctures and liquors. The grand old man, D. C. Bailey, came across Greeley county, having driven all the way from Waupaca, Wisconsin, and with his three sons, George, Harry and Frank, filed on land still held by him. W. D. Long, for years a leader in politics and now a highly respected land owner and farmer, took land close to the Baileys. About the same time too, O. S. Haskell and his cultured wife who had the honor of being the first to teach school in the upper half of the county, arrived from Illinois and settled in the same neighborhood. That same fall and early next spring other families came, among them Frank M. Cushing, Frank Chubbuck, Johnson

Gerry and Van Gorden, while Leslie Scott homesteaded a claim further down the river.

On the north Melville Goodenow was not long to remain the outpost; for in November of '72 the beginnings were already laid to Garfield county. The first settler was Charles H. Jones who came from Allegan, Michigan. He left his native state in 1870 and after two years of "roughing it" became the pioneer of the above mentioned county. As Mr. Jones became the founder of the important Willow Springs settlement, and was for many years the center of Garfield county civil and political life, we will let him tell his own story:

"On the 22nd of Feb., 1870, with $50 in my pocket I started west. With no definite idea of destination I entered a ticket office in Chicago and called for $30 worth of transportation in the direction of Colorado, and got a ticket to Kearney, Nebraska.

"Learning from passengers that the country about Kearney was quite sandy, I got off the train at Columbus (Feb. 24, 1870) and went to work choring around a hotel at $10 a month and board. My possessions when I landed at Columbus were $5.20, the ticket to Kearney and a big revolver. In the spring of 1870 I squatted on a claim and made some improvements thereon and in the spring of 1871 sold the right for $150. I then sent for my wife and boy and in February of that year in company with thirteen others in wagons made a trip up the Loup to look at the country, going up to where Elba now is, then turning back. On this trip I captured a pony from the Sioux Indians. The party returned to Columbus on the 8th of March. The surveyors went out the first of April to run the township and section lines in Nance, Greeley, Howard and Sherman counties. Mrs. Jones and son (Will) having arrived in June, I hired "Jim" North to take us up the Loup to Howard county where I located a claim nearly opposite the present townsite of Elba. At that time there were few settlers in Howard county—the first of them being four months in advance of us. The life of our family at this time was quite strenuous—for six weeks after settlement we lived on potatoes and salt alone.

"I was a member of a party that made a trip to the cedar canyons in what is now Garfield county in the spring of 1872, after piling for a bridge at St. Paul. At that time the surveyors were at work in Valley, Wheeler, Loup and Custer counties. The nearest settler to the cedar canyons was Mr. Scott, who resided just above the present townsite of Scotia. In the fall of 1872 I sold my claim, hired a couple of teams and six men and pulled out for the canyons. After a strenuous trip during which it was demonstrated that barefooted horses could cross ice by using; woolen blankets for foot gear, the party arrived (Nov. 10, 1872) at what was afterwards known as "Jones' Canyon." The men helped erect a log house, cut wood and haul water and then left for their homes, leaving the Jones family established twenty-two miles beyond the nearest settler. During the winter Messrs. Messenger, McClimans, T. Freeland and others arrived, and in the spring of 1873 several others located here. Deer and elk were numerous and the settlers had plenty of meat."

The above data was taken from Mr. Jones' "Early Events" as set forth in the *Burwell Tribune* of Dec. 31, 1903. The writer, who is now an old man, is evidently mistaken about some of the details mentioned. For the sake of accuracy it is but just to state that the second settler was Trueman Freeland who arrived very soon after Jones had squatted at the mouth of the cedar canyons. With him came Thomas McClimans. The latter therefore may be considered the third settler. William Pierson and A. R. Harper arrived in February of 1873, and may claim rank as fourth and fifth settlers. Richard McClimans came in the early part of 1873, and about the same time came the Messengers, William Draver, William Smith, Mrs. Bumpus, George Leffingwell, Captain Alger, Frank Webster, I. W. White, George McAnulty, Ike Bartholomew, George Horton, Stephen Chase, William Wertz, A. A. Alderman, and Ross and William Woods.

VII

Organization of Valley County— Early Politics

> From age to age man's still aspiring spirit
> Finds wider scope and sees with clearer eyes,
> And thou in larger measure dost inherit
> What made thy great forerunners free and wise.
> —James Russell Lowell, "Ode"

Wherever in the history of our country a handful of American citizens have settled down to set up for themselves civil government their first and chief aim has been to become a loyal part of the general commonwealth. During the winter of 1872–73 our colonists on the North Loup took active steps towards such an organization. The state legislature had already, March 1, 1871, provided for the organization of a congressional county to comprise townships 17, 18, 19, and 20 north, Ranges 13, 14, 15 and 16 west—this was Valley county. Governor Robert W. Furnas was petitioned to take the necessary steps for further organization, and accordingly he issued a proclamation ordering an election to be held at the residence of George Larkin on the 18th day of March 1873. This was a memorable day in the history of Valley county. It meant much more than an election usually means. Upon this day was settled for good and always the question of county seat location.

George Larkin's residence was a small dugout, built in a hillside just north of the present flag-station Olean, and was thus a sort of half way point between the upper and lower settlements. On the day set the entire countryside, counting some 50 odd voters, assembled bright and early. Heman A. Babcock, George Larkin and Ash G. Post were appointed judges and A. L. Clark and H. Collins clerks of election. As the day progressed a spirited though, upon the whole, friendly contest developed. All said, the great question upon which all else hinged was, shall the upper colony become predominant in the county's politics or shall it be the lower? This naturally involved the matter of county seat location. The notice of election was strangely enough silent upon this matter; indeed some members of the North Loup colony aver to this day that there existed a tacit understanding to the effect that the countyseat question should be left open till the first regular fall election. However this may have been, some misunderstanding ensued; many of the North Loupers neglected to vote on the question and departed early for their several homes, not learning till too late that the matter was being settled then and there. Some people have even hinted that our sturdy fathers from the upper colony "worked" the North Loupers by letting these vote first, and then later in the day when the coast was clear and a majority assured, cast an almost solid vote for the location of the county seat on Section 21, township 19, its present location. Thus the day was won and the prize was gained for the time being, at least, for the upper colony. But right here originated a struggle between the two halves of the county for the final disposition of this plum. Let no one for a moment think that this first defeat discouraged North Loup. This was only the first chapter in an interesting struggle which it took several years to terminate. "The bridge incident" told below formed its climax and virtually closed the matter. The March election, aside from this contest, was very satisfactory to all concerned and resulted in the election of John Case, D. C. Bailey and L. C. Jacobs, Commissioners; W. D. Long, clerk; E. D. McKenney, treasurer; Oscar Babcock, judge; H. A. Babcock, sheriff; Thomas McDowell, surveyor; and Charles Badger, superintendent of schools.

On page 22, of "Miscellaneous Records No. 1," now preserved in the archives of the county, the following interesting resolution appears:

> RESOLVED, That the. Co. Clerk shall make the following resolution a part of the Co. Commissioners records:
> To-Wit: Whereas, the legal voters of Valley Co., Neb., did by a large majority, at the election held March 18, 1873, for the organization of said county, declare the county seat of said County of Valley to be located on, Section Twenty-one (21) Town Nineteen (19), Range Fourteen (14); and whereas, the Secretary of State did send a certificate of said location to the Co. Clerk of said Valley County, Neb., and whereas, the Statutes of Nebraska make it necessary for said certificate to be placed on record in the Book of Miscellaneous Record; and whereas, the County of Valley has had no Book of Miscellaneous Record up to this date

Organization of Valley County

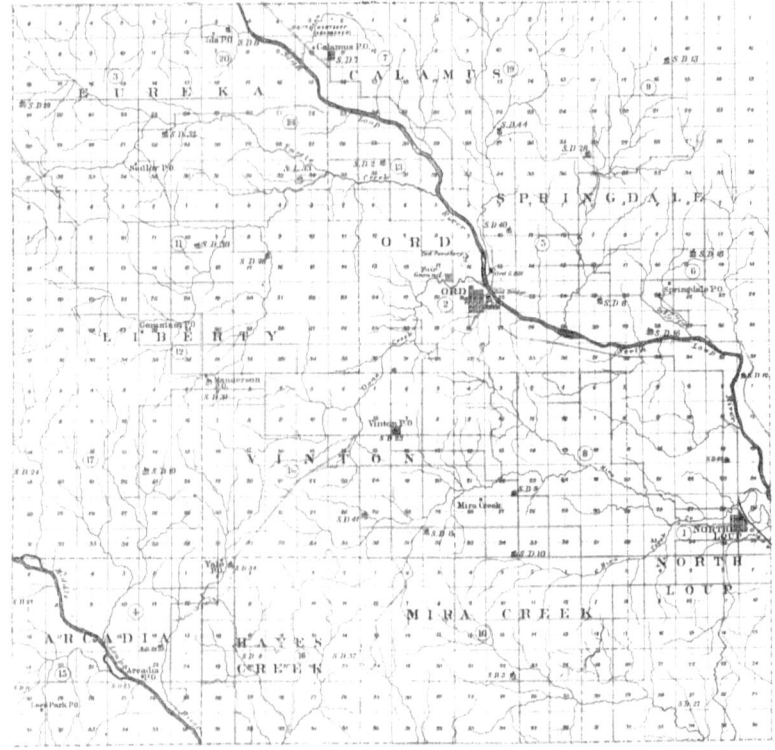

Old precinct map of Valley county.

—Now, therefore, be it resolved by the Co. Commissioners of said county, that they do hereby order the county clerk to place said certificate of location on record immediately after said book comes to hand of said Co. Clerk of said Co. of Valley, together with this resolution.

July 16th, '74
R. W. Bancroft, Chm.
Com's. Present. L. C. Jacobs
John Case, Members
Attest: W. D. Long, Clerk

Here follows the "Certificate of Location" mentioned in above resolution, with date of record, spelling, capitalization, punctuation, etc., exactly as given in the original.

Chapter VII

CERTIFICATE OF ELECTION: Dept. Secy of state, Lincoln Neb. Apl, 21st 1873.

This is to certify that at an election held in the County Co of Valley and State of Nebraska on the 18th day of March 1873, the legal electors therein by a clear majority of their Votes declared that Sec. Twenty-one (21) Town nineteen (19) range fourteen (14), shall be the County Seat of Said County of Valley. (SEAL)

John J. Gaskon, Secy, of State
Recorded July 17th 1874. W. D. Long, Co. Clerk
A. T. Stacy, Dep'ty

It will be noticed that the above commissioner's resolution was made by a new board elected at the first regular fall election, the name of R. W. Bancroft appearing here in place of that of D. C. Bailey, and that for more than a year no record had been kept of the certificate of election. We must not from this get the impression though that the first board did not do its work well. Far from it, they took hold of their duties with creditable energy and considering what they had to work with, did remarkably well. To give the reader some appreciation of early county affairs some of the first meetings of the board are here introduced. Before the erection of a court house these meetings were "held around" at the most convenient place. The matter of taxation came before the commissioners at their first meeting, the minutes of which read as follows:

June 23, '73. Present L. C. Jacobs, Ch'm., John Case, and D. C. Bailey. Attest E. D. McKenney, Co. Clerk.

First assessors appointed—Geo. B. Rood for south side and Q. S. Haskell for north side. Horses $5.00– $70.00; Oxen $25.00–$70.00 per yoke.

This in brief tells the story of the first steps taken to defray the expenses of the new county government. The following list gives in full the first ten warrants paid with the money thus collected:

No.	Amt.	Date	Services	To Whom Issued
1	$131.90	Jan. 19, 1874	Books, blanks, etc.	Acres & Blackmar
2	2.00	"	Clerk of Election	D. A. Post
3	7.00	"	Road Commissioner	D. A. Post

4	21.90	"	County Commissioner	John Case
5	10.85	"	County Commissioner	John Case
6	48.00	"	County Commissioner, etc.	L. C. Jacobs
7	7.00	"	Sundries	Charles Badger
8	46.55	"	County Clerk, etc.	E. D. McKenney
9	98.45	"	Making out tax list of 1873	W. D. Long
10	2.00	"	Clerk of Election	J. H. Collins

The minutes of February 23, 1874, are rather amusing. As will appear later in our story the settlers found it "desirable and expedient" to organize a militia company for protection against the Indians. Of this company O. S. Haskell was elected captain and M. B. Goodenow lieutenant. It further appears that there developed considerable feeling over the matter of guns furnished by the government. Some of the "boys" brought their grievances before the county commissioners who made the following rulings:

> RESOLVED: That O. S. Haskell be ordered to restore to Wm. Hobson the govt. gun and ammunition and accoutrements that he has taken from said Hobson, and now in possession of said Haskell.
> RESOLVED: That M. B. Goodenow be ordered to restore to Mr. Wood the govt. gun issued to said Wood together with ammunition belonging thereto; also that said Goodenow be ordered to deliver the govt. gun that D. A. Post left in his care, to C. C. Post or his order.
> RESOLVED: That the needle-gun taken from Wm. Cronk and given to Herbert Thurston shall remain in possession of said Thurston subject to the order of the Co. Comm's.

We read too how early blizzards raging unchecked across the virgin prairie, and river torrents unspanned by bridges on occasion kept the county fathers from their regular board meeting. Of this the following minutes are illustrative:

> County Clerk's Office, Valley Co., Neb, Apl, 21st, 1874
> The County Commissioners met at the office of the Co. Clerk. When meeting was adjourned for want of a quorum caused by a heavy snowstorm. Present R. W. Bancroft:
> *Attest, W. D. Long, Clerk*

Chapter VII

> County Clerk's Office, Valley Co Neb, Dec 7, 1874.
> No session of the County Commissioners held by reason of the North Loup being in an uncrossable condition.
>
> *Attest, W. D. Long, Clerk*

Now to revert to the county seat controversy hinted at in the first part of this chapter. The North Loup party though defeated in the first test of strength did not lose courage, and hoped against hope sooner or later to be able to wrest the countyseat from the upper settlements. The matter which ultimately settled the sorry affair was the so-called "bridge incident." The story of this matter is in brief as follows: Settlements were rapidly springing up on both sides of the river and the demands for a river bridge were becoming imperative. For many months of the year it was impossible to cross from one side to the other. Now in case a bridge was to be built, the all important question would be where to build it. The strongest settlement on the north side of the river was the Springdale settlement immediately across from the Dane Creek settlement. Both these settlements, and indeed all the people in the upper half of the county, would favor a bridge as near as practical to the newly voted county seat. North Loup naturally enough advocated some point on the river near their own settlement; or, for sake of compromise, a location midway between the upper and lower settlements.

As affairs stood in the summer of 1874, two of the county commissioners, Case and Bancroft, not alone favored building the bridge, but were determined to see it built where it was needed the most—and that with them meant near the new county seat, Ord. The third member was Jacobs of North Loup, who would build the bridge at his home town or not at all. If the people should vote to issue bonds for a bridge the building of the same would be in the hands of the commissioners, and this would under present conditions mean a victory for Ord.

Township map of Valley county.

Organization of Valley County

It came to a test, and an election to vote bonds was called for August 25, 1874. When the vote was counted the bond issue was found to have carried by a good majority. Even yet the North Loupers did not lose hope. There was some question as to the legality of the election, just what it was the author has never been able to ascertain. At any rate the contesting faction sent the sheriff, who was a North Loup man, all the way overland to West Point, to apply to the District Court for an injunction to stop the issuing of the bond. Time was now precious. A commissioners' meeting must be held, the bonds must be issued and sold, all in a legal manner and before the injunction could be returned and served. We may rest assured that the up-river men did not let the grass grow under their feet! A purchaser for the bonds was already at hand in the person of John Means, the Grand Island contractor and bridge-builder. The required three days' notice was given and the Board of County Commissioners met bright and early on September the 9th, 1874, at the residence of Chairman Bancroft—that is, all with the exception of Mr. Jacobs, who flatly refused to have anything to do with the proceedings.

The meeting, although hurriedly called, was nevertheless held in absolute conformity with the law, as the clerk's minutes show. They read:

> Commissioners' meeting, Sept. 9th, '74
> "The Co. Clerk being ordered by the Comm's., brought forth the abstract of votes cast at an election held in and for said Valley county, Neb., on the 25th day of August, 1874, wherein the proposition of issuing the bonds of said county to build a bridge across the North Loup river was duly submitted to the qualified voters of said county, and upon examination of the same it was found that said proposition had carried in the affirmative. Whereupon the commissioners resolved to issue the said bonds and let the construction of said bridge to private parties."

But such prosaic records fail to tell the story by half. The excitement, the fear lest their efforts might be frustrated by a too early return of the sheriff, lent a zest to the commissioner's proceedings which none but the chief actors themselves can ever fully appreciate. As soon as the above resolution was adopted the commissioner proceeded to issue the bonds, when it appeared that no one present could tell just how such documents ought to be formulated, and to make the matter worse there was not a solitary law book nor a single

Chapter VII

Grandpa Daniel Cooley Bailey at the age of 85.

copy of the Nebraska Statutes at hand! At his dire extremity D. C. Bailey was dispatched post haste to Grand Island to procure the necessary information. This of course meant a long adjournment, and meanwhile the injunction might appear! But patience, Providence has decreed that Ord must win! Do you remember, good reader, how upon a certain night in January of '78 Washington's army lay entangled in miry roads between the Delaware and the Assinpink, hemmed in by the exultant Cornwallis, when all but the commander-in-chief had despaired of safety, that suddenly the elements came to the patriots' succor, freezing the roads and providing an avenue for escape? So now these same elements came to our fathers' rescue. Heavy rains in the eastern part of the state made travel difficult and delayed the sheriff's return from West Point, where a misguided judge had granted him the dreaded injunction. Westward rains were delayed just long enough to allow Mr. Bailey to return from the "Island" with his precious law dryshod. Then indeed did the sluices of Heaven open up! And every creek and gully go on a rampage, flooding the lowlands far and wide. But neither flood nor storm could stop our stalwart minion of the law. Homeward he struggled through rain and mire, much delayed though not disheartened. Yet it was to avail him nothing. At eight o'clock sharp on the morning set for the adjourned meeting the crudely formulated bonds were produced and sold to John Means, who, as the sole bidder, was also given the contract to build the bridge. At just five minutes past eight o'clock the meeting adjourned. Ten minutes later the baffled sheriff drew rein in front of Mr. Bancroft's residence, but—too late! It must have been a dramatic spectacle indeed to have seen the sheriff lashing his foaming and nigh spent horses uphill and down hill, across creeks and canyons, on the south bank of the river, cursing his luck, but hoping against hope to be in

Remains of the first frame house in Valley county. This structure was erected by Orson S. Haskell on his claim northeast of Ord in the summer of 1872.

time; while Means, the bond-owner and contractor, on the opposite bank, was leisurely cantering away toward Central City, the important documents snugly hidden in his waistcoat pocket!

Such then was the "deed" by which the bridge was secured and the county seat question finally disposed of. But to get the bridge built and paid for was, as it will appear, not so easy. The specifications called for a pile and plank structure 831 feet long; for this the contractor was to get $12.00 per running foot, or $9972.00. Work was soon under way on the bridge-pilings, a levy of two mills was ordered on all property to pay the interest on the bonds, and everything seemed

Chapter VII

in fair way to success, when Mr. Means found himself unable to handle the bonds and turn them into cash. Work on the bridge was consequently discontinued and the bonds were turned over to the county board. July 13, '75, the commissioners determined to make a second attempt at bond sale and this time they were successful. Under a new contract, entered into Sept. 8, '75, Mr. Means agreed to build the bridge at the rate of $9.00 per running foot and have the structure completed by October 20th of the same year. This contract was faithfully executed and final settlement was made Nov. 29, 1875. The cash cost was $7479.00, which the county settled with warrants amounting to $9719.30, placing their face value at 70 percent. The bridge, which in our day would have seemed a very crude affair, answered its purpose very well and was for many a year the chief connecting link in the traffic between the two sides of the North Loup.

Before closing this chapter on odds and ends it may be of some interest to know how the county procured its first iron safe—the one now to be seen in the county clerk's office at Ord. In time as valuable documents began to accumulate on the commissioners' hands, it became a serious question to know what to do with them. By 1875, some sort of a depository had become absolutely necessary, and it was unanimously decided to purchase a "safe." The board had no ready money, not even enough to pay the freight, as the appended agreement will show and warrants were not held in much favor, so the safe became an expensive one. It was purchased through one Chas. L. Wundt, representing a Cincinnati house, and was to cost $1000.00 and freight, the latter to be prepaid by the selling firm. Furthermore, the warrants given in payment were to run "till the B. and M. railroad taxes could be collected" and at this particular time that was a vexing question with the board. The safe laid down in Grand Island cost just $1058.27 plus the freight charges from that place to Ord. When eventually paid it represented an outlay of fully $1200.00. The same safe could today easily be purchased for one-sixth of that amount. Here are the agreements in the original, just as they appear on the record:

AGREEMENT: E. L. Wundt vs. Co. Comm's. Valley County, Nebraska, Apl. 6th, 1875.

To the Hon. The Board of County Commissioners of Valley County. Neb. Gents.

Organization of Valley County 111

I hereby agree and bond myself to pay the freight on the safe this day ordered from Cincinnati, Ohio, to Grand Island. Nebraska, and take warrants for same at their actual cash value.

Chas. L. Wundt.

"July 13, 1875.—Warrants 74 to 75 issued to Chas L. Wundt for safe and freight on same, as per contract of Apl. 6th.—75—One Thousand and Fifty-eight and 27–100 Dollars."

Emily C. Bancroft and William A. Hobson. To settle a much-disputed question among the old-timers as to who was the first couple married in Valley county the writer offers the following taken from the county records: Nels Andeson (age 29) and Johann Mortensen (age 22), married by Elder Oscar Babcock, July 6, 1873; Wm. A. Hobson (age 27) and Emily C. Bancroft (age 17), married by Elder I. A. Bristol, August 10, 1873. The dispute originated in the fact that Mr. Anderson neglected to take out a license to marry.

An early photograph of the Ord court house and square. The trees have now grown so large as to almost entirely hide the building from view.

VIII

The Memorable Year 1873

In the heaven's, in the cloud's, oh! I see
Many spots—many dark, many red;
In the heavens, oh! I see
Many clouds.

—Uncas' Chant

The Battle of Summit Springs in July 1869 practically put an end to the Sioux War and soon thereafter a treaty was signed, which remained unbroken till the invasion of the Black Hills by miners, consequent upon the discovery of gold, led to the desperate war in 1876–77, which culminated with the Custer Massacre. But for years after the peace-signing the Sioux made free use of the hunting-grounds in the North Platte country. They would sally forth from the agencies along the South Dakota border and hunt up and down the Nebraska river courses. Occasionally war parties stole away from their agencies. Breaking through the sand hills, they would trail the courses of the Cedar and North Loup, suddenly to fall up on their ancient foes, the Pawnees, on the Nance county reservation.

On such marauding expeditions it was not unusual for the Indians to run off outlying settlers' cattle and horses and make life as a whole unsafe.

The Loup Valley settlements were repeatedly harried and for a while it looked as though these incursions would put an entire stop to the influx of the settlers. Then the government came to the rescue and built Fort Hartsuff, after which time there was no further danger. The first real trouble occurred in the month of March 1873, when a band of Pine Ridge Sioux fell upon the Post settlement north of Turtle Creek and ran off much valuable stock. This affair culminated in the burlesque of an Indian hunt usually known as "the Battle of Sioux Creek." Right here might the history of many of our valient fathers have ended had the Indians been as eager for scalps as they were for good saddle horses. As a matter of fact the settlers organized a party to hunt the thieves down, and to recover if possible, the stolen property. But so inadequately were the members of this party equipped and so unskilled were the majority of them in Indian warfare that the great wonder is that a single man returned to tell the story. Indeed the foolhardy pursuers could readily have been led into an ambush and all massacred had the Indians been so disposed.

The battle as here reviewed is from Peter Mortensen's article in the *Ord Democrat* of March 2, 1894, and is here given almost verbatim. Speaking of the Turtle Creek settlement, Mr. Mortensen says:

"The young blood of the Posts, who had been asking for a real tight with the red men, did not have to wait long. One morning in the latter days of March '73 a fine mare and her yearling colt were missing from the corral. The footmarks of Indian ponies were noticed around the stables and their trail with those of the stolen horse and cult were plain, leading southward toward the hills and up the Turtle Creek Valley. All the settlers were notified and requested to respond at once for the purpose of overtaking the red rascals, to recover the stolen horses and such other booty as they might have in their possession and to teach them such a lesson as would forever prevent them from again stealing any horses from the white settlers. To this call responded, as quickly as possible, 'Happy Jack' a trapper, Indian scout and regular frontiersman, who the previous fall had moved his camp from near the chalk hills in Greeley county to the canyon bearing his name, near Mr. Goodenow's farm; also A. G. Post and his son Frank, John Case, Doctor McKenney, Frank Curtis, the three Post boys, David, Charles and Calvin, Falle Moller and Chris. Frey (the latter two returning home after the first day and before the battle the following morning) and the writer, who received the news while plowing on his farm with his ox team. The oxen were immediately liberated from their yoke and on the back of a borrowed horse, without a saddle, a borrowed gun and a belt with a shot bag containing 27 rounds of cartridges, he hastened to meet his companions, who had been preparing sufficient provisions to last the company several days. The company were all on horseback with the exception, I think, of Mr. Case and A. G. Post, who rode in a spring wagon containing the provisions, camping utensils and blankets. It was estimated from the trail that the Indians were about twelve in number. There were eleven of us when we started out with 'Happy Jack' as our leader, who it was reported had single-handed defeated as large a band as the one we were about to annihilate. And there were the younger Posts. Their blood was just more than boiling with enthusiasm enough in each to fight the band single-handed. We were armed 'to the teeth.' Frey brought his old musket, loaded to the muzzle with large buck-shot enough to kill several of the red bucks if they had been conveniently arranged. He had forgotten to bring any extra ammunition. Moller brought his double barreled shot gun, also heavily loaded. The writer brought a borrowed Springfield needle-gun and 27 rounds of cartridges, but on account of some defect in his eyesight and inexperience in handling such a dangerous weapon might as well have brought a willow club. Even 'Happy Jack' did not carry a breech-loader, but a double-barreled gun, one barrel of which was used for shot and the other for ball. Mr. Curtis and Frank Post, I think, both carried Spencer carbines, which experience had proven were sure to overshoot their marks from ten feet to ten rods, according to distance. The rest of the company were armed with muzzle-leading guns and muskets of more or less improved patterns. With such arms no wonder we were certain of victory against a foe, who, as we found out later, were armed with nothing but Winchester repeating rifles!

"After receiving our instructions from 'Happy Jack' we left Uncle Billy at home to protect the two ladies, Mrs. Post and Mrs. McKenney, and the remaining horses, about ten in number. Jack was as sure in following a trail of Indians as a bloodhound is in following a nigger trail in the South, and with him in front, Messrs. Case and Post behind in a buggy with our provisions, we started in hot pursuit after the offenders of the Common Law and of the Statutes of Nebraska. A few miles up the north branch of Turtle Creek the trail divided, the largest body of the Indians crossing the creek toward the south, while a trail of two or three Indians and the stolen mare and colt continued on up the creek. This appeared to be in our favor. The prospect now was that we would have to fight but two or three instead of a dozen. That it would have been very convenient for those Indians who had left the trail to have followed us up and in one of the deep draws which we occasionally had to cross to have massacred us all did not enter our minds, and probably not theirs, for as it will appear later they were not planning for human blood but to steal more horses. Occasionally along the trail which we continued to follow we noticed pieces of red cloth, which 'Happy Jack' explained to us was to warn us not to follow them, as they would fight us if we came too close. The trail continued to lead up to the head of Turtle Creek, over the divide to Sioux Creek in Loup county and down that creek to the North Loup Valley. When we reached the valley it was sundown and we decided to go into camp

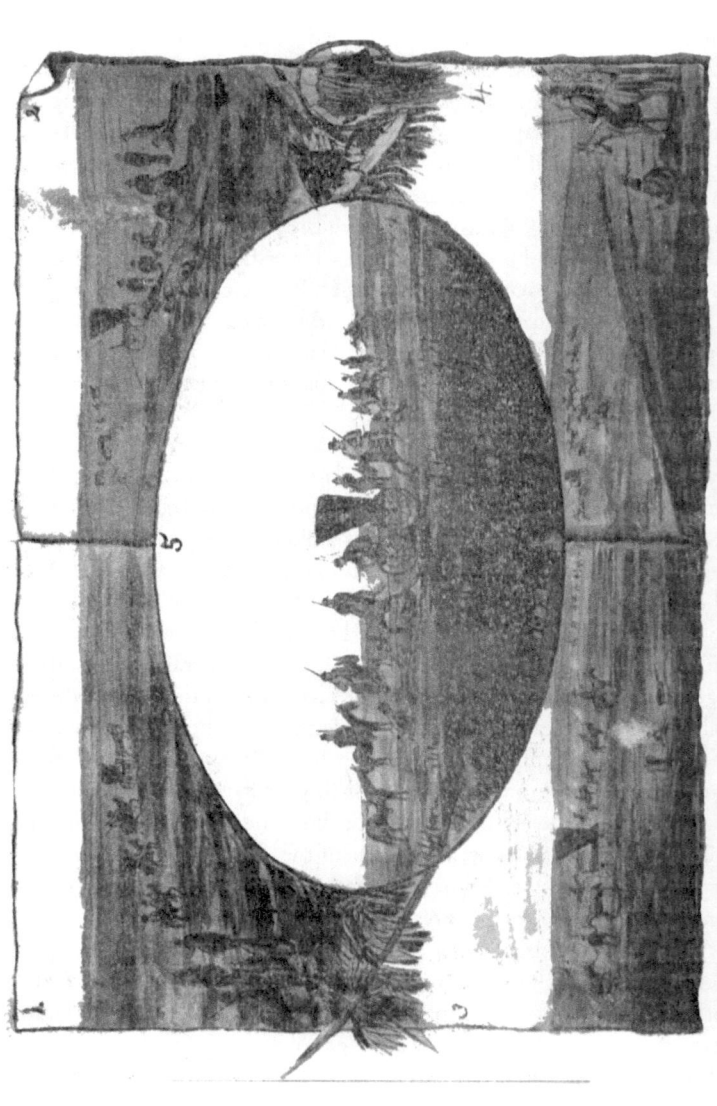

The Battle of Sioux Creek in Five Acts: (1) The valiant settlers in pursuit of the thieving Sioux; (2) In camp at night; (3) Sudden approach of Indians; (4) Homeward bound with the Red Skins in hot pursuit; (5) Safe, but utterly exhausted. (Copied from a watercolor drawing made by an English artist in July 1878 and now in the possession of Hon. Peter Mortensen.)

on Sioux Creek in a cottonwood grove with plenty of water and dry wood. After partaking of a hearty meal of fried bacon, bread, dried venison and coffee some of us, sore and tired, tried to sleep on the damp ground while others were scattered around our camp to guard us against sudden surprise. But even those who were permitted to sleep were but little benefited. The howl of a coyote or wolf in the still air or the neighing of the horses tied in the brush would startle us or call us to arms by the guard.

"Before sunrise we had finished our breakfast, broken camp and were again in the saddle, following the trail up the Loup Valley. We had not travelled more than an hour, probably 8 or 10 miles, when we heard fierce yelling behind us. We were startled to say the least. Our enthusiasm went down into our knees and made them shake. The blood rushed to our heads and made us dizzy. There they were within 80 or 100 rods of us, eight, ten or twelve, more or less. On their little Indian ponies, they looked like giants and with their flowing red blankets and feathered hats like knights of the Dark Ages. It would have been a grand sight had we been in a mood to appreciate it, but we were not. Where was Calvin and Frank Post? Where was our hero and leader 'Happy Jack'? There he stood his pony between him and the Indians, and as pale as a corpse. I offered him the service of my needle gun and my 27 rounds but he declined and advised us not to shoot. 'If you don't shoot at them they will go on and not molest us,' he said, but they did.

"Soon one of the warriors was seen to leap from his horse and deliberately take aim at us with his Winchester over his pony's back and the ball went whiz-z over our head. Soon he was followed by others and the balls went whiz-z! whiz-z! whiz-z! Our horses became excited. They had caught our enthusiasm and began to run, not towards the Indians but in an opposite direction towards the river. The balls kept a whizzing, and some were seen to strike on the ground near us. A few times we would change front and send a volley after the red skins, who would mount their ponies, circle around a minute and then again commence to fire at us. During our retreat Charles Post and the Doctor, I think, were riding in the hind end of the buggy facing the Indians and keeping up a constant firing, even after the stock of the Doctor's rifle had caught in the buggy wheel and broken its stock. How long our retreat lasted or what distance it covered I have no distinct recollection. We might have covered a mile or two when we reached a high bank near the river. Here I handed my gun to

Chapter VIII

A hand-to-hand encounter.

Frank Post and made myself useful holding the boys' horses while they opened fire on the Indians at a rather long range, and I fear to little effect. When I turned my gun over to Mr. Post I had but 7 rounds left, and as I had not fired once I must have lost the other 20 in the excitement. The Indians soon got tired of being targets for us to shoot at and took up the trail after their companions where we had left it and no doubt soon overtook them and over their camp fire had a good laugh over the panic they had caused and the trick they had played us.

"On our way home a valuable mule belonging to A. G. Post and hitched to the buggy died some distance west from where Burwell is now located. Whether the cause was from a wound received during the fight, a sudden attack of colic, or from excitement, opinions have very largely differed, and the facts have never been established. We reached home before night where Uncle Billie and the ladies, with tears in their eyes told us of the trick the red rascals had played on us. That portion of the Indians whose trail we had left on Turtle Creek, and who we supposed had left the locality post haste, had hid themselves in the hills and after we had passed they very cooly and deliberately returned and before the eyes of Mr. Post and the ladies, who were powerless to offer any resistance, drove off the rest of their horses, nine or ten in number.

"I don't mean to infer that 'Happy Jack' was a coward. While his actions were, to say the least, very strange, his superior knowledge of Indians and Indian warfare may have shown him the folly of forcing a fight in which the settlers certainly appeared at a disadvantage against their better trained and better armed opponents, and thus saved our lives, if not our reputations as Indian fighters.

"Thus ended the first conflict in the North Loup Valley between the pioneers and the savages, but it was not the last, as may be noted later on. The direct loss to owners was indeed a heavy one, as it represented many years of hard earnings. Estimated in dollars and cents it could not have been less than $1500, but the indirect loss in retarding immigration and the development of the Valley was many times greater."

In every way considered, this first experience with the Indians was a disastrous one, and satisfied even the most daring among the settlers that they were no match for the well-armed, hard-riding Sioux, who had been trained by the great Red Cloud. This was indeed a serious matter. Accordingly a council was called, and after careful consideration Messrs. John Case and A. G. Post were delegated to report the raid to the Commandant of the Department of the Platte, stationed at Fort Omaha, and petition the government for protection. As an immediate result the War Department, ever mindful of the welfare of the frontier settlements, ordered Captain Mix with a company of cavalry to make a scouting expedition up the valley. The soldiers spent a part of April 1873 on the Loup; and then started on a return trip to Grand Island to report conditions as they found them here. The company made the return by way of the Middle Loup, having crossed the divide somewhere up in Loup or Cherry county. Just as they reached the site of present day Loup City in Sherman county, the terrible storm of April 13, of which more will be said hereafter, burst with sudden fury on the devoted heads of the troopers. So terrible was the blinding blast of the blizzard that the hardy men had to abandon their horses and mules in some plum brush, under a high bank of what is to this day called Dead Horse Run, to seek shelter in the little store building of Frank Ingram, one of the two houses which then comprised Loup City. For three long days the sixty soldiers comprising the company were imprisoned here by the storm and when finally released it was to find their mounts, to the number of fifty, dead along the creek bottom. This meant a march on foot through the snowdrifted hills to Cotesfield in Howard county, where the soldiers arrived after much suffering, cursing the settlers for causing them to leave their comfortable quarters in Fort Omaha to which they returned as soon as means of transportation could be secured.

In May of the same year a second command under Captain Munson came into the Valley and went into camp at "Happy Jack's Gulch." "While this," says Mr. Mortensen, "to some extent allayed the fears of the community, it did not disperse them. The Pawnee tribe was at that time on their reservation in what is now known as Nance county. The Sioux tribe had full sway over the northwestern part of the state. Between these two hostile tribes a continual warfare was kept up and the trail between their reservations lay close to the North Loup Valley. Occasionally a raid would prove unsuccessful and the raiders would run out of provisions. And provisions they must have, either by begging or stealing, as best suited their purpose, from the poor settlers. An effort was made to get the soldiers to erect temporary quarters and remain in the Valley over winter, but the comforts and social privileges of Fort Omaha were too much for the settlers to overcome, and the effort failed.

"The return of the soldiers to Omaha in the fall of '73 again brought fears and uneasiness to the settlers. Hunters and others would circulate reports that bands of Indians had been seen in this or that part of the county, and settlers in a neighborhood would often gather with their families in some of the largest and strongest houses, from which scouting parties would be sent out in different directions, scouring the country in search of Indians and Indian trails. In some localities earth works were erected, behind which the settlers could gather with their families, in case of Indian outbreak." One of these fortifications was built near the present school house in District No. 6, Springdale Township. Traces of another may yet be seen at an elevation in the meadow-lands of the old Ash Post farm, owned by Jorgen Moller. This was the fort erected by the Post boys.

Mrs. Emma Haskell, wife of O. S. Haskell, the founder of Ord, narrates the following graphic incident in one of these Indian scares—indeed the very first one, which resulted from the Sioux Creek fight. "Every prairie schooner that came," says she, "was hailed with delight for it meant more neighbors. The Baileys arrived in the summer of '72 and lived at Springdale in the Harter house while building their own. Dear Auntie Bailey! How good she was to me! I shall always love her for it. Here we all gathered at the time the Indians ran off the horses

D.C Bailey's first home.

Chapter VIII

on the south side of the river—and what a scene it was! It requires an abler pen than mine to do it justice.

"A few days before this a number of families had gone up the river to look for land. I do not recall the names of any except two families by the name of Chubbuck. I think the others all left. There was a sick woman with them. Her husband stopped with her at our house that she might rest, and I remember that they were people well advanced in life. It was he who afterwards told us the Indians were coming. He had seen Uncle Bailey up the river, who did not forget us. In the afternoon we saw a team coming at an unusual rate and wondered what was the trouble. It took him only a minute to say in excited tones, 'the Indians are murdering the women and children and burning the houses. See the smoke. I am sent here by Mr. Bailey to tell you to go to his house. Get up!' He whipped his horses until they fairly ran, while the sick woman, sitting in the bottom of the wagon box was tossed and thrown from side to side as they passed through the prairie dog town, till I feared she would be thrown out, but she only demanded to go faster. In a very few minutes our horses were harnessed to the buggy, provisions and a few of our most precious belongings put in, and I wanted to go fast too, for we also had seen the smoke. Orson said, 'see! there are no Indians in sight, we have plenty of time to get there before dark, and it would kill you to ride like that.' I think we were about forty men, women and children in one room that night. The wagons were arranged in a half circle around the end of the house having the entrance-way and the horses were placed in the corral thus formed. Next, lest the roof be set on fire by burning arrows, all tubs and buckets on the place were brought in filled with water. In crowding for standingroom, the water was spilled on the floor, babies cried, dogs barked, horses kicked, men talked very loud—and you can imagine the rest. All the men had some kind of a weapon, even feeble minded Dick Geary, and the wonder is that no one was shot. Long before morning I was so tired I did not care whether the Indians came or not. There was a bed in the room, only it was taken by babies smaller than I. In sheer exhaustion, I think, I found what I supposed a vacant corner, for I remember that Mrs. Frank Chubbuck gave me a good shaking and warned me that I was sleeping on her baby (I suppose I owe that baby an apology to this day), so I slipped down by the foot of the bed onto a keg of onions and slept soundly until morning, when we scattered for our several homes."

Clifton Hill, one of the many strange loess formations in Garfield county.

Now before going any further into our Indian history we should pause for a brief space of time upon a natural phenomenon which came so suddenly and was so awful in its effects that those who experienced its visitation will never be able to dismiss it from memory. We refer to the great snowstorm which raged with terrible fury through the Valley from April 13 to 16, 1873.

All prairie dwellers have had their experience with the western "blizzard," the dreaded winter stormwind of the plains, which is wont to burst into a marrow-chilling fury over the plain but lately bathed in a flood of sunshine, surprising man and beast far from home and shelter, tossing them about with all bearings lost, till chilled to the heart and exhausted they sink dying into the drift, the whistling, howling wind singing their last requiem. Of late years these storms have been less frequent and of shorter duration than in early days when the winds could sweep for hundreds of miles over the unbroken prairie. Perhaps the most destructive storm of this kind in Nebraska was the April storm of '73. Easter Sunday, April 13th, was remarkably mild, and gave every promise of coming spring. Plowing and seeding were already well under way and the settlers were rejoicing in renewed outdoor activity. As the day advanced the atmosphere became murky and early in the afternoon a mild rain began to fall. By nightfall the rain was falling freely. But who could have dreamed of what was in store for the settlements!

Sometime in the early night the wind veered to the northeast and later to the northwest, and burst with a roar over the Valley. The rain became frozen to a fine, powdery snow, which was hurled horizontally through space, stinging and blinding, working its way through the smallest aperture, and in a surprisingly short time had filled every cranny and corner in any way exposed. The first shock of the storm left the earth surprised and paralyzed in an enshrouding ice-sheet, which rapidly lost itself in heaping drifts of snow.

Before morning men lay shivering in bed, so intensely cold was it getting; and cattle and horses, where not properly housed, were perishing. Dwelling houses and hay sheds were in many instances entirely buried. In places the settlers were unable to reach their barns and cattle sheds till the third day, and then at the risk of their lives. A few succeeded in feeding their stock a little grain—to get bulky fodder to them was practically out of the question. Heroic measures alone saved the settlements from great loss. Many a farmer saved his domestic animals by bringing them right into the house with the family. In the Dane Creek settlement the only loss of any moment befell Adam T. Morris, a brother-in-law of Sam A. and O. M. Stacy, who the preceding fall had filed on the southeast quarter of section twenty-six, adjoining the townsite of Elyria, and who had just arrived with his family and stock at the George Miller dugout. When the rain began to fall Mr. Morris's best team was sheltered in a new barn built by Nels Anderson on the latter's claim, one-half of a mile distant. When the storm had abated sufficiently to allow the owner to reach them, he found the stable drifted full of snow to the rafters and both animals dead. The family and the only remaining horse were saved from certain death by George Miller, who had them move from their prairie schooner into his dugout—family, horse and all.

George W. Larkin, down near Olean, found his shed full of snow on the morning of the first day. With almost superhuman effort he succeeded in extricating his ox-team from the drift. These he then led into the dugout—the same in which the first county election was held—and for three long days shared his narrow quarters with his bovine friends.

Austin Terry of the North Loup colony lost his only span of horses, and Elder Ira Bristol of the same locality, his only cow. Elder Oscar Babcock awoke late in the forenoon to find the room in inky darkness. His dugout was entirely snowed under, and only after digging an eight foot tunnel did he find daylight. L. C. Jacobs, the county commissioner, had an unique experience. He found it necessary to bring all his stock, horses, cows, pigs and chickens into the one-room dwelling house. To make room for all he rigged quarters for his family up under the rafters, on a sort of a swinging platform. Here they spent several never-to-be-forgotten days.

The great wonder was that the upper Valley escaped with as light a loss as it did. It is almost impossible for us now to conceive of the fury of this storm or to appreciate the amount of snow that fell. Thus John Sheldon of North Loup tells us that canyons forty feet deep were filled with snow to the very top, and that it became hard enough for a man to walk across on the crust. Snow lay in the ravines till late in June.

Farther down the Loup the losses were much more serious. We have already heard how Captain Mix lost practically all his cavalry mounts at Dead Horse Run in Sherman county, and in Howard county which was older and had more to lose, conditions were still worse. "Horse stables and cattle corrals were covered with the whirling snow, and there the cattle and horses were obliged to remain without food, for so blinding was the rapidly falling snow, driven by the violent winds, that it was impossible that any human being could go to them to care for them. It was almost sure death for anyone to venture out even for a short distance from the house. During the storm nearly one-half the cattle in the county perished.

"Among the settlers, a great deal of suffering was experienced. Several perished during the storm, the details of whose death is truly sad.

"One of those who died was Miss Lizzie Cooper, who had taught the St. Paul school the previous year. Mr. Cooper was absent in Grand Island on business. The only son was also away. Mrs. Cooper and her two daughters, Lizzie and, Emma, were left alone. Lacking fuel, on April 16th, the girls determined to so to a neighbor's for relief. After carefully wrapping Mrs. Cooper in blankets and covering her in bed they started out. The cold was so intense and the snow so blinding they very soon lost their way. Still they struggled bravely on, hoping against hope, that they might reach some habitation and procure relief for their aged mother. Soon they began to be so exhausted that it was almost impossible for them to move. Seeing that there was now no hope of reaching the homes of any of their neighbors, they tried to

Chapter VIII

The original Dowhower log-house six miles north of Ord. Erected in 1872–73.

reach an abandoned dugout in a canyon, which they thought they could find. Pressing on, sometimes stumbling, through the rough lands just off from the Cotesfield road, Lizzie soon dropped from sheer exhaustion and could go no farther. This was partially under the bank of a canyon. Emma did all she could to urge her sister on, but it was impossible for her to move. Lizzie was soon dead. The devoted Emma remained with the dead body of her sister all that day and all night. Being partially protected by the bank above, the snow soon drifted over her, and this saved her life. By continued struggling she managed to keep from smothering. In the morning she left her dead sister to try to find some habitation. Half dead and nearly crazed from the effects of grief, hunger and cold, she rushed madly on, hardly knowing what she did. The storm had now abated, but the snow, driven by the heavy winds, made it almost impossible to find the way. As she passed the home of W. P. Wyman, on the farm of Capt. Munsen, she was seen to be rushing wildly on, sometimes on hands and knees, and sometimes on her feet. So nearly unconscious was she that she passed only a few rods from the house without seeing it. She was stopped, taken in and cared for. As soon as the poor girl could speak, she managed to let them know what had befallen her sister, and that her mother was left alone the day before. A party soon organized to go to the relief of Mrs. Cooper.

"When they arrived at the house they found she was gone. Looking for her on the road they frequently found pieces of clothing, and all the indications that the woman had pushed on, frequently falling from exhaustion, and then recovering her strength had again struggled on. In a short time, her dead body was found partially covered with snow and stark and stiff. It is supposed that on the day the girls started out she became alarmed at their protracted absence and started to look for them, and soon perished. With a mother's guiding counsels and an older sister's love so suddenly withdrawn, Emma has since led a sad and lonely life."

But the above were not the only lives lost in this terrible and long-to-be-remembered storm. Dillon Haworth and his family, consisting of his wife and two children, were living on a pleasant farm that they were just opening up on Spring Creek. Becoming frightened at the long continuance of the storm they started, it is supposed, to find a neighbor's house. At all events the dead bodies of the entire family, except the babe, one half year old, were found dead the next day after the storm some distance apart. The babe was the only one found alive, and she was clasped to her mother's breast.

Such, in brief, was the April storm of '73, a storm which the hardiest of the old-timers cannot recount without an involuntary shudder.

IX

Indians and Grasshoppers

> The Lord only knows which harmed the poor settlers the more, the prowling Red-skins who were wont to sally forth from the hills and uplands or the green imps of satan the grasshoppers, which pounced upon us in bewildering hordes—both literally took the bread out of our mouths.
> —An Old Pioneer

The summer of '73 was a busy season in the settlements. Whitetopped prairie schooners with their quota of brawny homeseekers were now common sights in the valley. Everywhere were there signs of settlement.

The older colonies steadily grew outward, and the space between them was steadily becoming smaller, till indeed farm-places occupied the river course in a continuous chain from Scotia to Willow Springs at the mouth of Jones' Canyon, and were even pushing beyond The Forks into the unorganized territory. From St. Paul and Loup City settlers were pushing northward along the Middle Loup and settling that part of Valley county. Early in '73 the foundations of Brownville, or Arcadia, were laid and an interesting community, whose history will be chronicled in later pages, took its beginning.

Much prairie was broken during the months of April, May and June, and quite a large acreage of sod corn planted. The "back-setting" of the previous season was sown with small grain, or planted with corn and potatoes. Considered as a whole the yield was fair; and this was indeed fortunate for disastrous years were even now to come upon the settlements.

The summer passed away peacefully enough. The prowling Indian for some reason steered clear of the Valley, and had not since the Sioux Creek fight molested any of the farmsteads. Fall and beautiful Indian summer came, and still no signs of him. But with the setting in of winter Indian signs became numerous. And hunters and trappers began to encounter small parties in the hills east of the river. Soon bands returning from unsuccessful raids upon the Pawnees, driven by hunger, openly entered the settlements, begging and stealing. This led to another fight, the most memorable in our

Chapter IX

George McAnulty of Scotia, as he appeared when he came to the Loup in 1873.

frontier history—the so-called Battle of Pebble Creek. George McAnulty who was one of the chief actors in this tragic fray recounts the causes and chief points of interest thus: "During the spring and summer of '73, quite a number of settlers, attracted by the great beauty of the valley at that point, and by the fertility of its soil, took claims in what was called the Goodenow settlement, the writer—then a boy of twenty-one—being one of the number, had homesteaded the laud now known as the Jas. Barr farm, near Burwell. On the east side of the river the settlement extended up as far as the old town of Willow Springs, or as it was known then, "the mouth of Jones' Canyon." The settlers were all more or less afraid of the wandering bands of Indians, that from time to time passed near the valley on their way to the Pawnee reservation, but as month after month passed in safety it seemed as if the Sioux had decided not to favor us with any further visits. This feeling of security was suddenly dispelled.

"On the evening of Jan. 18, 1874, a cold, stormy Sunday afternoon, with the wind driving the snow in blinding sheets over the wild, unbroken prairie, in a lull in the storm, some hunters of which the writer was one, beheld a large party of Indians surrounding the residence of Richard McClimans, near Willow Springs. Mr. McClimans' family at that time, consisted of himself, his parents and his brother Newton, and that home was one of great hospitality, Mrs. McClimans being noted for her kindness of heart, extending to all a sincere welcome which was never lost on a weary traveller. But on this occasion the good lady's hospitality was sadly abused. The Indians dismounted, crowded into the house and proceeded to hold high carnival. They devoured everything eatable in the house and were even then far from satisfied. They prowled around the place like so many wolves, eating everything they could find, finally killing all the chickens within reach. And at that time chickens were very valuable on the frontier. At last, about three o'clock in the afternoon, without any friendly thanks for what they had received, they left the McClimans ranch, and to the relief of the family started up the river.

"About half a mile above McClimans' was the home of the trappers, and who of the old settlers do not remember the trappers, as they were called. Their house was a red cedar one, strongly built. At this particular time, Cy. Haney, Bill Wirtz, the Sawyer boys, the Baker boys, Charley White (Buckskin Charley) and Marion Littlefield were out on a hunting and trapping trip, leaving Steve Chase alone at home; and just at the time of the Indian visit he was getting some wood in the canyon, a quarter of a mile from the house. The writer, from the opposite side of the river, saw the redskins break open the house and take possession. Knowing the boys were away from home, I ran to Bob Hill's house and told him to come with me to see what they were after. We crossed the river on the ice and were nearly through the willows on the east side, when we saw them leaving the shanty, taking with them everything of any value, skins worth perhaps a hundred dollars and all the clothing and provisions. It was a rich find for the rascals and they lost no time in making off with the booty. When we were within four hundred yards of the house the last Indian came out, his arms full of blankets and coats. Just as he was trying to mount his pony I fired at him. The ball must have whizzed too close for comfort, for he dropped his load, jumped on his pony and soon overtook his party. When we reached the house we found it completely looted: not a thing they could carry off remained. About this time Steve Chase came with his wood. He was a picture of righteous indignation when he found what had occurred during his short absence. Late that night the rest of the boys returned home. They reported having seen Indians on Pebble Creek, three miles up the valley, where they had gone into camp. The Indians took a cow from Harry Colby's farm on their way and were having a royal feast.

"A meeting was held that night at the trapper's shanty, and it was decided that I should notify settlers on the south side of the river as far down as the Post settlement, which I accordingly did, making the trip from M. B. Goodenow's to David Post's and return in about three hours. Unfortunately "Happy Jack" was not at home, being in camp about thirty miles up the river, where his traps were set. No one slept in the frontier settlement that night for it was known that in the morning the Indians would be asked to return all the stolen goods and pay for the property taken and destroyed, and if they refused, then, large as the party was—about forty in number—it would mean a fight, even though we could muster only sixteen men.

"The next morning, Jan. 19, 1874, was the coldest morning of that year, but in spite of this bright and early we were on the way to Pebble Creek, under the command of Charley White or as we knew him best, 'Buckskin Charley.' Just at dawn we were within three hundred yards of the big 'tepee.' Cautioning the men to keep silent, White entered the camp and demanded the return of the property. Here White no doubt made a mistake. He found the redskins breakfasting on the remnants of their last night's feast, and in no humor for compromise. Charley, who knew a little Sioux jargon, talked with the chief, who emerged from the tepee, took a cartridge from his belt, held it above his head, summoned his followers, and standing in their midst in the gray light of the morning uttered the Sioux war chief's battle cry, always terrible in its character. Many a time since I have heard that same peculiar chant, but never when it sounded more awe-inspiring. We now saw that it was impossible to avert trouble. White rejoined his little command and ordered them to seek shelter under the bank of the Loup river. The Indians opened fire as we reached the bank. It was promptly returned, and for ten minutes the roar of musketry was like that in other days experienced at Rosebud Creek, the lonely bluffs of the Loup echoing the sharp crack of the rifles of white men and red engaged in mortal combat. It was soon discovered that owing to the extreme cold the shells were sticking in our guns, retarding our fire; and right here I must mention what I believe was the coolest act I ever saw a man do in time of extreme danger. Steve Chase, a little in advance of the rest of us, finding the cartridge stuck in his gun, sat down and cooly opening his pocket knife, proceeded to pick the shell out while the bullets flew so thickly around him that to this day it is a mystery to what strange providence he owed his escape.

"The Indians now divided, half of them crawling along to our rear, protected by a little ridge running parallel with the river. They saw we had the advantage of a perfect protection from their bullets. While we were under the bank we could return their fire without exposing ourselves. It was to get better range at us, that they divided. The first we knew of their intentions we were greeted by a volley from the southeast. At this juncture Marion Littlefield arose to fire. He

A second view of Jones' Canyon.

exposed his head to the enemy and just as he pressed the trigger of his needle gun there was an answering report and he fell dead on the bank of the river. The shot that killed him was almost the last of the fight. The Indians withdrew. What loss they had sustained we never knew, but that they lost several men was nearly certain. With heavy hearts we raised our dead comrade and carried him further down the river to a place of safety. Here we kindled a fire to warm our guns, expecting every moment to be again attacked by the now invisible savages. Mr. McClimans' wagon now arrived, arrangements having been made that we should have some supplies sent out to us in the field. The body of Littlefield was carried back to the settlement in this wagon, accompanied by White and Haney. The rest of us went back to the battleground, but no Indians were to be seen. We dispatched two of their ponies left on the field terribly wounded. About nine o'clock we returned to McClimans' ranch. In a little while reinforcements came, but it was decided not to follow the Indians, as by this time they had a fair start.

"Thus ended the Pebble Creek fight. The next day a sad party passed down the valley, the friends of Marion Littlefield taking his body to his home near Sutton, Neb. He was a promising young man, only 21 years of age, and a favorite with all his friends. His death was a fearful blow to his parents and relatives and the sad affair cast a gloom over the whole settlement for a long time."

The summer of '74 was blessed with an abundance of rain and warm weather. Corn grew rank and was surprisingly forward for the season of the year. The small grain too gave promise of exceptional yield. Farmers in the Valley were beginning to make preparations for harvesting and housing the crop which should at once place them in easy circumstances, when a calamity as complete as it was unexpected with one fell stroke destroyed all their calculations and for a time left them stunned and almost broken in spirit. It came in the shape of one of the plagues of ancient Egypt, and it is doubtful whether the Nile-dwellers could have felt greater dismay at the sudden down pouring of this curse than did the Loup-dwellers when—the "grasshoppers" came.

Nothing perhaps in the natural history of our state has excited more general interest than the migrating locust. The particular species formerly such a pest in our part of the country is the Rocky Mountain locust (Melanoplus spretus), and is native to the dry plateau-lands of the Rocky Mountains, lying between latitude 43 degrees and 53 degrees north. Its permanent habitat, according to the United States Entomological Commission of 1877, covered an area of about 300,000 square miles. "The most favorite breeding places in this area were the river bottoms and the uplands or the grassy regions among the mountains." Whenever the weather conditions were favorable they hatched here in astonishingly large numbers. And the favoring conditions were exceptional dryness and warmth. In the early days two such dry seasons were sure to bring on a locust migration. During the last twenty years, however, the character of these early breeding grounds has been greatly changed. "Settlement and agriculture have so restricted the permanent haunts in Montana, Idaho and Colorado that the danger from future incursions is very slight. Indeed the locust has practically been driven beyond the borders of the United States, and now breeds freely only in portions of British Columbia."

After the insects hatch in the spring it takes about seven weeks before they reach a mature state. They go through five moultings and after the last, acquire wings. Their appetite becomes voracious, and as they are most numerous in hot and dry seasons when vegetation is scant, it takes but a short time for this to become exhausted. It is now that they manifest their peculiar instincts. With a common impulse they take to wing, swarming in a southeasterly direction. They usually rise between 8 and 10 o'clock in the morning and continue their flight till the middle of the afternoon, when they come down to feed. A fall in temperature or a head wind suddenly precipitates them to the ground in great numbers. They move not so much in sheets as in great columns from one to five thousand feet thick, resembling great fleecy clouds propelled onward by some strong but hidden agency. Moving, as we have stated, in a southeasterly direction, those that leave their breeding grounds in southern Montana and Colorado in spring will reach Nebraska in July, while those from northern Montana and Canada do not appear till August or September.

An exceptionally destructive year was 1856, when the insects swarmed over Nebraska, Kansas, some parts of Missouri and Texas, into Iowa and Minnesota, and through Colorado and Utah. In 1870 and 1871 they again threatened the states west of the Mississippi, and in 1873 committed very serious depredations. "The most serious locust year known in the United States, however, was 1874 when enormous swarms invaded the settled portions of the Mississippi Valley west of the ninety-fourth meridian. Colorado, Nebraska, Kansas, Wyoming, Dakota, Minnesota, New Mexico, Indian Territory, and Texas were overrun by swarms from the northwest, mainly from Montana and British Columbia.

"The loss in this region was estimated at $50,000,000 in the actual destruction of crops. In 1875 the young insects hatched in immense numbers over an area embracing portions of Nebraska, Kansas, and Missouri, entailing destitution and suffering among a population of 750,000 people. In 1877 the young insects died in great numbers and those which acquired wings flew toward the northwest in the direction of Dakota and Montana, the region of permanent breeding grounds."

The month of July was about half spent when the locusts reached the North Loup Valley. Corn was "laid by" and in tassle;

the small grain was heading and full of promise. Then dawned the fatal day. By noon a strange haziness overspread the clear, blue sky, and the bright sunlight took on a sickly, yellowish tint. Had anyone taken the trouble to look at the sun through some proper medium he would have discovered the cause of this gradual transformation in the day. Myriads of insects were flitting by the disk of the sun. But people were not looking for trouble and so allowed the phenomenon to go unnoticed. In a short time, however, everyone had cause to become wide enough awake. The clouds of locusts suddenly began to settle over the earth. With a strange whistling sound of wings and myriad bodies they came on, pelting the appalled earth; hustling and tumbling they came, clinging to whatever they happened to strike, devouring every planted thing from Indian corn to garden truck.

At first some of the settlers made vain attempts to scare the pests from their fields, but this was usually rewarded by having the clothes literally eaten from off their limbs. As time advanced the number of insects grew. In places branches of trees are said to have been bent almost to the ground under their living burden. The corn fields were speedily stripped of their leaves, and soon all but the toughest portions of the stalk were devoured. We hear of thrifty housewives attempting to save favorite flowerbeds by spreading over them bedquilts and carpets for protection, who to their chagrin found the locusts as eager to devour the spreads as they were the flowers.

Ah, those were sad days in the settlement! Gone were now the hopes and day dreams of many a sturdy pathfinder! The last dollar had with many been spent in the hope of speedy returns from good crops. What now would be the future? How to span over the coming winter and eke out an existence till another crop could be gotten became serious questions. Had it not been for the abundance of game in the adjacent hills and the logging industries, and more particularly still, the building of Fort Hartsuff, which gave work at good wages to scores of men up and down the valley, many would perforce have left their farms and returned, to the older settlements.

X

Fort Hartsuff, Its Rise and Fall

> We loved the wild clamor of battle,
> The crash of the musketry's rattle.
> > The bugle and drum.
> We have drooped in the dust, long and lonely:
> The blades that flashed joy are rust only,
> > The far-rolling war music dumb.
> > > —S. Weir Mitchell, "The Song of the Flags"

The Pebble Creek fight led the settlers to petition the National Government to establish an army post on the upper North Loup River. A mass meeting was called to meet at Willow Springs and a committee consisting of Melville B. Goodenow, John Case, E. D. McKenney, W. A. Harper, and G. W. McAnulty were selected to bring the matter to the notice of Congress. The first step was to draw up a petition and place the same in the hands of Hon. Frank Welsh, who represented the congressional district of which the Loup country at that time formed apart. Congressman Welsh seems to have recognized the urgency of the case, as he lost no time about getting the bill through the Lower House of Congress. United States Senator Hitchcock piloted the same bill through the Senate. It called for the appropriation of $50,000 to be expended for the purpose of establishing a permanent military post near the head of settlement on the North Loup River. This appropriation was later increased to $75,000, but even this was increased. A fire in the partially completed structures swelled the eventual outlay to fully $110,000

The actual work of construction did not begin till September 1, 1874. Meanwhile Company C, 9th U.S. Infantry, Captain Samuel Munson commanding, came into the upper valley and forthwith allayed all fear of further Indian trouble. Later in the summer the old Civil War veteran Gen. E. O. C. Ord—after whom the city is named—arrived and with him came a corps of engineers who should help locate the fort. The site chosen had some strategic importance, and was not far from the excellent gravel beds on Gravel Creek and but a short distance from the Clifton and Jones Canyons, which

Fort Hartsuff taken from the Hills; officers' quarters in the foreground.

furnished the bulk of the timber needed in the construction of the several buildings.

The building of the fort in the fall of '74 was a most fortunate event in the history of the Valley. The swarms of locusts had earlier in the season destroyed every vestige of crops, and starvation actually stared the settlers in the face.

But just in the nick of time came the fort and with it an abundance of work at good wages for every man who cared to take it.

The buildings were to be constructed from concrete of gravel and cement. This called for a great deal of hauling. There were the sand and gravel to be moved from the pits four miles south of the fort, and the timber to be cut and drawn from the canyons eight miles north. The lime was to be carted from the kilns on "Dr. Beebe's" ranch forty miles down the river, and every sack of cement and all the finishing lumber came from Grand Island, eighty miles by road.

Every team for miles up and down the river was requisitioned and every man and boy who could wield a shovel was given something to do. Indeed, settlers came all the way from the Platte River country and from the Middle Loup to seek work. A saw mill was erected near the site of the fort. Here all the rough timber for use in roofs and floors was prepared.

In one way only did the erection of the fort work ruin to the valley. Through the wholesale destruction wrought in the cedar canyons. "The Jones Canyon," says Truman Freeland, "which is now a dreary waste of broken cliffs and naked ravines with scarcely a bush ten feet high, was then heavily timbered; the tall graceful pines stood by the thousands on the hillsides, while the cedars grew so close together in the canyons that a team and wagon could with difficulty make a way through them. Tall cottonwoods, three and four feet in diameter, were found here and there along the canyon. Boxelder, hackberry, ash and elm were also in abundance, and in places on section eight there towered fine groves of poplars.

"This evergreen forest" he continues, "was the haunt of thousands of bright plumaged birds, and the shelter from the bitter winds of the surrounding prairie for hundreds of deer and other game-animals, and bore not the mark of a single stroke from the woodman's axe in 1871." But now,—what a desolation!

Fort Hartsuff was a fort in name only: it comprised a number of officers' quarters, barracks for the privates, commissary buildings, stables, and other structures arranged in a hollow square. The only

Fort Hartsuff taken from "Skunk Hollow" Watch Tower; stockade and windmill may be seen in background.

Fort Hartsuff, Its Rise and Fall 141

defensible part of the fort was the waterworks, which lay on the hills back of the officers' quarters. This was protected by a circular stockade, accessible from the fort by an underground passage. This stockade which might well have remained a lasting memorial of the pioneer days was some years back ruthlessly destroyed and sold as old lumber. The completion of the first buildings in December '74 was celebrated with a grand ball to which the entire country side was invited. Everybody was proud of Fort Hartsuff. Indeed it was from the first considered by officers and men alike, the prettiest and in every way the most desirable station in the Department of the Platte.

Captain S. Munson was the first commander of the new fort. His Company was relieved April 14, 1875 by Company A 23rd Infantry, under the command of Capt. John J. Coppinger, a son-in-law of the statesmen James G. Blaine. A further change was made in December 1876, when Company K, 14th Infantry, under Captain Carpenter, came to garrison the post. Finally, in November 1878, Captain Munson again assumed command, which he retained until the fort was abandoned in May 1881.

At the close of the Sioux War of '76 the broken remnants of the warring tribes were settled upon their reservations in the two Dakotas, and since that time they have never been much of a menace to Nebraska settlers. The Pawnees had already been removed to their new home in Oklahoma. It thus came about that Fort Hartsuff early outlived its usefulness as a defense against the old-troublers of the valley, and it was accordingly discontinued as an army post

Its later history is quite prosaic. The buildings, erected at such great cost to the government, were sold in July 1881, to the Union Pacific Railway Company for the paltry sum of $5000.

The reservation, comprising two sections, was sold later, at public auction, and purchased by Peter Mortensen, Ed Mitchell, and Mrs. J. L. McDonough of Ord. It is now used as a stock ranch by Collison Brothers and Lindquist.

Life at Fort Hartsuff was such as one usually finds at the American frontier post. There was the usual routine of drill and guard-mount, of scouting trip and hunt; the same old round of balls and gaming and idleness—a life which unfortunately too often has led to vicious living in one form or another. Our fort was no exception to this rule, and a certain looseness is yet to be marked in a few families of the old campfollowers, which remained in the vicinity where the post was abandoned. This should not, however, be taken as a reflection

Chapter X

Return of the lost Alderman children: George and Emma Alderman, seven and five years old, wandered from home and were lost for three days. They were found by Sergeant Myers and Corporal Schreck under shelter of a washout, their only protection a faithful Newfoundland dog. (Retouched from an old picture in the possession of Judge Herman Westover of Ord.)

on the many good citizens of Valley, Garfield and neighboring counties, who were directly or indirectly identified with the fort. It is of interest to note that Joe Capron, the prosperous Ord real estate dealer, was quartermaster's clerk at the fort from 1878 to '81, while George Clement of Mira Valley was one of the government contractors who built the fort. Hon. Judge Norris, who now holds high office in the Philippine service, was 2nd Lieutenant in Company K. Ed. Satterlee, for many years proprietor of the Satterlee House, and Arthur Schaefer, whose business career in Valley county ended so sadly some years back, were both members of Company K. John Luke of Ord held the position as musician in Company A, and George McAnulty of Scotia was a member of Company C.

XI

Village Organization

>   ...and over the
> roofs of the village
> Columns of pale blue smoke, like clouds of
>   incense ascending,
> Rose from a hundred hearths, the home of
>   peace and contentment.
>   —Henry Wadsworth Longfellow, "Evangeline"

The Seventh-Day Baptists settled the rich bottom lands of the North Loup and Mira Creek valleys, and were well content to live pastoral lives in their new Arcadian realm. This seemed in fullest harmony with their simple religious system. The village organization had therefore no part in their system, but materialized rather in spite of it, as a part of our gregarious Teutonic system. The first step in that direction came with the creation of a post office, called North Loup, with Elder Oscar Babcock as postmaster.

Prior to this time the nearest postoffice was at Cotesfield in Howard county. The Star route was extended to Valley county in the fall of 1873, in charge of A. G. Gillespie as carrier and contractor. The latter at one time controlled the mail routes on both sides of the river between St. Paul and The Forks. His "Pony Express" and stage coach were for many years the chief means of communication between the settlements and the outer world. Thus we hear that Truman Freeland used to carry it from Cotesfield to Calamus and Willow Springs on the north side of the river, and that Mrs. S. S. Haskell at one time managed the route between Ord and The Forks (Burwell). Mr. Gillespie is still living, a hale and hearty patriarch, at his home in Scotia; he has just filed his one hundredth year, which marks him the oldest resident in the Loup country, if not indeed the oldest man in our state.

Shortly after the postoffice was established the North Loupers decided to build a school house. These people were indeed people of education and knew how to appreciate good schools, and they proposed to make the right kind of a start. Accordingly a dugout, fourteen feet square, was constructed—a humble enough beginning,

The beginnings of North Loup, 1878. (From a picture in the possession of Frank L. Green.)

Village Organization 145

but inestimably better than nothing at all—and Miss Kate Badger, now Mrs. J. W. Holliday, was installed as teacher. This was in the summer of 1874. Here then we have the first school in Valley county. A few months later the county was districted for school purposes. All the south half was designated as District No. 1, with North Loup as the centering point: the north half became District No. 2. with its only school held for a time in the Mortensen dugout, north of Ord, in charge of Mrs. Emma Haskell, wife of Orson S. Haskell, one of the founders of Ord.

At North Loup the dugout schoolhouse was early discarded for a neat little cedar log cabin, erected on Elder Babcock's land, at the edge of the present townsite. In the fall of 1873, W. J. Holliday opened a general store on his homestead, not far from the postoffice and school house. Here naturally enough the center of interest came to be, and other buildings were soon springing up and making the beginnings of quite a village. Just then the grasshoppers came, and with the loss of crops everything came to a stand still. The village,

A plat of North Loup showing the original townsite and a number of later additions.

though, managed somehow to survive, and was regularly surveyed and platted in 1877, in anticipation of the heavy influx of settlers which commenced the very next year. The original plat of North Loup, as may be seen from the cut herewith given, comprised six blocks only. The streets, denominated as 1st and 2d, and A, B, and C, were all 80 feet wide. Lots were 4 to the half block; alleys were 25 feet wide. The miscellaneous records show that the townsite was surveyed and platted by C. H. Webster, that A. J. Davis and Eddie Babcock were chainmen, and J. A. Green, axman. The plat was subscribed and sworn to before County Commissioner Oscar Babcock, March 6, 1877, and received for record the 7th day of March 1877.

The year '78 marked the beginning of a steady growth in the valley. In '81 the railroad question came to the fore. The Republican Valley Road was contemplating a northward extension. North Loup township helped matters along by voting bonds to the amount of $4000.00. The grade was at once begun, and by the spring of 1882, had been completed from St. Paul to North Loup. As soon as the railroad became an assured fact, there was a rush of settlers to the village, and soon numerous, substantial buildings were under erection. In a year the population increased from a hundred to more than double that number. This has slowly been added to in the course of later years till now, in 1905, the village counts 510 all told. North Loup can never expect to become much of a city, but is just a thrifty little residence town, an ideal place if one wishes to retire to a moral Christian atmosphere, where churches are wide open and saloons and drinking places are kept closed.

The history of Ord, the county seat and principal town in Valley county, really begins with the organic election in 1873, when it was made the official town of the county. But for more than two years the town was without name, nor was a single house built upon its site during that time. The county officials were satisfied to keep their books and records at their respective residences—in dugouts and in log cabins—and for all practical purposes they got along very well indeed.

In May 1874, the first steps were taken towards building the town. Then O. S. Haskell of Valley county, O. C. Haskell of Chicago, and A. M. Robbins of Dixon, Illinois, who had purchased the land from the Burlington and Missouri River Railroad Company, made a first plat of the proposed town. For some time it was known among the settlers as "Chin City," a name which it took from A. T. Stacy,

Joseph A. Green on his way to North Loup from Pardee, Kansas, in 1872. This was the first frame house in that town. (Enlarged from a small picture belonging to Mr. Green.)

or "Chin" Stacy, so named for a certain facial peculiarity, and who lived in the only house anywhere near the townsite, in what is now the Woodbury Addition to Ord. But this is how it took its real name: During the summer of 1874, as we will remember, General E. O. C. Ord, who was then in command of the Department of the Platte, came into the valley to locate Fort Hartsuff; and in honor of this old, war-scarred veteran it was decided to name the town Ord.

In the summer of 1875 the town was carefully platted, and the first efforts were made to induce the people to build on the site. To this end the townsite company proposed to give the county every fourth block in the plat—eighteen blocks all told—on condition that the county build a court house of equal value with the eighteen blocks, on the townsite prior to July 4, 1880. The proposition was promptly accepted by the board of commissioners on behalf of the county. The townsite company now immediately executed a $2000.00 bond for faithful performance. This instrument was approved by John Case, chairman of the board of commissioners Nov. 16, and properly recorded Nov. 25th of the same year. The eighteen blocks were appraised at about $50.00 each, and on this basis the plans and specifications of a court house to cost between $800.00 and $900.00 were drawn up and bids asked for. The contract was let to our friend the bridge builder, John L. Means of Grand Island, November 17, 1875, consideration to be even $800.00.

Specifications of Court House

Building to be 16 × 24 feet; 9 feet high
Sills 6 × 8 inches
Studding 2 × 4, set 16 inches from center to center
Lower joist 2 × 8, set 18 inches from center to center
Ceiling 2 × 4, set 16 inches from center to center
Collar beams 1 × 6 on every set of rafters as shown in plates, double, 2 × 4
Rafters 2 × 4, 24 inches from center to center

This unpretentious little structure was reared near the south side of the present Court House Square, which was then a treeless plat of virgin prairie. After being used for court purposes for some twelve years it was removed to give place for the present, modern building. It was carted to the east side of the square, where it may yet be seen—a forlorn bit of the past.

Village Organization 149

The court house was completed in February 1876, and a couple of months later Herbert Thurston commenced the erection of the first residence on the townsite. Nothing further developed till the fall of the year; then the grand old patriarch, S. S. Haskell, set up the first hostelry, general store, and postoffice, in what in those days was considered a very pretentious frame building, situated in the east part of the present town on the road from the river bridge. This structure has been variously known as the Ord City Hotel, the Dies House, and is now in a somewhat remodeled form, the Transit House, near the north side of the square.

Sylvester S. Haskell, the Father of Ord.

No further improvement was made in the townsite till the fall of 1877, when W. H. Mitchell moved his paper, the *Valley County Herald*, from Calamus, and began its publication in a small log building, moved from the above-named place, which had until this time, on account of its location near Fort Hartsuff, been the principal town of the county.

During the year 1878, there was quite a large immigration to the county, and Ord began to grow quite rapidly. In the spring, E. S. Harter moved his stock of goods over from Springdale Postoffice, and built a store twenty-two by forty feet in size, two stories high, and put in a large stock of general merchandise, hardware and drugs. Herman Westover, an attorney, moved here from Calamus and erected a dwelling. W. A. Hobson and L. E. Post each erected blacksmith shops and dwellings. W. H. Mitchell sold the *Valley County Herald* to J. C. Lee, then built a dwelling and began the practice of law. In September, H. W. Nelson moved his paper, the *Valley County Courier*

The Ord Townsite Company.
O. S. Haskell   O. C. Haskell   W. W. Haskell
A.M Robbins

Village Organization 151

from Vinton. There were now two newspapers until the *Herald* failed in November.

The year was further noted for the removal from Calamus to Ord of Z. K. Ferguson with a good stock of general merchandise. Early in 1879, Joe Capron purchased Henry Nelson's paper, the *Courier*, and established the *Valley County Journal*. Soon afterwards Case & Mortensen opened the first exclusive hardware store in Ord, and indeed in the county. J. A. Collins and John A. Bales established a harness shop, Copp & Westover opened a nice new law office and Henry Nelson built the first livery stable. S. L. R. Maine and H. M. Deegan moved down from Calamus and re-established themselves at Ord. S. S. Haskell, H. A. Babcock, M. E. Getter, J. H. Collins and others added to the growing little town by erecting dwelling-houses.

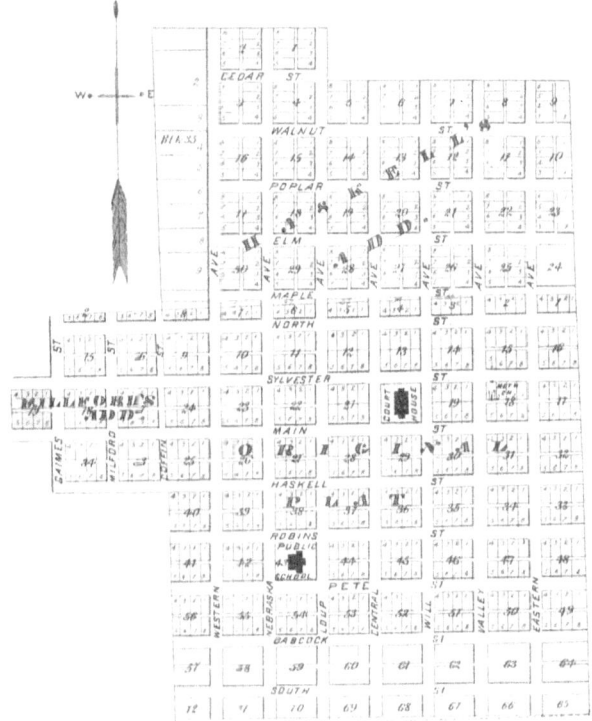

An early plat of Ord showing the original townsite, and S. S. Haskell's and Finn Milford's addition.

Chapter XI

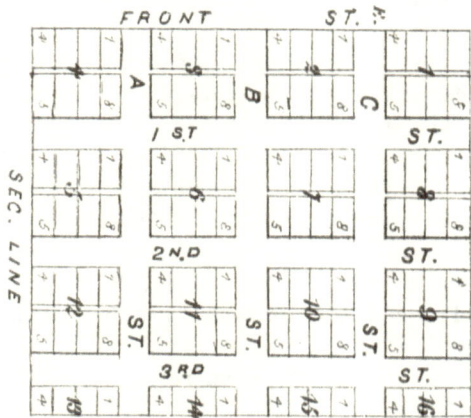

Townsite of Calamus.

When Fort Hartsuff was built it immediately became the center of interest in the county. Men with an eye to business flocked thither; and, as might have been expected, a thriving little town was soon springing up on the very edge of the fort reservation. This was Calamus. For a year or more it was the liveliest town in the county. Under the patronage of Lieutenant Thomas Capron of the fort, the townsite was platted and quite a start was made. Sixteen blocks and half blocks were laid off, pretentious streets, 100 feet wide, were planned, and every preparation was made for the expected boom. Stores of the several kinds were opened, and many residences sprang up. The town had the undivided support of the fort garrison and of many outlying settlers. But Ord was altogether too near, and then came the rumors of the fort's speedy abandonment. The bubble burst and in three years' time the town was to all practical purposes—dead.

As we have seen above, what was Calamus's loss became Ord's gain. For from Calamus came newspaper men, lawyers, physicians and business men. In many instances these not alone moved their business to Ord, but the very houses thither. Thus died ambitious Calamus.

The following record and affidavit is taken from the Valley County Miscellaneous Record, No. 1, and is reproduced, spelling and all, just as it appears there:

State of Nebr.,
Valley County

To the Co. Clerk of said County:

The Undersigned Surveyor being employed by Lieut. Thos. Capron, to Survey Mark and Plat the Town Site of the Town of Calamus in said Valley County according to law and for that purpose he did Employ George Ferguson and C. R. Hutchins, Sworn chanemen on Such survey and did on the 16th 17th Days of Sept proceed to Make such Survey of which the foregoing is a correct and True Plat of the same being made on the North West ¼ of the S. W. ¼ of Sec. (11) Eleven in Township (20). R. (15) W and extending South 36 ft. on the S. W. ¼ of the S. W. ¼ of said section (11) Tp 20 N. of Range (15)
Dated and signed this Sep 24th, 1874.

Levi G. Perce, Surveyor

Affidavit (to above)

I G. Ferguson and C. R Hutchins do solemly sware that we will support the constitution of the United States and the constitution of the State of Nebraska and faithfully and impartialy discharge the duties of Chainmen according to law and the best of our ability.

G. Ferguson
Chas. R. Hutchins. W. D. Long,
Filed Oct. 5th, 1874. Co. Clerk

In those early days towns were projected rather promiscuously on the virgin prairie by ambitious organizers. Natural demand had little to do with such enterprises; the idea was to *make* a demand. Thus the town of Vinton came into existence. In 1876 the town was planned but very little was accomplished for a couple of years. Early in 1878, Henry W. Nelson established a newspaper there, which he called the *Valley County Courier*. For some months this courageous boomer did all in his power to attract settlers and investors to the new town, but so seemingly hopeless was the outlook that, despairing of success, Mr. Nelson moved with his paper to Ord. On Nov. 18, 1878, the Burlington and Missouri River Railway Company made an out-and-out donation of the townsite, but even now no marked progress was made.

The Vinton Townsite Association was incorporated May 11, 1882, and the following well known men were elected directors: H. C. Perry, Thomas G. Bartlett and A. W. Travis. The plat on file locates

Vinton townsite.

the town in the S. W. ¼ of the S. W. ¼ of Sec. 7, in Township 18, Range 14 West. Sixteen blocks were platted; of these, block six was designated as the "Public Square." But the town had no future; there was no demand for another town within seven miles of Ord, and Vinton too—died.

Of the four towns here mentioned Calamus had a meteoric existence and then died; Vinton was still-born and came to nothing; North Loup has become a prosperous and promising little city; and Ord has developed into a strong, progressive business center. It is almost pathetic now in the new Ord of 1905, with her many business houses and fine residences everywhere springing up, to read of the slow progress of those early days. Years of grasshoppers and droughts, of hailstorms and windstorms, all did their share in keeping her in the embryonic state. But when she finally burst into bloom it was done with a substantiality engendered in the years of rest. The above statement should however be qualified somewhat. The first half of the decade 1880–90 was indeed remarkable for steady growth and substantial progress. The general standstill in affairs came later as a result of poor crops and hot, blasting winds which for a time threatened ruin to all the Valley

The following paragraphs on "Later Improvements" and "Local Matters" in Ord of 1882 are quoted verbatim from Andreas's History of Nebraska, and should now after almost a quarter century prove interesting reading, and at the same time impress the reader with the many great changes that have come to the County Seat since that time:

"In 1880, the little village began to make rapid progress indeed. So great was the improvement that it is impossible to mention it in detail. About thirty-five buildings were put up. Over one-half of these were business houses. The total value of buildings erected that year is estimated at $21,225. The population had by the end of the year increased to 250.

"During the years 1881 and 1882, Ord continued to progress steadily, and its population will number about 500. All branches of business are well represented, and the trade of the town is in a prosperous condition. On November 8, 1881, bonds amounting to $5000, were voted to the Union Pacific Railroad for the purpose of securing the early building of the railroad up the North Loup Valley.

"In 1881, the entire town was threatened with destruction by fire. Though the village was saved, the livery stable of H. W. Nelson was burned to the ground.

"In the spring of 1882, a fire broke out on the south side of the public square. It was caused by a defective flue. Before it could be stopped, several buildings, including the office of Judge Herman Westover, were completely destroyed.

"Ord was incorporated as a village on June 23, 1881. The following is the first Board of Trustees appointed on the above date by the County Commissioners: H. G. Rodgers, S. S. Haskell, B. C. White, R. F. Milford and H. W. Nelson.

"Manufactures.—The Ord Flouring and Grist Mill was commenced in the year 1880 and completed early in 1881, by R. F. Milford. It was built at a cost of $5000, and for the quality of flour manufactured, it is second to none in the state.

"In 1880 John Drake & Co., started a brick yard and the first year about 100,000 bricks were manufactured, since which time the yard has been kept up and a very superior quality of brick is made.

"Banks.—The Valley County Bank was established in October 1880. A general bank and collection business is done. The affairs of the bank are in a prosperous condition. J. D. Bacon is President, and Frederick L. Harris, Cashier.

"The Ord City Bank was established and commenced business on March 15, 1882. A general loan and collection business is done, and the bank starts in with very favorable prospects. H. C. Metcalf is President, and George A. Percival Cashier.

"Hotels—Besides the restaurants and boarding houses the hotels are two in number. The Ord City House is the old hotel built by S. S. Haskell, and is now owned and operated by James Dies, who keeps a good hotel.

"The Satterlee House, E. D. Satterlee, Proprietor, is centrally located, is well kept, and is doing a good business.

"Churches.—The different church societies are represented by the Methodist Episcopal, Baptist, Presbyterian and Seventh-day Baptist denominations. The first two named have capacious and comfortable houses of worship, which were completed in the spring of 1882. All these societies are liberally supported by the moral and intelligent citizens of Ord.

"Schools.—The Ord school is provided with able instructors, and is well sustained by the intelligent and education-loving citizens. One of the first things looked to in the foundation of the town was a good school, and no money or labor has been spared to make it such a one.

"Societies.—Ord Lodge, No. 90, Independent Order of Odd Fellows, has an organization of over fifty members. The society owns a hall and are in a prosperous condition. The order was organized December 1880, with thirty-six members. W. J. Wilson was the first Noble Grand.

"Foote Post, No. 40, Grand Army of the Republic, was organized late in the year 1880, with W. H. Williams Post Commander

"Pilot Lodge, No. 57, Independent Order of Good Templars, was organized at a quite early date. They have a large and working membership.

"Newspapers.—The *Valley County Journal* is published here by Capron & Wolf. It is a bright and well edited weekly, Republican in politics, and a five-column quarto in size. The *Journal* was founded in February 1879, by J. H. Capron, who had purchased the *Courier* and changed the name, and published it but a few weeks until his office was burned, when the paper discontinued for a short time, until a new office could be fitted up. Since that time the *Journal* has continued to be published. In August 1881, Charles E. Wolf purchased a half-interest in the paper.

"J. H. Capron came to Nebraska in September 1874 and located at Fort Hartsuff, where he was Quartermaster's clerk until December 1875, when he went to Manitowoc, Wis., and took charge of a newspaper published there until February 1878, when he again entered Government employ in Wyoming Territory until December, when he located at Ord, and soon afterward started the *Journal*. He was born in Beloit, Wis., September 14, 1856. He learned the printer's trade in the office of the Freeport, Ill., Journal, beginning in 1871, and remaining until going to Fort Hartsuff, Neb. He was married February 15, 1882, to Miss Mary F. Ramsey.

"Charles C. Wolf, the junior editor of the *Journal*, came to Nebraska in June 1881, and in August he purchased a half interest in the *Journal*. He was born in Freeport, Ill., March 3, 1855. He learned his trade in the office of the Freeport Journal, beginning in 1872, and working there until he removed to Ord.

"The *Ord Weekly Quiz* is a bright and sparkling paper, Republican in politics, and was founded on April 6, 1882, by Will Haskell, of Chicago. The paper starts out with good prospects for future success."

XII

The Middle Loup and Arcadia

> The Creator's richest blessings have been given unto thee,
>   Nebraska, dear Nebraska.
> The air with incense laden blows across thy prairies free,
>   Nebraska, dear Nebraska.
> Loyal hearts are beating true, dear Nebraska, e'er for you;
>   Thy glory ne'er shall dim nor honor fall.
> Over valley, hill and plain shout again the glad refrain:
>   Our Nebraska, dear Nebraska, leads them all.
>   —Will M. Maupin, "Nebraska"

While we have been telling the story of the North Loup, the Middle Loup in Valley county and its history has not for a moment been lost sight of. It was indeed purposely held back for the present chapter in as much as this part of the work really forms its own unit whole.

For the beginnings of the Middle Loup settlement it becomes necessary to go back to the spring of 1873, when the pioneers arrived. First came one George McKellar, together with his father and mother. He settled a claim which later has been known as the John Wall farm, near Arcadia. Mr. McKellar was a man of irascible temperament. When under the influence of liquor he was positively dangerous. To him belongs the unenviable notoriety of having been the first person tried in Valley county on a criminal charge. Porter Brown and family arrived from Louisa county, Iowa, during the early days of April '73. He had just reached the protecting woods on Hawthorne Creek when the terrible storm of April 13 broke. As good fortune would have it shelter was found in a trapper's cabin, which alone saved him and his devoted family from certain death. Porter Brown entered a claim near the present townsite of Arcadia.

During the summer of '73 the "yellows" were more than usually destructive in the fruit sections of Michigan. They came to Berrian county and there ruined the peach-orchards of Mingerson Coombs, who in despair left the Wolverine State to seek his fortune in the West. Thus it came about that "Ming." Coombs arrived on the Middle Loup early in September. He immediately took a homestead and a timberclaim, lying respectively two and three miles from the present-day Arcadia. About this same time a widower by the name of W. H. Fradenburg arrived and took a claim two miles east of Arcadia. Alonzo Fradenburg with family was the fifth settler to come into the settlement. Next spring came Samuel A. Hawthorne with family, and settled near the present townsite. It fell to the lot of Boone Hawthorne to settle where Arcadia now stands.

To narrate in full the story of these first comers would in reality be to retell the narrative of the North Loup settlements. There was the building of suitable dwelling-places, and the hauling of red cedar logs to older settlements. Corn was planted, and then came the locusts in great swarms, destroying every vestige of planted things. When the Indian scares fell upon the North Loup Valley, the Middle Loup was affected also. A stockade was erected on W. H. Fradenburg's farm, whither the settlers might congregate at the first intimation of danger. Fortunately, however, the settlers were not troubled by hostile bands. Several times much excitement was caused by the approach of begging Pawnees, who, as some of the settlers will have cause never to forget, were mistaken for the terrible Sioux.

At first the settlement was practically isolated from the outer world. At length, in 1874, a post office was opened on Samuel A. Hawthorne's place, and mail was then brought in from Loup City twice a week. When it came to the matter of naming the post office all were united in calling it "Brownville" in honor of Porter Brown, who was considered the real father of the settlement, George McKellar having been eliminated from consideration through his own misdeeds. It soon appeared, however, that there was already one Brownville in the State; then the present euphoneous name—Arcadia—was adopted.

"Arcadia has from the earliest time been noted for her interest in education. The colonists had no sooner become settled in their new home than they determined to open a school for the education of their children. A teacher was found in the person of Mingerson Coombs, and the sod house of Boone Hawthorne furnished the necessary school-quarters. Here then was the school taught. Seven children, all told, assembled daily from the sod-shanties scattered up and down the valley, and here was laid the foundations to the learning of many men who are making the history of Arcadia today.

But soon there arose a cry for better accommodations for holding school. Why not issue bonds and build a structure worthy of the community? Thus argued one Ingersoll from Loup City, and he found a willing tool and coworker in George McKellar, who together with Samuel Hawthorne comprised the school-board.

It was proposed to vote bonds in the sum of $4000.00 which Ingersoll was ready to accept in lieu of cash, provided of course that the contract be given him. A hurried election was held and the bonds were declared carried. But the proceedings were soon found illegal, as it was quite apparant that the notice provided for by law had not been given. A second election was ordered, and again, after some "strenuous" work on the part of McKellar chiefly, the bonds carried by a small majority.

The sum called for was now $3000.00. Ingersoll got the bonds and the contract for the school house. The site chosen was about one mile east of the present town. Here the work of erection was commenced. The framework was actually raised: but that was as far as the work ever proceeded. Ingersoll left for parts unknown and the new community was left wiser though poorer for their experience.

Much bad blood was engendered as a result of this fiasco. Staunch Samuel Hawthorne had bitterly opposed the bond deal, and as a result had trouble with George McKellar, who was arrested on a charge of assault and battery. The prisoner was carried overland to Peter Mortensen's dugout, three miles north of Ord, and there for the first time in the history of Valley county was a man tried on a criminal charge. Orson S. Haskell presided as judge and after a careful hearing and much deliberation, fined the defendant a good round sum of money, and then let him go with an admonition to keep the peace or worse things would befall.

It may not be altogether out of place here to follow out the checkered career of this George McKellar, the first settler of the Middle Loup. He, as we have said, was ever quarrelsome, and this was particularly true when he was in his cups. It appears that he had fallen out with a man named Chapman, who lived across the line in Sherman county, about a pig. In February 1877, the two chanced to meet in Loup City, when McKellar was very much under the influence of liquor. Chapman went into a grocery store there to purchase some tea, and as he came out, was shot by McKellar and fatally wounded. A surgeon was called but the victim died within forty-eight hours. Immediately after the murder, McKellar coolly saddled his horse and rode away, while the men who stood about did not attempt to stop him, as they were waiting for the sheriff to procure a warrant for his arrest. After the escape followed a week of excitement in pursuit of the criminal. A reward of $500.00 was offered for his arrest. After a week, however, he was brought to Loup City, by his own father and given up. He was then placed in jail and securely guarded until the time of his trial in April. He was found guilty and sentenced to the State penitentiary for life. Here, we are told, he was shot and killed by a guard some years ago, while attempting to escape. Thus ends the life story of George McKellar, the first settler on the Middle Loup in Valley county.

The story of the Middle Loup in Valley county is of late years centered in the rise of Arcadia. The first postoffice it will be remembered was established on the homestead of Samuel A. Hawthorne, a short distance from the present townsite. For some years no move was made to build a town. The settlers made Loup City and St. Paul their trading points. This seems a long distance for us now to go to dispose of one's butter and eggs and to get groceries in return; but in early days the inconvenience of the thing was not taken into consideration, and then, too, all in all considered, time was not so valuable as now.

In 1880 there came up the Middle Loup a man, every inch of him a practical business man—this was John Wall, today known as one of the grittiest and most successful lawyers and business men in his part of the state. It struck him forcibly that the lands adjacent to the river bottom and Hawthorne Creek would make an ideal site for a town. The valley was fast filling up with settlers now and the railroad was bound soon to follow upon their trail. So why not stake out a town and become its founder! The project soon took form and Boone Hawthorne's homestead was chosen for the original townsite. While the beginnings were made in 1882 the town was not properly platted till some three years later. The plat was put on record, Oct. 3, 1885, and shows that Parley Round, Alice Round, John Wall and Isabella Wall were all associated in the new enterprise.

The first store in town was a general merchandise establishment, operated by Ed. Fuller. W. B. Reynolds soon afterwards opened a hardware store. Then came W. S. Owens with a harness shop and George Hastings with another general merchandise store. The Landers Block and the first good hotel were erected and Mrs. Sylvina Gilchrist moved the postoffice to town from her farm one and a half miles out from the new site. These business places were practically all the accessions that the town could boast for several years. But the last half of the decade 1880–90 saw substantial additions made to Arcadia, both in the business quarter and the residence portion of the town. Then came that season of disasters, 1890–91.

In the fall of this year the very heart was burned out of the business street. Some eight leading firms were put out of business, several of them never to reopen. To this day the scars of the conflagration can plainly be seen. And now right on the heels of the first calamity came the first dry season and Arcadia naturally enough came to an absolute standstill. From 1891 to 1896 and even later the young town saw some distressing times. Many of the population became absolutely disheartened and pulled stakes and left the country. A number of houses were actually moved from town and transformed into farmdwellings. Arcadia was on the retrograde. But this is only telling over again the story of every other town in the Valley.

By 1900 the rallying point had been reached. The population was then 350. In 1902 it reached 374, and in 1905 it has increased to nearly 700. Modern dwelling houses are springing up in every part of town. John Wall has lately completed a fine brick business house to take the place of the one destroyed by tire some time ago, entailing a net loss of $25,000; an up-to-date Odd Fellows' Hall is under construction and ground has been broken for the new Kinsey bank building. Substantial cement walks are rapidly supplanting the old wooden structures; beautiful shade trees and well kept lawns begin to mark a prosperous, growing community.

The Arcadia Champion sets forth the year's growth in the following language:

What We Have Done

A summary of the improvements which have been built and are now in building or for which contracts have been let might prove interesting. Here is the list:

Mrs. Salisbury, cottage	$800.00
Mrs. Salisbury, residence	1000.00
O. D. Henyon, cottage	750.00
A. Lane, house	500.00
Arthur Lane, house	300.00
H. E. Sawyer, cottage	650.00
E. H. Peck, cottage	500.00
E. P. Milburn, residence	1250.00
C. Landers, cottage	800.00

Peter Christian, two houses	500.00
F. H. Davis, residence	1000.00
F. H. Kinsey, residence	3000.00
C. O. Blomquist, residence	1400.00
H. O. Cooley, residence	1150.00
G. H. Kinsey, barn	1500.00
G. H. Kinsey, bank	4000.00
Odd Fellows' Hall and Opera House	6000.00
W. L Phillips, lumber office and sheds	1500.00
M. L. Fries, lumber sheds	700.00
J. P. Leininger Lumber Co., lumber office and sheds	3000.00

This foots $30,300. Comment is unnecessary. Bring on your improvements, you towns.

And again a week later:

Besides the sum of nearly $35,000 that is being spent in new buildings in this city this year, the following sums have been expended in building additions to buildings already here:

Peter Christian	$1000.00
E A. Donnell	350.00
E. L. Quinton	300.00
S. E. Leininger	100.00
D. O. Hawley	400.00
G. W. Scott	350.00
J. M. Robinson	350.00
E. G. Robinson	200.00
H. H. Waggoner	300.00
W. L. Bruner	150.00

Besides this there have been cement sidewalks built by Hastings, Raish. Boyce, Cooper Bros, and Landers at a cost of about $40 each. This adds $4000 more to the amount spent in improvements this year, which added to the $35,900 as shown in the Champion of last week makes a total of over $39,000 spent in improvements in this city this year.

Home of Hon. A. E. Bartoo at Arcadia.

A chronicle of the Middle Loup Valley would not be complete without a passing glance at Lee's Park, lying some five miles southwest from Arcadia. The "Park" is a beautiful valley lying on the border line of Valley and Custer counties, right between the Middle Loup river and Clear Creek. It is surrounded with hills and unfolds itself in many gentle undulations. This remarkable valley, containing some 4000–5000 acres, is one of the choicest farming and fruit raising regions in the entire state. The soil is a rich, dark loam, capable of withstanding almost any amount of dry weather.

The valley takes its name from the first settler, James Lee, who reached the hills overlooking it in September 1874. The wild beauty of the scene struck a romantic chord in this pioneer's breast, who immediately selected a choice spot at the center of the valley and squatted there. In '75 he pre-empted one quarter and entered an adjoining quarter as a timber claim. Thus settlement was begun.

Mr. J. L. H. Knight, one of the enterprising stock raisers and farmers of Lee's Park, may here be allowed to take up the thread of the story. He says: "Mr. Lee kept bachelor's hall in a sod house, and began to subdue the native soil. He evidently succeeded, as his first wheat crop of one acre testified. He obtained from it forty bushels of wheat, which is supposed to be the largest yield ever raised in the park. The following spring he continued his operations on the farm, and planted some trees on his timber claim, but the grasshoppers again found him, and ate up his corn crop, and also all of his small trees. During these years, as hunters and adventurers passed through, they occasionally stopped at the bachelor's sod mansion, and the fact of his being the only settler, and working with his trees on his timber claim, caused the travelers to name the valley 'Lee's Park.' Here then this settler dwelt, year after year, in solitude—farming, planting trees, and doing his sewing, cooking and washing. He tried to get others to locate, but no one volunteered. Nearly four years had passed by, and his courage, which had remained firm for years, began to wane, and he at last decided to leave his beautiful half section of land.

"About this time, however, Frank Wright offered to locate in the park, providing Mr. Lee surrendered to him his pre-emption, on which was his house and well. This Mr. Lee agreed to do, and soon after, Mr. Wright started to claim his new possessions. On his way he fell in with some land seekers who seemed to be headed for Lee's Park, so they went together and on arriving at Mr. Lee's, Wright asked for the papers, which were immediately surrendered. Soon after, however, this Mr. Wright sold the place for $25 to F. E. Morrison. These land lookers were William and Joseph Murray, who, in February 1878, took claims in the park, and their families arrived in May the same year. Soon after this, in March, Benjamin Knight located in the Park, and returned to his Wisconsin home to claim the hand of his 'best girl,' and together they journeyed to their frontier home. From this time on, settlers flocked in rapidly, and James Lee, no longer alone, decided not to leave. His pre-emption right, however, being gone, he proceeded to the extreme end of the park and filed on a 160-acre piece as a homestead, on the bank of the little stream afterwards known as 'Lee's Creek.'

"In July Messrs. Overton, Chandler True, Jay Hamlin, George Hamlin, Jr., E. Stephens and William Vanalstine settled. In August, T. J. Johnson and Amos Smith; then followed Parish Freeman and his son Charles; William Hall, Joseph Peacock, and James Thompson. In 1879 Edward Knight, Phillip Lynch, James Wisely, N. Mehrhoff, Nelson Potter, Sam Minchell and Mr. Abel located here. In 1880, David and Archie Todd, F. E. Morrison, James Bradford, and Thomas, John and Sam Berridge arrived. Next year J. L. H. Knight settled permanently here with his father, Edward Knight, who had arrived two years prior to this.

"The early settlers of Lee's Park underwent many hardships and privations. Corn stalks and willows were the main reliance in those days for fuel. The mail service at first was not very good; for a while their postoffice was at Loup City, a distance of twenty-two miles; afterwards there was an office established at Wescott, which was twelve miles distant, but shortly it was arranged to have an office on Clear Creek, four miles west of the park. This was quickly followed in the fall of 1878 or '79 with Uncle Sam's locating one in Lee's Park.

"During the fall of 1878, the first district school meeting was held in Lee's Park, which was then organized as Joint-District No. 11, of Custer and Valley counties. This meeting was held at the house of Parish Freeman, and it was decided to build a sod school house, which was completed the following spring. During the summer of 1878, a Sunday School was organized with Benjamin Knight, as superintendent. It was held from house to house, and occasionally Father Cook, a Baptist minister living on the Middle Loup, came over and preached. After the schoolhouse was built the Sunday School and preaching was held there. This sod schoolhouse was occupied for years, until it was declared unsafe, when a sod building was rented of F. E. Morrison, to hold school in. During these years, the school district being large, and in two counties, caused much disagreement. Some wished it divided, while others wished it to remain as it was. Finally the south end was allowed to go off with District No. 91. This, however, did not settle the matter, and school meeting after school meeting was called, which finally resulted, in 1889, in dividing the district on the county line. The following summer, these districts built new frame schoolhouses, one in Custer county, and one in Valley county.

"In April, 1884, the town of Lee Park was laid out in Custer county on the town line, and the same year, the Lilly and Houder addition to Lee Park was laid out, adjoining the original town, and in Valley county, with the postoffice in Valley county. Then came quite a boom for the new town. A general merchandise store was built by Lilly & Houder, to which the postoffice was removed; then followed a blacksmith shop, a hotel, a wagon shop, and a feed stable. This little town was progressing finely when the B. & M. railroad concluded to outdo the U. P. railroad, and so built past Loup City, the terminus of the U. P. railroad, and stopped at Arcadia, five miles from Lee's Park. The little town held out for a while, but the railroad town of Arcadia took away its vitality, and after some struggles, the town of Lee Park was no more. All the buildings were torn down or removed, and an attempt was made to take away even the postoffice. The attempt was nearly, or quite successful, as the office was actually removed to Arcadia, but prompt action was taken by patrons of the office, and an order came for its return, only a day after its removal. The postoffice was afterwards removed from Valley county across the line into Custer county, where it still remains. The fact that originally the postoffice was in Valley county, and is now in Custer county, has caused some confusion as to the real location of Lee Park, some thinking it in Valley and some in Custer county. The name of the town and postoffice has also been confused with the name of the valley. Originally the postoffice had the same name as the valley, but Jay Hamlin, while postmaster, had the name of the office changed to Lee Park, consequently the name of the postoffice is Lee Park, and the name of the valley is Lee's Park.

"The farmers of Lee's Park are honest and industrious, and are not of the shifting kind. Most of the old settlers are still residing here, and seem to have no idea of soon changing their location. This makes it difficult to purchase a farm in Lee's Park, and when one is sold, it is at good figures."

XIII

The Further History of Garfield County

> Everywhere is the grasping hand,
> An eager adding of land to land;
> And earth, which seemed to the fathers meant
> But as a pilgrim's wayside tent,—
> A nightly shelter to fold away
> When the Lord should call at the break of day,—
> Solid and steadfast seems to be,
> And time has forgotten Eternity!
> —John Greenlief Whittier, "The Preacher"

The story of the first comers to Garfield county has been touched upon in a former chapter. It remains for us to tell, in the passing, something further about their frontier experiences—for be it kept in mind, they were now the extreme outpost on the north. The Battle of Pebble Creek, Jan. 19, 1874, was distinctly *their* fight. It was fought practically in their midst and one of their number lost his life in the fray. Then relief came with the building of Fort Hartsuff. For two years the Indians kept to the hills and were rarely seen. But the great "Indian year"—1876—was at hand, growing out of the gold discovery in the Black Hills and the consequent expulsion of the Red Man from those favorite haunts. Everywhere the Sioux were on the war-path. Even now it is doubtful whether there would have been any trouble in the valley had not the settlers themselves precipitated the trouble.

The story, in brief, of the last encounter between the settlers and the Sioux Indians—the so-called "Battle of the Blowout"—is as follows: A small band of Indians was discovered in the hills near Jones' Canyon. The settlers, aided by local trappers and gold seekers on their way to the Black Hills, immediately took the trail and, after a running fight of several miles, brought the redskins to bay in a large blowout above Pebble Creek. A messenger had meanwhile been sent post haste to Fort Hartsuff for reinforcements. A young and inexperienced lieutenant by the name of Hyle led a squad of soldiers

Chapter XIII

The North Loup River near the old mill, Burwell. (By the courtesy of Mrs. Anna Johns.)

to the battleground. In a ridiculous and unwarranted charge upon the blowout First Sergeant Dougherty fell mortally wounded. The besiegers now realized the folly of trying to drive the Indians out of their excellent retreat, and accordingly settled down to a siege. But, strange as it may seem, that very night the Indians escaped under cover of darkness, and this in spite of the cordon of men surrounding the blowout.

Mr. C. H. Jones has written his version of the battle, which I cannot forbear repeating here. He has retold the story so often to appreciative listeners these thirty years past that it has inadvertently become somewhat enlarged. His personal prowess especially seems to be greatly overdone. But this touch of egotism may be readily overlooked in the lace of the fact that the story is very interesting:

"In the spring of 1876 the Sioux were on the war-path. One morning Tom Hemmett came down the canyon from his claim just as we were eating breakfast, and coming to the house asked me 'what those bareheaded men were doing up there on the hill?' I asked, 'where did you see any bareheaded men?' 'Right up there,' looking over the top of the hill about 350 yards from the house. 'Bareheaded men, h—l! they are Indians,' I yelled, and grabbing my gun went around the point on a double-quick. I went up a 'pocket' and peeked over very carefully but they were gone. I went to the spot and discovered tracks and followed the trail until I saw they were headed for the west canyon. Running back to the house I sent Tom down the valley to get out the boys and have them meet me at the forks of the west canyon.

"I went back, took up the trail and followed the Indians. They knew they had been seen and had stopped just over the bank of a canyon half way between the east and west canyons and were lying down watching the back trail. Instead of following the trail I trotted up the west canyon. I went up very cautiously, knowing almost exactly where they would cross it. Every point I approached very carefully, looking through the grass at the top, and lucky I did so, for at the last one I found them not more than 100 yards distant and on the lookout over the back trail. My heart thumped so loud I was afraid they would hear it, but I guess they didn't, for in about twenty minutes they moved west. I waited a few minutes, then went up the bank and peeked again. They were in plain sight, six of them well armed and watching everything. I kept to the left towards the canyon so that I could see the boys when they came up. The Indians finally went down into the south pocket of the west canyon and I circled around expecting them to come out at the head of it, but after waiting a long time I made up my mind that they had slipped out toward the valley, so I started back on the north side of the pocket, keeping a sharp lookout. Finally I discovered just a little smoke in the canyon, and slipping along peeking over cautiously, I discovered them around a little fire eating a turkey they had stolen the night before from Dolph Alderman. How I wished for the boys then! But there was a misunderstanding. Instead of coming where I told them to they mounted their horses and went up the valley to head them off.

Tom Hemmett, as he looked back in the seventies.

"When I got home and found out why the boys had not shown up, I saddled my pony, went back and found that the Indians had gone and then pulled out for Pebble Creek, to the north of the canyons, looking for their trail. Just as I neared the head of the creek I saw some of the trapper boys coming and two of them came over to where I was. They had gone four miles beyond, and seeing nothing had turned back. I told them the Indians were hidden somewhere in the canyons near Pebble Creek and they went to looking. During this time others had joined us, most of them on foot, however. Two of us remained north of the canyons to see whether they would appear again and, sure enough, in about thirty minutes the footmen routed them out of Pebble Creek, but no shots were fired. As soon as they came out we gave the alarm and went for them. Alter about a mile of hot chase the Indians threw away everything except guns and ammunition. When I came up I dismounted and picked up a cartridge belt of Indian manufacture with 16 44-calibre empty shells in it. The belt I wanted as a memento, and I have it yet after nearly 30 years. After joining the advance it became evident that we would have to throw out flankers, as they would stop over every hill and let fly a couple of shots, but they could not hit a barn after running as they had.

"In our party were four mounted trappers and three young men who were en route to the Black Hills—James Flint, Elmer Raymond, John McNutt, and myself (C. H. Jones). The trappers and strangers took the flanks and left us the center. There had been only five or six shots fired by our side when we lost the Indians in the sand hills just to the north and east of the head of Dry Creek. We knew they were somewhere, therefore we commenced looking in the blowouts and in so doing our party became scattered over a mile of territory. Some of the trapper boys were to the northwest, the rest east, and my party to the west and southwest of the blowout where the Indians were. Will Wirtz and two of the Black Hills men were about 300 yards to the north and a little west. Steve Chase and his partner were about 200 yards east and a little north. Dave Shroyer and George Baker were southeast 100 yards. McNutt and I were south 175 yards, Jas. Flint was 200 yards southwest and Elmer Raymond had stopped on a knoll 200 yards west. Now I will go back and bring up the reserves.

"When the trapper boys started to head them off above Pebble Creek and left me alone with the Indians. Newt. McClimans mounted a horse and made for the Fort, yelling 'Indians!' as he went. He dashed into the Fort and told Capt. Coppinger and immediately thereafter

Original log house built by Mr. William Draver south of Burwell in the early seventies.

the bugle sounded 'boots and saddles.' In less than 15 minutes after McClimans got there Lieut. Hyle dashed out at the head of 15 mounted men and went flying up the valley. The Indians were about two miles from the Calamus valley. These troops rode up the Calamus above where we were, but scout 'Buck Shot' being with them and having a powerful glass was taking advantage of the high places to look over the country and discover us.

"At about this time I had located the Indians in a blowout and yelled to Raymond. But he, having sighted the soldiers, paid no further attention to me. Dave Shroyer heard me and asked me where the place was,—Dave was in the valley between the parallel ridges and about 150 yards from me. I pointed north and he turned and dashed up the hill to the very edge of the blowout, in fact the horse's head was over the edge. Just then a shot rang out and Dave's horse wheeled and plunged down the hill, blood spurting from his neck. Immediately after an Indian jumped out of the hole and shot again, then started down the hill after Dave. Then another Indian joined the chase.

I jumped off my horse and told McNutt to hold him but he had skipped down the slope about 30 feet. I yelled at him to stop, telling him that I would shoot him if he didn't, and then ran down the hill and gave him my horse and told him to stay there, and ran back just as the last Indian was getting out of the hole. I dropped down, rested my gun over the top of the hill, took sight and fired. The Indian threw up both hands and fell with a yell backward into the hole. The other Indians looked around in time to see him disappear and just then George Baker opened fire. The Indians immediately broke for the hole again and went in much quicker than they came out. I got another shot at them just as the last one went over the edge, but not being a good wing shot I missed him. I then fired a couple of shots into the hole. The Indians now made an attempt to escape by the north side but three shots from the Wirtz party put them back. Steve Chase was standing on the hill to the right and shortly after two shots in quick succession came from the Indians and Steve dropped out of sight. I left Fling and Raymond and went around to see what had become of Steve. I found him lying on the slope out of range with his partner holding the horses. I asked him if he was shot and he said 'no, but I don't see how the d—l that Indian shot on both sides of me at once.' He said the balls didn't miss him on either side over five inches. I told him two Indians fired at the same time. I gave my horse to the man holding Steve's and we crawled up to the top of the hill, one to watch while the other shot. A shot or two was fired. Then the Indians replied, the first shot striking just between us. We moved a little and then began a fusillade. It wasn't long till the Indians ceased firing. Then we hollowed to Dave and George to come out. They were behind a little knoll just large enough to cover them, but too low down to fire from at the blowout. They came out and everything was quiet for awhile. Then the Indians raised a rag on a gun and shook it. I afterwards thought they wanted to parley but at the time of it I didn't think a black flag denoted anything but blood, so I let drive a shot and the flag disappeared. (The fact of it was, they didn't have any white cloth, but I didn't think of it at that time.) Now, I never felt just right over this matter for I believe that the Indians either wanted to surrender unconditionally or else get us out from under cover and shoot one or more of us to even up the score. But we will never know just what their intention was. At all events that was the last shot for awhile.

"Dave Shroyer suggested when he joined us that perhaps they wanted to surrender when they made the signal. But I told him that I thought they had adopted the wrong course in raising the black flag, so the only consolation I have is to blame the government for not furnishing their good Indians with white handkerchiefs to use when they got into a hole and chances were desperate.

"When 'Buckshot' saw Raymond's signal he dashed down the hill, joined the soldiers and led them on a gallop over the country to our position. As the soldiers came over a point about 250 yards from the blowout the Indians fired two shots at them. One of the shots cut the mane of a horse, next to Lieut. Hyle. After Hyle had asked a few questions he told us that this was no way to fight Indians. 'Why didn't you go up in a body and take them out?' he asked. You may believe I was somewhat taken aback as I thought we had done very well. Hyle then told us that his experience of three years with the Apaches was to go right after them and keep them going. By this time I had gotten my wind. 'Lieutenant,' I said, 'they're in the blowout; go and get them.' After a little parleying seven of our party took a position on the top of a knoll to keep the Indians from firing on the soldiers as they advanced, and the soldiers with Lieut. Hyle on the right and Sergt. Dougherty on the left, advanced up the hill. Sergt. Dougherty got to the top first and came in sight of the Indians. He stepped back, motioned to Hyle that they were there; then, with gun ready, stepped back' to the edge of the blowout when an Indian fired, shooting him through the heart. This threw the soldiers into a panic. They squatted down holding their guns over their heads and fired into the hole without effect—all except Lieut. Hyle. He deliberately stepped to the top, took aim and fired but missed, and the Indians fired three shots at him but missed him. After the soldiers fired they all ran down the hill and when Hyle stepped back to reload he found himself alone. He could not get any of his men to go up after Sergt. Dougherty's body. Bill Wirtz and one of the Black Hills men finally joined the lieutenant and recovered the body. The lieutenant stood and looked at the body of the dead sergeant and then at his cowardly squad of men without saying a word. Finally one of the strangers spoke to him and he roused up, and sent one of the soldiers to the Fort after more men and the ambulance. It was then sundown. Pickets were put around the hole. James Flint and one or two others and I left for home. The reinforcements arrived about midnight and at daylight another advance was made, but the Indians were gone.

"In about three weeks we got word from the Rosebud Agency that our party of six had come in almost naked and that one of them had a bad wound, being shot across the breast from right to left and that the bone on the right side was splintered. I knew then that he was my Indian and that if I had shot two inches farther to the left he would have been a good Indian."

As an immediate result of this brush with the Indians, a number of families feeling themselves insecure in life and property abandoned their claims and left the frontier. Thus the settlers McNutts, Harpers, Raymonds, and others set their faces southward, away from the settlement.

Mr. Jones, nothing daunted, constructed an almost bulletproof fort at a short distance from his house, and placed Tom Hemmett in command. Under him was a garrison of two. The ruins of this fortification are yet traceable on a sharp ridge, at some 85 to 90 yards distance from the old Jones cabin.

But the Indians had gone to rally around Sitting Bull and other chiefs in a vain hope to drive back the regulars which General Miles was beginning to hurl against them.

Aside from the Indian troubles just narrated, life in the upper settlement was much akin to that of the lower settlements. The "Gillespie Star Route" was at an early date extended as far as Willow Springs on the north side, and to The Forks on the south of the river. Truman Freeland carried the mail, in 1874, from St. Paul to the "Springs," via the Springdale-Calamus route. That same year Henry Maxon opened the first postoffice at The Forks, that being the northern limit of the route extending from St. Paul, through Cotesfield, North Loup, and Ord.

Here too were the settlers jealous of the education of their children. In the summer of '75 a very neat, shingled loghouse was erected and Almira J. Freeland installed to teach the first school in the county.

But, all considered, the settlers experienced some fearfully hard years; and yet, as was said of the early New England Pilgrims, not a one of the real settlers lost heart and wished himself back to the flesh-pots of the East. Neither loss of crops by grasshoppers and hail, with consequent shortage in bread, nor winter storm and summer drought could dishearten them, and they lived to see their part of the valley bloom like a rose—great farms, well stocked with choice cattle, and growing marvelous crops. Carefree, with larder well filled and good balances in the bank, they may now take the well-earned rest which is

The Further History of Garfield County 177

theirs. They opened the Trail of the Loup, and those who came after do them honor.

For more than eight years after the first nucleus of pioneers has reached what we now know as Garfield county, that part of the state continued as "Unorganized Territory." For judicial purposes and for purposes of taxation, all that portion lying immediately north and west of Valley county was attached to the latter county. But this condition of things was never satisfactory; accordingly a new county, Wheeler, was organized. This took place on the 11th day of April 1881. The act provided for the organization of a territory forty-eight miles east and west, by twenty-four miles north and south, comprising the present counties of Wheeler and Garfield.

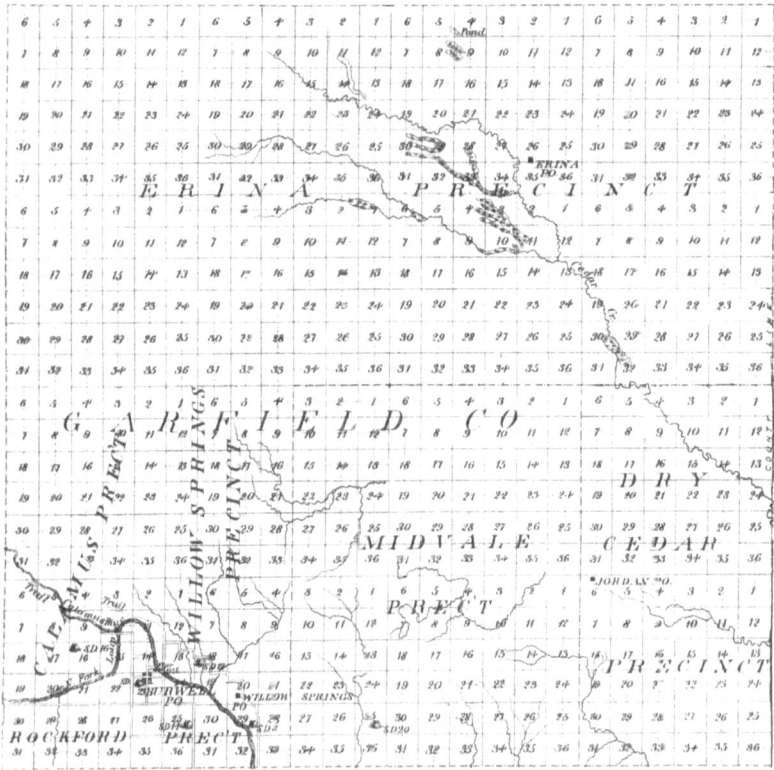

Old precinct map of Garfield county.

Chapter XIII

J. F. Cummings was elected County Clerk and for some time he kept the county records at Cumminsville on Beaver Creek, which may therefore be termed the first county seat. But this place was altogether too far east to suit the settlers living in the western part of the county. So it came about that a new county seat, Cedar City by name, was founded near the middle of the county, on Cedar Creek, or as it is now often designated—"River." This town proved, however, to be a "bird of passage" only, for as soon as Wheeler county was again divided, in 1884, and Bartlett made the permanent county seat, Cedar City passed away so rapidly that today its very foundations are no longer to be seen.

Since the organization of Wheeler county there had been considerable dissension among the settlers relative to an eventual division of the county into regular congressional counties. In 1884 such a division actually took place and Garfield county was organized. Burwell was by gubernatorial proclamation made the temporary county seat, and an election was called to be held at the store of Mr. Graber, at Burwell, December 30, 1884.

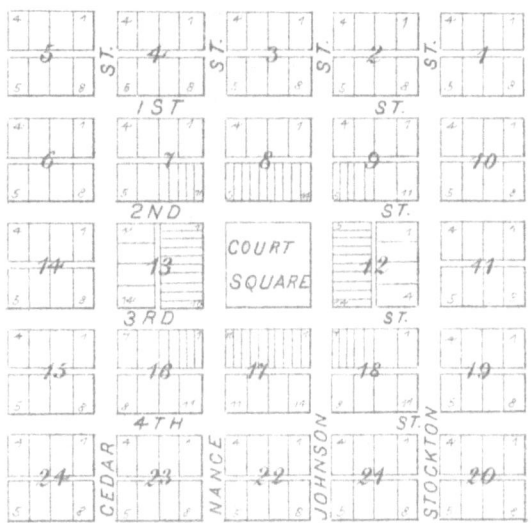

Plat of the defunct Cedar City, first county seat of the original Wheeler county.

The Further History of Garfield County

Incident from the Garfield county Seat Fight: Sheriff Johns serving the "Writ" on the County Clerk. (From the *Willow Springs Illustrated Gazette*.)

The ante-election campaign brought out three rivals for county seat honors—Willow Springs, Burwell and Midvale. A bitter struggle ensued, wherein county officials and settlers took sides and joined the faction which seemed at the time to suit their own ends best. All Garfield county was divided into rival camps. However, election day dawned and even before the formality of a regular count had been gone through with, it was seen that Willow Springs was the winner with votes to spare. But the law provides that where more than two contesting points are voted on, a second election shall be called to choose between the two getting the highest vote in the first election. Midvale had received the smallest vote and was therefore dropped. The second election was set for January 30, 1885.

Another month of bitter campaigning and full of anxiety passed, and election day was again at hand. Both factions were out in force as the vote all along had promised to be a very close one. In this respect no one was disappointed, for out of a total vote of 277, Willow Springs received 142 and Burwell 135, a difference of only seven votes. But this result was not satisfactory to the south siders, who asked and received from the State Supreme Court, a writ of mandamus issued April 9, 1885, whereby a recount of votes was ordered.

The Loss of the Ballot Box: an interesting act in Garfield county history retold in pictures. (From the *Willow Springs Illustrated Gazette*.)

The Further History of Garfield County 181

This recount took place April 18, and resulted—Willow Springs 105 and Burwell 128. Such a remarkable figure was the direct result of gross irregularities. It seems that before the canvassing board had time to count the returns, the entire "Dry Cedar" vote was done away with. The story goes that there are those still living in Garfield county who could, if they were so inclined, tell the secrets of that remarkable *coup d' etat*. But howsoever this may be the machinations proved of no avail, as the Supreme Court set aside the alternative Writ after a careful hearing of both sides in the contest. The judges subsequently gave the certificate of election to Willow Springs, declaring that town the legally chosen county seat.

Now ensued a spectacular fight for the possession of the county records. The County Clerk, Henry W. Mattley, and County Commissioner O. E. Randall, insisted that Burwell was and should remain the county seat. A majority of the board, James Butler and M. E. Guyer, on the other hand, were as insistent on making Willow Springs the county seat. The county records contain some very interesting reading in this connection. First the county clerk called a meeting of the commissioners as follows:

> Commissioners of Garfield county will please meet at my office on Saturday, May 16th, 1835, for the purpose of declaring Burwell the county seat of Garfield county, Nebraska.
> *May 8th, 1885. Henry W. Mattley, County Clerk*

Then it appears that two of the members ignored this call entirely as the minutes here appended show:

> Office of Clerk. Burwell, Nebraska, May 16, 1885.
> In accordance to above call Mr. O. E. Randall appeared at office and as he was unaccompanied by either of the other commissioners, no business was done.
> *Attest: H. W. Mattley, Clerk*

But all this time the other two members of the board were planning to organize the county government at Willow Springs. To that end a meeting was called for June 2. On their minutes we read these terse, epigrammatic statements:

Chapter XIII

Willow Springs, June 2, '85.

H. W. Mattley ordered to appear instanter—fails—Sheriff sent after him.

W. E. Johns, Sheriff.	James Butler	Comms present at meeting
John W. Abbott, Clerk Pro Tempore	M. E. Guyer	

It would appear from the above, and from statements of eye witnesses and participants, that at first the clerk flatly refused to move his books from Burwell to Willow Springs, and that there was talk of holding the temporary court house by force of arms if need be; but better judgment finally prevailed, so that when the sheriff a second time crossed the river for Mr. Mattley, he was found in waiting on the south side of the river, willing to be transported to the victorious "Springs."

But the end was not yet. In 1887 the Burlington and Missouri River Railroad in Nebraska commenced building northward, up through the valley, on the south side of the river. From Ord it extended its grade to Burwell, and on to Butka on the Calamus. This was a death blow to Willow Springs. Poor "Springs"! Had she not been living in the almost certain hope of getting an extension of the Union Pacific which had these many years had its terminus at Ord? And, now, at one fell stroke she was utterly ruined! As was expected, a new election was ordered, and this time resistance was simply hopeless. February 16, 1890, decided the county seat question forever. Burwell received 288 votes, while Willow Springs could muster only 148. Thus the change was made and Willow Springs passes out of history.

The above is a terse outline of the bitter struggle which for years set neighbor against neighbor in Garfield county, almost threatening for a brief time internecine war. But fortunately this is all over now, and though not entirely forgotten, has long been forgiven; so that those who participated in the fight, are again on as good terms of comradeship as when they first, as brothers, toiled over the Trail of the Loup.

No one person, perhaps, was more vitally interested in the county seat struggle than H. C. Jones of Willow Springs He furnished much of the "sinews of war,'" and when all was lost and Burwell won, it meant financial ruin to him. It is but proper then that he should

The Further History of Garfield County 183

be allowed to tell his story of the matter, and in his own way. The narrative gives many sidelights and is, in the main, correct, though his memory may at times err in minor details. He says:

"In 1884 the proposition for a division of the county was submitted to the people and carried. Frank Webster had laid out a townsite the year before and there were five or six buildings up at that time, and perhaps more—I have forgotten—and it had gotten the temporary county seat. Tom Hemmett and the Acrees had laid out a town a quarter of a mile west of my store and called it Willow Springs. Frank Webster's town was named Burwell. John Acree at that time was our main politician. He was a talker, a great schemer of very nervous disposition and never at his best unless well loaded with Hostetter's Hunki Dori Bitters of which I kept a good supply.

"The same year, I think, the location for county seat of the new county of Garfield came up. The contest was very warm between Burwell and Willow Springs. In the contest Willow Springs won with the aid of our friends in the north and east part of the county. As soon as the result was known Tom Hemmet and the Acrees began to put up a building for county offices. At the end of the time allowed for canvassing the vote it was found that the ballots, poll book, etc., of Dry Cedar precinct had been stolen and the Burwell people had the clerk (who was a Burwell man) declare in favor of Burwell, but soon after he wanted to take it back as his own brother was going to scalp him. About that time there was a strong talk of war—a war of extermination. Most of the citizens on both sides of the river denounced the act, and on account of it the feeling was very strong in favor of Willow Springs.

"In less than two hours after the clerk had announced the result, men were riding over the country on different missions; one to Cedar City after a certified copy of the poll book, another to the district judge for an injunction, etc., and a letter was written to the governor to "head off" the clerk's returns, and everything was done that could be thought of to get our rights by law. Wise council prevailed and there was no resort to arms, but the matter was kept in the court for some time, Willow Springs winning.

"The building was completed in the meantime and a store started in the lower room thereof. Other buildings went up and by the first of June 1887, Willow Springs had two general stores, one grocery, one newspaper, two drugstores, one bakery, one hardware, one bank, one blacksmith shop and several dwellings. I then bought

Chapter XIII

the Hemmett building, had it remodelled and moved my store up there but found it too small. Just before I moved, the county records were brought over from Burwell by sheriff W. C. Johns, who had a little squabble with the Burwellites to obtain possession of them, and we had the county seat in fact. But the B. & M. Road built to Burwell and we had to fight for our existance. Some of the newcomers got skittish and made arrangements to move their buildings to Burwell and give up our town. As soon as a start was made away went everything but one other and myself. I had doubled the size of my buildings and had the largest stock of goods in the county and held a good share of the trade. But the fight for relocation of the county seat was kept up continually by Burwell. Whenever they got up a petition we got up a counter petition which carried more names than theirs, consequently the commissioners would not grant their petition.

"About this time W. Z. Todd started the *Enterprise* at Willow Springs. Soon after Geo. Gill came out from Ohio and started a hardware and tinshop and Willow Springs was 'looking up' again. Burwellites got out another petition; we got out a remonstrance and hired men to canvass the county with it. When the commissioners met there was considerable oratory and wire-pulling but the board decided not to call an election. The Burwellites applied for a mandamus. H.W. Todd was sent to Grand Island to look after the interests of Willow Springs and succeeded in knocking them out. I wish to go back a little and show what we had to do to keep up our end of the fight.

"At the time our town had reached its best we wanted a bridge across the Loup. The county wasn't able to build it; a bond was out of the question, so we had to hustle. $780 were subscribed towards the building of a bridge. $100 of this amount was subscribed by Commissioner Jackson and others, of Burwell, who when they discovered that the bridge would not be located just where they wanted it, promptly withdrew their subscriptions.

"Then we got busy and laid out a road on the south side of the river and one on the north side, both terminating at the river, and demanded a bridge. It was then up to the board. We agreed with them to make up what the county lacked in funds to put in the bridge and it was built.

"All this cost me money. And to make matters worse a hailstorm destroyed the crops about this time and I was compelled to do a large credit business and had to borrow money to pay my bills. We had gotten tired of the continuous fight on the county seat. Burwell folks raised about $1200 to use in the election in 1889 and came over to see some of our friends. They sent them to me. I told them if they would give me a lot in Burwell and move my store onto it and would provide for W. Z. Todd and Geo. Gill, I'd quit. They agreed to it. Todd and Gill were moved over and my goods and building were also moved. Then the election returns showed Burwell to be victorious.

"The result of the fight was disastrous to me. I was compelled to sell out at 75c on the dollar and eventually lost my home also. One part of the county never went back on me—Erina, and I never lost a cent by them, Bless the people of Erina. May they always prosper."

Burwell is the only town of consequence in Garfield county. It may in a way be said to be the outgrowth of "The Forks" postoffice, located down near the old mill on the river road. The townsite lies at a bend in the river not far from the point where the Calamus blends its waters with the eddying North Loup.

As to the origin of the name there are several stories told, more or less reliable. One has it that it was given to perpetuate the name of a certain young woman, the betrothed of one of the Webster

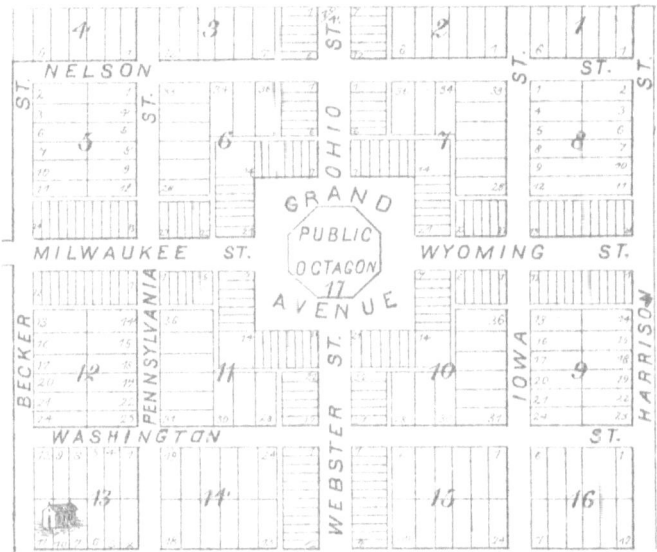

Plat of Burwell showing "Public Octagon," which has been disfigured by building upon it, and the streets meeting the square at the middle of the sides.

Chapter XIII

Home of D. S. Beynon at Burwell.

family platting the town, but who died before the nuptials could be solemnized. The writer will not, however, vouch for the truth of this rather romantic christening.

The town was platted by Frank Webster on his home farm and was for many years "Webster's town." This gentleman's ideas of what an ideal townsite ought to be were certainly remarkable and may best be understood by a glance at the erection of the public square. This is very large, but instead of being approachable by streets intersecting at its far corners, they approach it as bisectors of the four sides.

Even this would not have been so bad had the inside plat of ground been dedicated to the city as presumably first intended. When Mr. Webster later sold his interests to the Burwell Townsite Company it appeared that the inside of the square had not been so dedicated. Accordingly he began selling this in parcels for building purposes. A protest and threat on the part of the townsite company led to a compromise and a division of lots on the "inside square." This unfortunately has for all time spoiled the appearance of the public square.

The first store building at Burwell was that of Wm. N. Becker & Co. This was in 1883. Alfred A. Graber soon followed with a small hardware store. Almost at the same time Frank Webster commenced building. A very few residences were added and we have Burwell's

The Further History of Garfield County

embryo. In 1884 Garfield county was created and the governor of Nebraska made Burwell the temporary county seat. Frank Webster's store became the depository for the official records and documents. Here the temporary county government met. Then came the county seat troubles and Webster's store was for a time the objective point in the operations.

A. A. Graber et al.'s writ of mandamus was overturned by the very court which had granted it and Willow Springs was declared the county seat. This made the Burwellites pretty glum for a time. But the gloom was not to last long, for in 1887 the B. & M. commenced building up the Valley. The old rival was overthrown utterly and was only too glad "to move over" and become a part of the new county seat. As if by magic Willow Springs residences and stores left their "anchorage" and in an incredibly short time became a part of Burwell. Thus the town grew at a moderate pace and had a population of 150 when the decade of general prosperity closing with 1890 terminated. During the next ten years its progress was not marked. In fact between 1890 and 1896 it experienced a considerable set-back. The remaining four years of the decade were spent in getting the town back on a normal footing.

In 1900, and more particularly since 1903, Burwell has made good strides onward. In the latter year the town had less than 500

Beautiful home of Robert Wicks, Burwell.

Chapter XIII

Comfortable home of Mr. Cram, Burwell.

inhabitants; now it is almost 700. Four years ago there was hardly a modern house on the townsite; now on the other hand, as so aptly illustrated in the cuts in this chapter, Burwell boasts a surprisingly large number of very fine houses. Excellent cement sidewalks are rapidly displacing the old wooden structures. A new eight-room school building was completed in the fall of 1903 at a cost of $10,000. The city owns its own waterworks system, and a private corporation furnishes an ample supply of acetelyne gas to light the streets and homes of all who desire it. It is safe to prophecy that Burwell will continue to prosper and to grow. By degrees the sand-hills to the north will be reclaimed to fruitfulness and the town's territory will as gradually become more and more populated.

Garfield county is in main a grazing district, well adapted to raising cattle and sheep. The Loup Valley part of the county alone is fit for true agriculture. But the despised sand-hills will yet be the making of the county. Alfalfa grows well in the draws and lowlands. Bromograss and English bluegrass will soon spread their green, succulent mantle from hill to hill and make this one of the richest hay producing belts in the entire country. Such is pretty sure to be the future of Garfield county.

Statistics

Population (1903)	2800
Area	576 sq. mi.
Miles of railway	4.17
Best tillable land	$25.00 to $60.00
Fair tillable land	$15.00 to $25.00
Hay and pasture land	$4.00 to $6.00

*Description by Townships**

Range 13

T. 21. North half and southwest sixth mostly level, fertile: rest rolling, fair soil.

T. 22. Cedar valley, quite sandy; rest sand hills and hay flats.

T. 23. Southwest quarter Cedar valley, sandy, but tillable; rest sand hills with few hay valleys.

T. 24. Northeast quarter rolling, mostly tillable; rest sand hills and hay flats.

Range 14

T. 21. Rolling, fertile; mostly tillable.

T. 22. Mostly sand hills; some fertile land in south third.

---

* From the *Bulletin of the Bureau of Labor,* Lincoln, Neb., 1902.

The largest ear of corn ever grown on the North Loup: taken at Burwell with Postmaster Beynon as driver.

T. 23. Sand hills and hay flats.

T. 24. Cedar valley, fertile; about four sections on north, sand hills.

Range 15

T. 21. Southwest half in North Loup valley, fertile; rest quite rolling, mostly fertile.

T. 22. South half rolling, fertile; north half sand hills and hay valleys.

T. 23. Sand hills and hay valleys; some shallow lakes.

T. 24. Cedar valley, fertile; rest fair, rolling land, interspersed with sand hills.

Range 16

T. 21. North Loup valley, fertile; rest very rolling, fertile.

T. 22. Southwest quarter mostly tillable; rest sand hills and hay valleys.

T. 23. Sand hills and hay valleys.

T. 24. Sand hills and hay valleys.

Public school building of Burwell.

XIV

Loup County and Its Possibilities

> Thy spreading fields are yielding recompense for honest toil,
>   Nebraska, dear Nebraska.
> The smile of God is beaming ever on thy fertile soil,
>   Nebraska, dear Nebraska.
> Once the dainty golden-rod peeped above the virgin sod,
>   Where today we see the beet leaves green and curled.
> Grain and cattle from thy fields nature's richest bounty yields,
>   And Nebraska, our Nebraska, feeds the world.
>   —Will M. Maupin, "Nebraska"

Loup county was settled in 1874. The first settlers to trail the Loup beyond the Garfield county settlement and squat within the confines of Loup county were Rodney P. Alger, John R. Goff, D. L. Bowen, B. J. Harvey, A. M. Gurnsey and Wm. Burns with their families. A few months later, when work on Fort Hartsuff was begun, a number of additional families became temporary dwellers within the limits of the territory.

In the spring of 1875 an Indian scare seized the outlying farmsteads; the growing crops were abandoned and the whole community assembled in the little, well-known park on R. P. Alger's farm, and there erected temporary abodes. For greater security a stockade was erected and dubbed "Fort Rodney," in honor of Rodney P. Alger. The Indians, however, did not appear and shortly all the staunch-hearted among the settlers returned to their abandoned homes; a few timid ones only left the country for good.

Fort Hartsuff was soon afterwards completed and the colony freed from any further Indian experiences.

In the summer of 1876 and the following spring the colony was further increased by the arrival of the Rushos, T. W. Williams, D. A. Gard and G. C. Snyder, all with their families. These arrivals settled near where Kent and Taylor are now located.

During the winter of 1876–77 A. M. Gurnsey succeeded in getting a special postoffice established. Mr. Gurnsey was appointed postmaster and the office named Kent. For a time the mail was carried by volunteers who took turn about making the trip down to The Forks and back.

Grand Island, one hundred miles to the south, was in those days the nearest railroad connection. Thither did the settlers have to go for most of their necessaries of life. During the first few years of scant crops it was a common thing for the settlers to cart ox-loads of cedar posts all the way to York and Butler counties—a round trip of fully 300 miles—to exchange the same for flour, groceries and other necessaries of life. Ten days to three weeks were counted necessary to make the trip; and during all this time the hardy freighter was subject to the discomforts and hardships occasioned by the uncertainty of weather conditions—swollen and unfordable streams, sudden storms, and the like.

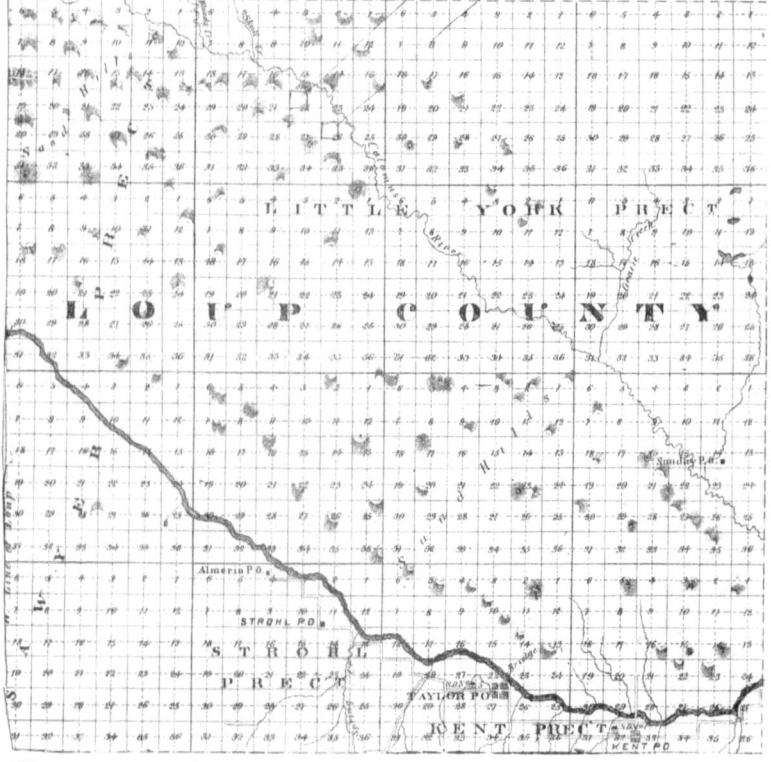

Old precinct map of Loup county.

"During the summer of '77," says David Gard, "we were all so busy breaking prairie and putting in crops, that no one had time to make a trip to the nearest grist mill, which was then fifty miles down the valley. For a while we accordingly ground our corn and wheat on hand coffee-mills."

The first school district was organized in 1876 under the jurisdiction of Valley county, where Rev. Oscar Babcock was at that time county superintendent. The district, which was designated as No. 9, was very large, containing more than thirty square miles. A sod house with dirt roof and stamped clay floor was erected on section 36, T. 21, R. 18. Rose Harvey was the first teacher employed to teach here, and her first term was only three months long.

The first general store in the county was opened by A. Kitzmiller at Kent in 1880. He was obliged to haul all of his merchandise from St. Paul, which point the Union Pacific Railroad had now reached.

Time passed and other families were added to the list already mentioned. There were A S. Moon, David McCord, Thomas Croughwell, William A. Clark, Jacob and Wesley Strohl, William Forbes, Henry Copp, John Burlingham, William Thomas, B. S. Sawyer, George Spangler, John Abbott, George Craven, Charles Copper, John Wheeler, George Abbott, Calvin L. Copp, Stephen Roblyer, Wesley Rains, H. Dunbar, Mrs. Phoebe Glover, and many others.

Loup county was at this time a part of the unorganized territory. As the population continued to increase it became expedient to organize the county. This was accomplished in the spring of 1883. The temporary county seat was placed at Kent with David Gard as temporary clerk. The first election was held May 3d of that year and resulted as follows: Clerk, F. H Sawyer; Treasurer, Joseph Rusho; Judge, B. J. Harvey; Sheriff, Arthur C Alger; Surveyor, A. J. Roblyer; Superintendent, A. S. Moon; Commissioners, G. W. Strohl, N. E. Fay and H. L. Reniff.

Next came the inevitable strife for the location of the permanent county seat. Kent lay too far east to be considered in the race. But Taylor, Almeria, and Clark's Point were all eager to land the plum. None of these places had been platted, but that mattered but little in those days. Locate the county seat and the town would spring up! Taylor lay very close to the center of population and was a logical claimant. Almeria became a dangerous rival because Kent might be expected to throw her support to a town as far away as possible from

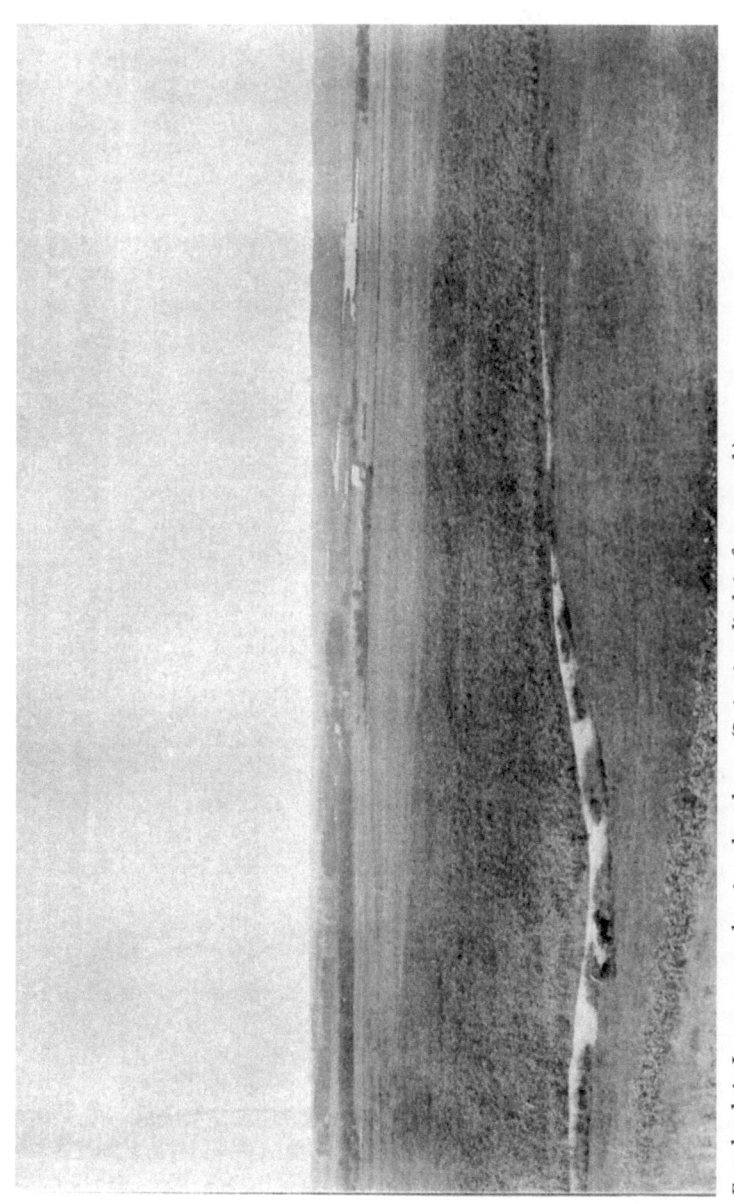

Farmlands in Loup county showing abundance. (Irrigation ditch in foreground.)

her own zone of influence. For Taylor once the county seat would mean death to ambitious little Kent. So it came about that the election was very close. Indeed Taylor won out by just two votes majority over Almeria.

Taylor was staked off on a farm belonging to and adjoining the homestead of Joseph Rusho. The original site contained 32 blocks, of which No. 13 was set aside as a public square.

The first store opened was that of Otto Witte, who carried a stock of groceries and drugs. This was very early in 1884 In a short time two additional stores opened. George Cleveland put in groceries and hardware and E. H. Snow, dry goods, boots and shoes. But these ventures were not to be permanent accessions to the town; they soon tired and left for more promising fields. The first permanent business house to become established at Taylor was that of Wheeler & Scott, which is still doing business under the name of George F. Scott. Half a decade later Taylor boasted five general stores, two banks, two hotels, two livery stables, two newspapers and many other business places. Many of those were built on the expectancy of getting an extension of the B. & M. which had reached Burwell in 1887. But, alas! Taylor was doomed to bitter disappointment and is to this day an inland town.

The dry years were hard on Loup county and her towns. Almeria, where G. W. Strohl and Fred Hoellworth had opened a general store, managed to hold her own and live through the crisis. Kent by degrees dwindled down till in 1905 there is nothing left but the postoffice, and this too will no doubt soon be discontinued. Taylor saw her banks close their doors for lack of business, and some of her business houses removed, stock, buildings and all. But here, as elsewhere, the tide turned in time, and today the town is slowly rallying from the staggering blow. A new bank has just opened its doors to business and the stores are all doing a thriving business. Geo. F. Scott and Rusho Bros. are carrying large stocks of general merchandise, George P. Emig has a first-class drugstore, Joseph Rusho a complete line of hardware. J. G. Wirsig is proprietor of the *Loup County News* and a thriving implement business. Joseph Kriegel has built up an excellent business in harness, saddles and trunks. The *Taylor Clarion*, the oldest newspaper in the county, is edited by E. Andrews. Everything considered, Taylor business men have cause to feel encouraged. The territory from which they draw their trade is rapidly developing, and with the increase in population which is sure to come the town is bound to grow. Taylor has from the beginning been handicapped because it is an inland town.

Chapter XIV

Several times it has looked as though the B. & M. would extend to it, but it has always ended in disappointment. First, when the Burlington built to Burwell in 1887, Taylor expected to get the line. Then when the same system extended up through Custer county the town became hopeful again. But this extension crossed the southwest corner of the county, passing south of Taylor and missing Almeria just four miles. Even now the situation is not hopeless. Two years ago a survey was made from Burwell up through the valley and Taylor may yet get a connecting line between the Garfield and Custer county branches.

Loup county is in many respects a remarkable county. It is chiefly a grazing district, well adapted for the raising of cattle, horses and sheep. But at least forty percent is made up of good tillable lands. The value of the county live stock is estimated at $500,000. This will increase rapidly hereafter. Alfalfa, bromograss, and English bluegrass are even now on the point of revolutionizing the cattle industry. When such remarkable grasses shall have had time to clothe the sand-hills with their mantle of green, these decried sections will become a source of untold wealth to the county; indeed they will be the making of a great and prosperous county. It is surprising how well fruit trees grow in the county. Some of the apple orchards in the valley and on the higher benches to the south can scarcely be excelled by any in the state. It is an eye-opener to the Easterner to see such orchards as are grown by L. F. Ruppel and others in this county. Since the passage of the Kinkaid homestead law, every section of land in the county has been snapped up and land is steadily increasing in value. To have land holdings in Loup county is now to be fortunate.

Hog ranch in Loup county.

Statistics

Population (1903)	1700
Area	576 sq. mi.
Best tillable land	$25.00 to $55.00
Fair tillable land	$10.00 to $20.00
Rich hay land	$20.00 to $25.00
Pasture land	$3.00 to $6.00

Description by Townships*

Range 17

T. 21. North Loup valley; rest rolling; all fertile.
T. 22. Calamus valley fertile in part; rest rough grazing land.
T. 23. Rough, sandy grazing land.
T. 24. Rough, sandy grazing land.

Range 18

T. 21. North Loup valley, three miles wide, fertile; rest rolling, fertile.
T. 22. Rough few farms in south, rest grazing land.
T. 23. Rough, sandy grazing land.
T. 24. Rough, sandy grazing land.

Range 19

T. 21. North Loup valley, three miles wide; rest rolling; good soil.
T. 22. North Loup valley, over two miles wide, fertile; rest rough.
T. 23. Rough, sandy grazing land.
T. 24. Rough, sandy grazing land.

Range 20

T. 21. Rough, sandy soil, used for farming and grazing land.
T. 22. Rough, sandy soil, used for farming and grazing land; Loup valley.
T. 23. Loup valley in southwest, tillable; rest rough grazing land.
T. 24. Rough, sandy grazing land.

---

* From the *Bulletin of the Bureau of Labor*, Lincoln, Neb., 1902.

XV

Scotia and Her Builders

> Behind the scared squaw's birch canoe,
> The steamer smokes and raves;
> And city lots are staked for sale
> Above all Indian graves.
>
> —John Greenleaf Whittier,
> "On Receiving an Eagle's Quill from Lake Superior"

We have already learned in Chapter VI how the committee of the Seventh-Day Baptists reached the chalk hills in Greeley county, opposite Scotia, on the last day of October 1871, and laid claim to the southern bank of the North Loup river for their constituents back in Wisconsin. But they were not the first comers in the Valley after all. For the northern bank of the stream was even then in process of settlement. In September, before autumn was fairly ushered in, the first band came. By handfuls they advanced up the north bank of the Loup through Greeley county by the old trail. The beautiful bend in the river where Scotia now lies, and immediately across from "Happy Jack's Look out," charmed them and held them fast. Here and up and down the valleys of Fish Creek and Wallace Creek they reared their homes and started life anew after their weary westward tramp.

The very first to file on a claim in all Greeley county was Alcie P. Fish of Fish Creek, whose papers were executed in October 1871. About the same time the grand old patriarch, William Scott, settled north of Scotia. Alza M. Stewart took a claim across the line in Valley county. John G. Kellogg, the well known Greeley county bard, and Alonzo Shepard settled in the same neighborhood.

Other early comers in the North Loup valley in this vicinity were James Harlow, Daniel Benson, George Babcock, W. Whitford, G. Craig, Patrick Coyne, J. J. Bean, David Moore, Horace Moore, Geo. R. Small, Fred Housmann, Henry Grosse, Ben Mullenbeck, James L. Wallace, George Ferrell, W. Cramer, Wm. Havens, Thos. Townley, Fred Stensby, Frank Roberts, Thos. Watson, John Vairy, the Skay and Gray families, John Dougherty, Andrew J. Gillespie, Jr., Simon Bilyeu, Jesse Bilyeu, George Hillman, Alfred Hillman, John A. Buchan, John V. Alderman, Leslie E. Scott, Loring E. Gaffy and Elihu Fish.

Chapter XV

Alcie Fish, first settler in Greeley county.

Up Wallace Creek came Joe Littlefield, D. C. Johnson, Henry Calvin, Elias Walker, Albert Barker, Elias Jeffries, Turn Miller, Joe Brown, Geo. Rutherford, Geo. Stubblefield, Joseph Hamilton, Maurice Johnson and Richard Johnson. On Fish Creek settled Fred Meyers, David Locker, John Phillips, W. Hayden, B. F. Griffith and William Halpin.

Of the old-timers here named only a very few arrived in '71. The great majority did not come till the succeeding spring and summer and even years later. The list contains but three or four who professed allegiance to the Seventh-Day Baptist Church. The Wisconsin colony, as a whole, settled on the south side of the river in Town 17, and more particularly in Town 18 in Valley county. For some five or six years settlement of Greeley county was restricted to the southwestern part. The rolling uplands, and Clear Creek and Cedar River valleys were not invaded till the spring of 1877. Meanwhile this little handful took measures to organize their county and elect county officials. Application was made to Acting Governor Wm. H. James, who issued a proclamation ordering an election to be held on the 8th day of October 1872. The election was held at Lamartine postoffice south of Scotia, where Elihu Fish was at that time postmaster. Thirteen votes were cast and the following officers elected: Commissioners, A. P. Fish, T. C. Davis and Alonzo Shepard; Clerk, E. B. Fish; Treasurer, S. C. Scott; Sheriff, G. W. Babcock; Judge, George Hillman; Surveyor, Mansell Davis; Superintendent, John G. Kellogg; and Coroner, C. H. Wellman.

The next question of importance to come up for settlement was the inevitable county seat location. This first contest was, however, but a friendly rivalry. The county commissioners held a meeting at Lamartine postoffice on January 20, 1873, transacting all business incident to the late organization of the county, and calling an election for the purpose of selecting a county seat. Said election was ordered to be held February

11, 1873. Two points were voted for, namely: The N. W. ¼ of the N. W. ¼ of Section 23, Town 17, Range 12, and the N. E. ¼ of Section 9, in the same town and range. The former location—Lamartine—won out by one vote and became the temporary county seat.

In November 1874, another election was held. The aim apparently was to draw the county seat northward. The two points in contest this time were scarcely two miles apart—the N. W. ¼ of the N. E. ¼ of Section 9, Town 17, Range 17 West, and the N. E. ¼ of the N. E. ¼ of Section 16 of the same town and range. The records show that in the election the former place received sixteen votes and the latter ten votes. Thus it came about that Scotia—so named from his old homeland by Sam C. Scott—was made the county seat.

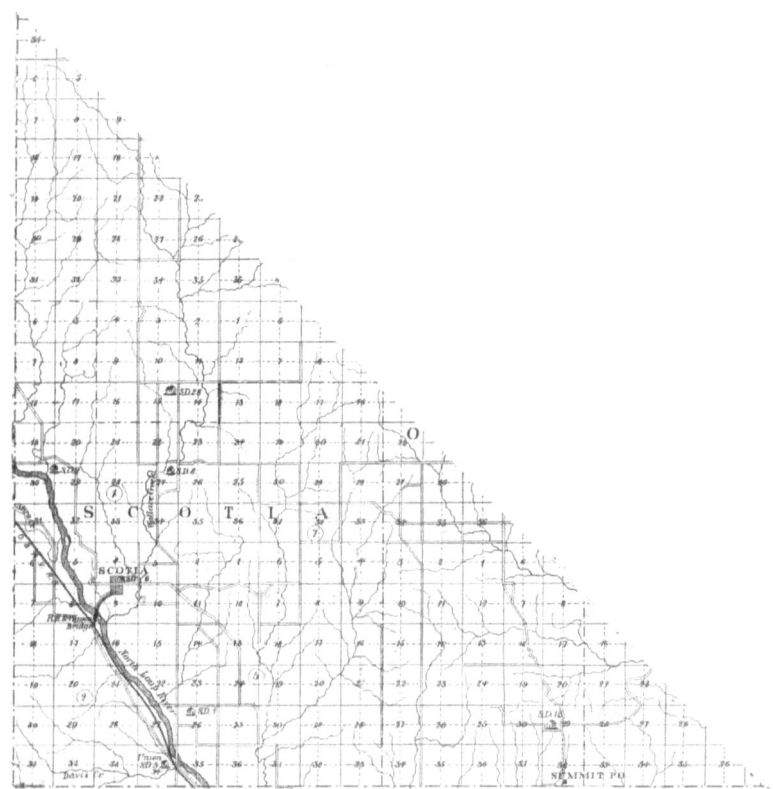

Old precinct map of Greeley county. Showing Scotia and vicinity.

Chapter XV

Plat of Scotia.

For a long time there was really no town. In the fall of 1875 a small court house was built. This humble structure was also used for school purposes. Thus we are told that Mrs. E. Craig used to hold school here in the same room where the county clerk would be busy over his records. Judge John J. Bean located at Scotia in May of 1876 and commenced the construction of a hotel. The same year Sam Scott moved the postoffice to town from his farm and relinquished it to Mr. Bean, who was regularly appointed postmaster in January 1877. In October of that year E. O. Bartlett and A. B. Lewis, two enterprising young business men from St. Paul, Howard county, established the *Greeley Tribune*, which did much to advertise the county and town. The first general merchandise store was opened by W. H. West of Grand Island, under the management of Ed Wright, in March 1878. The railways were beginning to exploit their lands in the North Platte country rather freely by this time. To further this end the B. & M. in Nebraska built a small immigrant house at Scotia. This home was in charge of the kind and public-spirited David Moore, one of the men who never lost faith in the possibilities of the beautiful Loup.

So far the village was a straggling, haphazard affair. But this same year, 1878, Lee L. Doane platted the site and a systematic though slow growth commenced. In 1881 the population was yet under one hundred. The business houses were few though these few had a good trade.

Just now too a cloud was rising on the horizon of Scotia's prosperity. Men of foresight had seen it coming for some time. It was again the same old question of county seat location. For some years the county had been rapidly filling up with settlers. Could Scotia then hope indefinitely to retain the county seat? Many realized that it would only be a question of time when some more centrally located town would rise as an aspirant for the honors. And the first mutterings of trouble came in December 1881, when O'Connor commenced a contest. But let us go back for a glimpse of the settlement of Greeley county at large.

David Moore of Scotia.

The first settler near the center of the county, so far as we know, was James L. Reed, who came in 1876. The next spring an Irishman by the name of Patrick Hynes arrived and became local agent for the Irish Catholic colonization association just then in its conception. General O'Neill seems to have been the originator of the plan which was no more nor less than to buy up vast tracts of land in Greeley and neighboring counties, which were to be colonized with his countrymen, both from the States and from old Ireland. 25,000 acres were purchased near the center of the county, and it was not long till some twenty Irish families were located on the land through the energetic Patrick Hynes. Other colonies sprang up in Cedar Valley and further north as far as Erina in Garfield county. The movement was organized for more than patriotic motives. Wherever Irishmen settle in numbers they will cluster around their church and parochial schools. The present case was no exception to this rule. Men high in ecclesiastical circles were from the first interested in the scheme. This was particularly true of the Right Rev. James O'Connor, Catholic Bishop at that time of Nebraska, Wyoming and Montana.

This great churchman was born in Ireland, September 10, 1823, and came to America in 1838. He was educated at Philadelphia and at the College of Propaganda, Rome. There he was ordained March

Chapter XV

Right Rev. James O'Connor,
Catholic Bishop of Nebraska,
Wyoming and Montana.

25, 1848, by the great Cardinal Franconi and soon after he returned to America, entering the diocese of Pittsburg, where he had charge of St. Michael's Theological Seminary for some years. He was also administrator of the diocese for a year. Then he was given charge of St. Charles Borromeo Seminary at Philadelphia for ten years. Later he was consecrated Bishop of Debona, and Vicar Apostolic of Nebraska, August 26, 1876. The same year he took up his residence at Omaha, where he established Creighton University, the Academy of the Sisters of Mercy, the Boarding Schools of the Ladies of the Sacred Heart and a number of parochial schools.

General O'Neill and John McCreary platted a town near the heart of the Irish land grant in November 1877, and called it O'Connor in honor of the bishop. For some reason this site was never used and a new town of the same name was later—August 1880—built only three and a half miles away on a site selected by the bishop himself. The town grew rapidly. Patrick Hynes opened the first store in October, and two months later Lanagan Brothers opened the second store. An imposing church edifice and parochial school buildings soon followed. R. H. Clayton established the O'Connor Democrat early in 1882, and a systematic agitation for the rights of that part of the county took its beginning.

The census of 1880 gave Greeley county a population of 1461, many of whom had to travel 25 miles or more to reach the county seat. Dissatisfaction with existing conditions grew with an increase in upper county population. Finally the county board felt constrained to call a new election. This was held December 6, 1881, and resulted, O'Connor 196, Scotia 171, and the county poor farm, 33. Fortunately for Scotia a two-thirds majority was required for removal and the county seat was for the time being saved.

In 1883, the Union Pacific built its spur into town and confidence was again restored, for was not Scotia the only railroad town in the county? Matters now moved along at an even tenor till 1887. The town grew slowly but surely. Then, like a thunderclap from a clear sky, came the news that the B. & M. had commenced to build across the county, apparently through O'Connor. This was bad news indeed for Scotia. Everyone realized what it meant. But while Scotia was sorely disappointed she could hardly have expected anything else; another town, which for the moment was jubilant in visions of coming prosperity, was, however, destined to an even sadder fate—this was O'Connor. Located in its beautiful, winding valley this town was on the logical line of the new road. The railroad authorities must also have been of this opinion for grading camps were established near the town and work actually commenced. The inhabitants were unfortunately too confident in their new position. They argued that the road could impossibly go elsewhere and were altogether too slow to meet the railroad's demand for right-of-way, station site and the like. The upshot of it all was that the grading camps were all abandoned and moved into the hills to the south. A committee with full power to grant every request made by the railroad was now sent hot haste to Lincoln. But to remonstrate and beseech was now in vain. O'Connor awoke too late. The B. & M. built a new town at a few miles distance, and called it Greeley Center. This town the Burlington system, with its old-time shrewdness for organization, decided upon as the political center of the new county and straightway formulated its plans.

Four generations of the Hillman family.
Mrs. Blueht.   Mrs. Chase.
Mr. Geo. Hillman.   Mrs. Hillman.
Baby Chase.

206   Chapter XV

Andrew J. Gillespie, Sr., the Centenarian of the Loup, who celebrated his 100th birthday at Scotia, June 4, 1905. Mr. Gillespie has 172 living descendents—nine children, 77 grandchildren, 80 great-grandchildren, and six great-great-grandchildren.

Scotia made one more desperate effort to hold her own. This came in the form of a gift to the county of a new court house built by Scotia Precinct at a cost of $5000.00. This was in 1887. The very next year the bitter struggle recommenced. The O'Connor constituency, still smarting from unhealed wounds, joined hands with Scotia and had the satisfaction to see Greeley's aspirations for the time defeated. But in the fall of 1890 the end came. Greeley Center won in the election and became the county seat. Considerable ill feeling and even personal animosity was engendered during these years. But these differences are how happily being forgotten. Neither faction could really be blamed. It is natural, I am sorry to say, in times like the above, for personal desires and gains to get away with one's better heart-promptings. But, as said, Greeley county is again getting united, and the less these old rifts be stirred the better for all concerned.

Scotia stood face to face with hard times. She had lost her chief point of prestige. The new court house stood empty and many prominent families left for Greeley Center. Her population decreased seriously. But she had staunch hearts in her midst. These stood by the old town during the hard years and never lost courage. The court house was turned into a Normal and Business College and did well till some untoward circumstances forced it too to close down. Then came abundant crops and Scotia rallied. New and modern homes are going up throughout the town; her population is increasing again. With the remarkably fertile farm districts round about her Scotia is bound to become a wealthy residence town with time. Her future is assured and the first comers will not have come in vain.

XVI

Harrowing Tales of a Third of a Century

> Then rose a sound of dread, such as startles
>   the sleeping encampments
> Far in the western prairies or forests that
>   skirt the Nebraska
> When the wild horses affrighted sweep by
>   with the speed of the whirlwind,
> Or the loud bellowing herds of buffaloes rush
>   to the river.
>   —Henry Wadsworth Longfellow, "Evangeline"

In the course of the years which have melted away since the Valley was first settled many things have transpired of a nature so distressing that even now, under the mellowing influence of time, it is hard to read them without shuddering. But in the reading our hearts involuntarily go out to the heroes and heroines who endured so much and endured so silently. The more we learn of their suffering, the more we honor them for their sacrifice, and the more we rejoice with them in their final triumph.

Several of these tales have already been narrated in previous chapters, and will not bear repetition here. Such were the Great Blizzard of April 13, 1873, and the Locust Plague following soon afterward. A few others may be added here. The first worthy of notice is the Great Fire of October 12, 1878.

To a person who has not actually lived on the frontier and with his own eyes beheld a great prairie fire in progress, it is almost hopeless to attempt to convey a true picture of its terrors. The awe inspired as the storm wind suddenly hurls great clouds of stifling smoke, mixed with cinders and burned grass, over the devoted settlement is beyond the description of pen. Then there is the sudden roar and distant glare; the crackling and crashing as the fire demon rushes onward; the rush of over-heated air; the distant glare and the final leap of countless tongues of flame from the seething, roaring hell-caldron coming on apace. Now, woe to the settler who has neglected all precautions for fighting fire, or whose guards are not broad and clear! Woe to him who has not prepared for the evil hour, for soon destruction will be upon him—the solid, destroying phalanx, burning several hundred feet deep, before whose scorching blast no living thing can stand! And now listen to what befell our North Loup settlements on the 12th day of October 1878: It was glorious autumn weather. Up and down the valley the farmers were at work threshing, and otherwise disposing of the bountiful crops of the year. The prairie grass was deep and matted, the growth of two seasons. It was dry as tinder and needed but a spark to start a conflagration. The farmers had on this account taken great care to throw up ample fire guards around their possessions.

But what protection are guards when the very air seems to be on fire! For several days fires had been burning on the Middle Loup to the west. At night the lurid glare was distinctly reflected on the peaceful sky.

On the eventful day as time advanced a breeze set in from the southwest. By degrees it increased in power till it blew a veritable gale. The wind swerved gradually to the west and by evening blew from the north; this fortunate circumstance alone saved the Garfield county settlements from destruction. Mira Valley lay immediately in the path of the fire-fiend and was the first to suffer. Here, in one place, three young men, Albert Cottrell, and William and Morris Greene, were at work building a sodhouse. Before they had time to realize their danger the conflagration was bearing down upon them. There was no time to backfire. Their only hope was refuge in flight. But, alas! what is human speed when measured with the fire fiend let loose! They were all quickly overtaken; and with a cry of despair threw themselves face downward, as the tongues of flame leaped and swerved round about their victims. From this bed Albert Cottrell was never to rise—he was burned to a crisp. The Green boys were more fortunate and lived through the terrible experience, though fearfully burned. And to the end of their lives will they bear the scars of the fire upon their bodies. Onward, across Mira Valley the fire swept, licking up hay stacks, leaping protecting guards, burning dwelling houses and outbuildings. In many instances the unfortunate inmates had barely time to reach some plot of plowed ground before the fire was upon them.

Mrs. John Luke, then a mere girl, saw the fire and in time sought a place of refuge. In several directions could she see burning property. On the farmstead where she chanced to be all the outbuildings were destroyed; the very pigs in their pens were roasted alive. At last the fire burst through the hills and rolled down into the river

Harrowing Tales of a Third of a Century 211

Advent of the prairie fire. (From a Kodak picture taken by Ina Draver.)

valley. At Dan Merritt's place it swept right through the stubble field and devoured a new threshing outfit, which the many farmers present were unable to save. George W. Larkin, living near the present day Olean, had just completed a comfortable log house. 250 bushels of wheat, all his previous yield, had just been stored away. Everything was consumed—house, barn, implements, grain and fodder. Mr. Larkin barely saved himself by falling prostrate onto the plowed ground. Heman A. Babcock lost practically everything he had, buildings, fodder and stock. As the deluge swept by Oscar Babcock's place his son E. J. Babcock had just time to leap into the protecting waters of Mira Creek. Judson Davis lost all his grain. At Jessie Worth's place practically everything of value was destroyed. And so the story might be lengthened almost *ad infinitum*.

    North of Ord conditions were scarcely any better. On Nels Andersen's farm another threshing outfit was burned; by desperate work only did Mr. Andersen save his home place, though much grain was lost. George Miller who was at Andersen's place when the fire became threatening undertook the foolhardy feat of outstripping it to his own cabin, a mile distant. This came near costing Uncle George dear. Had it not been for a convenient buffalo-wallow full of water, he would not now be living to tell the story. Such tales as these could be told of the Valley from Cotesfield to Turtle Creek. No farmstead in its path escaped the awful fire. That night beheld the valley scorched and suffering. Smouldering heaps of ruins marked here and there all that was left of the personal belongings of many a sturdy pioneer. Homes were gone; much cattle; the very grain for bread—and yet these men did not despair. On the morrow they were again at work to keep open the Trail—the Trail!

The next in chronological order of these stories is not so far-reaching in effect as some others here retold. But it is nevertheless of such a nature as to deserve relating. This is the August Hailstorm of 1885.

Meteorological observations as well as practical experience teach us that some localities in the west are more liable to be frequented by hailstorms than others. The fertile districts in Nebraska immediately south of the great sand hill belt are thus exposed. Any barren, sandy expanse heats and deflects a layer of air more rapidly than does a grassy and well protected loess plain. The result of this phenomenon may be observed on almost any hot summer day. Layer upon layer of overheated, moist air, over the sand hills, will in the afternoon heat, suddenly begin to expand and rise, forcing lower currents to rush in to fill the vacuum formed. The rising, heated current condenses and becomes visible to the eye the moment upper, cooler currents are encountered. These we know as cumulus or thunderhead clouds. If the evaporation does not chance to be very extreme, an afternoon thunderstorm and rainfall may result; but, in case the day has been intensely hot, the evaporation may become violent, and the upward rush of air so rapid as to create great disturbance in the upper cloud regions. A churning together of the hot and cold currents causes a rapid condensation of the moisture of the former into raindrops. These in turn freeze and are hurled around by a strange rotary motion now ensuing, growing ever larger as they receive coat upon coat of freezing moisture.

In our valley we may expect to find the surface currents blowing from the south on such a day as here in question. At the same time the upper currents, by degrees, begin a southward movement to fill the vacuum there formed. For a moment before the storm breaks all wind ceases. This is when the so called balance point in the opposing current is reached. As the upper current overbalances the lower the storm breaks. Now its advance is usually marked by a long roll of horizontally revolving cloudmass, from which showers of hailstones are precipitated to the ground as soon as these have grown large enough to overcome the centripetal force of the cloud itself.

It stands to reason that, in time, as the sand hills become more stable and receive a heavier matting of vegetation, these destructive storms will become less and less frequent.

August 5, 1885, was a hot and sultry day in the Valley. In the forenoon, and again in the afternoon the barometer acted in a most erratic way. About 3 o'clock in the afternoon great cloud masses began towering up on the northern horizon. That this betokened an unusual storm soon became apparent to all. A strange activity was shown by the way the cloud masses parted, moving in opposite directions—west and south—only later to retrace the first course, to come together a few miles above Ord. Here the horizontal roller cloud was formed, and came rushing down the valley. As it rolled on, dark and lowering, it seemed but a few hundred feet from the ground. With a roar the wind came out of the cloud, blowing at a terrific rate. Hailstones of enormous size were carried almost horizontally through space, so strong was the wind. For twenty long minutes all created things trembled under the fury of the storm. Outdoors all was destruction: indoors the roar of the storm was deafening. The howling of wind, the crashing of breaking window panes, the ripping of timbers torn made a veritable bedlam. When all was over ruin almost beyond description opened to one's gaze.

Not alone had the growing crops been hammered into the ground, but even the trees were stripped of leaves and branches, yes, the very bark was hammered into a pulp. To this day—after 20 years—may scars be seen upon the trees sufficiently strong to live through the storm. The story of the catastrophe is well told in the *Ord Quiz* of August 9, 1885, and runs as follows:

"Wednesday afternoon a threatening storm gathered in the north. It seemed to be drifting rapidly to the west, but about 5 o'clock it was met by another storm from the west. They met in the valley ten or twelve miles from Ord, and came tearing down upon us at a terrific rate. The storm burst upon the town at 5:40 and lasted 20 minutes. The wind amounted to a hurricane, the rain fell in torrents and hail of the regulation hen's egg variety fell. The ground was covered with hail.

Every exposed window—which means all north and east windows—regardless of awnings, shutters and screens, were beaten out; tin roofs were perforated and torn loose; nearly all north and east shingle roofs are ruined; trees are stripped of their leaves and battered and beaten beyond recovery, and there is nothing left of other vegetation. So much for the town.

"The extent of the destruction, however, does not seem to be general. At this writing it seems that very serious damage was done from only five or six miles above Ord, to three miles below. Toward Mira Valley damage extended no farther than Mr. Shinn's place, and in Springdale the limit of the damage seems to be at Mr. Coffin's place.

"The damage in the business portion of the town was sustained chiefly on the south and west sides of the square. A fair estimate of the damage on these sides is about as follows:

Cleveland Bros., store	$350.00
F. A. Witte	250.00
Wolf & Ehlebe	200.00
Miss Day, millinery	100.00
F. W. Weaver	200.00
Quiz Office	50.00
Perry & Stover	300.00
Dr. Bickford, residence and store	500.00
A. S. Martin	250.00
C. C. Wolf	50.00
D. C. Way	150.00
G. W. Milford	250.00
Woodbury & Mortensen block	400.00
Mortensen & Babcock	50.00
The First National Bank	100.00
Coffin & Clements' office	50.00
B. C. White, store and residence	400.00
W. J. Lloyd, stock	40.00
J. S. Bussell, bank building	100.00
W. T. Barstow, building	75.00
H. A. Walker	75.00
A. M. Robbins	75.00
Linton Bros., livery	200.00
Hotel America	500.00

"The chief losses on the north and east side of the square are:

D. C. Bell, yard and dwelling	$200.00
Frank Misko, shop	100.00
D. J. Martz	75.00
Odd Fellows' Building	100.00
Sorensen & Williams	350.00

"The balance of the buildings on those sides of the square are damaged mostly to the extent of the roofs. The loss on the other 300 buildings in town will average $50 each.

"It is a hard blow to Ord, but the extent of the storm being so limited it will not interfere with the trade to any considerable extent, the chief damage being the actual damage to property here. Had the crops of the whole county been ruined the loss in a business way would have been irreparable, but as trade will undoubtedly continue brisk, business men are inclined to look upon their losses optimistically.

"Our special reporter at Calamus reports that place in a worse condition than Ord. The new frame school house is a total wreck, including the foundation. Mr. McCaslin's house was torn to pieces and his wife and children were nearly killed. The windmill and smaller buildings at the fort were leveled. Will Duby's large new house was lifted, turned half way around and set down again. J. V. Alderman's splendid grove and nursery is nearly ruined. A mile north of Calamus no damage was done.

"Elton Cheesebrough lost one hundred young pigs.

"Bailey Bros.' cattle were stampeded and men were hunting them up yesterday. Two head of cattle were found dead in the yards.

"Charley Parks had 50 acres of fine oats uncut which were leveled to the ground.

"Lightning struck the rods and chimney of the public school building, but the damage was confined to these objects.

"Mr. R. Collingwood, of Sargent Bluff, Iowa, an old man, was crossing the small bridge southeast of town just as the storm struck him. He had a heavy load of lumber. The team became unmanageable and refused to face the storm. They turned with the storm and ran over the abrupt bank by Haskell's old brick yard, falling fully twenty-five feet. Mr. Collingwood's arm was crushed and the team badly injured. His family is in Iowa.

"The storm seemed to gather somewhere near W. B. Keown's place. The hail there was not heavy but the wind was furious. It totally wrecked his fine new barn and badly damaged his residence.

"Fred Dowhower says his crops are unhurt.

"Damage on Haskell Creek was light and Elm Creek escaped entirely.

"Dave Quackenbush's buildings were blown down and one horse killed.

"Jens Jensen lost a horse in the storm. He does not know what killed it.

"J. A. Ollis' building was blown down. In this part of Mira Valley damage by hail was done, though it was not so serious as around Ord.

"Comparatively little damage was done by hail on Haskell Creek at Lounsbary's and none beyond there. Plain Valley, Rose Valley and Bean Creek all escaped."

Barely a month had passed since the hailstorm struck Valley county, when another storm of a tornadolike nature struck the already badly shattered Ord and vicinity. Such an impression did the great hailstorm and this new windstorm of the evening of September 11 leave upon the minds of our people that for years to come they could not behold the uprolling of a stormcloud without a feeling of uneasiness creeping over them. This storm is described in the *Quiz* in the following language:

"Last week, Friday evening, the elements were in an exceedingly unsettled condition, but aside from the quickly changing sky and the swift coming and going of flurries of clouds nothing noteworthy was visible. At dusk a long narrow cloud extending from the western to the northern horizon appeared in the northwest, but no one gave more than passing notice to it, and each one in our busy little city went to his home thinking, if he thought of the storm at all, that it was over. But at 10:20, suddenly, without a moment's warning, a cyclone burst upon us from the southwest. Its fearful fury was spent in an instant, but that instant meant sad destruction to property. The destructive whirlwind dashed through our town and was followed instantly by a heavy gale from the northwest. As soon as the frightened people recovered from the shock, and safety permitted it they ventured out with lanterns to learn the extent of the damage and render assistance if needed. The Baptist church was leveled to the ground in irreparable ruin. The skating rink was swept away with the exception of the foundation. The roof was hurled against Wentworth's carpenter shop knocking the northwest corner clear away and wrecking the building badly. Very serious damage was done to the court house walls. With the exception of the corners, they were leveled as far down as the basement. The little building near O. S. Haskell's brick yard was blown into the river bodily. It was occupied at the time by three of Mr. Haskell's hands, all of whom escaped from the building during its passage to the river without injury excepting Frank Rogers, who was struck by a board, dislocating and slightly fracturing his elbow.

"Finding that no good could be accomplished by traversing the town our people at last went to rest anxious to see what new ruins the light of day might disclose. Of course much damage was done to buggies, sheds, etc., all frail buildings suffering a greater or less degree of injury.

"It was hoped that the damage was mostly confined to the town, but the next day and for a few days following reports of damage have kept coming in from all points in the track of the storm. The storm seems to have commenced its destruction in the neighborhood of Judge Laverty's farm in Geranium Township, whose house and contents were totally destroyed. His sick son was fortunately kept from getting wet, though Mrs. Laverty received a severe blow from some heavy piece of furniture.

"It would be almost impossible to enumerate the men who lost by the storm, for the track was wide. The damage to hay and grain stacks is very general in all parts of the county, from Mira Valley north. The last serious damage done by the storm reported at this writing was at the house of Messrs. Charley Parks and R. Burdick, northeast of town. Their sheds and out-buildings were destroyed though fortunately none of the inmates were injured.

"But bad as this and the recent hailstorm were, many places in states east of us have suffered far worse than we have in this most exceptional year of storms."

Several years may now be passed over and we come to 1888 and the Historic Blizzard of January 12. No other winter storm in the history of our plains, it is safe to say, was ever more destructive than this. For that matter the storm was general throughout the whole country, and its chilling blast was felt from the Rockies to New England. Yet the windswept plains of Dakota and Nebraska fared worse than sections farther east. Loss to human life and property was on the plains, in places, simply appalling. Entire families were lost; in some instances the bodies were not recovered till the snows began melting in spring. On this occasion the Loup Valley was almost miraculously saved from the loss of life. To be sure many narrow escapes from death by freezing are chronicled; and in numerous instances only the most heroic efforts saved those imperilled from death.

The morning of the 12th dawned damp and gloomy. A mist had been falling during the night; and the wind, which blew gently from the south, was just cold enough to turn the moisture covering all nature, into a light hoarfrost. Before noon the frost had disappeared and every indication pointed to an early clearing of the sky. But this was not to be. At just 11:35 o'clock in the forenoon a terrific stormblast struck Burwell, and 25 minutes later reached Ord. In a moment the heavy leaden clouds were blotted out. A bewildering, blinding sheet of dustlike snow was whirled horizontally through the air; the thermometer began sinking at a rapid rate and before 4 o'clock reached 25 degrees below zero. The wayfarer, caught far from home, soon found his pathway obstructed by drifts of snow and every familiar guidemark obliterated. His bearings once gone would mean certain death unless he should chance in his blind gropings to stumble upon some human habitation or friendly stack of hay or straw in his path.

As the early part of the day was so mild many people had ventured far from home. Scores of farmers were caught in town, where they had to remain for several days, chafing under the restraint, but absolutely snowbound. Others, less fortunate, who were caught on the road, in the valley or out in the hills, soon found themselves in a terrible predicament. Some were wise enough to unhook their teams and seek the nearest refuge; others, with their bearings lost, allowed their horses to lead them to some haven of safety. The writer knows of at least seventeen farmers in Valley county alone who shivered that terrible day and succeeding night to an end in straw stacks. Here is a solitary instance of this nature taken from the press of that month:

"Mr. Banlemiah, a German, and his son, a lad of 14 or 15 years, got lost in the storm. After driving along till the cold began overcoming them, they abandoned the team and, digging a hole in the snowdrift, sought shelter there. But fearing they might freeze to death they again got up and staggered along till they chanced upon a strawstack, which saved their lives. When rescued they were both pretty badly frozen about the head, feet and hands. It is feared that Mr. Banlemiah will be obliged to have his hands and feet amputated."

Stories without number could be told of narrow escapes throughout our Loup region. Here are a couple:

"On the day of the blizzard Ebert Gaghagen of Vinton started after a load of hay, and when about a mile from home the wind upset the load. Ebert wandered around, lost, and did not reach a place of shelter till 4 o'clock in the afternoon. Then he was so exhausted that he had to be assisted into the house."

"Professor Tipser of Haskell Creek was caught four miles from the nearest house. His horse refused to face the storm. He then got out and led the horse till almost exhausted. He next attempted to build a fire by burning his sleigh, but even this failed. In despair he dragged his frozen limbs along till he finally found shelter at the home of a Mr. Moses."

Some of the rural school teachers had harrowing experiences that day, and it seems almost Providential to us now that they should be able to have gotten their flocks of little ones home without a single casualty. Especially is this true when we know that Custer county, our sister county on the west, chronicles fifteen victims, young and old.

Mrs. Powell, who taught the so-called Hardscrabble school in Valley county, heroically determined to outweather the storm right in the schoolhouse. The coal could be made to last for some hours and, divided into small rations, there would be lunch enough in the dinner pails till aid should come. But in the course of the day Mr. W. Thompson and others living near at hand came as a rescuing party and carried all to places of safety.

While many other instances of snowbound people could be told we will not now weary the reader with them. However it seems that the story of the January blizzard is never considered complete without the story of Minnie Freeman, the Midvale heroine. We therefore reiterate it here, and add our personal views on the matter. The *Ord Quiz* of January 20 contains the following:

"The manner in which this modest and unaspiring school teacher saved the lives of all her pupils during the great storm of Jan. 12, 1888, has won for her wide renown. The forenoon of that day was mild and damp, with a warm breeze from the south. But just at noon, without a minute's warning, a hurricane blast came from the north. In an instant the temperature fell several degrees below zero, and the flying snow made it impossible to see but a few feet away.

Chapter XVI

The first blast broke in the door of Miss Freeman's school house. With the aid of her larger pupils she closed and nailed it. A moment later the door gave way again and was irrepairable; and to add to the dilemma, a portion of the roof was torn away also. Something must be done at once. There was no alternative. Her sixteen pupils must be taken to the nearest house, a half-mile against the storm. At the peril of her own life, and with calm presence of mind and forethought she hastily but carefully covered the faces of her younger pupils and to prevent them from being lost—for in the terrible storm to wander away a few feet was to be certainly lost—she tied them together. The older pupils she placed in the lead, and to see that none faltered, she brought up the rear. Thus was the heroic march begun and successfully accomplished."

The *Headlight*, in a late issue, tells us that "her school consisted of nine small children, and when the blizzard struck the school house and tore off a large portion of the roof, she gathered her children together and, tying them with a cord, one end of which she took in her hand, she started for the sod house above, about half a mile distant, where she arrived safely, after suffering from fatigue and cold, for which heroic act her name has been immortalized in story and song. Miss Freeman is now the wife of Mr. Penny, a prosperous merchant of Lexington, Neb."

Again, in the *Lincoln Daily Star* of June 17, 1905, we read that "as Iowa had her Kate Shelley so Nebraska has her Minnie Freeman." Now all this lauding to the sky would perhaps not be so much out of place did we not, in so doing, forget the other heroes and heroines of that never-to-be-forgotten day. It never has seemed quite just to us that this one young woman, noble and unassuming though she were, alone should receive the ever ready acclamation of a hero-worshipping world, and alone be "immortalized in story and song," when a score of others were just as deserving as she. In another sense it is hardly doing Miss Freeman justice. She was "modest and unassuming." She asked for no newspaper notoriety, for none of the presents or praise, such as overwhelmed her, coming from every part of the country. And then again, persons who are well acquainted with the actual facts in the case are naturally enough inclined to blame Miss Freeman as wishing to take for herself all the credit of the act, to the exclusion of everyone else.

The newspaper articles quoted above variously put the number of pupils rescued at nine and sixteen. A magnificent gold watch received by Miss Freeman from an admirer in California bears this inscription: "A. Andrews of San Francisco to Minnie Freeman, of Mira Valley School District, Valley County, Nebraska, for her heroism in saving the lives of thirteen pupils during the storm of January 12, 1888." The back of the case is set with thirteen rubies to represent the thirteen lives she saved. Thus we have the numbers nine, thirteen and sixteen. And so it is with the other particulars of the story too—they have grown and been distorted from the first. After sifting all the facts to the bottom, we are ready to offer this version of the story. When the first blast struck the rickety sod school house the door was burst inward, and the unanchored board roof partially lifted. Miss Freeman, then, with the aid of her older pupils, grittily enough, braced the door, and nailed it shut. But this gave but a moment's respite. Again the door was torn open, and this time the storm carried a section of the roof entirely away. To remain was to perish, for the room was rapidly drifting full of snow. The children were accordingly bundled up as well as the wraps at hand permitted, and in a body they were started for the George Kellison home, one-half mile distant. The children, so say eyewitnesses, were not tied together to keep them from straying away. The Headlight, quoted above, would even have it appear that Miss Freeman led her whole school by this cord to Mr. Kellison's home—and safety. To Miss Freeman's praise it must be said that she was everywhere present—at the front, at the rear, and on the flanks of her little band. But she was not alone about this. The older boys and girls aided her in every way. Why not give them who so unflinchingly led through the drifts, aiding and encouraging the younger children all they could, and without whose assistance the youngsters could hardly have reached safety, some of the credit? Why not give honor to ALL to whom honor is due?

The latest and in point of destructiveness the most disastrous of all the storms that have visited the Loup Valley is the Burwell Tornado of September 15, 1905. This came as suddenly as it came unexpected. Never before in history has a real twister of any great dimensions passed over our region. The so-called "cyclone" which struck Ord in September 1885 could in no wise be compared to this either in velocity or in thoroughgoing destructiveness.

The season 1905 was unusually satisfactory to our farmers. An abundance of rain interspersed with spells of hot weather resulted in bumper crops in valley and highland. The latter part of the summer only was somewhat unusual in its meteorological manifestations. The latter part of August and the first part of September marked a dry spell which, while it matured the corn rapidly and thus brought it beyond the danger of frost, yet drew the moisture out of the ground at such a rapid rate that fall plowing fast became an impossibility. Then the change came. September 2nd saw a great area of low pressure slowly settle over Nebraska and other western states, which marked the beginning of a series of rain and windstorms seldom equalled in western history. Friday, September 15th, marked the climax of the great atmospheric disturbances. All throughout Nebraska and up and down the Missouri Valley, in Iowa, Missouri and Kansas, the winds blew with varying fury and deluges of rain and hail caused untold damage. That evening Burwell was visited by her destructive tornado.

The first intimation given the dwellers in the lower valley of any such catastrophe was some more or less incoherent messages by wire; then came the following postal card extra printed immediately after the storm by the *Burwell Tribune:*

> *The Tribune Post Card Extra*
> *Burwell, Neb., Friday Evening, 8:30.*
> A cyclone struck the north part of Burwell at 6 o'clock this evening, demolishing sixteen buildings, Mrs. A. E. McKinney, wife of E. B. McKinney, being instantly killed, and Mrs. Geo. Dinnell, Mrs. Leeper, Clifford Dinnell and Frank Hennich being hurt, the latter seriously. M. Saba's general store is a wreck and the dwellings of these entirely demolished: Costello, Hanna, J. Dinnell, McKinney, Scribner, Leeper, the Star, R. L. Miller, Mrs. Dinnell, Mrs. Aikens. Many others more or less damaged. Storm formed in The Forks west of town, was narrow, and extended only a mile and a half southeast of town.

The full extent of the ruin wrought could not be learned till Saturday morning. It then became apparent that good fortune alone had spared the town from a much more disastrous visitation. Had the wind column veered but a few rods to the southward it would have plowed its way through the heart of the hapless town and quite a different tale might now have been told. As it was, it certainly was bad enough, and years must pass before the storm trail can be entirely effaced. The *Burwell Tribune* in a supplement to the issue of Thursday, September 21st, tells the story of the disaster in the following language:

"Friday, September 15, 1905, will be remembered for years by the present inhabitants of Burwell as the day of the great tornado.

"Weather conditions that day were very peculiar. The day dawned clear and bright, but within an hour or two a dense fog enveloped the earth. This lifted and the sun shone brightly for a short period of time. Then fog again descended and obscured the landscape. The afternoon was hot and close; clouds black and threatening festooned the horizon to the north.

"About six o'clock the death-dealing funnel-shaped cloud appeared to the northwest of town and in a few moments death and destruction were dealt out.

"But few of the people of the town saw the awful creature of the elements. Those who did took hasty refuge in storm cellars. Others did not know that anything more serious than a rain storm was brewing till the alarm was sounded.

"The tornado seemed to form in The Forks—the confluence of the Calamus and the Loup—just northwest of town a couple of miles. Its first work was on the farm of M. J. Scott, close to where the funnel formed, where several grain stacks were promiscuously scattered over the country. A cornfield near Scott's was demolished. Then the residence of Mr. Costello was razed. The family had gone to the cellar and thus escaped injury.

"C. W. Hennich's stable and outbuildings were next destroyed. Frank Hennich was in the stable when the storm struck it and attempted to get into the house when a flying timber struck him down, crushing his ribs and injuring him internally. He grittily crawled to a clump of bushes and waited for the passage of the storm. His mother and sister were frantically trying to get to his aid and were tossed about by the wind but happily escaped injury.

"The storm passed east from this point, demolishing stables, cribs and outbuildings at Kirby McGrew's, destroying part of the Bartholomew house, occupied by Leslie Baker, then swinging a little south, it overturned John Dinnell's dwelling and razed Mike Saba's store.

"R. W. Hanna's home, north of Saba's store about two blocks, a fine two-story dwelling, was totally destroyed—smashed, I guess would express it about as well as any detailed description. Mr. Hanna, his wife, their son, and Mrs. Hanna's mother were in the house at the time and how they escaped unharmed is nothing less than a miracle. The building was picked up bodily, carried a few feet and literally crushed into kindling wood. The four people were right in the midst of the wreckage and yet escaped without a scratch.

"The Haas house north of Hanna's, occupied by Ed. McGuire, escaped destruction, but the barn, outbuildings, trees, etc., were swept away. Martin McGuire lost a horse, wagon, harness, etc.

"J. H. Schuyler's fine home, a little south and east of Hanna's, was perforated by flying timbers, racked and wrecked. Clothing which hung in a closet in the house was whisked out of the window and disappeared. The house is almost a total wreck. His stable was entirely blown away.

"Wm. Kester's house, just east of Schuyler's, was partially unroofed. His stables and cribs were carried away. The debris from these buildings was carried eastward.

"The home of E. B. McKinney, east and a little north of Kester's, was the scene of the greatest calamity. Both Mr. and Mrs. McKinney were in the house when the storm struck it. The house was reduced to kindling wood. Mrs. McKinney was killed almost instantly. Mr. McKinney was carried up into the air but escaped with slight injuries.

"Mrs. Geo. Dinnell's home, south of McKinney's, was swept out of existence. Mrs. Dinnell and son Clifford were carried away and up into the whirling mass of cloud and debris and thrown to the earth close together. Mrs. Dinnell sustained bruises and cuts about the head and body and is hurt internally. Clifford had his arm badly lacerated and broken.

"Geo. Bell's livery barn was unroofed and wagons and buggies were carried away and broken and twisted into all conceivable shapes. One new wagon belonging to Frank Schuyler was found away down the road east, with the wheels gone and the spindles twisted off.

The roof of Bell's residence, just across the street from the barn, had a large chunk taken out of the center, the damage looking as though it had resulted from something having been blown through it.

"Mrs. Gring's residence, just east of Bell's, was badly damaged by wreckage blowing through it.

"McGrew's old store building, occupied by J. H. Schuyler as a pump house, was demolished. The Star store, used in part as a storehouse and part as a dwelling-house by Wm. Jeffries, was razed. The family narrowly escaped death.

"North of McKinney's the wreckage of houses lies westward. Here Mrs. Scribner's home was made into matchwood; the house occupied by Mr. Wheeler and family shared the same fate. Mr. and

Mrs. Wheeler and three children were in the house at the time but escaped without serious injury.

"Fred Woodworth's house (the Hoyt property), a concrete house, was unroofed and wrecked, the windmill, outbuildings, trees, fences, etc., being entirely destroyed.

"H. C. Woodworth's barn was destroyed and his team taken on an aerial trip. The horses were found near W. L. McMullen's home, nearly a half mile southeast, unscratched.

"Mrs. Aken's dwelling was blown to smithereens, as was also that of Mrs. Leeper, wherein Mrs. Leeper was badly hurt

"I. W. McGrew's fine home is almost a wreck although not torn up badly. Timbers were driven through it and it was carried off the foundation and generally wrecked. McGrew's barn was totally destroyed, buggies, harnesses, outbuildings, etc., went with the general wreck to the southeast.

"D. E. Sawdey's place, next east of McGrew's, was a scene of desolation. All his outbuildings, windmill, dray wagon, harnesses, etc., were totally wiped out. His barn was destroyed, the horses blown over the house into the field southward and there escaped unhurt. The dwelling house was picked up sent a short distance into the air and jammed onto the ground just off the foundation. It is almost a total wreck.

"R. L. Miller, who lives just east of Sawdey's, says the storm passed him on its first trip through, but after cleaning up R. B. Miller's place (the Carson farm adjoining town on the east), it swung back and completely wrecked his home—the two-story part of his dwelling being lifted up and deposited wrong side up in the yard. The family had seen the storm coming and had taken refuge in the cave. Every bit of furniture in the house was broken to bits except a large mirror.

"R. B. Miller's place was hard hit and Mrs. Miller and the children had a very narrow escape. Indeed it seems incredible that they could have escaped injury in the mix-up that occurred in the house. Barns, cribs, granaries, fences—everything on the place except the dwelling house itself was entirely swept away—some of the wreckage being carried south, part north. The dwelling was taken up, spun around and jammed into the earth and foundation. Furniture, plaster, debris from the storm, the lady and children, were mixed up indiscriminately but yet the folks escaped unhurt. One horse and several head of hogs were killed on this place. The storm passed southeast, sweeping away grain stacks, wrecking cornfields—in places shucking the corn and digging potatoes, crossing the Loup between H. T. Johns' and Ed Brown's places and entering the hills where it wiped out Wayne Waldron's farm house, barns, etc., and carried off his team. No further trace of the tornado can be found.

"Will Post's new barn in the Harrison addition was snatched out from among the dwellings roundabout and literally carried away. The only other damage done was the upsetting of Mr. Bilderback's house which was under course of construction."

"A relief committee, composed of L. B. Fenner, John Brockus, Guy Laverty, A. Mitchell and Fred J. Grunkemeyer, was appointed by a mass meeting of the citizens of Burwell Saturday afternoon to solicit funds and look after the unfortunate victims of the tornado. The meeting was called by W. C. Johns, chairman of the village board. Contributions are coming in nicely but a great deal more cash can be used and contributions of clothing, etc., would not come amiss.

"The cornice of the Burwell State Bank building was wrecked.

"Windmills, cribs, etc., at Cram's stockyards were demolished.

"The front of Janes & Sons' store was blown in, as was part of the front of Johns & Mitchell's.

"One of the city's windmills went through the window of Baker's barber shop.

"Nearly everybody in town lost a chimney or two.

"The front of Murphy's saloon went out.

"Arlo McGrew hung to a fencepost between the barn and the house until the storm had spent its fury. The ground around him was covered with timbers, but he escaped injury.

"Charley Rupel lost a valuable cow in the mix-up.

"One would bet money to marbles that a rabbit couldn't have escaped from where the Hanna family did without injury.

"Mr. Costello's house was insured for $600.

"The only cyclone insurance carried by any of the losers was $300 by Mrs. Scribner, $1400 by J. H. Schuyler and $750 by Mr. Carson.

"Mike Saba, John Dinnell and J. H Schuyler, and Rev. E. Maleng, who were in Saba's store when it went up, had miraculous escapes. Mike found himself hung to a telephone pole near the Star store, Jerry flew out and grabbed a pole, John went out and up, landed and was knocked down by timbers several times. The preacher remained in the building until help arrived. All escaped without serious injuries.

"A potted plant stood between McKinney's house and the gate, a distance of not over five feet from the house. It was uninjured.

"Mrs. Ed McGuire's canary bird was hanging in a cage on the porch and was carried away. The cage was found Saturday about half a mile away but no canary. Sunday morning the canary returned to the house and is now installed in a new cage.

"A part of a wooden hoop from a barrel was driven through a tree in I. W. McGrew's yard.

"Half of M. McGuire's potato patch was dug by the tornado.

"It is a difficult matter to estimate the property loss. Many of the minor losses are not recorded. Following is a partial list. The loss will total more than $50,000:

Costello	$1000
Hennich	500
Hanna	3000
Schuyler, J. H	2500
McKinney	2000
Saba	5000
Murphy	100
Dinnell, Mrs. Geo.	500
Dinnell, John	500
McGrew, I. W.	2000
Scribner	600
Leeper	500
Woodworth, Fred	800
Miller, R. L.	2000
Miller, R. B.	500
Sawdey	500
Carson	1000
Schuyler, John	500
Akens	500
Coon	400
Brownell	150
Bell, G. W.	1000
McGrew, Kirby	250
McGuire, M.	350
Williams, R. T.	125
Star Store	350
Hathaway	100

Ziegler, Orville	100
Post	250
Cram, W. I.	200
Telephone Co.	500
Raster, Wm.	200
Woodworth, H. C.	200
Beatrice Creamery Co., notes, cream cans, etc.	5000
Garrison, Fred	300
Otte, Will	200
Barr, Jas	100
Thurman, Tan	100
Miscellaneous	10,000
Beauchamp, Ross, corn	200

XVII

Changes Down Through the Years

> What constitutes a state?
> Not high raised battlement, or labored mound,
>   Thick wall or moated gate;
> Not cities fair, with spires and turrets crown'd;
>   No:—Men, high-minded men,
> With powers as far above dull brutes endued
>   In forest, brake or den,
> As beasts excel cold rocks and brambles rude:
>
> —Alcaeus, "The State"*

The first regular election held in Valley county after its organization took place in October 1873, and resulted as follows: L. C. Jacobs, John Case and R. W. Bancroft, Commissioners; W. D. Long, Clerk; E. D. McKenney, Treasurer; Oscar Babcock, Judge; H. A. Babcock, Sheriff; Thomas McDowell, Surveyor; and Charles Badger, Superintendent of Schools. At an election held October 13, 1874, R. W. Bancroft was re-elected Commissioner and Peter Mortensen and Mingerson Coombs were elected respectively Treasurer and Surveyor, to fill out the ticket.

At the regular election held on October 12, 1875, Mingerson Coombs, A. S. Adams and C. H. Woods were elected Commissioners; Thomas Tracy, Judge; M. B. Goodenow, Sheriff; H. A. Babcock, Clerk; Peter Mortensen, Treasurer; Oscar Babcock, Superintendent of Schools; Charles Webster, Surveyor; and Charles Badger, Coroner.

On Nov. 7, 1876, Oscar Babcock was elected County Commissioner. Herman Westover was appointed County Superintendent to fill Mr. Babcock's unexpired term.

At the next annual election, held on Nov. 12, 1877, H. A. Babcock was elected Clerk; Byron K. Johnson, Commissioner; Peter Mortensen, Treasurer; Herman Westover, Judge; H. W. Nelson, Surveyor; M. Coombs, Superintendent of Schools; and E. D. McKenney, Coroner.

---

* Editor's note: Likely translated by Sir William Jones.

Chapter XVII

The election of November 1878 resulted in the election of Oscar Babcock to the State Legislature from the Forty-fifth Representative District. W. B. Keown and A. V. Bradt were elected Commissioners.

At the general election on November 4, 1879, B. H. Johnson was elected Commissioner; H. A. Babcock, Clerk; Peter Mortensen, Treasurer; Herbert Thurston, Sheriff; S. L. R. Maine, Judge; H. W. Nelson, Surveyor; and M. Coombs, Superintendent.

In November 1880, H. C. Perry was elected County Commissioner.

The regular election on Nov. 8, 1881, resulted in the election of Arthur C. Lapham, Commissioner; H. A. Babcock, Clerk; Peter Mortensen, Treasurer; John Mosher, Judge; Herbert Thurston, Sheriff; John F. Kates, Superintendent; C. J. Nelson, Surveyor; and E. D. McKenney, Coroner. In the November election of 1882, H. A. Chase defeated his opponent for Commissioner by a vote of 422 to 33.

Now, as the county increased more rapidly in population, much of the old, neighborly feeling was beginning to wear away, and party lines to be more closely drawn. In the regular election of 1883 a bitter contest ensued between Arthur H. Schaefer, the Republican nominee and Ed. Satterlee, Democrat, for the Clerkship. Mr. Schaefer was elected. A. D. Robinson was chosen to succeed Mr. Mortensen who had refused further re-nomination to the office of Treasurer. All the other officials were re-elected.

The election of Nov. 3, 1885, resulted in a complete Republican victory. J. J. Hamlin was elected Commissioner; A. D Robinson, Treasurer; A. H. Schaefer, Clerk; A. A. Laverty, Judge; W. B. Johnson, Sheriff; John F. Kates, Superintendent; D. C. Way, Surveyor; F. D. Bickford, Coroner.

In November 1886, J. A. Ollis, Jr. was elected County Commissioner, and E. J. Clements, County Attorney.

The election held November 8, 1887, was closely contested as a new element—the Prohibitionist—showed remarkable strength. The Republican nominees were, however, elected with the one exception of Superintendent. For this place the Democratic candidate, Stephen A. Parks, defeated Mrs. Emma Gillespie by some 50 votes. The other Republican candidates elected were Jacob Lemaster, commissioner; Abe Trout, Treasurer; Jas. A. Patton, Clerk; A. A. Laverty, Judge; R. C. Nichols, Sheriff; C. J. Nelson, Surveyor; and Ed. McKenney, Coroner.

In the election held November 6, 1888, the main issue before the people was the question of township organization versus the

Commissioner system. The township supervisor idea seemed to meet with general approval, and carried at the polls by a vote of 826 for to 381 against. At this election B. H. Johnson was chosen Commissioner, the last under the old organization.

A spiritless campaign, characterized by Republican disaffection and general dissatisfaction, marked the fall of 1889. When November 5 came the best the Republicans could do was to elect treasurer, clerk and coroner; the other offices all went to the Democrats. Those elected were Abe Trout, Treasurer; J. A. Patton, Clerk; J. R. Fairbanks, Judge; W. H. Beagle, Sheriff; S. A. Parks, Superintendent; Bennett Seymour, Surveyor; and F. D. Bickford, Coroner.

By 1890 the Farmers' Alliance was entering politics and the Populist party was in the making. A great shifting in party affiliation was taking place. And this to such an extent that the Republican party was soon to lose control of both county and state. November 4, 1890, saw the election of Charles Munn, a former Republican, to the county attorneyship; this marked the beginning of Valley county's change in political affiliation.

The next year, Nov. 3, 1891, every office with the sole exception of county clerk was won by the "Independent Party." George Hall was the only Republican elected, and he went in with the small majority of 59 votes. The Independents elected were: I. S. Fretz, Treasurer; F. C. Cummins, Judge; A. V. Mensing, Sheriff; J. H. Jennings, Superintendent; Wm Hill, Surveyor; J. M. Klinker, Coroner.

In 1892 and again in 1894 Charles Munn was re-elected county attorney. The election held November 7, 1893, did in nowise change the political complexion of the county officials. The only changes were the substitution of Vincent Kokes, Republican, for George Hall, Republican, and Dougal McCall, Independent, for J. H. Jennings, Independent.

The year 1895 was marked by a rather vindictive campaign. The chief light was on the clerkship, now the Republican citadal. Vincent Kokes and his opponent, Jorgen Miller, were both strong, clean men. The Republican forces were, however, marshalled in such a manner that Mr. Kokes retained his office by a large majority. The Republicans now regained control of the county board, the vote standing: Republican, 4; Independent, 3. The Republicans also regained the offices of sheriff and surveyor. Those elected were: Vincent Kokes, Clerk; H. A. Goodrich, Treasurer; R. L. Staple, Judge; Adam Smith,

Chapter XVII

Sheriff; D. McCall, Superintendent; C. J. Nelson, Surveyor; E. J. Bond, Coroner.

In 1896, while the nation went for McKinley, Nebraska and Valley county voted for Bryan. J. H. Cronk, an Independent, was elected to the state legislature and A. Norman, a Democrat, was elected county attorney.

The next year, 1897, was in many respects an off year. The results of the November election were rather mixed. Vincent Kokes was re-elected clerk; W. B. Keown, Republican, defeated H. A. Goodrich, the incumbent, by only two votes; R. L. Staple was re-elected, as was also Adam Smith; Lorenzo Blessing, Republican, defeated D. McCall, likewise S. G. Gardner, Independent, defeated C. J. Nelson. Drs. F. D. Haldeman and E. J. Bond each polled 719 votes for coroner. Dr. Bond later drew the lucky straw and was declared elected. As it was thought that Valley county had now a population which under the law would allow the maintenance of a separate office for Clerk of District Court, candidates were put in the field for this office. Frank Koupal, Independent, was elected.

The election held November 5, 1899, was a victory for the Independent party; but it was also their last one. W. B. Keown and Lorenzo Blessing were the only Republicans elected. The other officials chosen were: Horace Davis, Clerk of District Court; Frank Koupal, County Clerk; R. L. Staple, Judge; H. D. Heuck, Sheriff; F. J. Ager, Surveyor; and R. A. Billings, Coroner.

In 1900 the Republican party won in nation, state and county. Victor O. Johnson, the popular Independent who had been appointed County Attorney when Charles A. Munn resigned to become District Judge, was elected by a bare 14 votes. Everything was preparing for the Republican victory of 1901.

The census of 1900 showed conclusively that Valley county was not entitled to the separate office of Clerk of District Court. This was therefore ordered discontinued. In the election held November 5, 1901, only two Independents were elected. These were Judge Staple and Superintendent Ira Manchester. Everything else went Republican. The new set of officials were: Alvin Blessing, Clerk; W. L. McNutt, Treasurer; John Kokes, Sheriff; C. J. Nelson, Surveyor; C. A. Brink, Coroner.

The year 1902 proved still more conclusively the Republican ascendency in local politics. The election held November 4th of that year saw the election of Peter Mortensen, one of the first settlers in our county, to the post of State Treasurer; M. L. Fries of Arcadia was elected to represent the 15th Senatorial District in the state legislature; Dr. A. E. Bartoo, also of Arcadia, was elected State Representative; and Arthur Clements of Ord defeated Victor O. Johnson for county attorney by 196 votes. These were all Republicans.

The general election of November 12, 1903, saw the end of Populist regime, so far as administrative offices are concerned. Every Republican of the previous administration was re-elected, and Hjalmar Gudmundsen was chosen to succeed Judge R. L. Staple, and Alta Jones to succeed Mr. Manchester as superintendent.

Our last election was held in November 1904. On that occasion M. L. Fries, A. E. Bartoo and Arthur Clements were all re-elected by good majorities.

One of the greatest drawbacks in the settlement of a new section of country is a lack of means of easy transportation. The settler on the western plains early found it impractical to stray very far from a railway base. For, after all, he had to depend upon this as a depot to supply him with the necessaries of life, and in return to take his output of grain and livestock. When the Loup valley was settled, its southernmost colony was fifty miles from the nearest railway, and the Loup county colony fully twice that distance. In 1872, and for many years after that time, our fathers had to cart every pound of provisions and every foot of finishing lumber from Grand Island. That this was the direct cause of much hardship, and materially retarded the development of the Loup region, goes without saying. A trip to the "Island" was fraught with all manner of difficulties. There were rivers and creeks to be forded, for bridges were few and far between in those days. The early wagon-roads were mere trails and made hauling heavy loads impracticable. And finally there were the elements, summer storm and winter blast, to be reckoned with. It is therefore not to be wondered at that the pioneers should rejoice when the Republican Valley 7 (Union Pacific) Railroad commenced building northward from Grand Island. The new road was completed to St. Paul in 1880 and thereby shortened our distance to market by some twenty-five miles.

To the Federal Government's praise it must be said that it has always done what it could to furnish outlying settlements with good mail service. The frontier star routes usually entailed a considerable annual deficit, but in spite of this they have been kept up as an encouragement to settlement. By 1880, mail and stage routes permeated every part of our region; and daily and tri-weekly service was furnished the whole valley. The mail time-card here printed gives some idea of the completeness of this service, such as we knew it in 1882:

Mail Movements

Arrives from the East

Arrives from St. Paul, via Scotia and Springdale, daily except Sunday, at 6 p.m.

Arrives from St Paul, via Cotesfield and North Loup, on Tuesday, Thursday and Saturday, at 6 p.m.

Arrives from Dannebrog, via Kelso, Bluffton, Mira Creek, Vinton, and Geranium, every Saturday at noon.

From the West

Arrives from Willow Springs, Fort Hartsuff and Calamus at 5:30 p.m., daily except Sunday.

Arrives from The Forks and Ida on Monday, Wednesday and Friday, at 6 p.m.

Departs for the West

Leaves for Calamus, Fort Hartsuff and Willow Springs, at 7:00 a.m., daily except Sunday.

Leaves for Ida and The Forks at 7:00 a.m. on Monday, Wednesday and Friday.

Going East

Leaves for Springdale, Scotia and St. Paul at 7 a.m. daily, except Sunday.

Leaves for North Loup, Cotesfield and St. Paul at 7 a.m., on Monday, Wednesday and Friday.

Leaves for Geranium, Vinton, Mira Creek, Bluffton, Kelso and Dannebrog, at 2 p.m. on Saturdays.

Stage leaves North Loup on Tuesday for Mira Creek, Vinton and Arcadia, returning on Wednesday.

Stage leaves for Geranium and other points between Ord and West Union on Friday morning, and returns next morning.

In the spring of 1881, the air was full of persistent railroad rumors. The Union Pacific would extend northward from St. Paul to North Loup and Ord, it was said. Mass meetings were held at both of these places and much enthusiasm was manifested. April 8th, Ord voted the Union Pacific bonds amounting to $5000.00, as an inducement to hasten the extension; about the same time North Loup township voted the sum of $4000.00 for a like purpose. The grade on the extension was at once begun. Within a year the first train entered North Loup amid general rejoicing. But Ord was doomed to wait long years before her cherished hope became reality Not before midsummer of 1886 was the track completed to Ord, which is yet the terminus of the line.

Great preparations were made to celebrate the event. It was the intention to make this a banner day in Loup history. Citizens turned out en-masse to make the necessary arrangements. That preparations were thorough-going can be gathered from the minutes of the mass meeting here appended:

The Railroad Celebration Meeting
Ord, Neb., July 5, 1886

As per special call of committee previously to arrange for a celebration at Ord on the completion of the railroad the citizens met at the court house. By unanimous vote Judge Laverty was made chairman, and H. A. Walker secretary. The committee reported their doings and were discharged. Upon motion the chairman appointed the following named nine gentlemen as an executive committee: J. M. Provins, C. B. Coffin, H. C Wolf, Peter Mortensen, H.A. Walker, Fred Cleveland, D. N. McCord, George Stover, and E. M. Coffin. H. A. Babcock A. D. Robinson and D. N. McCord were retained to further correspond with the railroad company in regard to excursion to Ord. The following committees were appointed: on invitation of speakers and special invitations, J, H. Ager, D. B. Jenckes, Geo. A. Percival, and Wm. Haskell; on finance J. L. McDonough. J. K. McConnell, E. K. Harris, and John Beran; on program, A. A. Laverty, G. W. Wishard, L. Moore, J. M. Klinker and A. M. Robbins; on shade M. J. Coffin, Wm. Wentworth, John Maresh; reception, A. M. Robbins, G. W. Milford, W. B. Johnson, E. J. Clements, P. L. Harris, W. D. Ogden, J. M. Provins, C. C. Wolf, W H. Williams, Geo. O Ferguson, A. H. Schaefer, T. R. Linton, Rev. Dodder, E. A. Russell; on music, Geo. A. Percival, D. Quackenbush, J. G. Sharp; on printing, editors-in-

Chapter XVII

chief of North Loup Mirror, Arcadia Courier, Ord Democrat, Ord Weekly Quiz, and Valley County Journal; marshal, W. B. Johnson, with A. W. Travis, John Wentworth, Bud Likes, Wm. McKenney, Fred Bartlett and Steve Weare assistants; on ammunition, Chas. Feiger, J. C. Heddle, Ezra McMichael, with request that they secure a cannon from Grand Island, if possible. The executive committee were empowered to appoint any subcommittee advisable. A motion carried inviting citizens, farmers, mechanics, tradesmen, and secret organizations to take part in a general industrial parade, Wm. Wentworth being manager. It was decided we celebrate on or about July 23d, 1886. Meeting adjourned subject to special call of executive committee.

H. A. Walker, Sec.

The date of the celebration was later definitely set for the 29th of July. The fete was liberally advertised and every preparation made for a glorious ratification. Then at the last moment word came from railway headquarters stating that it would be impossible for them to furnish the desired train by the specified time. The result was a great disappointment and ended by the celebration being definitely called off.

The year 1887 had a surprise in store for the Loup region. It was the unheralded coming of the Burlington and Missouri River Railroad. To be sure surveying outfits had been passing through the valley at various times during the spring, but that was not taken very seriously as the Union Pacific experience had made most men rather pessimistic on railroad questions. But when one bright day in March, gang after gang of graders commenced filing through Ord on their way up the country, the doubter received a sudden set-back. By April 1st, grades were beginning to take form all along the route and the whole valley rejoiced. The following appeared in one of the newspapers at that time:

"Last Saturday a B. & M. grading outfit came into town without ceremony or forewarning. It consists of 60 mule teams and about 100 men, all provided with abundance of new implements. Monday they pitched their tents at various points up the river as far as Meeks' place. The first camp is on Dane Creek just north of town, and the dirt is flying in grand shape. This move on the part of the B. & M. was the greatest possible surprise to the Ordites and naturally enough they are elated over this good luck and rejoice over the boom that must inevitably come. It has been a question in what direction the B.

& M. will connect with their main line, but that is pretty well settled now. The line will run from Central City to Greeley Center and from thence to Ord leaving Scotia out in the cold. In this way Ord will have a direct B. & M. line to Lincoln and a competing line to both Lincoln and Omaha. The object of the B. & M. starting work at Ord first is evidently to cut off all possibility of the U. P. going farther up the stream. It will have the line completed to Ord as soon as the grade above this place will be ready for the ties. It is undoubtedly true that surveyors of the Northwestern railroad are at work headed for Ord. The company has already made a survey to this place and the second visit means something. With the U. P., B. & M. and the Northwestern Ord will be a great railroad center indeed."

The coming of the B. & M. was important in more ways than one. In Greeley county is settled the fate of Scotia so far as being the county seat is concerned. Greeley Center, near the geographical center of the county, lay in the path of the new road. This settled the county seat controversy in its favor. The B. & M. was the making of Burwell in Garfield county, and as completely the undoing of poor Willow Springs on the opposite side of the river. Loup county, too, was greatly benefited by the railroad for, although it did not tap the county, Taylor and Almeria were brought fully 20 miles nearer railroad communications by its coming.

Arcadia and the Middle Loup had long awaited the building of some railroad. The Union Pacific filed a plat of extension of the O. & R. V. R. R. up the Middle Loup, with the county Clerk October 27, 1886, and Arcadia lived in the happy expectancy of its early advent. The road was built from St. Paul through Dannebrog and Boelus, to Loup City, but that is up to the present time its terminus. For here, too, the Burlington played a lucky hand. From Palmer in Merrick county, it quietly built westward through Saint Paul to Loup City, and then followed the identical route selected by the Union Pacific up the Middle Loup to Arcadia, cutting out the latter at Loup City. Lately the B. & M. has been extended from Arcadia to Sargent in Custer county, and may in time be projected further northwestward.

XVIII

The Newspaper and the Valley

> In the United States a constant interest in political or social affairs, complete freedom from censorship or restriction, except that provided by the liberal laws, have given five percent of the population of the world forty percent of its newspapers.
> —Investigator

The printing press was set up at an early date in our Valley, and from the very first has it been one of the most potent factors in our development. The early newspaper became the mouthpiece of the pioneers, calling upon the older settlements to send their quota to re-inforce the small bands upon the frontier. It rallied the settlers when they were discouraged. It held them together and molded sentiment and public opinion. In the later day it has this power still. It advertises us abroad and interests the world in our possibilities; at home it chronicles our common history and speaks our sentiments in social and political affairs

The *Valley County Herald* was the first newspaper published in the county. It was established at Calamus in the fall of 1875 by W. H. Mitchell, a lawyer, and was published there for two years, when it was removed to Ord. Calamus proved in the days of its boom a very profitable newspaper town, but when the first signs of the early decadence of Fort Hartsuff appeared and the county seat began to take form, Mr. Mitchell decided to take time by the forelock and get out while there was yet time. Thus the *Herald* became an Ord paper. Meanwhile a competitor had entered the field. This was the *Valley County Courier*, established at Vinton early in 1877 by Henry W. Nelson and L. P. Granger, who hoped through the medium of their paper to draw investors to the new townsite. However, after printing the *Courier* for six long months in a lone dugout on the prairie, the partners despaired of making the venture a success. Mr. Grander sold his interest to Mr. Nelson, who now as sole owner moved to Ord and re-established the *Courier* there as the first newspaper at the county seat. In a very short time the *Herald* was also in the field. But as both papers were Republican the picking became mighty slim and Mr. Mitchell was glad to sell the *Herald* to J. C. Lee, who changed the paper to a Greenback sheet, in accord with the greenback sentiment of the times. But unfortunately for the new venture, our people did not fancy the Greenback doctrines, accordingly the *Herald* failed. This was just after election. Later, we are told, the plant was removed to Grand Island where it became the nucleus of the *Grand Island Democrat*.

On February 3, 1879, Henry W. Nelson sold the *Courier* to Joe H. Capron who changed its name to the *Valley County Journal*. Mr. Capron had learned the printing trade at Freeport, Illinois, but through the solicitation of his brother, Lieutenant Capron, became Quartermaster's clerk at Fort Hartsuff. As was natural, however, he was glad to get back to his chosen profession. No sooner had the new paper got into good working order than misfortune overtook it. On the night of March 23, its printing office was burned to the ground, entailing an almost total loss. But the new editor did not despair. A new outfit was immediately ordered from Chicago and arrived after much tedious waiting. For those were times of slow transportation, as the last sixty-five miles of the route were overland. Meanwhile, as there was no other printing office in the Valley where the paper might be published temporarily, the *Journal* suspended publication till the new office could be put into shape. On May 7, the rehabilitated paper was again in the field, better and brighter than ever. August 5, 1881, Charles C. Wolf associated himself with Mr. Capron in the management of the paper. The *Journal* was published by the firm of Capron and Wolf till Dec. 31, 1883, when Mr. Wolf retired to become post master of Ord.

On July 14, 1881, another lawyer by the name of C. S. Copp established the *Independent*. This paper also was Republican in politics and found the field already pretty well taken up. After less than three months the management of the paper was changed. It now appeared with Wininger and Clayton as publishers and R. H. Clayton as editor. The latter was an able newspaper man and in almost any other newspaper field than in that of Republican Valley county would have made a marked success. He made the *Independent* a fiery opposition sheet and throughout the campaign of 1881 and for some months thereafter put up a plucky fight against "Republican corruption." But this paper weakened for want of support. On January 16, 1882, it met its fate and was discontinued.

The *Ord Quiz* was established April 6, 1882, by W. W. Haskell as a Republican paper, and will soon be able to celebrate its quarter centennial anniversary under its original founder. Mr. Haskell has this to say about the founding of the paper: "On the day after election in 1881, I appeared on the scene with an eye to the newspaper business. There seemed to be no room for three papers so I awaited the death of the *Independent,* which seemed inevitable. The expected occurred and the first *Quiz* outfit was ordered. This arrived during March 1882, and April 6, the same year, the first issue appeared." During the twenty-four years of the *Quiz*'s publication it has been known as a staunch Republican paper. Through foul report and fair, it has been loyal to its party; never for an instance has it hesitated in its allegiance to the principles that it represented. And as a reward the *Quiz* finds itself today the strongest and most popular newspaper in our part of the Loup Valley.

Meanwhile, the county grew in population and the Democrats came to feel the lack of an organ of their own persuasion. To make amends for this M. Randall and other Democrats circulated a subscription paper to aid in the establishment of such a paper. In the fall of 1884, Evans Brothers arrived from Iowa and started the *Standard*. After a few months John Evans retired from the firm and his brother Jack pegged away till February 1885, and then turned the plant over to Provins and McDonough. The new management evidently not wishing the public to be left in doubt as to the politics of their paper, re-dubbed it the *Ord Democrat*. Mr. Provins, taking sick, sold his interest to Byron Griffith, who in turn sold out to J. L. McDonough. December 10, 1886, J. R. Clayton, of the defunct *Independent,* began to edit the *Democrat* on a salary and got along very nicely till the paper was sold to the true-blue Jeffersonian Democrat A. W. Jackson. This was April 16, 1888.

Between 1886 and '88 a remarkable prohibition sentiment manifested itself in Valley county. July 7, 1887, C. C. Wolf bought the *Valley County Journal* and changed its name to the *Prohibition Star.* Mr. Wolf unfortunately found the new venture a losing one. Shortly after election The *Star* was merged with the *Quiz*. The printing plant was used in the new *Willow Springs Gazette,* established by Rogers and Haskell at Willow Springs in Garfield county. Less than a month after the appearance of the *Star,* O. S. Haskell and Rev. B. F. Hilton embarked upon a new prohibition venture called the *Blizzard*. Rev. Hilton soon tired of the paper and withdrew, leaving O. S. Haskell as sole proprietor. Early in 1890 Mr. Haskell was carried away on the populist tide and changed his politics. The *Blizzard* now became a populist organ. O. S. Haskell soon sold out to Dr. J. M. Klinker who changed the *Blizzard* to the *Ord Journal*. The latter published the paper till October 16, 1893, and then sold out to B. A. Brewster. He, in turn, relinquished his paper to the experienced, old newspaper man J. L. Claflin, of St. Paul. This was February 13, 1894. Some six weeks after this, March 30, Mr. Claflin also bought the *Democrat* from A. W. Jackson and merged the two under the name of the *Ord Journal*. But the pioneer populist newspaper in Valley county was the *Independent*, founded by Leonard Brothers in December 1890. They barely made ends meet and were glad to dispose of their plant to D. J. Martz, who in turn changed the paper's name to the *People's Advocate*. But this paper never prospered; and after barely existing for some time, Mr. Martz moved the entire outfit to Oklahoma.

The passing of the *Advocate* left but two papers in the field, the *Quiz* and the *Journal*. Of these the *Journal* was destined to go through still further changes. Thus in October 1894, and just before election, Mr. Claflin for some reason sold out to A. W. Jackson. But this Simon-pure Democrat did not relish writing populist editorials and again, in January 1894, the paper was re-sold to Mr. Claflin. From this time on till January 1890, the *Ord Journal* remained under his management. Then Mr. Claflin sold out to Charles Smith, expecting to leave the newspaper work for a new field of activity. But for various reasons the *Journal* once more passed into Mr. Claflin's hands. Since that time it has been published variously by Horace M. Davis, Miles Brothers, Davis and Parks, and now, in 1905, again by Horace M. Davis who is making it one of the newsiest and strongest papers in our Valley.

January 27, 1887, L. J. Harris founded the *Real Estate Register* at Ord. It lasted only a few months and then died a peaceful death. In May 1897, the *Valley County Times* was founded by Harris and Leggett. But in November of the same year Harris retired from the firm leaving H. D. Leggett the sole proprietor. The paper was Republican in politics. It was well edited and enterprising; but there was hardly field enough to support two Republican newspapers at the county seat. In November 1901, Mr. Leggett therefore sold his paper to the *Quiz*. As things now stand Ord has but two papers: the *Quiz* and the *Journal*.

The press was first represented in North Loup by the *Mirror*, established by R. S. Buchanan in June 1882. Mr. Buchanan emphasized that "the Mirror shall be pure in tone, enterprising in business and news, lucid and strong in editorials and staunch in favor of the Republican doctrine." Judge N. H. Parks soon after this entered the field with the *Herald*, a Democratic paper of much merit. the *Mirror* suspended publication and the *Herald* was succeeded by the *Farmers' Advocate*, an independent paper. It was first edited by one F. C. Beeman and later by E. E. Chamberlain. It too suspended publication on the approach of the hard years.

The only newspaper in North Loup to show much vitality is the *Loyalist*, which has quite an interesting history. When the *Burwell Bell* was burned out and forced to give up the ghost its press, practically all that was saved from the fire, was purchased by E. W. Black, who moved it to North Loup to become the substantial part of the *Loyalist* plant there. The first issue was printed October 13, 1885. That there should be no mistake about its politics, Mr. Black gave his paper this motto: "For the party that saved the nation and remembered the veteran, the widow, and the orphan." Mr. Black who was quite a naturalist and had many and varied interests did not devote much of his time to local affairs. This naturally did not suit his subscribers. When the irrigation boom was on at North Loup, the *Loyalist* was the mouthpiece for those interests. R. R. Thorngate edited the paper for a couple of years as Mr. Black had other irons in the fire. Finally, on November 14, 1895, it breathed its last in a very caustic editorial, in which Mr. Black took occasion to charge North Loup and North Loupers with things which would look anything but complimentary should they be repeated here. For two years and a half the *Loyalist* lay dormant. Then, April 15, 1898, it was resurrected by E. S. Eves who published it for six months only. In turn H. L. Rood and Horace Davis took charge of the plant and promised to issue the poor old *Loyalist* as a "non-partisan" paper. Now the former of the two editors was an ardent Populist while the latter has been a life long Democrat. No wonder then that the *Loyalist*, in spite of promises to the contrary, came to have certain "demo-pop" proclivities. However, it was a good paper. In May 1899, Walter G. Rood, the present editor, purchased the plant and re-established it as a Republican paper.

The *Arcadia Courier* was the first paper established in Arcadia. This was in April 1886, and its owner and editor was O. D. Crane. The paper, like its successor, the *Champion*, was Republican in politics. The paper continued publication till late in 1890, when it suspended. At that time Arcadia's future looked anything but bright—the drought had killed the crops and fire had burned out the heart of the business quarter of the town.

No wonder then that the editor got discouraged and quit. For five years Arcadia had to get along as best she could without a newspaper. Then in 1895 the *Champion* was started by C. L. Day. The first five years it eked out a precarious existence under an ever-changing management. In March 1900, the present, hustling editor, Harold O. Cooley, got control of the paper and under his management a new future is opening up before it.

The *Willow Springs Gazette* was the first newspaper in Garfield county. It was established in 1884 by W. W. Haskell of the *Ord Quiz*. The paper was Republican in politics and was placed under the management of a Mr. Rogers. When Willow Springs lost the county seat the *Gazette* was moved to Burwell where it continued publication under the old management till it was sold to Jack Evans and backers in 1887. It now became a Democratic sheet and was rechristened the *Lever*. But Garfield county was getting more papers than it could well support, and accordingly the *Lever* was suppressed in 1889.

The first newspaper actually established on Burwell townsite was the *Burwell Bell*, which first appeared Friday, March 6, 1885 with L. M. Hart as editor and publisher. Of the paper's politics the editor had this to say in this first issue: "Some would call us a Republican because we favor a tariff; others would say we are Greenbacker because we oppose the national banking system; and still others would insist that we are a Democrat." Mr. Hart evidently intended to run an independent paper, a thing pretty hard to do, especially in a small country town. He said: "We have come to stay if we can make it pay." Evidently he did not make it pay for after a few short weeks the *Bell* tolled its last and was no more.

When the *Gazette* removed its printing plant from Willow Springs the business men there induced William Z. Todd to establish a new paper. This he called the *Willow Springs Enterprise*. It was first published in 1888. But its career here was destined to be a brief one. The warring business interests of the rival towns came to a final understanding in 1889, whereby the remaining Willow Springs business houses were removed to Burwell. This general exodus forced Mr. Todd to follow suit and re-establish himself as best he could in that town. His paper now became the *Garfield Enterprise*. Meanwhile W. T. Harriman had founded a second Burwell paper, the *Quaver*, in 1887. Mr. Todd purchased this paper and merged it with his *Enterprise* in 1891. Three years after this he sold his newspaper interests and went to Colorado. But he soon longed for the flesh-pots of the Loup and came back in 1896, and leased his old paper, now for sake of variety, called the *Progress*. The name evidently did not suit Mr. Todd who speedily redubbed it the *Mascot*.

Back in 1888 the *Taylor Republican* and *Loup Valley Alliance* were bought by a stock company and moved to Burwell. The new sheet was issued to promote the interests of the Independent party just springing into being. Its editorial staff changed rather frequently. Thus in the course of its very brief career Wm. Evans, Adolph Alderman, Tom Day and Van Mathews all took turn about running it. Then R. L. Miller got control of it, changing its name to the *Eye*. The *Mascot* in turn absorbed the *Eye* in 1898. S. Hoyt assumed charge of the *Mascot* in 1899 and changed its politics to the Populist faith and the county was without a Republican organ. Now Todd founded such a paper and named it the *Tribune*. But the end of changes was not to be here. In 1902 Guy Laverty got control of both papers and merged them under the name of the *Mascot*. For a little over a year this gentleman published it as a Populist paper. In October 1903, the last change took place. Then Mr. Todd bought the *Mascot* and changed it to the *Tribune*, making it at the same time a good Republican paper. The *Blade*, lately started by S. Hoyt, as a Republican organ, became superfluous and was soon merged with the *Tribune*, which is the only newspaper in Burwell today.

Loup county's newspaper history is not so varied as that of Garfield county. The *Loup County Clarion* was established by H. A. Phillips at Kent in 1883, and was subsequently moved to Taylor. It changed editors from time to time but politics only once. Thus William Croughwell and later J. B. Lashbrook had charge of it. Then came Wm. Evans, who ran it for a couple of years as a Populist paper. It was again re-established as a Republican paper by E. Andrews, who edits it at the present time under the name of the *Taylor Clarion*.

The *Loup County News,* another Populist paper, was founded by R. S. Schoffield in 1902. Within the last few months it was sold to J. G. Wirzig who says he will make it non partisan.

Scotia had one of the earliest newspapers in the entire valley— the *Greeley Tribune,* established by R. S. Buchanan in 1878. For three years the paper was issued as the Republican organ of Greeley county. Then Mr. Buchanan moved his plant to North Loup and founded the *Mirror*. A. B. Lewis immediately purchased a new outfit and re-established the *Tribune*. Next appeared the Democratic paper, the *Index,* edited by R. F. Clayton, who bobs up from time to time in our newspaper history. But his sheet died young and may be passed without further comment. The history of the *Tribune* is anything but thrilling. Continuous change in the editorial head and even name will just about tell the whole story. Thus in the fall of 1885 Hamlin W. Sawyer came into possession of the plant and changed the name to *Loup Valley Gazette*. In a brief time again it became the property of George McAnulty, who saw fit to re-dub it the *Greeley County Graphic*. Late in 1888 Mr. McAnulty sold out to W. T. Faucett, who called his paper the *Scotia Republican*. The latter editor actually stayed by the paper two whole years and then sold to Henry Alnut, who renamed it the *Independent*. In 1893 W. E. Morgan got possession of it and played a bad trick on Scotia by moving paper and all to Greeley Center. Here he merged the *Independent* with the old *Greeley Leader* under the name *Leader-Independent*. This paper is yet published at Greeley Center by Tom Hardesty. For almost a year Scotia had to get along without a paper. Then, in 1894, Henry C. Waldrip commenced publishing the *Scotia Register*, a Republican paper, which has since been the only paper in the town. Away back in 1884 Judge N. H. Parks established the *Scotia Herald*, a strong, well-edited Democratic paper, which continued till 1891 when it also was moved to Greeley Center.

XIX

The Critical Period in Loup Valley History

> Smiling and beautiful, heaven's dome
> Bends softly o'er our prairie home.
>
> But the wide, wide lands that stretch away
> Before my eyes in the days of May,
>
> The rolling prairie's billowy swell
> Breezy upland and timbered dell,
>
> Stately mansion and hut forlorn—
> Are all hidden by walls of corn.
>
> All the wide world is narrowed down
> To the walls of corn, now sere and brown.
>
> What do they hold—these walls of corn,
> Whose banners toss in the breeze of morn?
> —Ellen P. Allerton, "Walls of Corn"

Nebraska became a state in 1867. Five years of statehood brought much prosperity to the new commonwealth. But soon, after sundry warnings, the financial storm of 1873 burst over the nation and state. Times became desperately hard. All classes suffered and the rural population in particular became greatly disaffected. The granges which had long existed as social organizations, entered politics, forced as it were by prevailing economic conditions. "The farmers," they averred, "worked harder and more hours than the artisans, had poorer food and fewer privileges—while the men who handled the farmers' products were better off than either farmers or mechanics and were rapidly getting rich." The granger movement had an amazing growth. By midsummer of 1873 more than 250 granges had been organized.

The state government was charged with incompetency, existing systems of taxation were declared inadequate and unjust. Their chief grievance was against the great railroad corporations doing business within the state. Nor was this without foundation. The Union Pacific

Chapter XIX

The Elms home of J. R. Williams, Ord.

and Burlington systems stubbornly refused to pay taxes on their land grants. Various excuses for not paying were trumped up and for years were many communities throughout the state unable to collect taxes from these corporations.

In Valley county, for example, bonds had been issued for public improvements based on calculations to collect the Burlington railroad tax. The county commissioners could not collect a cent for years, and amusing as it now sounds, were threatened with arrest should they not desist. This condition of things put our local government in desperate straits. And naturally enough left a grudge against the railroads. When the issue was finally forced to a head a compromise was agreed upon and one-half of all the assessed taxes had to be accepted as sufficient payment of all claims.

The inadequate revenue system in the state, as mentioned above, was another grievance. Many counties flatly refused to pay their taxes. Indeed one-third of all the taxes levied in the state between 1869 and 1873 remained unpaid. At the close of 1873 there were $300,000 in state taxes delinquent, and $400,000 in local taxes. Money became extremely stringent and farm produce brought shamefully low prices. Then right on top of all this came the grasshoppers and devoured the crops and "there was real destitution in the sod houses and dugouts along the border." But it is not the

The Critical Period in Loup Valley History 249

purpose to re-tell this sad story now. Let it suffice that the Nebraska Relief and Aid Society disbursed $68,000 among the sufferers. Congress appropriated both money and seed-grain, and in sundry ways aided the homesteaders. Some of this aid reached the Loup, and did much to keep the wolf from the door.

The year 1875 was a dull one on the Loup. The loss of crops of the year before coupled with the general depression existing throughout the entire state kept newcomers out of the Valley. To add to the gloom crops again became a partial failure. Dry weather and locally hatched locusts damaged the growing grains and reduced the yield seriously; 1876 was an exact repetition of the previous year.

But a change came. The growing season of 1877 was very favorable and farmers harvested abundant crops. The state, too, was slowly recovering from the panic of 1873. Once again the attention of homesteaders was called to the possibilities of the beautiful Loup Valley. Many who had lost in the desperate game of chance in the days of wildcat speculation back East, and others seeking cheap lands, came pouring into the Valley. The year 1878 more than quadrupled the acreage of cultivated lands. That year, and again 1879, were marked for their fine crops. A population of almost 2200 was now scattered from Scotia to The Forks and further up the Loup.

White Towers; home of A. M. Daniels, Ord.

Chapter XIX

But these were small things when compared with the great movement of settlers just about to begin. The decade 1880–90 marks a new era of prosperity in Nebraska. The long "nightmare of depression" resulting from the panic of 1873 was at an end. A substantial class of settlers came out of Illinois, Iowa, Wisconsin and other states, eager for homesteads and glad to purchase relinquishments from restless pioneers. Wealth and population increased many fold. The railroads began building new lines to keep up with the general movement. The F., E. & M. V. threw open the northern part of the state. The Union Pacific, Burlington and other lines initiated a system of expansion, running a network of branch lines throughout their part of the state and up every available watercourse and into every promising farming community.

Prior to this time only the choicest pieces of land had been settled. Now white-topped prairie schooners were everywhere visible. Homesteaders and pre-empters quickly culled out the remaining good tracts. But the eager scramble for claims did not cease with that. The dry cattle country was invaded, and even the sand-hill ranges did not escape. Nowhere was the movement more marked than on the Loup. Valley county alone increased her population more than 30 percent in six months. All the Valley lands were snapped up. The

A modern farm home on the Loup; beautiful "Cedar Lawn Farm," owned by A. J. Firkins, Ord.

The Critical Period in Loup Valley History 251

The Evergreens; home of Dr. F. D. Haldeman, Ord.

river bluffs showed signs of settlement. On the edge of the sand-hills sod houses and strips of breaking could be seen. It was all one mad rush for land—land in any shape or condition. A cycle of wet years had set in. Crops grew luxuriously everywhere. Even the high plateaus in the western and northwestern parts of the state blossomed like the rose.

Nebraska entered upon a real estate boom of vast dimensions. The speculative fever seized the people. The east had idle capital to invest in western lands. A period of borrowing was at hand. People who had no idea whatever of making their permanent home there filed on sand-hill claims and reared their sod huts close by the smoking blow-out. The headwaters of the Loup and Calamus had their quota of these fortune hunters. Unscrupulous loan agents, more intent on earning their commissions than on serving their eastern principals, were eager to loan money on any kind of land. Security for the money seemed to trouble them but little. The New England Loan and Trust Co. and other great corporations did a rushing business in sand-hills and other worthless lands, and to this day do they regret ever having heard the name Nebraska spoken. Heaps of crumbling sod yet mark the place where some of these sand-hill speculators reared their roofs.

Chapter XIX

Home of Hon. Tom Doran of Burwell. Under construction.

Another unfortunate feature of all this "easy money" was the borrowing habit into which so many fell. All manner of expensive machinery, bought on credit, could be seen littering the barnyard or standing unsheltered at some fence corner. The top buggy and carriage began to displace the good old lumber wagon. Sundry extravagance was the mark of the times. But a day of reckoning was fast approaching when "tight money" and contracted loans were to force many an unfortunate, improvident farmer to the wall.

The cycle of wet years came to an end at last—in 1890. That year the growing season began propitiously enough, but as time passed the needed rains failed to come. Instead, week after week, the hot, burning sun glared down from a cloudless steel-blue sky. The dread hot winds blew in from the south. Day after day they continued. All fodder, small grain and corn were cut short. Where farming had been carried on extensively rather than intensively the yield amounted to preciously near nothing. The careful expert got some returns for his work, though small. The northern part of our Valley fared better than the districts lying farther south, where in many places there was not enough fodder gathered to carry the stock through the winter. Those of the settlers who had come here poor, and who had borrowed freely while money was plentiful, now faced a crisis. The bubble of

The Critical Period in Loup Valley History

speculation suddenly burst. Pay-day was at hand and where should the money come from?

Right here the critical period in Loup Valley history begins. The years from 1890 to 1896 were crucial in our development, and may justly be marked as the most important six years we have known. The importance of this test period can hardly be overestimated for it marked the commencement of a struggle for the betterment of economic conditions, which has already led to a more solid prosperity in our Valley. The year 1890 found the nation entering a period of financial stringency. This taken together with crop failures resulted locally in hard times, chronic dissatisfaction and much real suffering. The cry against existing conditions of things came from the farm. The Farmers' Alliance, at first a purely agricultural organization, entered politics to find a panacea for the ills of the times. Memorable days were at hand. Midsummer of 1890 beheld 1500 Farmers' Alliances in the field with a membership of 50,000. "There were no crops to gather so the people gathered in numbers never seen before or since, out in the groves away from the towns. Farmers' Alliance parades seven and eight miles long were among the sights of the campaign, and the enthusiasm of the monster meetings defied description. Everywhere there was a breaking away from former political affiliation, and the chorus, 'Good-bye, Old Party, Good-

The Charles I. Bragg residence, Burwell.

bye,' was chanted with religious ferver by thousands of throats." In the November election the new People's Independent party won an overwhelming victory, gaining control of the state legislature and electing two out of three congressmen. The work of reform began. On the Loup old-time Republican strongholds became in turn fastnesses for the new party. The farmer had spoken and—acted. In many respects he blundered, as all reformers will; but none can deny that much good has come and is yet to come from this political revolution—and it was a revolution. The People's Independent party may never live to reap the fruits of its efforts—for it was untrue to its own fundamental principles—but it has served a period of inestimable usefulness all the same, and the community, state and nation are the winners.

In a purely economic sense the hard years had a remarkable effect upon our community. The disgruntled ones and all who lacked the natural thrift to surmount the many hardships of those times became weeded out. This left the sturdiest and best of the old population in possession of the Valley, and opened the way for a new class of farmers and business men, possessed of better methods of farming and ample capital to make the most of the riches hidden in our fertile soil. But this is getting ahead of our story. To get back to the dry years:

Home of Harry Coffin, Burwell.

The Critical Period in Loup Valley History

Home of Vincent Kokes, Ord, with Eret's Band in foreground.

The growing season of 1891 fortunately yielded good crops and eased conditions materially. '92 and '93 were rather dry though fair crops were harvested where hailstorms had not already spared the garnerer his trouble. Then came the never-to-be-forgotten drought year 1894. And who can ever forget that year!

The spring and summer of 1894 was marked by unusual meteorological phenomena. Rainfall was withheld for months from the great plains and portions of the central prairies. All moisture seemed to disappear from the atmosphere. In sections even spring rains failed to come. There was hardly enough moisture in the soil to germinate the seed. Where it sprang up it was only to be withered by the blasting winds. The sun set at night in a sickly yellowish glare only to rise morning after morning upon a hopeless, steel-blue sky. Crops died. The loose soil from the dusty fields filled the stifling air or was heaped by the winds in dunes in the tall, dead grass of former seasons. Was it surprising that men should despair then? Fodder for stock could not be procured locally. Those who had none laid by from the pittance of past years were obliged to sell their stock or almost give it away. The market was glutted with lean cattle and hogs so that it shortly fell to a shamefully low figure. Many a farmer slaughtered his old work-horses to help keep a few brood sows alive over winter. Destitution in our central and western counties became great. The

256   Chapter XIX

Street scene, Burwell.

legislature appropriated $250,000 for seed and food for the sufferers, besides $28,000 received in private donations. The Loup suffered with the rest of the state, and for the first time in its history had to accept aid from the outside. And yet it is but fair to add that most of those who accepted aid were of the improvident class who have long ago left the Valley.

But the dread summer came to an end at last. A mild, open winter followed providentially. Much cattle which might otherwise have perished came through the season in fair condition. Then came spring and summer of 1895 and with them an increase in rainfall.

Unfortunately many of our people had lost heart and did not dare to risk too large a seeding. Others were too poor to put in much of an acreage. This resulted in a fairly good though limited acreage for the year. It was a season of beginnings—of preparations for greater things to be. The spring of 1896 was auspicious and the sluices of Heaven opened to a grateful earth. Abundant crops sprang from the rested soil and people tried in their joy to forget the nightmare of the past.

The storms were indeed past. An adverse fate left the Valley-dwellers wiser and better equipped to cope with the problems of the future. They had passed through a stern school and experience is ever an exacting master. Six years of adversity had taught two important lessons—the value of money and the imperative need of a more intensive system of farming. Both lessons have taken deep root. The future can never again repeat the failures of the past. For the Loup the experimental stage has been safely passed. Our farmers have at last learned how to adapt themselves to our peculiar climatic conditions. In years gone by they clung to their corn and spring wheat. There was a strange notion abroad that winter wheat could not be grown with profit in the North Platte country. This delusion has long been exploded, and winter wheat is now one of our most important crops. Alfalfa has solved the fodder question. This remarkably prolific plant seems to have settled for good all fear of a repetition of dry seasons. Even should droughts again strike the Valley the alfalfa, the bromegrass and the English bluegrass would be pretty sure to give "roughness" sufficient to keep our large herds in plenty.

The past decade has wrought an economic revolution in the North and Middle Loup Valleys. Prosperity is manifest on every hand. The farmer has become independent. His granaries and sheds are full to bursting; his pastures are dotted with herds of blooded cattle. Fine modern homes supplant the humbler dwellings of yesterday. Dugouts and sod houses are even now becoming curiosities belonging to an era of beginnings now well-nigh spent. Towns and villages are taking on metropolitan airs. Modern conveniences which a few years ago would have been deemed luxuries are found in every well-appointed home. Real estate values have increased marvelously; and yet it is not an artificial increase but the legitimate result of prosperous times and continued good crops.

Three decades back this remarkable region was a great "unfenced buffalo pasture," its virgin soil all untouched by the ploughshare.

A group of Wisconsin colonists and their descendants. Taken a few years ago near North Loup.

Today it is the home of thousands of prosperous families and its annual output of crops runs high into the millions. Then there was not a school nor a church nor a printing press in the Valley. Today these are everywhere disseminating the wisdom and morality which has given us high place in the sisterhood of counties forming our great commonwealth. Today a race of clear-visioned, broad-minded men and women, dwelling on high-land plateau and in lowland valley unite in grateful praise of the first comers who opened the trail of the Loup and made all of this prosperity possible.

XX

The Brave Men and Women Who Opened the "Trail of the Loup"

Biographical

This section of the work is devoted to very brief biographical sketches of the brave men and women who opened the trail of the Loup. We should have said some of the brave men and women, for it has been practically impossible to see personally all who deserve a place here. It is to be regretted that all old-timers did not send in their biographies as they were invited to do through the press of the Valley. Space was offered free to every pioneer and if advantage was not taken of this the fault must lie with him rather than with the author. Some who are prominently mentioned in the main body of the text are not mentioned in this list.

Valley County

ADAMS, A. S.—Mr. A. S. Adams was born in Hounsville, N. Y., Sept. 18, 1832. When he was but three years old his parents moved to Pillar Point, in Jefferson county, N. Y. Here he lived till the winter of 1852 when being taken with the "Gold Fever" which was so prevalent at that time he set sail in the South Hampton, a store ship under Commodore Perry, and landed in Placer county, California, the following spring. He now lived the life of a miner till August 1861, when he enlisted in the Union army. Upon being discharged some three years and twenty one days later, he went to

A. S. Adams.

New York and married Miss Kathrina Nay in the fall of the same year. In the spring of 1874 he came to Valley county where he has since lived on his beautiful farm on Turtle Creek. His wife died October 28, 1901.

ANDERSON, NIELS—is one of the "original five" Danes who settled north of Ord in the spring of 1872. He was born at Arendlev, Denmark, August 12, 1841. In his old country home he spent much time in the Danish naval service. Thus during the Dano-German War of 1864 he took part in the battle of Heligoland where the Danish fleet defeated and put to flight the united German and Austrian naval forces. Soon after the war he came to America, spending four years in Illinois and Missouri. In April 1872, as told elsewhere in the book, he came to Valley county and settled upon the southwest quarter of the famous section 8, Ord township. Here, on July 6, 1873, he was married to Johanne Mortensen, thus making good his right to having been the first man married in the new county. They have six children who have grown up to be useful members of society. The Andersons still own their old homestead although they have for many years made their home on a timber-claim near Ord. They have accumulated much of this world's goods, and are growing old in our midst, respected and honored by all who know them.

AYERS, C. M.—is perhaps one of the best known of all the early settlers in the neighborhood of North Loup. He was born in Clark county, Ohio, in July 1838. His father died when he was but a small boy and so in 1854 he and his mother moved to Rock county, Wisconsin. In 1861 he enlisted in Co. E. 5th Wisconsin Infantry and served till July 1864. While leading the life of a soldier he was engaged in the battles of Williamsburg, Savage Station, Antietam, two battles at Fredericksburg, Gettysburg, Wilderness and several others of importance. In September 1872, Mr. Ayers was married and in October of the same year made a trip to the North Loup Valley where he took a homestead and then immediately went back to Wisconsin for his wife. He returned in April 1873, and has been a resident of Valley county ever since. In 1892 he retired from hard work on account of an injury received while in the army and subsequent bad health. He is now a resident of North Loup.

BABCOCK, HEMAN A.—who but lately died while holding the office of Deputy State Treasurer under Peter Mortensen, is one of the early trailers whose memory will long be cherished on the Loup. He came to North Loup, May 15, 1872, and located on a homestead in section 2, township 19, range 13. He was the first sheriff of Valley county, and held the office of clerk from 1876 to 1882. Later he was elected president of the First National Bank at Ord and then Auditor of the State of Nebraska. Since that time he has held many lucrative positions of trust under the various state administrations. He was born in Cattaraugas county, New York, May 19, 1842. He later removed with his parents to Wisconsin. He enlisted in 1863 in Co. G., Thirty-Seventh Reg., Wisconsin Volunteer Infantry and was mustered out in 1865 as Sergeant Major. After spending some years in Minnesota he joined the Seventh-Day Baptist colony of Waushara county, Wisconsin, at North Loup. He was married August 28, 1862, to Retta O. Bristol of Kenosha county, Wisconsin. They have two grown sons, Everett C. and Royal O.

BABCOCK. N. W.—was born in Shelby county, Ohio, in 1844. When he was ten years old his parents took up their home in Iowa where he lived till 1872. At this time he moved to Nebraska and took a pre-emption claim about three and one-half miles southeast from North Loup. In the following year he purchased his present farm and has lived there and in North Loup ever since. Mr. Babcock has always been a farmer and a glance at his well kept place will satisfy everyone that he has been successful in his chosen calling.

BABCOCK, OSCAR—Legislator, postmaster, farmer and stock-raiser, came to Valley county, Neb., and located on a homestead at what is now a part of North Loup, in November 1872. This is now a thriving village containing about five hundred people. The village was laid out by J. A. Green, under the supervision of Mr. Babcock, July 17, 1874, on the northeast quarter of section 35, town 18, range 13, with an addition laid out in June 1881, by Oscar Babcock; second addition made in May 1882. Mr. Babcock was president of a Seventh-Day Baptist colony which was organized in Waushara county, Wis., which colony settled in North Loup in May 1872. Mr. B. arrived with his family in November of the same year. His wife died in Waushara, Wisconsin, in the fall of 1872. They have four children—Edwin J., Arthur E., Myra and George J. Mr. B, with his small children, settled in a dugout fourteen feet square and lived there until the summer of 1873, when he erected a red cedar block house. He was pastor of the Seventh-Day Baptist Church for more than five years, preaching the first sermon in a small grove on the bank of the North Loup River, in May 1872, to a congregation of twenty-five pioneers. He was appointed agent of immigration for Valley county. He has been postmaster off and on ever since January 1873. He was born in Cattaraugas county, N. Y., March 15, 1834, and lived in his native state until 1849. His family then moved to Rock county, Wis., where he attended school for five years, then to Waushara county, Wis., being the first of the pioneers in the then wilds of central Wisconsin. He is a self-educated and thoroughly practical business man. His first wife's maiden name was Metta A. Bristol, of New York state. He was again married in 1877, to Miss Hattie E. Payn of North Loup, who died in February 1880. Mr. B. was a member of the Wisconsin Legislature in 1865–66; was elected Probate Judge of Valley county, holding the office one term; was County Superintendent of schools one term; in the Nebraska State Legislature in 1879. Elder Babcock is the president of the "Old settlers' Meeting" of the North Loup Valley and does much to further the interest in this organization.

BADGER, DR. CHARLES—was born in Kingsbury, Washington county, N. Y., on the 21st of March 1824. He lived in his native state until eighteen years of age, during the last three years of which he taught in the public school of his native town. From this time until the age of twenty-two he studied theology. From twenty-two to twenty-seven years of age he studied medicine and clerked in a store. On June 9, 1851, he went before Drs. Johnson and Bartlett, of Milwaukee, Censors of the State Medical examiners, and upon their recommendaton received the society's diploma at the hands of Alfred L. Castleman, who was then president of the society. In the same month he commenced the practice of medicine with A. L. Castleman at Delafield, Waukesha county, Wis. On March 31, 1853, he was married to Samantha L. Maxon. They have two children—Katie M. and Hettie S. Badger. While living in Wisconsin, Katie married Mr. W. J. Holliday, railroad contractor. Hettie S. married James Vernon, an English gentleman. Dr. Badger graduated March 14, 1871, at the Chicago Medical College,

Dr. Charles Badger.

the Medical department of the Northwestern University, receiving the college and university seals. He practiced medicine in Waukesha, Dodge, Dane and Rock counties, Wis., McHenry county, Ill., and Clinton county, Iowa. In the spring of 1872, he came to Valley county, Neb., and located on section 26, town 17; broke 120 acres, took a timber claim and broke forty acres, and planted twenty in trees. He practiced medicine in Valley, Sherman, Howard, Greeley and Taylor counties for nearly eight years, when overwork and failing health compelled him to abandon it. He was appointed by the Governor to register votes of Valley county; was coroner three terms, justice of peace one term, first county superintendent of public instruction for Valley county, fought through the first public highway, built the first bridge and gave to North Loup its name. The venerable doctor spends his declining years at the comfortable family home in the town he helped to found.

BAILEY, DANIEL COOLEY—the grand old man of the Loup, was born in New York State, October 15, 1820, which makes him now more than 85 years old. He was married April 6, 1845, to Susan E. Dale. They have four children, Mary, George, Harry and Frank. Leaving New York the Bailey family sojourned for some years in Wisconsin and came on west to Nebraska and the Loup in 1872. They came overland by way of Nance county and reached the site of their future home September 3, 1872. From the first Mr. Bailey was one of the pillars of the upper colony. When Valley county was organized in 1873 he was elected one of the first board of commissioners and as such performed his duty well. When the Indian scares of 1873 stirred the settlements his cabin became a rallying point; when later needy wayfarers happened up on the north side of the Loup, they could expect a hearty welcome from Grandpa and Grandma Bailey, for their latchstring always swung inward. Now that declining years are beginning to set their stamp upon these staunch first-comers they may at any rate have the satisfaction of having lived to see the once virgin valley become a part of the great American Commonwealth in riches and in fact.

BANCROFT, RUFUS W.—One of the first comers to the Loup and one of the first set of county commissioners, spent his early life in Michigan, where he was born in March 1826. He arrived with his family in Springdale early in the spring of 1873 and was for many years a leader in public life. Of his three children Emma C., S. T. and Libbie May, the former married William A. Hobson, August 10, 1873, and as such was the second white woman married in Valley county. Mr. Hobson set up the first blacksmith shop in the upper Loup, first in Springdale and later at Fort Hartsuff where he became the post smith. After a time again he moved his shop to Calamus and then to Ord. He died after a lingering illness, June 13, 1883, leaving a wife and one daughter Cora, behind.

BARKER, THOMAS O.—one of the first settlers of Mira Valley was Thomas O. Barker. He was born in Almond, Alleghany county, New York, July 24, 1838. In 1856 he moved to Milton, Wisconsin. He celebrated New Year's Day of 1861 by taking Miss Mary A. Needham as a helpmeet. Because of failing health he came to the Loup country in June 1873, taking one of the first homesteads in Mira Valley. Mr. Barker died July 8, 1897. Mrs. Barker and the two oldest sons now farm the homestead. The youngest son is a physician in one of the leading hospitals of London, England.

BARTZ, FREDERICK—was born in Pommerania, Germany, November 4, 1844. Here he lived till he was about 18 years old when he moved to the vicinity of Berlin. When 28 years old he married Miss Augusta Schoning. Hearing of the possibilities of this country through his brother-in-law, Mr. Otto Schoning, they came to the U.S. in the fall of 1877 and settled in Valley county about six miles north of North Loup. Here they have lived since.

BEE, N.—is a native of West Virginia in which state he was born in 1837. He moved to Minnesota in 1865 where he lived for twelve years. In 1877 he moved to Valley county and settled on a farm near North Loup. Mr. Bee has followed farming principally as an occupation although he did spend four years as a merchant in North Loup.

BENSON, DANIEL—Mr. Daniel Benson was born in Steuben county, New York, October 31, 1839. When he was twelve years old his parents moved to Lake county, Illinois. Here he grew to manhood and on August 2, 1862, enlisted in Co. G. 96th Illinois Volunteer Infantry, and served till June 11, 1865. On December 26 of the same year he took unto himself as a wife a Miss Shotswell. They came to Platte county, Nebraska, in 1869, only to remove to the Loup country and homestead in Greeley county in 1873. Here they resided till Feb. 2, 1899, when Mr. Benson died. Mrs. Benson bought her present home in North Loup in 1903 and has since made this her home.

BOETTGER, CONRAD—was born near the city of Cassel in Germany in 1841 where he lived the first 24 years of his life. Then coming to America he spent several years in New York, Pennsylvania

Settlers of the "Trail of the Loup" (Bios)   267

and Maryland. In 1869 he arrived at Wautoma, Wisconsin, and in the winter of the year he married a Miss Hannah Nickell. In the spring of 1874 they came to Mira Valley and on May 9 homesteaded their present home farm. Mr. Boettger is one of Mira Valley's prominent farmers and is very much interested in horticulture.

BOWER, CHARLEY— Although Charley Bower was born in Baden, Germany, in 1851 it is hardly possible that he remembers very many experiences that took place in the old country for his parents moved to America when he was but six months old. His first home in this land was in Freeport, Illinois, where he resided until he came of age. The next three years of his life were spent in Omaha, after which time he came to the North Loup valley and settled on this present farm in 1874. Mr. Bower has always been a successful farmer and stock raiser.

Charley Bower.

BURDICK, AMOS R.—was born April 27, 1827, in Scott, Courtland county, N. Y. Here he grew to manhood and on August 27, 1852, married a Miss Martha Spencer. Immediately they went to Waupaca county, Wisconsin, where they resided till shortly before the Civil War when they moved to Milton, Wisconsin. In 1861 Mr. Burdick enlisted in the 13th Wisconsin Infantry, Co. B., and for four long years he served as a soldier of the federal government. In the spring of 1872 they homesteaded in Valley county just across the river from the old Stewart place. From 1883 to 1889 these people lived in Rushville, Neb. They then took up their residence in Plimona, California. Here they resided till in 1903 when on a visit to their daughter, Mrs. Stewart, Mr. Burdick died. His wife still lives in Plimona.

CHASE, HENRY A.—was born in Jefferson county N. Y., in 1837. He received the rudiments of his education here and when eighteen years of age moved to Wisconsin. Here he completed his education at Albion Academy. He enlisted in the Union Army and

Chapter XX

Henry A. Chase.

served till August '65. His war record is a very honorable one. He was seriously wounded in the explosion and succeeding disastrous charge before Petersburg. Later he was present at Lee's surrender at Appomattox. At the close of the war he returned to Wisconsin; thence he moved to Minnesota and later to Missouri, where he dwelt thirteen years. In 1859 he married Delia Babcock, a sister of Oscar and Heman A. Babcock. He has one daughter, Nellie E. Black. The family came to North Loup in 1879, when Mr. Chase bought one quarter of the section on which North Loup is located. Mr. Chase has been a lifelong Republican, casting his first vote for Abraham Lincoln. He has been a member of the county board off and on for twelve years and a member of the North Loup school board for more than twenty years.

CHRISTIAN, PETER—is probably one of the best known men from the neighborhood of Arcadia. He was born in Denmark May 18, 1848. In 1867 he came to Wisconsin where he lived as a farmer till 1874. He then moved to Indiana from which place, after a three years' stay, he came to this valley. At first he bought some railroad land at $1.25 per acre and in 1880, being well pleased with the country, he took up his claim about three miles north from Arcadia. In 1884 he purchased his present farm near town.

COLBY, H. M.—was born in the state of Maine in February 1836. When 17 years old he came to Wisconsin, which state remained his home till 1876. On July 24, 1861, he was married and nine days afterwards enlisted in Co. I., 2nd Wisconsin Infantry. From this time on to the time of his discharge he never received a furlough and never saw his bride. In February of the following year Mr. Green re-enlisted in Co. E, 9th Illinois Cavalry and served eight months. During his life as a soldier he fought in many of the most important battles of the war, including 2nd Bull Run, Antietam, Gettysburg, Wilderness, Spottsylvania, Cold Harbor, siege of Petersburg and several others.

After the war he returned to Wisconsin where he lived till September 1876, when he came to Greeley county, Nebraska, and took up a claim about four miles northeast of North Loup. In 1882 he moved to town where he has lived ever since.

COLLINS, W. G.—was born in Alleghany county, New York, in 1845. In 1863 he moved to Wisconsin where he lived for nine years, engaged as a farmer. In 1872 he came to Valley county and settled on the same farm on which he now resides. Mr. Collins is one of the best known and most highly respected citizens of this valley.

H. M. Colby.

While a member of the first militia organized in this county, he was called out three times on account of Indian scares but never came into any active engagement. His daughter, who was born January 30, 1873, bears the distinction of being the very first white child born in Valley county.

COOMBS, MINGERSON—is a native of Knox county, Me., and when 13 years of age moved with his parents to LaPorte county, Ind., where he worked on a farm until of age. He then opened a store in New Carlisle, Ind. His next move was to Berrien county, Mich., where he bought a fruit farm, and four years later, in 1873 sold out and came to Valley county. He located a homestead and a tree claim, and has probably accomplished what no other man in the United States has, to-wit, taking a timber claim under the original timber culture act, which required the actual planting and cultivation of forty acres of timber. This he successfully accomplished and now has one of the finest bodies of timber in the state, many of the trees being two feet in diameter. He still owns both quarter sections, with 230 acres under a high state of cultivation, besides 67 acres adjacent to Ord with 50 acres under cultivation. Mr. Coombs has been a prominent factor in Ord having held many positions of trust and honor. He has creditably filled the offices of County Commissioner, County

Surveyor, County Superintendent of schools and Mayor of the city. He is also a representative business man and one of the most highly respected citizens.

COON, J. L.—was born in Alleghany county, New York, in 1840. His parents moved to Wisconsin when he was but a child and this continued his home till 1860. Then he went to Minnesota and lived there as a farmer till 1877 when he came to Nebraska and settled near Fort Hartsuff. In 1893 he went to Oregon but like most of the other folks who move away from the Loup Valley he returned in 1895. He is now engaged in the feed business in Burwell.

CRANDALL, ALPHA M.—was born in Milton, Wis., December 11, 1852. When 14 years of age his parents moved to Illinois where he was raised as a farmer. Late in October 1878, he came to Valley county and homesteaded six miles from North Loup. On May 25, 1882, he married a Miss Rood. Then for ten years they lived on their farm. In 1892 they moved to North Loup where they still live.

CRANDALL, MAXON—one of North Loup's oldest inhabitants was born in Alleghany county, N. Y. away back in 1827. He was brought up and received his schooling there. For many years he followed the profession of a mechanic. He was early married to Elizabeth Lily, by whom he has had six children, three of whom are living. When he took up the westward march it was to halt for some time in Wisconsin and Minnesota, and finally in 1879, to move to Nebraska. Here he has farmed and in various ways made an honest living. He is now retired at the ripe age of 78.

DAVIS, A. J.—Though not of the first immigration to Valley county, another early settler is Mr. A. J. Davis of North Loup. He was born in Salem county, West Virginia, December 21, 1829. When but a boy of nine his parents moved to Ft. Jefferson, Ohio, where Mr. Davis gained his majority. Soon afterwards he went to Peoria, Ill. Later he removed to Welton, Iowa. Here he met a Miss Esther S. Worth whom he married on October 25, 1857. In May 1874 these people moved to North Loup and here Mrs. Davis passed away November 22, 1893. Mr. Davis has carried the mail ever since the railroad came to North Loup.

DAVIS, HENRY S.—was born in 1844 in Louis county, N.Y. At the age of twelve he came to Walworth county, Wisconsin, and grew to manhood there. He was a member of the 22nd Wisconsin Regiment and served actively for three years. After the Civil War he moved to Minnesota where he pursued farming for twelve years. He came to North Loup in 1877 and took a homestead three-quarters of a mile from town. Later he was proprietor of the Union Hotel of North Loup for three years. Since that time he has been at different times liveryman, farmer, etc. September 28, 1867, he was married to Abbie F. Greene. They are the parents of six children.

DAVIS, NEWTON—was born in Ohio in 1834. When but ten years old his parents moved to Rock county, Wis., where he lived for nearly twenty years. In 1861 he married a Miss Clement and after two years took up his home in Minnesota. In 1868 they turned their faces towards the west and after spending six years in Iowa finally landed in this Eldorado of the West, the great North Loup Valley. Their home was now on a farm about eight miles south of North Loup. In 1891 they came to North Loup where Mr. Davis died in June 1903, his sorrowing wife surviving him.

EAST, HENRY T.—was born in London, England, in 1826. Here he followed the occupation of his forefathers, that of a tanner, until 1847 when he came to the United States. He enlisted as a soldier in the Mexican War and was at the surrender of Mexico City. When discharged he went to Vincennes, Indiana, and engaged as a merchant. He married a Miss Presnell in 1853. In February 1865, he enlisted in Co. K. 149th Indiana Regiment and continued as a soldier till September 27th of the same year. In 1867 he moved to Wisconsin where he stayed for six years. At the end of this time he came to Nebraska and settled in Valley county. He worked at the occupation of tanning for a long time. He died in June 1902, leaving a wife and family behind to mourn his loss.

Henry T. East.

FLINT, E. R.—was born in Lincolnshire, England, in 1850. He was married in 1869. He was a farmer until 1870 when he moved to Sheffield, England. While here he worked for one of those big steel manufacturing companies which make Sheffield cutlery so famous all over the world today. In 1874 he came to the United States and settled in the Loup Valley. While here he worked on Fort Hartsuff. Two years later he moved to Kent county, Michigan, which remained his home till 1888. At that time he returned to the Loup Valley. Since 1888 he has lived for five years in Cotesfield and the remainder of the time on Davis Creek and near North Loup.

FLYNN, MARILLA—The first white woman in Valley county was Marilla Frederick who came here with her father in July 1872. She was at that time a young lady of about 15 years of age. In 1877 she went to Omaha where she met a young soldier named Flynn who was stationed at Ft. Omaha. He was soon afterwards transferred to Ft. Laramie, Wyoming, where they were married the following year. In July 1885, they returned to Valley county where they lived on various rented farms till Mr. Flynn's death, April 18, 1895. In 1900 Mrs. Flynn bought her present farm just cornering on her father's old homestead in Springdale.

FOGHT, EMIL JOHN,—the father of the author of *The Trail of the Loup*, was born sixty-four years ago in historic old Fredrickshall, Norway, the son of a well-to-do merchant and ship owner. He was educated in the Latin school and nautical school of his native town and at an early date went to sea. While yet a stripling boy he was made first mate and soon after captain of the schooner Aurora, which sailed chiefly between the Baltic and French ports. In the seventies the Aurora was lost on the French coast and Captain Foght received command of the large bark Laura, so named after his wife, Laura Arneberg Foght. This vessel was owned chiefly by the Foght family and proved more or less of a hoodoo from the first. To several severe losses caused by storms at sea came the serious competition with swift steamships then just beginning to make inroads on the shipping of the sailships. After a long and hopeless fight against the new carriers he gave up and retired to terra firma. Then after some unfortunate mercantile ventures at Fredrickshall he came to the United States in 1879, making Yankton, Dakota Territory, his home for a few months. Here he took service as a government freighter, going first to Fort Robinson and later to the newly constructed Fort Niobrara. At the latter place he was joined by his family in the summer of 1881, they having made their journey of 7000 miles from old Norway alone. For a few months the Foghts squatted on a claim near Rosebud Agency but were forced into the fort by the Spotted Tail-Crow Dog uprising. They now left overland for Ord, where they arrived early in September

1881. From that time on the family has been associated with Valley county and its development. Of the seven children living, the oldest daughter, Valborg, is married to Jorgen Miller, and the oldest son, Harold W., who has also penned this book, married Alice Mabel, youngest daughter of A. M. Robbins of Ord.

FREY, CHRISTIAN—was one of the "original five" in the Danish colony above Ord. He was of course a native of Denmark and came to the United States in 1871, hoping here to better himself financially. We have already told how he reached Valley county and about his first exciting adventure here. He remained a bachelor on his claim for a number of years, when he returned to Denmark where he met and married an estimable Danish lady, who returned with him from a home of affluence to share his frontier life. Five children have been born to them of whom four—Mary, Kate, Ericka and James—are living. Mr. Frey remained on his old homestead through all the years of beginnings and hardships and has succeeded in laying by a goodly bit of property for a rainy day. A few months ago he disposed of his old homestead, returning to old Denmark with the intention of spending the rest of his days there. But the call from over the ocean blue was too strong for him and he is again back in the Loup where he will no doubt be content to remain for the rest of his days.

GOODENOW, M. B—"It is something to be able to say that for a whole season I was the outermost settler on the Loup. No man dwelt between my claim and the Black Hills." This boast could truly be given by Mellville B. Goodenow in the summer of '72. Then he was our outpost. But that has been told elsewhere. He was born in New York state in 1844 and was brought up by his grandparents as his mother died when he was born. In '61 when only 17, he enlisted and served through the Civil War. He was mustered out in the spring of '66 and then moved to Woodbury county, Iowa, remaining there till 1872 when he set out across country for the Loup. He married a Miss Coffin in 1869 and has four children—one son and three daughters.

GREEN, H. I.—was born in Walworth county, Wis., in 1859. When he was but four years old his parents moved to Minnesota. In the fall of 1877 he moved to the town of Calamus just south of Fort Hartsuff. During the next spring he moved to his present farm about two and one half miles northwest of North Loup. Mr. Green has always been a farmer and a glance at his place will be enough to convince any one that he has been successful in this line. He held the office of county supervisor in 1901–1902 but has held no other public office. He was married in 1883 to Miss Emma Brace.

GREEN, JOSEPH A.—a native of the Green Mountain State, was born in 1832. When but a child his parents moved to Berlin, New York, where he stayed till 1853. During the next few years he traveled through New Jersey, Illinois and Kansas, stopping at various places in these states but never making his home at any place for any length of years. In 1872 Mr. Green came to Valley county and settled one and one-half miles south of North Loup and has lived there ever since. He at one time owned forty acres of the original townsite of North Loup. Mr. Green is a farmer by occupation yet his ability as a mechanic came in handy in the early years when all sorts of machinery was scarce.

W. B. Green.

GREEN, W. B.—was one of those natives of New York state who has spent most of his years in this western country. He was born in Alleghany county, New York, March 25, 1849. When but five years old he moved to Milton, Wis. Here he spent his time as a farmer until 1873 when he came to Nebraska and took up a claim on the very place on which he now resides, about five miles southwest from North Loup. Mr. Green worked on Fort Hartsuff during the summer of 1875. He was married in 1877. In 1878 he was with Albert Cottrell in that terrible October prairie fire in which Mr. Cottrell was burned to death. Even to this day Mr. Green bears scars that remind him of that awful disaster.

GREEN, W. L.—is a native of New York, who was born in Jefferson county in 1833. In 1855 he was married and started toward the west. Only one year was spent in Illinois while the next eight were spent in Wisconsin. In 1864 they moved to Minnesota which place remained their home until they came to Nebraska and settled in Valley county in 1877. Mr. Green has always been a farmer and has worked his farm which lies two and one-half miles north of North Loup until about eight years ago, when he moved to town where he has lived ever since.

HARRISON, W. H.—has, by his sterling qualities, shown himself worthy of carrying the name of a former president of the United States. He was born in Louisville, Kentucky, in 1853. Here he lived for six years when he moved to Missouri where he lived till after the Civil War. At this time he moved to Kansas and finally in 1874 to Nebraska and settled on the place where he now lives, about nine miles southwest from Ord.

W. H. Harrison.

HASKELL, S. S.—Sylvester Smith Haskell, the father of early Ord, was born December 7, 1822, at Stockholm, St. Lawrence county, N. Y., where his early life was spent. His father was a millwright, and living in the pine region the son naturally enough became a sawyer, which trade he followed many years. He came of sturdy stock, the Putnams of revolutionary times being among his lineal ancestors. December 5, 1843, he was married to Miss Harriet E. Soper and for a few years they lived in St. Lawrence county, but in 1849 he removed with his family to DeKalb county, Ill., and filed on a quarter section of land in that then wild country. He had a hard struggle here to make ends meet as he came west a poor man. Two years of toil in the saw-mills at Two Rivers, Wis., enabled him to build a comfortable dwelling house on the Illinois claim, but this unfortunately was burned to the ground on the very day of its completion. The set-back was a severe one, but he accepted the situation bravely and clung to the farm in spite of misfortune and hardship, and called it home for twenty five years. During this time he reared his large family and saved a fair competency with which to build anew in the promising west of which he was continually getting news from his children who had preceded him there. In the fall of 1875 he sold out and moved to Ord. The next summer he erected the first store building on the townsite lately platted by his sons. Old-timers will all remember this general store and hostelry and later postoffice, where every wayfarer received a kindly welcome and shelter. When hard times came to the Valley dwellers and starvation almost stared them in the face, Haskell fed them till he could no more. His capital exhausted, he was forced to close his doors and failed in business. But by the indomitable energy of self and wife he got on his feet again and could proudly boast of paying his creditors dollar for dollar what he owed. Mr. Haskell has been called the father of Ord. And not without reason, for not alone did he build and operate the first store here, not alone is a large section of the town built on his early farm, but he was a father to all in need. Nor was any early timer more public spirited than he. Charity and public enterprise depended on him for aid and co-operation. When he was laid to rest March 1, 1901, just 78 years, 2 months and 21 days old, the whole community mourned the loss of a father and friend. In Ord the business houses were closed and the deceased was accorded a public funeral such as had never before been known in the history of the Valley. His many children have all taken their part in making the history of the Loup. Of these the sons, O. S. Haskell, O. C. Haskell and W. W. Haskell, platted the original town-site of Ord; the daughters, Cynthia C. Robbins, Rose I. Williams and Mary E. Jones and the son, A. R. Haskell, were all old pioneers and have grown up with the Valley and seen it become what it is—a garden spot in our state.

HONNOLD, R. T.—Richard Truman Honnold was born in Coshocton, county, Ohio, September 12, 1851, and removed with his parents to Marion county, Iowa, late in 1862. In 1874 he was married to Miss Eceneth McMichael and immediately loaded his possessions into a covered wagon and started for Nebraska. He lingered at St. Paul and put in a few acres of wheat there, meanwhile looking about in search of a good place to homestead. He finally located in Mira Valley where he yet resides. Mr. Honnold is one of those pioneers who has gone through the hardships incident to grasshoppers, fire, hail and drought, and still stands up for Nebraska. He had many exciting experiences with the Indians in those days; from the first, indeed, he has been closely identified with the history of his county.

Note:—Since the writing of the above biography Mr. Honnold moved to Ord where he was stricken with Bright's disease, death resulting Monday, April 23.

JOHNSON, BYRON H.—is another of those very early settlers of this Valley who has always been interested in its development and closely connected with its history. He was born in Rhode Island in 1847 but lived there only one year. His parents moved to Wisconsin in 1848 and it was here he grew to maturity. In 1866 he went to Minnesota where he lived

The Byron Johnson family.

for five years. In 1871 he made a trip to Valley county, Nebraska, in order to see the country which was destined to be his future home. He returned to Minnesota to get things in shape and then moved to this valley in November 1872, and settled on a claim about six miles north of North Loup. In 1878 he bought his present farm just one and one half miles north of town. Mr. Johnson was a member of the first militia organized in this county. He helped to build Fort Hartsuff during the grasshopper years. He held the office of supervisor several terms but beyond this has taken but slight interest in active politics. He married a Miss Stewart in 1880.

KEOWN, W. B.—Bedford Keown's name is closely associated with the settlement of Valley county. He was born in Ohio county, Kentucky, in 1849, and came with his parents to Missouri when but a babe. The Keowns remained in that state till 1874 when they arrived in Valley county. Here Mr. Keown secured the quarter first filed on by one of the Post boys, which later on became the townsite of Elyria. He remained on this fine tract of land till he sold it to the B. & M. railroad company in 1887. Then he moved with his family to Ord and engaged in business. He has been prominent as a hardware man and has been engaged in the drug business and other enterprises. Several times has he been honored with places of trust and profit by his fellow-citizens. The last of these was the county treasurership which he held for two terms. At the present Mr. and Mrs. Keown are beautifully situated on their fine farm two miles above Ord and across the river. They have three children living—Anna Williams, John, and Emma Mayo.

Chapter XX

KRUSER, MARTIN—Mr. Martin Kruser was born in Kolding, Denmark, in 1853. Here he lived and received his education. In 1872 he came to the United States and for three years made his home with the grandparents of Mr. M. Goodenow. In April 1878, he came to Valley county, Nebraska. For eight years he then worked for Mr. Goodenow. In 1880 he homesteaded his present farm though it was some six years before he made his permanent home upon it. Mr. Kruser is a single man.

LEE, JAMES—Perhaps no one in the southwestern part of Valley county is better known than Mr. James Lee who was the first settler in the Park which now bears his name. He was born in Ontario, Canada, April 28, 1847, where he lived till 1874 when he came to Valley county, Nebraska, and took up his claim in that section of the Valley called Lee's Park. Mr. Lee has always been a farmer, though he worked for two years on Fort Hartsuff during the grasshopper years.

LUEDTKE, AUGUST—is a successful German farmer who, born in a foreign land, came to this country to better his condition. He was born in Pommerania, Germany, in February 1841. Here he lived till 1866 when he came to the United States and settled in Wisconsin and afterward spent a few years in Kansas and Texas. In April 1873, he came to Nebraska and worked between Omaha and Wood River. He came to Valley county in the spring of the following year with Mr. Frank Ohms and a trapper named Murphy and settled on his present farm about five miles northwest from Arcadia.

LUKE, JOHN—is a native of the state of Connecticut but while quite young moved to New York city. He lived there till he was seventeen years old, when he joined the army as a drummer boy. In April 1875, he came to Fort Hartsuff with Co. A, 23d U.S. Infantry, commanded by Capt. John J. Coppinger. In

John Luke.

Settlers of the "Trail of the Loup" (Bios)   279

October 1876, after having served eight years in the United States army he was honorably discharged and at once settled down in Valley county to make it his home. He was married to a Miss Stewart, November 9, 1876. Mr. Luke has long been known as a lumberman. Until recently Mr. Luke has had charge of one of Ord's rural routes.

MATTLEY, MRS. E. J.—Although Mrs. E. J. Mattley was born in England yet most of her life has been spent in this country. When but four years old she came to Iowa and after staying there for five years moved to Missouri. While here she met Mr. Mattley whom she married in 1875. In 1877 they moved to Nebraska and settled on the farm on which she now resides. Mr. Mattley died in November 1903, but as his wife was a business woman, the farm has been operated successfully nevertheless.

MOLLER, FALLE—who was one of the members of the Danish colony which settled above Ord during the spring and summer of 1872, is a native of Denmark, coming from a small village near Haderslev in Slesvig. He comes of good old Danish stock, well-to-do land-owners who have ever bitterly resented the encroachment on Danish soil by the German coalition. After the Dano-German War of '64, so disastrous to little Denmark, the Mollers concluded to leave their homeland and seek a new home in America. Accordingly, in 1872, the family, comprising the parents and four children, Marie, Elizabeth, Jorgen and Laura, set out for the United States and, as told in another chapter of this book, reached Valley county and settled on their old homestead on lower Turtle Creek. During the early years Falle Moller's substantial log house was an asylum for wayfarers in the Valley. The log cabin door always swung inward for needy immigrants. When Indians were threatening the Loup Mr. Moller was ever ready for the front. On several occasions in those days did settlers flock thither when rumors of Indian raids filled the air. The Danish colonists have

Jorgen Moller.

practically all remained true to their early religious teachings in the Lutheran faith, and in the seventies no more beautiful picture could be imagined than to see these sturdy northerners, who had outstripped both their church and pastors, assemble on a Sunday for church services. On such occasions Falle Moller would usually conduct the Danish service of song and sermon reading in a manner worthy a well tutored preacher. Down through the years Mr. Moller and his son Jorgen have accumulated much worldly goods, comprising chiefly farm and ranch lands and cattle. Falle Moller may justly lay claim to being one of the most travelled men in our Valley, having crossed the Atlantic thirteen times within the last thirty-five years.

MURRAY, WILLIAM P.—was born in Dundee, Scotland, in 1839. Until he was 13 years old he changed his residence several times back and forth between his native land and Ireland. When he reached this age he came to the United States and settled in Westchester county, N. Y. Here he lived till 1861 when he moved to Oswego county. The next few years he spent as a rambler, visiting nearly every part of the country. In 1878 he came to Nebraska and settled on the place where he now resides, about six miles west from Arcadia. Before coming to Nebraska Mr. Murray was a stonemason and quarryman but since he has been a farmer.

NELSON, HENRY W.—located with his parents in Omaha in 1862, where he lived with them for twelve years. He learned to be pressman in the Omaha Bee office, and in 1874 he came to Valley county, Neb., and located a homestead and timber claim containing 320 acres, seven miles south of Ord on Section 10, Town 18, Range 15. He was born in Sweden, March 5, 1852, and came to America with his parents in 1862. He was married in Ord, August 3, 1879, to Miss Lura Abel, a native of Ohio. He was a member of the I. O. O. F. of Ord. He has been county surveyor of Valley county for five years; edited the *Valley County Courier* one and a half years, beginning in 1878. At the present Mr. Nelson is located at Billings, Montana.

OHMS, FRANK—bears the distinction of being the first settler in Custer county. He was born in Prussia, Germany, in February 1844. Here he lived till he was twenty-five years old when he came to the United States and settled in Jefferson county, Wis. While in the old country his work was varied. Three years were spent with a confectioner, another three years were spent in a large depot restaurant, while three more were spent in the army. He was engaged in the war between Germany and Austria in 1866. He fought in the battle of Sadowa. He received his discharge in 1868. The next year he came to this country. He stayed in Wisconsin only one year and then went to Douglas county, Nebraska. Here he farmed for four years when he came to his present home on the Valley county line.

PIERCE, DWIGHT—and family left their old Wisconsin home in the spring of 1878 and set out for the Loup Valley with a whole carload of household goods, implements, horses and cattle. "In Grand Island," says Mr. Pierce, "we stored our goods and set out to seek a home. The farther up the Valley we came the better we liked the country. At the Big Bend of the Loup lay Byron Johnson's homestead. This just suited me and I purchased the land." Mr. Pierce died Jan. 22, '06, after a short illness.

D. Pierce.

POST, CHARLES W.—is the only member of Post clan now dwelling in the North Loup Valley. The others, like the frontiersmen that they were, moved westward and ever westward, till the Pacific now forbids a further migration.

Mrs. D. Pierce.

Charles was born December 3, 1847, on the frontier of Michigan. When he was five years old his parents began to drift westward by easy stages. Thus he saw life in Wisconsin, Iowa, Minnesota, Kansas and Missouri. When the Civil War broke out the Posts found it expedient to leave the state and move back to Jasper, Iowa, their old home. He enlisted in '64 when only 16 years old and saw much service before the war was over. The Posts next spent some years in Harrison county, Iowa, and in the spring of '72 they set out for the North Loup Valley, carrying with them horses, cattle and all other belongings. They came via the Beaver and Cedar and entered the Loup near Cotesfield. Charles filed upon the northeast quarter of section 26-20-15, the townsite of the present Elyria. Later he filed on a pre-emption and secured a school quarter on which he made his eventual home. In June 1881, he married Marie, the eldest daughter of Falle Moller. He is the father of three children, Willie, Falle and Magdalene. Charles Post came to the Valley in time to participate in all early hardships and disappointments but has out-ridden them all and is now beginning to spend his older days in partial retirement.

POTTER, HARVEY—was born in La Salle, Ill., on December 18, 1846. When but a small boy his folks moved to Minnesota. Within the next few years his home was changed to Lexington, Kansas, Jasper county, Iowa, and finally in May 1873, to Valley county, Nebraska, where he has resided ever since. Mr. Potter is one of the oldest settlers in Valley county and as such has been interested in the growth and development of the Loup Valley. He was married in July 1882.

PRENTICE, WILLIAM A.—was born in Dakota, Wis., in July 1851. Here he lived till June 1873, when he came to Valley county and took up a claim in Mira Valley. He was married in 1872. In 1881 he came to North Loup and began to work as a carpenter. He took a course of study in law and was admitted to the bar in 1891. Mr. Prentice was a justice of the peace for several years but outside of this has had no political aspirations.

W. A. Prentice.

ROOD, CHARLES J.—is one of the older sons of Charles P. Rood, and was born in Waushara county, Wisconsin, July 4, 1851, where he boasts being the first white child born

Settlers of the "Trail of the Loup" (Bios) 283

in his particular township. He grew to manhood in Wisconsin and was given what was then considered a pretty good education. He too was one of the second locating committee to come to the Loup. In 1872 he homesteaded just outside of North Loup. He spent much time as a teacher in those days, and as such had the honor of being the first to teach school in the village of Ord. For some years he farmed on Davis Creek but moved to North Loup in 1895 to give his children the advantage of the better schools in that town. In 1875 he was married to Rosa P. Furrow. They are the parents of ten children.

ROOD, CHARLES F.—now long passed to his reward, is one of the early North Loupers who deserves more than passing mention in a history of the Loup Valley. He should have much credit for the part he played in the settlement of North Loup by the Wisconsin colony. He was a member of both committees and but for his determined stand and flattering reports of the land, the enterprise might have been altogether abandoned. He was born in Vermont, May 30, 1823, and after a brief sojourn in Canada moved with his people to Cataraugas county, N. Y., where he grew up and married Marianne Thorngate. The family moved to Milwaukee and later to Waushara county and became a part of the Seventh-Day colony there. The large family of nine children born to him have practically all taken active and leading part in the development of the Loup and most of them live in or near North Loup today.

Mr. Rood lived for some time on Section 32, Town 18 Range 13; but homesteaded over in Mira Valley somewhat later. He was a public-spirited man, strong in his convictions of what was right. He was quite a lay preacher and really the head of the Good Templar movement in North Loup. He died March 17, 1878.

ROOD, W. H.—beheld the beautiful Loup in 1871, when he came here as one of the second committee from Wisconsin. From the first he was satisfied with the country and determined to make it his home. This he did

W. H. Rood.

Chapter XX

Mrs. W. H. Rood.

in the spring of 1872 when he came as one of the Seventh-Day Baptist Colony. Mr. Rood was born in Rock county, Wisconsin, in 1840. He enlisted in Co. G, 37th Wisconsin Infantry, in 1864 and served till August 1865. Although he was in active service his regiment never took part in any serious engagements. At North Loup Mr. Rood farmed for a number of years. Later he engaged in mercantile pursuits and was for years proprietor of the North Loup hotel. At present he is a carpenter and builder. In 1880 he married a Miss Pierce. He was a member of the militia company organized for protection against the Indians in 1873 and has held every township office in his home township.

SCHONING, OTTO—Another of Germany's sons is Otto Schoning who was born in Plathe, Pommerania, Germany, September 23, 1841. His early life was spent on a farm. He served two and one-half years as a state regular, but soon after getting his discharge he was recalled because of the war with Austria in 1860. Six months later he was discharged. Upon hearing rumors of a threatened Franco-Prussian war he left for the United States, landing at Baltimore in September 1868. Securing work in Wisconsin he remained there till 1872 when he came to Valley county and homesteaded his present farm, four and one-half miles from North Loup. May 7, 1878, he married Miss Amelia Brown. They have a beautiful farm.

SHELDON, JOHN—was the first of the North Loup colony to choose land in Valley county; this he did when he located his claim three miles southeast of North Loup, November 6, 1871. From that day to the present he has been a loyal trailer. Mr. Sheldon was born in Germany, August 31, 1848, and came to America when only five years old. He was one of the early Seventh-Day Baptist locating committee and together with the Roods and Mansell Davis made the long trip from Wisconsin and back in 1871. The next spring he moved onto his farm, remaining there seven years. After leaving the farm he lived for a few years in Scotia; then he moved to North Loup where he still resides. He has spent his time variously on the farm, as a proprietor of livery barns, in the mercantile business, and as a real estate dealer. He married Mary Brown of Wisconsin and is the father of four sons and daughters.

SMITH, A. J.—is another of those natives of New York state who came west to better their condition. In 1874 he came to Iowa where he was married the following year. In 1879 the Smith family moved to Nebraska and settled in Valley county. The first seven years of their Nebraska experience was spent on a farm near the place where Mr. and Mrs. Melville Goodenow now live. In 1886 they moved to Ord, making the county seat their permanent home.

SNOW, CYRUS A.—was born in Alleghany county, New York, April 23, 1847. When he was only six years of age his parents came to Union Mills, Erie county, Pennsylvania, and ten years later they moved to a farm near Centreville, Michigan. In the fall of 1877 he came to Valley county and worked on the historic Mortensen place for two years. He then timber-claimed his present farm southwest of Ord. In July 1879, he married Miss Ella M. Jackson.

STACY, SAMUEL AUSTIN—was born in Hocking county, Ohio, in 1851. His parents early set their faces westward and moved to Clark county, Iowa, where Samuel grew to manhood and received a common school education. July 1, 1874, he left Sloan, Iowa, on horseback and after twenty-six strenuous days arrived in Valley county, where his sister Mrs. A. T. Morris had preceded him. That summer was spent in visiting, hunting and in general enjoyment. He did not, however, make this his home till February 20, 1877, when he filed on a homestead in Mira Valley. After building a humble dugout on the claim he went to Aurora, Neb., for his bride, Alice E. Likes. This was

Samuel Austin Stacy.

286 Chapter XX

October 25, 1877. After getting a few essentials for housekeeping, the young couple had just $6.10 with which to start out in life. But Mr. Stacy was not cut out for a farmer. He moved to Ord and clerked for a time in Doc. Harter's new store. Then he worked for B. C. White and later became a member of the firm Stacy, Johnson & Co., general merchandise. He has at various times been engaged as a real estate dealer and in the meat market business. He has also held office as town treasurer of Ord township. When Co. B, 2nd Regiment N. N. G., was organized, Mr. Stacy was made Second Lieutenant. Later he was raised to the rank of First Lieutenant, Captain, and Adjutant of the 2nd Regiment, successively. June 1, 1898, he was made postmaster of Ord; he was reappointed by President Roosevelt, May 28, 1902.

THORNGATE, GEORGE—was born in Cataraugas county, New York, in 1834. When but twelve or thirteen years old he removed to Wisconsin in which state he afterward taught school. In May 1861, he enlisted in Co. E, 5th Wisconsin Infantry. He engaged in the battles of Antietam and Williamsburg. In the latter battle he was wounded in the chin and sent home on sick leave. He was discharged in the spring of 1862. However, he reenlisted later in the 13th Wisconsin Light Artillery which was then stationed at Baton Rouge. He was mustered out in July 1864. In the fall of the same year he was married to a Miss Crandall and the young couple took up their home in Missouri. The following year, 1878, they came to Valley county and settled at North Loup. Mr. Thorngate died in December 1893, but his wife still survives him.

TIMMERMAN, LEVI D.—is another of our early settlers who came originally from New York. He was born in Jasper county, that state, July 22, 1849. In 1878 he came to Valley county and being well pleased with the county bought the south eighty acres of his present farm. In August he returned to New York and married Miss Mary Dennis. The following April they came to their new home on the Loup where they have since resided. It is interesting to know that for his first eighty acres of land Mr. Timmerman paid but $140.00. He now has one of the finest farms in this county.

TRUE, CHANDLER—was born in Clayton county, Iowa, December 1, 1854. Here he lived as a farmer until June 1878, when he moved to Nebraska and settled on his present farm about four miles west of Arcadia. He was married December 25, 1878, to a Miss

Knight and they have eight children living. Mr. True is a successful farmer as a glance at his well-kept farm will show.

WEAVER, MARSHAL N.—came to Nebraska in September 1873, in company with George McAnulty. He settled at the head of the "Big Island," where he trapped and hunted during the winters of '73 and '74. He then returned to his old home in Latiabe, Pennsylvania, where he lives a prosperous man. It is safe to say, however, that he never forgets the beautiful North Loup Valley, the scene of some stormy adventures of his youth.

WEBB, SAMUEL S.—was born in Floyd, New York, in August 1825. Here he lived till 1857 when he moved to Illinois. Two years later he married a Miss Davis and in 1861 moved to Wisconsin. Three years later they moved to Minnesota which remained their home till 1877 at which time they came to Nebraska and settled in Valley county. Mr. Webb is essentially a farmer, though now retired from active work. At the ripe age of eighty he lives in comfort in his North Loup home, respected and highly honored by all his townsmen.

WELLMAN, M. A.—Among the early trailers of the Loup and a man identified with the business interests of North Loup for a number of years was M. A. Wellman. He was born at Windsor, Mass., May 28, 1842. When a child his parents moved to Waushara county, Wisconsin, where he grew to manhood. On May 18, 1866, he married Miss Mary Francisco. Five years later they moved to Greeley county. In 1886 they moved to North Loup and purchased their present home. From that time to his death on May 4, 1899, Mr. Wellman was engaged in the grocery business in North Loup.

WHEELER, JOHN S.—was born in Sullivan county, New York, in 1854. Here he lived for twenty-four years, being engaged during the latter part of this time in the printing business. In 1878 he came to Valley county and has lived here ever since. Until 1904 he farmed a place near Geranium but when this was sold he bought a farm near Elyria on which he now resides.

WIGENT, D.—was born in Berrien county, Michigan, August 17, 1859. Here he lived and attended school till 1877 when his parents came to Valley county and homesteaded on Turtle Creek. When Mr. Wigent came of age he took a homestead on the north branch of Turtle Creek. April 22, 1884, he married Miss Agnes Pecas. Three years later they sold out and bought near the present Hillsdale schoolhouse. In 1891 they moved to Barton county, Missouri. Here they lived for ten years when returning to Valley county they

Chapter XX

William Wiygent.

purchased the farm in Springdale where they now reside.

WIYGENT, W. H.— One of the early settlers of Springdale was W. H. Wiygent who came to Valley county in 1875. Mr. Wiygent was born near Syracuse, New York, July 25, 1843. When he was but a small child his parents moved to Michigan where he grew to manhood. In November 1862, Mr. Wiygent enlisted in the Union Army and served till August 1865. On December 23, 1866, he married Miss Myra Drake of Van Buren county, Michigan. He helped build the first bridge across the Loup river at Ord. Early in 1876 he homesteaded his place in Springdale, where he has since made his home.

WRIGHT, CHAUNCEY—was born on a New York farm in 1813. Here he lived till 1874 when he came to Nebraska and took up a claim about three miles south of Ord. Mr. Wright was married to a Miss Standish in 1837 and to them five children were born. One of them, a daughter, married a Mr. Chaffee in 1860 and settled in Wisconsin. Mr. Chaffee enlisted in the fall of 1864 and served for one year. After being discharged from the army he returned to Wisconsin where he died in 1877. Mrs. Chaffee now came to Nebraska to live with her parents who soon afterwards moved to North Loup, where she has lived ever since.

Garfield County

ABBOTT, WILLIAM—has followed the "star of empire" in its course toward the west. He was born in Alberg, Vt., in 1844. When but a baby his parents moved to Clinton county, New York, and it was from here that Mr. Abbott moved to New Jersey in 1866 and began to work his way westward. After a short stay in New Jersey he moved to Pawpaw, Ill. In 1869 he came to Iowa and after living there for nine

Settlers of the "Trail of the Loup" (Bios)   289

years moved to this valley and settled near Burwell. He farms a piece of land in Jones' Canyon.

BARKER, F. A.—was born in Alleghany county, N. Y., in April 1848. When but a boy of five years of age he moved with his parents to Wisconsin. Here he received his early education and grew to manhood. In July 1873, he came to Nebraska and homesteaded in Valley county. In 1891 he moved to Louisiana where he lived till 1897. He then returned to Nebraska and settled in Burwell. At present Mr. Barker is engaged in the bakery business.

BARR, JAMES—comes of good Scotch parentage, having been born at Glasgow, in April 1845. The Barrs left old Scotland in 1850 and immediately came to Chicago. His father was a stone-mason and contractor as well as bridge builder. The elder Barr thus had charge of constructing all the masonry on the old Galena and Chicago Union Railroad and put in the masonry on one of the first bridges to span the Mississippi. After attending school at Belvidere, Illinois, "Jim" entered the army at the early age of sixteen. He became a member of the famous Scotch regiment under Colonel Stewart, which marched more miles, fought in more battles and suffered greater losses than almost any other regiment east or west. Mr. Barr's army history reads like a romance and would fill books to narrate. How he surrendered to "Stonewall" Jackson at Harper's Ferry, scouted in eastern Kentucky or saved the life of the rebel colonel, or how he severely wounded was brought in contact with the young woman—Esther Ann Tilden—whom he later married, cannot unfortunately be told in this brief sketch. In the early seventies O. S. Haskell arrived with his family in Valley county. Mrs. Haskell being a first cousin of Mrs. Barr had perhaps something to do with inducing the latter and husband to come west. At any rate the Barrs arrived in the Valley in 1874. For a year or so Mr. Barr worked for the government at Fort Hartsuff. Now and later he

James Barr.

was one of the chief government freighters between Fort Hartsuff and Fort Niobrara. In 1875 he filed on a pre-emption three miles southeast from Burwell, first held by George McAnulty of Scotia. This together with some additional land comprises the comfortable Barr farm of today. The author has had the privilege to read some of the numerous letters which have passed between Mr. Barr and men high in army and governmental affairs, and from it he feels free to state that had Mr. Barr been so inclined he might today have been in high office. But he was content to be a plain Scotchman. He has always taken active part in politics and could have held important offices had he wished. Thus he refused the nomination of representative from his district. As commissioner of Wheeler county just before its division, he drafted the petition for the organization of Garfield county and suggested the name which it came to bear.

DEAFENBAUGH, J. A.—first saw the light of day in Tuscaroras county, Ohio, on July 4, 1846. Evidently he was pleased with the celebration for here he spent the first 29 years of his life. However, in 1875 he decided to cast his lot in Illinois, only to move again April 1878, to Garfield county, Nebraska. Here he took a homestead in the Loup Valley about three miles from where Burwell now is. In the winter of the following year he took unto himself a wife in the person of Miss Rose M. Schreier of Illinois. In 1903 they sold their old homestead and moved to their present farm. Mr. Deafenbaugh is an energetic farmer and has a beautiful place.

DRAVER, WILLIAM—comes from a country from which we receive many of our most reliable citizens. He was born April 13, 1840, on the Isle of Westray off the coast of Scotland. Here he received his education and remained till the age of twenty-eight. In 1861 he was married to Miss Ann Randal. His parents coming to the United States, he came with them and they all located in West county, Iowa, remaining there five years. Mr. Draver is one of the earliest settlers of Garfield county, coming here in 1873. He still lives on the old homestead. When one learns that he and his children now own about twenty-six hundred acres of land, they are tempted to forget the early privations endured by Mr. Draver's family—poverty, drought, and sickness—all met with true Scotch fortitude which must characterize one who overcomes.

FREELAND, TRUMAN—"was born in Rock Island county, Illinois, on February 22, 1852. His parents were among the pioneers of northern Illinois. Mr. Freeland assisted in the construction of the first bridge thrown over the waters of the Platte in the state of Nebraska. He acted as lead chainman in the original survey of what is now Custer and Loup counties. He built the first actual settler's residence (a dugout) constructed in the valley of the North Loup river above Haskell Creek; and his nearest neighbor on the river valley was then twenty miles away. He was the second settler of what is now Garfield county (Mr. C. H. Jones having preceded him a few days.) He carried the first United States mail brought into what is now Garfield county. He cut and hewed the logs for the first school house built in the county, and on his pre-emption was broken the first sod turned in Garfield county. He built the first frame residence in the county constructed of lumber shipped from the East, and hauled the lumber from Grand Island, a distance of nearly eighty miles. Mr. Freeland is an author of no mean ability, his writings having appeared in some of the leading publications of Nebraska and other states. He is also the author of a volume of poems soon to appear in print. He is decidedly a man of peace and never took any prominent part in the various conflicts with Indians in the early settlement of his neighborhood nor did he ever lose anything by them, except once when they stole his coat while he was felling a tree a few rods away. Mr. Freeland was married in 1874 to Miss Jane Russell of Rock Island county, Illinois. Mrs. Freeland taught the first school held in what is now Garfield and Wheeler counties. Mr. and Mrs. Freeland are the oldest residents now residing within the boundaries of Garfield county and have witnessed all the changing conditions from the days when the buffalo, elk, deer and antelope roamed over the prairies and woodlands to the time when all these have passed away and given place to modern civilization.

Truman Freeland.

GROSS, ALEXANDER—is a native of Poland in which state he was born in 1855. He lived here 18 years and then sailed to New

York. He went from one place to another for the first three years after coming to this country. In 1875 he arrived in Hall county and the next year moved up the valley to Valley county. He lived here till 1901 when he bought a farm in Garfield county only a short distance from Burwell. Mr. Gross is a successful farmer.

HEMMETT, TOM—was born in Niagara county, New York, March 9, 1850. While yet a lad of five years he removed with his parents to Pelican county, Michigan, where he grew to manhood. In the early '70s a number of neighbors had moved out west and several had reached the Loup. The western fever seized young Hemmett and we soon find him making his way thither too. Early in 1875 he arrived on the North Loup and filed a pre-emption in the timber on Jones' Canyon, just above the claim of his old Michigan neighbor, C. H. Jones. He later took a homestead in the valley, a place which has developed into one of the most productive and beautiful farms in this part of the state. Mr. Hemmett early became identified with Loup history. He played his part in the early Indian skirmishes and took quite a part in the county seat drama. He has for years been actively engaged in politics. When Wheeler county was divided in 1884 he was clerk of the county, but as his interests were in the new Garfield county he resigned his office. In 1904 he was elected clerk of Garfield county, serving three consecutive terms. After a brief interregnum he was again elected to the office, this time as a Populist. Mr. Hemmett has lived through more actual history than most men in his county.

Tom Hemmett.

JOHNS, W. C.—one of the citizens to whom we point with pride is a native of Green county, Wisconsin, born there forty-two years ago. In 1878, he came with his parents to what is now Garfield county. His early manhood was uneventful, being spent chiefly in receiving a good education in the public schools of Wisconsin and

Settlers of the "Trail of the Loup" (Bios)

Nebraska. In 1892 Mr. Johns was married to Miss Anna Beauchamp of Fort Hartsuff, Nebraska. He was for some time a teacher and also a farmer and rancher He is half owner of the grocery of Johns & Mitchell. The people have shown their appreciation of him by electing him to be sheriff of Wheeler county before the organization of Garfield county, as county superintendent and county treasurer. He is now serving his second term in that capacity. He is a Republican.

MESSENGER, H. A.—was born in Wisconsin in 1853. He lived here until May 1874, when he started toward Nebraska with ox teams. He arrived in Garfield county about two months later and took up his home just north of Burwell at the place where he yet resides. He is a farmer by occupation and has spent his whole life in following this kind of work. He is one of Garfield county's oldest settlers and has been closely connected with its history throughout all its stages of growth. He was a member of the old militia of which R. P. Alger was captain.

ROBKE, FREDERICK—has surely had a varied experience. He was born in Germany in 1834 where he lived until twenty-four years old. As a young man he spent four years of his life as a soldier, taking active part in the early war between Prussia and Bavaria. His occupation while in the old country was that of a wagon maker, which work he followed for a number of years after he had come to the United States. In 1868 he arrived in the land of his adoption and located his home in Chicago. In 1870 he made a trip to Colorado but returned to Chicago six months later. In 1873 he moved to Nebraska and settled on his present home about three and one-half miles from Burwell. Since coming to this Valley he has been a farmer.

Frederick Robke.

SMITH, MRS. M.—is another of those sturdy people who though born in a foreign land came to this country and made themselves a home. She was born in Scotland and came to Iowa in 1858. Here she lived till 1873 when she moved to Nebraska and settled in Garfield county. In 1871 she married a farmer by the name of Smith. In 1884 they moved into Burwell and have run a boarding house ever since. Mr. Smith died in 1891 but his wife has shown her ability as a business woman by continuing the business in a very successful way.

WEBSTER, FRANK A.—Among the early "Trailers of the Loup" who have since moved to other communities none is more worthy of mention than Frank A. Webster. Mr. Webster was born in Crawford, Pennsylvania, in April 1852. When but three years old he moved with his parents to Adams county, Wis. Here he grew to manhood and learned the printer's trade. In April 1873, he came to Omaha and accepted a position with the *Omaha Bee*. Here he remained only till the following fall when he came to the Loup Valley. Later western Burwell was platted on a part of his old homestead. For several years Mr. Webster was engaged in newspaper work in central Nebraska; among these papers was the *Howard County Advocate*. In 1878 he married Miss Ella M. Bowen. The Websters moved to Rathdrum, Idaho, several years ago where they still make their home.

WOODS, WILLIAM—has come a long way to find this garden spot on the Loup River. He was born in Surrey county, England, November 28, 1833. However, being attracted by the greater possibilities in a new country he came to Canada on May 6, 1857, and located about fourteen miles west of Toronto. Mr. Woods then moved to the United States in 1856. He has since lived in several different states, New York, Wisconsin, Iowa and Nebraska among others. In 1865 he enlisted in the Union Army and served till the end of the war. Mr. Woods came to Garfield county in 1874 where with the exception of a couple of years he has since resided. In 1878 he homesteaded the farm on which he now lives.

Greeley County

BEEBE, Dr. J. B.—One of the most prominent figures on the Loup river from '71 to '77 was "Doc" Beebe. He came to the North Loup Valley in 1871 and for years "Beebe's Ranch" was one of the best known places in the Valley. His wife and charming daughter Susie were notable pioneer women. In 1890 Mr. Beebe went to Oregon where he died a few years later.

BILYEU, J. W.—was born September 20, 1841, in Clinton county, Ill. When he was twelve years of age his parents moved to

Bond county, Iowa, where Mr. Bilyeu grew to manhood. On August 12, 1862, he enlisted as a private in the 130th Illinois Infantry. He was present at the siege of Vicksburg. Upon his discharge in August 1865, be returned to Bond county. On March 22, 1866, he married Miss E.C. File of Bond county. In the fall of 1877 he came to the Loup country and homesteaded near Scotia. In 1904 he purchased property in Scotia where he has since lived.

DAVIS, MANSELL—One of the very first settlers in Greeley county was Mansell Davis. He was born in Jamestown, New York, in 1848 and resided there till 1867, when he moved to Dakota, Wisconsin. While in New York he was engaged in mercantile pursuits. His western life has, however, been that of farmer. When in 1871 the Dakota Seventh-Day Baptists commenced casting about for new homes Mr. Davis became a member of the second or voluntary committee to explore the west. Thus he came to the Loup and became one of the first six to file on claims in Greeley county. In those early days Mr. Davis took quite an active part in politics. Thus he was the first surveyor of Greeley county, and later served in the capacity of county superintendent and county supervisor. At the present time he lives on his fine farm three miles southeast of North Loup.

FARELL, GEORGE—was born in Columbus, Indiana, January 10, 1857. In 1870 his parents moved to Caldwell county, Missouri, only to remove to Howard county, Nebraska, the following year, having filed on their homestead the previous year. Though only a boy he and a friend went up near Kent and squatted on some land there. However, being forced off his land in 1874 he returned home and in 1877 homesteaded his present farm. The same year he married Miss Emma Bixby. In the fall of 1882 they moved to Scotia only to return to the farm four years later.

FISH, ALCIE P.—The man who has the distinction of being the first settler in Greeley county was Mr. Alcie P. Fish. He was born February 18, 1822, near Brockport, New York. When he was 12 years old his father died and he was compelled to shift for himself. In March 1843, he married Esther E. Williams near the Niagara Falls. In 1848 they moved to Loraine county, Ohio, where their son Elihu B. Fish was born. Elihu is the only survivor of four children. In 1850 Mr. A. P. Fish came to Fond du Lac county, Wis. In 1861 he enlisted in the First Wisconsin Cavalry where he served till his discharge in November 1864. In October 1871, he came to Greeley and pre-empted. His son followed the next spring and homesteaded one mile north of his present residence. Mr. Alcie P. Fish was one of the first county commissioners. Indeed, the first election was held in his house. His son was first county clerk of Greeley county. In the fall of 1879 the younger Fish married Miss Julia McMillan. The father moved to Scotia in 1887 and died three years later.

GARDNER, ANDREW—was born in Buffalo, N. Y., in 1849. When but a child he moved to Green Bay, Wis., where he lived till 1861. At this time he changed his residence to Fond du Lac, Wis., where he lived until he came to Nebraska in 1878. Mr. Gardner has always been a farmer, although in early days he used to spend the winter trapping. He worked on his farm about eight miles southeast of Scotia until 1904 when he retired from active labor and moved to town.

GILLESPIE, A. J.—Andrew J. Gillespie, Sr., the grand old patriarch of the Loup, filled his hundredth year June 4, 1905. He is still remarkably hale and hearty for a man of his years. This wonderful good health he ascribes to the thirty four years he has lived in Nebraska "where people stay young longer than anywhere else on earth." Mr. Gillespie's name has long been associated with the North Loup Valley to which he came early in 1871. He first settled near Elba where he operated quite a ranch. His herd of cattle was the first to fatten on the grasses of the Loup. He also took the first contract to carry the United States mail up the North Loup valley, the route being fully seventy miles long. Often he drove the stage in person but never did his passengers dream that the man who guided his team with such skill over the difficult route had long filled his three score and ten. Mr. Gillespie was born in Kentucky, June 4, 1805, near the place where Abraham Lincoln first saw light four years later. Like Lincoln he spent his early manhood in Illinois, where he married Temperance Lee Bankston, daughter of Colonel Bankston, a life-long friend and comrade of Lincoln. Thirteen children were born to them, of whom twelve reached middle age. In 1836 the family moved to Iowa where they remained for many years. In 1871, at an age when most men are preparing to spend their declining years in peace, he sold his home near Dubuque and came to Nebraska. He became a great hunter and soon attracted the attention of leading plainsmen, who have ever held him in the highest esteem. At the age of seventy-five he is known to have killed deer at a distance of more than three hundred yards. The centenarian is tall and supple, showing in his carriage but slight indications of the burden of a hundred years of active life. His long line of descendants inherit his fine physique and remarkable stamina.

Thus his seventh son, Joe, won the trying horse race of many hundred miles from Chadron, Neb., to Chicago, when already past middle life. He has a remarkable lot of descendants living—numbering in all 172 souls. Of these nine are his own children, seventy-seven are grand-children, eighty great grand-children, and six great great grand-children. At a grand public celebration held at Scotia in honor of his hundredth birthday, in the neighborhood of a hundred descendants assembled to do the old man honor, and eight hundred guests were lunched and drank to his health and many happy years yet to come.

GRIFFITH, COL. B. F.—was born in Monroe county, New York, in 1845. When but five years old his parents moved to Pennsylvania which became his home. In August 1861, he enlisted in Co. H, 105th Pennsylvania Infantry and as a member of that regiment he fought through four long years. He certainly did his part in this great rebellion, having fought in many of the greatest battles of the war, Fair Oaks, Seven Pines, Second Bull Run, Antietam, Fredericksburg, Chancellorsville, Wilderness and Gettysburg. In the last named of these battles he was severely wounded in no less than three places and afterwards spent sixteen months in the hospital. After having been discharged he returned to Pennsylvania where he lived till 1878 when he moved to this valley. Mr. Griffith is a lawyer, having been admitted to the bar in 1882. He has twice been elected county attorney of Greeley county. His home is in Scotia.

Col. B. F. Griffith.

HILLMAN, REV. GEORGE—came to the North Loup Valley in April 1872, and settled in Greeley county. On May 10, 1872, he preached a sermon in the house of John Vanskike. Captain Munson sent an armed escort to guard the congregation from Indians. The first Methodist church ever organized in the Loup Valley was organized at the Hillman home, also the first Sabbath school. The first general election was held in his home on October 8, 1872 at which time he was elected county judge, being of course the first judge of Greeley county. Rev. Hillman was born in Banwell, Somersetshire, England, September 17, 1829; came to America in 1848; lived in Iowa until 1872 when he came to Nebraska. He was married to Miss Hannah Jenkins in 1853. Rev. Hillman and his good wife are now living near Scotia. They are in good health and still enjoy living. Mr. Hillman still preaches occasionally. The old settlers hold them in love and esteem, remembering the long years of right living this good couple have spent here in the North Loup Valley.

KELLOGG, JOHN G.—the minnesinger of the Loup, was born in Lake county, Illinois, January 15, 1846, where he grew to manhood and got all the schooling he ever had. Here he farmed and composed rhymes. When twenty-three years old he set his face westward and came to Platte county, Nebraska. Here he lingered till August 1871, when in company with Shepard, Scott and Stewart, pioneers spoken of elsewhere, he set out for the North Loup Valley. On the 7th day of September he selected his claim in Greeley county, lying above present-day Scotia. Mr. Kellogg was one of the organizers of Greeley county and became its first county superintendent. On January 30, 1879, he married Belle Scott, one of the earliest women to come into the Loup, who is more than usually conversant with all topics pertaining to early frontier life. They have five children living.

McANULTY, GEORGE W.—was born at Latrobe, Pennsylvania, in 1853. He lost both of his parents at an early age, his father losing his life in his country's defense during the Civil War, and his mother dying within the same year. At the age of eighteen he went to Texas and for the first time saw the great West. After some time spent in the Lone Star state he went to Illinois and thence back to Pennsylvania. But he had gotten his taste for the plains. Accordingly he came back and arrived in Nebraska and the North Loup Valley in 1873. He settled on the James Barr farm near Burwell. When Fort Hartsuff was established he helped to build some of the structures there. Later he enlisted in Captain Munson's company—Co. C, 9th U.S. Infantry—which was ordered into active service a few days after his enlistment. The company joined the rest of the 9th Regiment at Fort Laramie, Wyoming Territory. The Great Sioux War was on and the boys were on the frontier. Mr. McAnulty was with General Crook in the terrible campaign of 1876, and returned with his company to Fort Hartsuff two years later and was there discharged. He married Miss Lillie Moore in March 1880, and settled near Ord. In 1882 he moved to Scotia where he has since resided. He has three children, two sons, Fred and John, and one daughter, Louise. Mr. McAnulty is a believer in the North Loup Valley. Never, even during the darkest years, has his faith in it faltered.

MOORE, DAVID—one of the early settlers of Greeley county was born in Ohio in 1827. He came of good Quaker stock. His early life was spent in Indiana and Illinois. As a boy he knew Lincoln and often heard him address a jury in the old court house at Delavan, Ill. Later his parents settled in eastern Iowa, near Wyoming. Here he met and married Louise Standish in 1848. He served throughout the Civil War in Co. K, 24th Iowa Volunteer Infantry. He was with his regiment in some of the hardest fought battles of the war. He came to Nebraska June 1873, and settled in Greeley county taking as a homestead the northeast quarter of section 10-17-12, one mile east of Scotia where he resided for twenty years. In 1893 he moved to Scotia. He was most public spirited and untiring in his efforts to build up this part of the state. He was admitted to the bar in 1881 and practiced law for some years. In early days his home was noted for its generous hospitality and for many years David Moore was known as the friend of the settler. He died November 25, 1904, at his home in Scotia. His wife and three children survived him. His oldest son Horace Moore died June 23, 1905. Those still living are Dr. Mila S. Moore of Taylor, Neb., and Mrs. George McAnulty of Scotia.

NURTON, E. A.—of Scotia is a much travelled man. He was born in Dubuque county, Iowa, February 19, 1856, and here he spent the first twenty-one years of his life. In September 1, 1877, he and his father bought one and one-half sections of railroad land five miles from Scotia. In the fall he returned to Iowa and the next year worked his father's farm. However, in the fall of 1878 he returned to his land in Nebraska. In 1879 he again went back to Iowa and worked for nine months for his uncle. Then again he returned to Greeley county. On February 6, 1883, he married Miss Emma L. Woodward of Dubuque, Iowa. In 1886 he moved to Ord only to leave in 1888. The next year however he sold his farm property and moved to Scotia where he lives at present.

PRIDEMORE, JEREMIAH—was born in Lawrence county, Indiana, April 24, 1833. When but a child his parents moved to Clay county, Illinois, where he grew to manhood. In March 1859, he married Miss Sarah File of Bond county, Iowa. In 1861 he enlisted as a private in the 48th Illinois Infantry. He saw much active service and engaged in the battles of Ft. Donalson, Shiloh, Vicksburg, Chattanooga and Atlanta. After his discharge in September 1864, he returned to Bond county, Iowa, where he lived till he came to Greeley county in 1877. He still lives on his old homestead.

SAUTER, GEORGE C.—was born at Wittenberg, Germany, and came to America when but three years old. His parents spent some time at Detroit and Chicago, but later removed to Indiana where the boy grew to manhood. He came to Fish Creek in Greeley county in 1877 and homesteaded there. He married Anna Brandt of Indiana. Of his children none are living. The Sauters remained on the farm till 1893 when they moved to Scotia where they are now nicely located.

SCOTT, WILLIAM—Two of the first among early settlers in Greeley county were William Scott and his son, L. E. Scott. William Scott was born in Fairfield county, Conn., July 22, 1823. As he grew to manhood he learned the carpenter trade. He was married September 6, 1849. His eldest and at present only living son, L. C. Scott, was born in October of the next year. In 1855 the Scotts came to Freeport, Iowa, only to return ten years later to Connecticut. In 1866 they moved to Rosendale, Fon du Lac county, Wisconsin. In the spring of 1872 L. E. Scott moved on to Greeley county and was followed by his father in the fall of the same year.

William Scott.

STEWART, ALZA M.—The first settler in Valley county was Alza M. Stewart who came to this county in August 1871. Mr. Stewart was born in Binghampton, New York, May 27, 1843. When a small child his parents moved to Waukegan, Ill., where he lived till 1869. During this time he served for three years in the army. In April 1869, he came to Platte county, Nebraska, where he lived till he came to Valley county. In January 1872, he took out papers homesteading the first farm in Valley county. In 1874 he moved to his timber claim

Settlers of the "Trail of the Loup" (Bios)   301

adjoining his homestead but being in Greeley county. On July 4, 1874, he married Miss Mamie Burdick.

SHEPARD, ALONZO—is one of the first four settlers of the North Loup Valley. He was born in Canton, Mass., in 1836. When but six years old his parents moved to Illinois where he lived till 1867. At this time he decided to come to Nebraska and after spending six months in Omaha finally took up a pre-emption claim in Platte county. In the fall of 1871 he came to this valley and took a homestead in Greeley county whither he moved with his family in April 1872. Mr. Shepard was married in 1866 and to the couple but one child was born. Mr. Shepard was a member of the first militia but was never engaged in any fights against the Indians.

Alonzo Shepard.

VANSKIKE SETTLEMENT—No history of the North Loup Valley would be complete without mention of the Vanskike settlement. Three brothers, John, James and Jefferson, with their brother-in-law, Joe Conway came to the valley in the spring of 1872. They settled in Howard county, just below the Greeley county line. They were all typical pioneers. They cheerfully bore their part in the early years and made many friends. Their homes were noted for hospitality.

WALLACE, VIOLA—The first white woman in Greeley county was Mrs. Viola Wallace, wife of James L. Wallace. She arrived with her husband in December 1871. They settled on the creek which today bears their name, "Wallace Creek." A brother of Mrs. Wallace, George Wallace, came with them, taking an adjoining claim. Mrs. Wallace was a lady of education and refinement, born and educated in the southern city of Norfolk, Virginia. Mrs. Wallace was a brave little woman and bore the great change from the luxurious home in the city to a settler's cabin on the extreme frontier with wonderful fortitude. Mrs. Wallace (now Mrs. Thomas Grandberry) lives at Long Pine, Neb.

WEEKES, WILLIAM BYRON—grain and live stock dealer, Scotia, Greeley county, was born in Illinois near the city of Cairo, November 5, 1859. He is of English ancestry, and his father, Thomas Weekes, was a soldier in both the Mexican and the Civil Wars, was mortally wounded at Hartsville, Tennessee, December 1, 1862, and was taken prisoner by the Confederates, and soon after died in Libby prison. The mother of Mr. Weekes was in maidenhood Elizabeth Lindridge. After the death of her husband she cared for her children the best she could, and gave them the advantage of a common school education. Before he was sixteen years old, with an elder brother, Charles Weekes, William came to Nebraska and settled upon a homestead in Greeley county. This was in the fall of 1875, and since then Greeley county has been his permanent home. He was successful as a farmer and a stock grower, and for some years has been as successful as a dealer in stock and grain. In the quarter of a century that he has resided in Greeley county, he has seen the country about him converted into rich farms, and railroads and towns built up. He has carved his own fortune by industriously working, and is in independent circumstances. In the matter of politics he has always been a Republican. From 1886 to 1890 he served as treasurer of Greeley county, and in 1891 was one of the Board of County Supervisors. He is a Mason of the Royal Arch degree and is also a member of the Woodmen and the Tribe of Ben Hur. He is a member of the Methodist Episcopal church. He was married June 12, 1881, to Nora A. Whitehead, and has six children—Charles W., now a physician in Scotia, Edwin and Edgar, twins, Chester, Cecil and Edith Weekes.

Loup County

BROMWICH, URIAH—Mr. Uriah Bromwich was born in Chicago, Ill., in 1853. Upon the death of his father six months later, his mother went to Canada, soon however to return to Chicago. She next spent several years in southern Wisconsin, landing in Minnesota in 1858. Here Mr. Bromwich grew to manhood. He married Miss Elnora Fay in 1876. In October of 1878 he came to Loup county and pre-empted. He then homesteaded just across the line in Custer county in 1880. From Mr. Bromwich's home one has a fine view of the Loup Valley for miles.

CLARK, WILLIAM A.—is a native of Pennsylvania, where he was born in May 1854. He spent the first twenty-five years of his life in Juniata and LaSalle counties of that state, though he has lived the rest of his life in Nebraska. In 1879 he took up a claim in Loup county about five miles west of Taylor where he still lives. In 1898 he went to Burwell and spent two years in the implement business there, but he sold out at the end of that time and returned to his Loup county home. He was elected to the office of county treasurer of Loup county in the fall of 1903.

COPP, CALVIN L.—was born in Tioga county, Pennsylvania, in 1848. He left the old Quaker state when eight years old, and saw life in Missouri and Iowa before he came to Nebraska in 1869. He married Elizabeth Roblyer of York county and came to Loup county in 1879. He has spent twenty-five years near Almeria and Moulton farming and is now cozily homed in Taylor. Mr. Copp has yet large landed interests in the county. He has been a lifelong Republican, though he has never been actively engaged in politics. Mr. Copp never grows weary telling of the strenuous days when he had to haul whole loads of cedar posts to Grand Island to exchange for a sack of flour and a plug of tobacco.

CROUGHELL, THOMAS—was born in Hartford county, Connecticut, in December 1854. Here he lived until 1878 when he moved to Nebraska and settled in Loup county, about two miles west from Taylor. While in Connecticut he worked in a cotton factory where all kinds of cotton fabrics were made. But since coming to Nebraska he has successfully devoted his time to farming and stockraising.

FAY, STEPHEN—is one of the many men who believe in the future of the Loup county sand-hills. He was born in Wisconsin, near Fond du Lac, in 1863, though raised in Vivian county, Minnesota. He farmed in Freeborn county, Minnesota, many years. In 1879 he came to Loup county and settled two miles south of Taylor. He was a young man then and to make a way for himself had to become a "cowpuncher" on the Snake River range. He married Rosetta Caldwell in 1884 and has four children. At present he owns 400 acres of pasture and hay lands north of Taylor where he keeps his herd of cattle.

GARD, DAVID A.—was born in Morris county, N. J., and at the age of 18 years was employed in a store at Dover. At the breaking out of the war he was the first in the city to enlist. He was a member of Company B Second Regiment, N. J. Vol. Infantry, and was attached to Gen. Phil. Kearney's famous Jersey Brigade, and participated in all its battles from first Bull Run to the fall of Petersburg. He received five wounds, and was left on the field at South Mountain, being badly wounded while charging a battery. He was captured May 6, 1864, in the Wilderness and, with six of his comrades, made his escape the following day. He was married in 1866 and removed to Iowa, where he worked at the carpenter's trade for seven years. In 1876 he moved to Grand Island, Neb., and one year later, to a homestead in the unorganized territory now known as Loup county, then 100 miles from the nearest railroad. He was mainly instrumental in organizing the county and was its first clerk. He was one of the most successful homestead farmers of that region. On account of poor health, caused by injuries received in the army, he abandoned farming, and in 1889 removed to Ord, and for four years conducted the Transit House. In 1894 he was elected mayor of Ord on the anti-license ticket. For some years Mr. Gard has been one of the chief promoters of the American Order of Protection, a very flourishing fraternal insurance order. At the present he resides in Lincoln.

HENRY, G. S.—first saw the light of day in Lycoming county, Pennsylvania, on the 17th day of April 1873. He came with his parents to Adair county, Iowa, at the age of four and lived there until his removal to Loup county, Nebraska, in February 1884. Mr. Henry's education has been received in the schools at Cromwell and Fontanelle, Iowa, and of Loup county, Nebraska. His marriage to Miss Myrtle B. Messersmith occurred May 26, 1904. He is serving his first term as county clerk of Loup county, being elected to that office by his chosen party, the Republican.

HOOPER, HENRY—is surely a man of varied experiences. He was born in Ohio in 1843. Here he lived until 1867 when he moved to Illinois. He stayed here for about four years as a farmer when he moved to Nebraska, where he spent the next few years of his life as a hunter and trapper. He finally found his way to Loup county where he took to farming. Mr. Hooper saw considerable service in the U.S. army during the Civil War. He enlisted in July 1862, in Co. F, 90th Ohio Volunteers. He served for three years, being mustered out in July 1865. He engaged in the battles of Prairieville, Stone River, Chickamauga, and was severely wounded in the battle of Kennesaw Mountain.

ROBLYER, JACOB—was born in Pennsylvania in 1846. He went to Iowa in 1867 whence he moved to eastern Nebraska three years later. In 1879 he moved up the Loup Valley to his present home two miles southeast from Almeria. He was married in 1872 and has lived the life of a farmer ever since. Mr. Roblyer enlisted in Co. C, 171st Pennsylvania Volunteers in 1861, and after serving two years was mustered out in July 1863. In 1864 he re-enlisted in the 1st New York Light Artillery, from which he was given an honorable discharge in July 1865.

STEPHENS, WILLIAM—was born near Rockford, Ill., in 1849. When but five years old his parents moved to LaSalle county where he lived until 1878 At this time he moved to Loup county, Nebraska, and settled on the farm that he now works. He was married in the spring of 1888. Mr. Stephens has gone through many experiences in this valley, some of which were very unpleasant. He has seen the blizzards and hailstorms of early years, to say nothing of his experiences with Doc. Middleton's gang of horsethieves.

WILLIAMS, T. W.—Among the earliest of Loup county's pioneers was Mr. T. W. Williams, who like some others, had come a long way to find his present home. He was born in Wales, February 7, 1841. When but a lad of 13 years, he came to the old historic Schuylkill county, Pennsylvania. Here he grew to manhood and, on March 29, 1862, he married Miss Mary Lewis of Pottsville, Penn. In the summer of 1865 they came to Missouri and for nine years lived in Mason county. They then came to York county. The following year they went to Hamilton county, arriving in Loup county in 1876. Here they homesteaded their present farm. They have had thirteen children, seven of which are now living.

T. W. Williams family.

WOODS, L. W.—was born in Farmington, Iowa, in 1859. When but four years of age his parents moved to Missouri where he remained until 1875. At this time he moved to Nebraska and settled in Burt county. He came to this valley in 1877 and took up his home in Custer county, bordering on the Loup county line. He has lived in this place ever since as a tiller of the soil.

XXI

The Men and Women Who Are Making the History of the Loup Valley

In this section *The Trail of the Loup* is rounded off and completed. Former chapters have told the story of the first-comers, of those who blazed the trail. Their work is practically at an end. The energy and enterprise of a later generation is even now transforming the pioneer hamlet and village into the modern city. Embryo cities are indeed springing up in the Loup Valley. Their ultimate growth and importance will depend to a marked extent on the ability and enterprise of the men who are building them. We have been fortunate in this respect. The business men of Loup, Garfield, Valley and Greeley counties are, upon the whole, self-made men who have kept in touch with the world and its progress, who, indeed, have ever kept in the vanguard of its progress. The following pages tell the life-stories of a majority of the men and firms which are making our history today.

Ord

BAILEY BROTHERS—In course of years many of our prosperous farmers have turned their attention to breeding high grade cattle, and feeding these for the top market. One of the most successful firms of this kind in the Loup Valley is Bailey Brothers, whose fine stock-farm lies across the river and in sight of Ord. The Bailey brothers—Harry and George—are sons of Daniel Cooley Bailey, one of the fathers of the Valley. The brothers were both born in New York state in the early 50s and moved with their parents to Wisconsin in 1855. In the summer of 1872 the Baileys arrived in Springdale from Wisconsin. The next spring they moved onto the excellent farmsteads which they have done so much to improve down through the years. The brothers are expert farmers and stock raisers. Of late years—indeed beginning in 1890—they have taken to raising pure blooded shorthorn cattle. Their idea is that it is just as cheap to raise high grade cattle as scrubs, and on the market they are sure to bring better prices. Indeed it is a very ordinary matter for this firm to sell their sleek, corn-fed steers on the Omaha or Chicago markets and get the very top prices for them.

BARNES & McGREW—Charlie Barnes is one of the old-timers in Ord. Indeed he has been in the barber business here since 1884, thus laying a just claim to being the oldest established barber in the county. With him is associated the popular young barber, Clayton E. McGrew, who learned his trade from Mr. Barnes years ago when the latter operated his shop in the old Hotel D'America. The firm is located on the north side of the public square, where it owns its own building. Absolute proficiency has built up for the firm a large and evergrowing patronage.

BARTUNEK BROTHERS & NELSON—is the title of one of the newest firms to open business in Ord. Anton and Paul Bartunek had carried on a prosperous business at Walbach where they catered to a satisfied public for seven years. Prior to this Anton had worked in the largest business house in St. Paul and there gained invaluable experience. The Bartuneks are Bohemians by birth. Their early and commercial education was procured in the old homeland, which they left in 1883. Gus H. Nelson, the third member of the firm, is a Scandinavian by birth and was formerly engaged in the general merchandise business at Greeley Center. The firm is located in the fine new Misko block on the north side of the public square. Here they have a store room 24 × 80 feet large, well stored with general merchandise. Fine drygoods and shoes are one of their specialties. They are now doing a $40,000 business and face a bright future indeed.

Anton Bartunek.

BLESSING, ALVIN—who has lately resigned his position as county clerk of Valley county to accept the position of assistant cashier in the First National Bank at Ord was born December 11, 1871, at LaGrange, Michigan, from which place he came with his parents to the so-called "Michigan Settlement" in Valley county, in 1880. He has taught school and farmed, making a success of both. Four years ago he entered politics and was elected county clerk on the Republican ticket. Mr. Blessing is quite a landowner and has lately completed one of the most comfortable and commodious homes in Ord.

BOND, ANGIE R.—the only exclusive milliner in Ord, was born in Michigan in 1874. She came with her parents to Valley county in 1877 and spent some years in the so-called Michigan colony in what is now Michigan township. She served her apprenticeship as a milliner in the employ of Mrs. Lee, an oldtime business woman of Ord. The next ten years she spent in the employ of G. W. Milford and Frank Mallory. When she started in business for herself she had a millinery experience of twelve years. Her first venture was in Cedar Rapids, Nebraska, from whence she came to Ord in 1903. She carries a very excellent stock of goods and is known up and down the Valley for her fair dealing.

Angie R. Bond.

BOTTS, HOMER—was born in Iowa in 1873. He learned his trade of carpentry, in his home state and when he came to Ord in 1897, it did not take him long to make a reputation as a builder and contractor. Fine buildings constructed by him in Ord and Burwell attest to his unusual skill in his chosen profession.

CAPRON, JOE H.—the Ord real estate dealer, may justly lay claim to being one of the old-timers. His early history, told in the chapter on village organization, needs no repetition here. From quartermaster's clerk at Ft. Hartsuff he became editor of the *Valley County Journal*, which he continued to publish till July 1887, when he sold the paper to C. C. Wolf. It is as a dealer in real estate, rental and abstract work that Mr. Capron has made a name for himself. During his long residence he has become acquainted with every part of the Loup Valley, its people, products, prices, etc., and as such is now in position to give immigrants and investors the benefit of his intimate knowledge. Mr. Capron, who has become a man of means, is just completing one of the finest residences in Ord.

CLEMENTS, ARTHUR A.—county attorney of Valley county and one of the most successful young attorneys in the Loup Valley, was born March 20, 1870, in Allegan county, Michigan, when he came to Ord in 1893. Here he became associated with his brothers, E. J. and E. P. Clements, of the law firm of Clements Brothers; first as a student apprentice, later as a partner in the business. As county attorney he is now in his second term. On January 28, 1900, he was married to Adelheid Reithardt. They have two children.

CORNELL BROS.—No more energetic and enterprising business men can be found anywhere than Cornell Brothers of Ord, dealers in hardware, tinware, stoves, plumbers materials, etc. The genesis of their business is indeed interesting. The firm name was originally F. W. Weaver & Co., who used to run a small hardware store in partnership with Hans C. Sorensen, at the southeast corner of the square. In November 1884, this firm was dissolved and F. W. Weaver moved into the old Cheeseborough brick east of the post office where he operated a successful store for many years. Finally ill health forced him to give up business and he was succeeded by Cornell Bros., who came here from Alliance, well schooled in the details of a successful hardware and tinware business. The firm early found their quarters in the Weaver brick too cramped for their growing business and were obliged to move into the much more commodious Perry building west of the postoffice. But even this place of business has proven too small to accommodate the large stock that the Cornells have found it expedient to carry. Two large warehouses in other parts of the city are now used to store the goods which they usually purchase by the car lot. In the main store is carried a well chosen stock of builder's materials, carpenter's and machinists' tools, cutlery, stoves and ranges, tin, copper and sheet iron goods in great variety. The work shop turns out all manner of tin work, including roofing and cornice work. The construction of pumps and windmills, and general plumbing are also important factors in this complete establishment. It is interesting to know that the volume of business for a single month during the summer of 1904 exceeded $11,000. Last year they purchased the Perry building, and now having added a complete farm machinery line of goods, have put up large warehouses to shelter the goods.

ERET, GEORGE C.—was born in 1874 at East Saginaw, Mich. His early schooling was procured at Red Cloud, Neb., where he came as a child. From earliest childhood he showed a marked talent for music, receiving his musical education at St. Louis. He is especially fine on the violin and band instruments, having been leader of bands at Shawnee, Okla., Oklahoma City, Curtis, Neb., and other places. Coming to Ord in 1897, he engaged in the barber business but left this to devote himself entirely to his loved music. He was married in 1899 to Miss Mary Masin, an accomplished musician. He has been director of the orchestra for three years and of the Ord band since 1904. He deals in pianos and also does piano tuning and regulating.

FACKLER & FLETCHER—The firm of Fackler & Fletcher, though comparatively new in Ord, is fast making a name for itself through square dealing and correct business methods. Samuel Fackler, the senior member of the firm, came to Ord in the fall of 1898 and engaged in the grocery business in a small way. He was then located where Mr. Stara's meat market now is. But the venture prospered from the first and Mr. Fackler had to seek a more commodious store building. This was found in the Woodbury building on the south side of the square. Mr. E. L. Collin became a member of the firm in 1902; he retired two years later, having sold his share to L. C. Fletcher. The reconstructed firm continued prosperous and again had to seek larger quarters. Accordingly they moved to the large Milford building where they are now located. At the present they are occupying a salesroom one hundred and ten feet in length and one of the most spacious warehouses in the city. Theirs is today the only exclusive grocery in Ord. The annual sales exceed $20,000.

FIRKINS, ALONZO J.—is one of our most successful stock breeders. He was born in DeKalb county, Illinois, in 1863, where he grew up and spent his early years, getting well acquainted with all the outs and ins of farm life. In 1883 he came to Valley county and possessed himself of the famous Cedar Lawn Farm, half a mile from Ord. Here he has occupied his time at farming, stock raising and breeding. While he has spent some time in raising Shropshire sheep and Poland China hogs, he now gives his time principally to raising and breeding pureblooded Hereford cattle. His herd at the present numbers some of the finest specimens in America and his stock is sought after by breeders from every part of the United States. Mr. Firkins has thus had orders all the way from South Carolina and Virginia. Mr. Firkins has become a man of more than ordinary means during his twenty-two years on the Loup. He owns among other things a large ranch—the Klondike—in Garfield county. He was for years manager of the Ord Hardware Company and has been a member and president of the Ord school board for many years.

FIRST NATIONAL BANK—The economic history of any section of our country may be read in the history of its financial institutions. That the Loup Valley has made remarkable progress down through the years is nowhere more clearly demonstrated than through a study of its banking houses. Of these the First National Bank of Ord came into existence as a private bank in 1880. It was rechartered as a national bank May 1, 1885, with a capital of $50,000. The organizers were J. H. Bell, D. C. Bell, H. A. Babcock, Wm. C. Wentz, J. C. Post, Geo. A. Percival and P. Mortensen. H. A. Babcock was elected president of the board, but resigned and J. H. Bell was elected in his stead. Mr. Babcock now became vice president, Geo. A Percival, cashier, and P. Mortensen, assistant cashier. In January 1887, Mr. Mortensen was elected president, an office which he yet fills. Mr. Percival resigned his post as cashier in December 1888, and was succeeded by Fred Bartlett who in turn was followed by W. E. Mitchell. The latter held the responsible trust till May 1891. His brother E. N. Mitchell released him, retiring in January 1896, to be succeeded by the present cashier, Everett M. Williams. Other officers are G. W. Mickelwait, vice-president, and Alvin Blessing, assistant cashier. The First National Bank was founded by men of exceptional financial ability and has from its inception had the confidence of the public. When financial storms came and swept over the country, the First National found no trouble in weathering them all. Much of this success may no doubt be traced to Mr. Mortensen, than whom there is no greater financier in Nebraska today. His rise in the commercial world has been little less than phenomenal. From a dugout on the prairie to office in the state capitol, all in the space of three decades is a record for any man to be proud of, and this is what the president of the First National has accomplished. The bank has always been conservative in business and yet at all times ready to extend aid and assist in the growth of commerce whenever consistent with safe banking principles. It has indeed been one of the greatest factors in the development of the Loup Valley. The steady growth of this institution can readily be gathered from a comparison of its financial statements published from time to time. Thus in July 1885, its loans and discounts amounted to $17,558.30, while today the same items foot up to $344,660.38; then the deposits reached $20,000.00, now $302,000.00.

GARD, GEORGE R.—Ord's genial dentist, is most decidedly a Loup Valley product, his entire life having been spent among us. He was born September 6, 1879, at Kent, Neb., a village between Taylor and Burwell, of which his father was one of the founders. Coming to Ord in 1887, he entered the public schools, continuing the education begun at Kent. Being eager to enter upon his professional life, he did not complete his high school course but, after first serving a brief apprenticeship in the offices of the leading dentists of Ord, matriculated in the Dental Department of the University of Omaha. He continued in school here from 1898 until 1901 when he received the degree of D. D. S. Immediately returning to Ord, he opened offices in the Mortensen block and is still in the same location, having there a fine suite of four rooms. He does not confine himself to practice in Ord but makes regular trips to Arcadia and North Loup. In April 1904, he was married to Miss Breezie Parks, a young lady accomplished in business and musical attainments. They have built a most beautiful and convenient residence in the western part of the city.

GREGORY, JOHN WILSON—proprietor of the well known Turtle Creek Stock Farm, was born in Marion county, Iowa, in 1860. He spent his youth and early manhood on the farm still owned by his father. Here he gained much of the training which later stood him so well in stead as the expert stock-raiser. He procured his early book learning, too, while on the old home farm. Mr. Gregory came to Valley county May 10, 1884, and ever since has been actively engaged in farming and stock-raising. In 1887 he bought the Chris Keller farm on lower Turtle Creek and converted it into a first class stock farm. He has been intimately connected with the hog-raising interests in this part of the state for many years. His specialty is pure bred swine. Indeed, he is the owner of the oldest herd of recorded Poland China Swine in Valley county. Mr. Gregory has made quite a name for himself in this field and his stock is everywhere in great demand. Although a busy man, he has found some spare time for politics. He belongs to the People's Independent Party, and is now serving his third term as supervisor from the first district. In 1897 he married Miss Mary Tucker. Mrs. Gregory, who was born in Effingham county, Illinois, came to Nebraska in 1887, and to Ord two years later. She attended the Ord High School and the Fremont Normal and taught in the Ord schools from 1896 to 1897. The Gregorys have two children—J. W. Jr., and Joseph.

GUDMUNDSEN, JUDGE HJALMAR—is a native of Denmark, though coming from a good old Iceland ancestry. He was born at Nysted, Denmark, May 27, 1860, where he spent the days of his youth. His early training came from the hand of private tutors who advanced him through the Danish Latin School course. In common with other young countrymen, he early became anxious to make a way for himself in the promised land—America. Accordingly he sailed for Quebec, which he reached in 1878. After spending a year in Canada he journeyed on to the United States. Five years were now spent in the regular army, U.S.A. Receiving an honorable discharge, Mr. Gudmundsen was so fortunate as to receive the superintendency of the Shoshone Indian Training School. This he held till Cleveland's first administration, when he resigned to give place to a Democratic appointee. In 1884 he married Miss Katie B. Jensen, of Shoshone. The family came to Ord in 1888 and has resided here ever since. Mrs. Gudmundsen died in 1902, leaving seven children living.

Judge Hjalmar Gudmundsen.

Mr. Gudmundsen has filled various positions of honor during the seventeen years spent in Valley county. He was deputy county clerk under several administrations, and has served both as assessor and treasurer of his township. When the Spanish American War broke out in 1898 he was captain of Co. B, 2nd Reg. N. N. G., and in that capacity marched his company to the front. The company did not however get beyond Chickamauga. In November 1903, he was elected county judge, an office which he fills with much credit to himself and his party.

HALDEMAN, F. D.—Dr. Frederick D. Haldeman was born October 2, 1859, in Muscatine county, Iowa. He received his early education at West Liberty High School and then matriculated at the

Iowa State University. From early boyhood had he decided upon medicine as his chosen profession. To gain his end he entered the office of Dr. W. S Gibbs, at Downy, Iowa. He took his first course of medical lectures at the Medical Department of the State University at Iowa City. The remaining two courses were taken at Omaha, in the new medical school. Dr. Haldeman graduated from this institution March 23, 1882, and had the honor of being the valedictorian of his class. He immediately located at Ord and has through the years built up a very large practice. By his profession he has been honored, being in 1896 elected president of the Nebraska State Medical Society. By his fellow townsmen he is considered one of the most substantial of professional men. Dr. Haldeman was married to Miss Olive A. Newbecker of Ottawa, Ill., January 14, 1885 Two children were born to them—Irma and Keene—the death of the former resulting after a long sick spell, Dec. 25, 1905.

F. D. Haldeman.

HONNOLD, A R.—One of the youngest of the successful members of the Ord bar is Arthur Rankin Honnold. His father came to Valley county in 1874 and settled in Mira Valley. Here Arthur was born in 1876. He has thus grown up in and with Valley county. His early education was gotten in the rural schools and the Ord High School, from which latter institution he graduated in

A. R. Honnold.

1898. After completing a course in the Grand Island Business College he was appointed state accountant of the Insane Hospital at Lincoln. Two years later he entered the law department of the University of Nebraska, graduating with the law class of 1904. The same year he was associated in law practice with Victor O. Johnson at Ord. October 1, 1904, Mr. Johnson retired from the firm, moving to Oklahoma. This left Mr. Honnold in sole possession. He has been very successful. As an evidence of this he has purchased the extensive law library of the late Judge Chas. A. Munn. Aside from his legal practice Mr. Honnold deals in real estate and writes insurance.

JONES, ALTA BELLE—was born February 11, 1877, in Warren county, Illinois. She moved to Missouri in 1879 and received her early education there. In 1887 she came to Valley county with her parents. She graduated from the Ord High School in the class of 1893 and immediately commenced teaching. Her experience in this, her chosen field covers three years in the rural schools, five years in the Ord schools and two years in the schools of Colorado. While a busy teacher she has neglected no opportunity for self improvement. Thus she has attended summer school at the University of Nebraska, at Drake University, and at schools in Grand Island and Fremont. She was elected county superintendent on the Republican ticket in 1903.

KOKES, JOHN—was born in Bohemia March 16, 1864. He attended school in his native country for some twelve years, two of which were spent in the Bohemian Real School. He came to the United States in 1880 and settled with his parents on a homestead in Michigan township, Valley county. He later moved to the White River country and homesteaded a farm there. After spending some years out west he settled on the sand flats. Here his wife died in 1901. He now entered politics and was elected sheriff. In 1903 he was reelected to this office.

KOUPAL & BARSTOW—It is safe to say that of the many firms doing business in our Valley, none have been more successful along legitimate lines than has Koupal & Barstow Lumber Company. Frank Koupal, who manages the local yard, is practically a Valley county product so far as his business career is concerned. Though born in Bohemia—January 29, 1865—his education was practically all procured in the country of his adoption. He appeared before the public first as a trusted employee in the Jaques Grain Company and in politics as county clerk between 1898 and 1900. William T. Barstow, who now resides at Lincoln, is a New Englander and came to Ord in the early '80s. He clerked in the old B. C. White store for a while; but his unusual ability was soon recognized by C. M. Jaques, the grain dealer, who first took him into his employ and later into partnership. The Koupal & Barstow Lumber Company is incorporated with a capital of $50,000 and owns and operates yards at Ord, Greeley Center, Sargent and Ericson. It carries in stock enormous quantities of building materials of all kinds and is through its accurate and businesslike methods rapidly attaining an enviable position among the leading lumber firms of the state.

MISKO, FRANK—was born in Bohemia in 1853. He came from very good ancestry there. His parents sent him to school at an early age and later apprenticed him in the harness business. Thus time passed till he was twenty years old. He now spent three years in the Austrian Army. He came to the United States in his early manhood and first sought a career in the great northwest. Thus he alternately followed his profession and farmed in Minnesota, North Dakota and Iowa. He married Miss Mary Rayman while in Minnesota. Of this union six children were born, of whom four are living. Mr. Misko and family arrived at Ord in 1882. Here he immediately launched in the harness business. In 1882 he built a small brick shop on the north side of the square. But his business rapidly increased obliging him to build the large two-story brick building where he is now located. In 1904 he further built a large double two story building on the north side of the square. Mr. Misko is enterprising and public spirited and has done very much indeed to build up Ord. As a dealer in harness and other leather goods he is known up and down the Valley for many miles. Thus he is known to make regular sales in Custer, Garfield, Sherman and Loup counties. Mr. Misko's success in a business way is attributable to honest methods and exceptional ability.

MORTENSEN, PETER—treasurer of the state of Nebraska, belongs to the hardy race which comes out of the peninsula of Jutland, Denmark, where he was born Oct. 8, 1844. He came to America in 1870 and worked in coal mines and iron works at and near Warrensburg, Missouri, for a year or more. In the spring of 1872 he came as one of the first Danish colony to Valley county and entered the northeast quarter of section 8, Town 19, Range 14 where he erected the famous first combination dugout-loghouse in the county. From the very first has he been before the public eye in one capacity and another. His career is worthy of careful study and emulation. In 1872 he walked barefoot the long distance from Ord to Dannebrog with a sackful of plowshares on his back, which needed sharpening. Today he is the treasurer of our great commonwealth; all this he has accomplished through common honesty, sound business sense and pure grit. He was county treasurer of Valley county from 1875 to 1884; then he was elected assistant cashier of the new First National Bank of Ord. He soon rose through the position of cashier to the presidency of the institution which he yet fills. He has ever been interested in the development of the Loup region and is extensively interested in its real estate and gives much attention to agriculture and stock raising. He was married February 16, 1878, to Jennie H. Williams of West Paw Paw, Illinois, and has one son, Crawford.

NEWBECKER, MINERVA M.—was born in Harrisburg, Pa. Her early education was obtained here, she being a graduate of Harrisburg Female Seminary. She taught in her native town till 1870 when she moved with her parents to Illinois where she continued as teacher in Ottawa. In 1889 she entered the Chicago Medical College of the Northwestern University. On receiving her degree in 1893, she became interne in Chicago Hospital for Women and Children, and later practiced her profession in Chicago. She was in Omaha one year and was most successful for over six years as woman physician in the State Asylum for insane at Lincoln, Neb. She entered into partnership with Dr. Haldeman at Ord in July 1901. At the expiration of three years she entered into practice alone, first building herself an office on Main street and a most comfortable residence. She has built up a large practice and is very successful.

ORD NORMAL AND BUSINESS COLLEGE—while one of the newest institutions established in the city, promises fair to take rank with the best schools of its kind. Prof. L. R. Bright, its principal and organizer, is a gentleman of culture, well fitted to make the venture a success. The high quality of work done in all departments of the school the past school year insures a greatly increased attendance for the coming scholastic year, which opens in September. From the new catalogue we glean the following interesting facts: "The Ord Normal and Business College is just a year old, and starts on its second year with the satisfaction of knowing that the first year was a successful one. Not in any manner connected with the school that was established by C. W. Roush and which had so unfortunate an experience, the Ord Normal and Business College is a fixture in Ord, and is the home of Prof. Bright, the principal. Ord is a good place for such a school. The business enterprise of the city has placed it ahead of any town in the county and there is a certain vim and push about the town that becomes an incentive to a student coming here from other places. The public schools of Ord are among the best in the state, and a splendid educational tone permeates the city. Excellent lecture courses are maintained every season. The churches of the city are well attended and the pulpits ably filled. The young people of the various church societies will welcome you to their services."

Prof. L. R. Bright.

ORD QUIZ, THE—On the 6th day of April 1882, the first issue of the *Ord Quiz* was printed and issued from a small shack, now gone, on the east side of the public square. It was established by the present owner, then a young man, with no newspaper experience. He came here because he was financially interested in the original townsite and that was all he had on earth but a young wife and a few debts incident to several years of college going. Whether the town needed another paper he did not know, and whether he was at all likely to succeed did not enter his head. From his early youth he was determined to be a printer, and as it was practically impossible for him to start anywhere else, he started here. For some reason, the Lord only knows what, the paper has succeeded. It stands pretty well in the estimation of the public and among the newspaper men of the state. Most everybody in the county permits it to come to his home, and most of these pay for it. It has one of the best printing plants in the state, equalled only by the best offices in three or four cities, and is housed in a new building erected specially for it last fall by the publisher. The *Quiz* is one of the very few papers which have run for about a quarter of a century without a change in ownership. Its files, which have been preserved from the beginning, have been largely utilized in the preparation of the foregoing history, and are in many instances, the only authority extant.

ROBBINS, A. M.—attorney-at-law, was born in McHenry county, Ill., in 1849. Shortly after this his folks moved to Boone county, Ill., where he lived on a farm until the spring of 1866, when he struck out for himself. Going to DeKalb county, in the same state, he continued to work by the month as a farm hand until the spring of 1868, when he entered the Teachers' Institute and Classical Seminary of East Paw Paw, Ill., and commenced a course of studies. He continued his attendance at the institute (with the exception of winters when he was teaching) until July 4, 1873, when he graduated and had conferred upon him the degree of Bachelor of Science. A few weeks after he graduated, he commenced the study of law in the office of A. K. Truesdell, of Dixon, Ill., and was admitted to practice in the fall of 1875 before the Supreme Court of that state, and in December of the same year was admitted to practice at Omaha. On January 1, 1876, he opened an office at Papillion, Neb., and soon accumulated a successful lucrative practice. He continued in practice there until April 1881, when he moved to Ord. Mr. Robbins has now been a practicing attorney in Ord for almost a quarter of a century and has built up a large practice in this part of the state. He has represented his district in the state senate and held other positions of public trust in his community. As one of the original founders of Ord he has been extensively interested in real estate in and around Ord. He was married in 1872 to Miss Cynthia C. Haskell, a resident of DeKalb county, Illinois, who is also a graduate of the Classical Institute of Paw Paw, Illinois. They have seven children who have all graduated from the Ord High School and later, after pursuing courses of study in higher institutions of learning, entered upon honorable careers for themselves. The youngest daughter. Alice, is the wife of the author of "The Trail of the Loup."

STAPLE, R. L.—was born in Dodge county, Wisconsin, and moved to Grundy county, Iowa, when five years old. In 1879 he came with his parents to Wheeler county, Neb., where he spent some years on his father's ranch. Clerical work was, however, more to Mr. Staple's liking. Accordingly he went into the Albion postoffice as deputy. Two years later he was appointed to a position in the office of the clerk of Boone county. In 1884 he went into the real estate business with his brother, W. L. Staple, at Cumminsville, Neb., and that fall was appointed county clerk of Wheeler county. Two years later he retired to the practice of the law and further engaged in the real estate business at Bartlett, Neb. He was married to Miss Margaret

Erickson of Ericson, Neb., in September 1886, and is now the father of four bright children, two boys and two girls. He came to Ord with his family in 1892 and immediately hung out his shingle there. In January 1893, he was elected secretary of the Valley County Abstract Company, of which organization he became the sole owner ten years later. In 1895 he re-entered politics and was elected county judge, and was re-elected in 1897, and again in 1899 and in 1901. When the last term expired he retired to private life and to the many duties of a growing legal and abstract business. Mr. Staple's specialty is the examination of titles, in which he has had twenty years' experience. He is also extensively engaged in insurance and real estate business.

TAYLOR, DR. GEORGE W.—was born at La Porte, Indiana, in 1877. His early education was gained at the La Porte High School. Later he studied at the University of Tennessee, which he left to enter the Dental Department of the University of Illinois. Here he received his degree in 1901. After being associated with a firm of dentists in Chicago for some time, Dr. Taylor came to Ord and entered the partnership of Holson & Taylor. This was in the fall of 1901. In 1903 Dr. Holson retired, leaving the latter in possession of the business at Ord. Dr. Taylor has built up here a good practice and is well known for his expert workmanship.

WATSON & HALLOCK—The firm of Watson & Hallock, barbers, was established in 1903. J. E. Watson, the expert tonsorial artist, was associated with Charlie Barnes from '99 to '02. Ernest N. Hallock learned his trade in Omaha where he spent a number of years. This popular firm recently moved into the new Quiz block. Their new quarters are equipped with baths and all the latest appurtenances which go to make up a first-class barber shop.

Arcadia

BARTOO, DR. ALBON E.—was born in Eden, Erie county, N. Y., in 1862. After completing his studies in the district school he entered Springville (N. Y.) Academy where he attended two fall terms. During the winter months he taught school and later attended for one term each the academies at Forestville and Hamburg. In the fall of 1885 he matriculated in the Medical Department of the University of Buffalo, from which he graduated as president of his class in 1889. For six months he practiced in Angola, N. Y., then removed to Wescott, Neb., and nine months later, in 1890, to Arcadia, where he has since

Dr. A. E. Bartoo.

lived and where for a time he was one of the proprietors of the Crystal Drug Store. The doctor is a member of the Custer County Medical Society and the ex-secretary of the Loup Valley District Medical Society. In the fall of 1896 he married Miss Rosetta F. Potter and the following year built a cozy residence in the southern part of town. Dr. and Mrs. Bartoo are the parents of two children, daughters. While always interested in politics the doctor never sought any office till in response to unanimous nomination in the Republican county convention for representative in the fall of 1902, he accepted and was elected the first Republican to fill that office for twelve years. He was chairman of the Insane Hospital Committee, and a member of Committees on Irrigation, Medical Societies, Corporation, and Public Lands and Buildings. It was largely due to his work that an appropriation for rebuilding the Norfolk Asylum was secured. He was re-elected representative in 1904.

FRIES, HON. M. L.—one of the best known business men and politicians of our state, was born on a farm at Winchester, Virginia, October 15, 1856. His parents were poor, the father indeed dying before the boy was born. The mother too died before he reached manhood. Thus he early learned to hustle for himself, a habit which his record shows he has been true to ever since. When Mr. Fries was but twelve years old the family moved to Jasper county, Missouri. Here he spent his winters in the country schools and managed by dint of hard work to get a year's instruction in the Carthage High School. Determined as he was to get an education the young man succeeded in getting through and graduating from the Scientific Department of the Northern Indiana Normal School. Then some years were occupied at teaching school in Indiana and Illinois. But failing health forced a change in climate, and for the next three years Mr. Fries held the responsible position as president of the Sierra Normal College at Auburn, California. This was between 1881–1884. Then for a year he was associated with Heald's Business College, San Francisco. In the spring of 1886 he located at Arcadia, Valley county, and engaged in the lumber business, which he has pursued successfully for almost twenty years. Indeed he has now one of the best equipped lumber yards in the state, and to judge by his books, does probably as big a business as any individual dealer in Nebraska. Mr. Fries is nothing if not public-spirited. From the day he first came to the state he has been active in politics. Thus he has served as county supervisor for a number of terms. He was on the state ticket as a McKinley presidential elector in 1896, and has been twice elected state senator from his district. He was one of the important special committee that drafted the new revenue law. Mr. Fries has during these years of public activity won many friends over the state who speak of him as a logical Republican candidate for the gubernatorial nomination in 1906. He would indeed make a strong candidate and an excellent chief executive. He was married to Cora Anderson in Streator, Illinois, in 1883, and has one daughter, aged nineteen. The Fries family has a pleasant home in Arcadia and is exceptionally prosperous.

Hon. M. L. Fries.

ROBINSON HOTEL—There is perhaps nothing more essential to the life of a town than a good, first-class hotel. For seven years prior to the establishment of the Robinson Hotel in June 1905, Arcadia had been without this essential. Joshua M. Robinson, the proprietor of the new hostelry, was born in Mercer county, Ill., October 17, 1872. When seven years old his parents moved to Nebraska and homesteaded seven miles southwest of Loup City. Five years later they removed to a quarter which they had pre-empted four miles northeast of Arcadia. Here Mr. Robinson grew to manhood. At the age of seventeen years he went to Alliance, near which place he taught three very successful years of school. He then attended the Scotia Normal and Business University till he graduated, August 3, 1893. For two years he now taught in the country and was afterwards principal of the High School at Scotia for the same length of time. For the next three years he kept books for W. B. Weekes & Co. of Scotia. March 1, 1905, he bought his present hotel property and after extensive improvements, opened his house June 11, 1905. The Robinson Hotel is a fine three-story structure. It is fitted with all the modern conveniences. The rooms are large and airy and heated with hot water. In fact it is as good a $2.00 a day house as there is in this part of the state. In February 1902, Mr. Robinson married Miss Gertrude B. Sturgeon of Alliance. They are the parents of two fine boys.

SORENSEN, WALTER—Walter Sorensen, one of the leading citizens of Arcadia, and who owns a beautiful residence in Arcadia, was born in Ribe, Denmark, in 1874. He came to this country in 1891. He went to work on a farm near Loup City, Sherman county, which he followed for two years, when he entered the barber shop at Loup City as an apprentice. He followed the barber business for two years at various points in the Loup country, and in 1895, he came to Arcadia, with but 75 cents in his pocket, but with a carload of grit. He bought the barber shop, and started business for himself. The fact that today he owns this beautiful home, and is in comfortable circumstances tells its own story. This is but another example of what can be done in the Loup country by one who sticks to it. He was married in June 1899, to Miss Nina Landers, and one daughter has been born to them.

North Loup

BABCOCK, E. J.—The most prominent member of the North Loup bar for many years has been E. J. Babcock. He was born at Dakota, Wisconsin, and came to Valley county in 1872. He received his first college education at Doane College, Crete, and later spent some years in Alfred University, New York, from which institution he received his Ph. B. in 1884. Later his alma mater granted him the degree of Ph. M. for post-graduate work. His law studies, which were commenced in New York, were continued under the veteran Tom Redlon at North Loup. He was ultimately admitted to the bar in 1886. Ever since that time Mr. Babcock has practiced law before the courts of Nebraska. He is considered one of the most successful barristers in this part of the state.

BABCOCK & GOWEN—The firm of Babcock & Gowen, general merchandise, is one of the most enterprising of North Loup business interests. While the partnership is only one year old at the present writing, it does a surprisingly large annual volume of business. The stock, which was $3000.00 at the commencement of business in November 1904, has gradually been increased till it now amounts to $10,000. Mr. Eddie Babcock, one of the partners, is a son of Elder Oscar Babcock and has been identified with North Loup from its very inception. He is well educated, having graduated from Michigan University Law School. For eleven years he practiced his profession. This was before he entered upon his new business in 1904. Mr. W. E. Gowen, the other member of the firm, was a Minnesota boy who came to North Loup in the early '70s. He too has been identified with many business ventures these last twenty or more years.

DAVIS, H. E.—North Loup's successful furniture dealer, is comparatively speaking an old-timer. He was born in Lewis county, New York, in 1855 and ten years later moved to Freeborn county, Minnesota. In 1878 he again turned westward and settled on a farm one and three-quarter miles northwest of North Loup. Here he farmed for some years and then moved to North Loup and opened a first-class furniture store. He carries a very complete stock, invoicing about $7000.

FARMERS' STATE BANK—In August 1882, Messrs. Lee Love and George W. Post established the Loup Valley Bank, the first banking institution in North Loup. The same year the firm name became Sears Bros. & Love, to be changed again in May 1883 to Sears Bros. During the last twenty years the town has had a rather varied banking history, coming to a climax with a failure and close-down during the dry years. But in May 1900, tried and practical bankers took hold of affairs and opened the Farmers' State Bank. The organizers of the institution were Guy Dann, A. U. Dann, Sam McClellan, O. S. Potter, W. E. Gowen and George Johnson. Of these A. U. Dann was elected president and Guy Dann cashier. The first financial statement of the bank was issued when the institution was two months old and is interesting particularly for the substantial growth shown when compared with the statement of May 19, 1906. After a management of the bank covering almost five years the Danns retired, giving way to a completely new management, composed as follows: Samuel McClellan, president; George E. Johnson, cashier; and Robert Johnson, third director. In February 1906, L. E. Pugh was elected cashier and George E. Johnson elected president and the capital stock of the bank increased to $10,000. A statement made at the close of business May 19, 1906, discloses the following status.

Resources		Liabilities	
Loans and Discounts	$44,283.88	Capital and Surplus Paid In	$10,000.00
Overdrafts	1335.26	Undivided Profits	936.60
Furniture and Fixtures	500.00	Deposits	67,664.32
Expenses	582.88		
Cash and Sight Exchange (Legal Reserve)	31,945.90		
Total	$78,647.92	Total	$78,647.92

HUTCHINS BROTHERS—is a firm of prosperous implement dealers, comprising G. L. Hutchins and E. A. Hutchins, both of whom were born in Minnesota. In 1866 they moved to Cedar Rapids, Iowa, where they spent the most of their youth. In 1884 G. L. Hutchins came to North Loup where, with the exception of two years spent in Colorado, he has lived ever since. His brother, although he came to Valley county in 1885, did not make this his permanent home till years afterwards. In 1892, G. L. Hutchins commenced business as an implement dealer. However, his stock was very small, scarcely invoicing $300. In 1898, E. A. Hutchins bought an interest in his brother's prospering business and since then they have worked together. The firm has now a large, growing business and carries a stock of implements which will invoice at least $4000.

JOHNSON, FRANK—One of the best appointed general merchandise stores in North Loup is that operated by Frank Johnson. He occupies the most pretentious brick structure in town and covers a very large floor space. In 1901 he bought the George Stover stock which invoiced about $5000.00. Since then the business has made rapid strides upward, so that now he carries a stock of at least $12,000. Mr. Johnson, who is a son of Robert Johnson of Davis Creek, was born in Jasper county, Iowa, in 1873. When he was but three or four years old his father moved to Hall county, Nebraska, but in 1881 moved up the Loup to Davis Creek. Young Frank determined to enter the commercial lists and to that end came to North Loup and entered the field. For a man so young as he is Mr. Johnson has done remarkably well.

JOHNSON, GEORGE E.—is one of the most enterprising and successful of Valley county business men. From a farmer he has risen to be one of our most prominent bankers and dealers in lumber and grain. He was born in Jasper county, Iowa, in 1862 and spent his early manhood there. When seventeen years old he came with his parents to Hall county, spending three years there on a farm. In 1882 the family removed to Davis Creek where both the father and son George homesteaded. The younger Johnson moved from the farm to North Loup in 1886, and there commenced his business career. He bought the old Allen coal business and a year later commenced buying grain for an Omaha firm. This he continued for four years and then began operating his own elevator. In 1902 he opened a lumber yard in connection with his other business and prospered from the first. The grain elevator was burned to the ground in 1905 but was immediately rebuilt larger and better than before. An inspection of the Geo. Johnson interests at North Loup impresses one with what general thrift and shrewd business ability can accomplish. Mr. Johnson has for a number of years been a director of the Farmers' State Bank of North Loup and was elected cashier of the institution March 15, 1905. He married Eva Redlon in 1885. They are the parents of five children.

MANCHESTER, I. A.—The lands of the Valley adjacent to North Loup have proven to be remarkably well adapted for raising seeds of various sorts. Some years ago W. P. Everingim opened a small seed house, contracting popcorn with eastern firms. After some twelve years he sold his holdings to Ira A. Manchester who is now rapidly enlarging the business by putting in approved machinery in his cleaning and sorting rooms. Not alone is he contracting for popcorn, but for barley, oats, macaroni wheat and several other cereal seeds. His shipments go to every part of the United States. Thus, last year he shipped 300 carloads of seed, a most remarkable feat.

MOORE, GEORGE W.—dealer in hardware and stoves, was born in Cedar county, Illinois, February 7, 1832. Here he grew up, attending the so-called subscription schools of those early days. He married Mary C. Frazier of Indiana and is the father of eight children, four of whom are living. The Moores have seen quite a bit of shifting about. Thus they came to Iowa in 1863—Mr. Moore farming for years where Missouri Valley now stands—later they moved to near Hastings, Nebraska, and finally to northern Sherman county. In 1893

Mr. Moore traded his farm for Charles Thrasher's hardware store at North Loup. He is well stocked with general hardware and stoves, and is doing a good business.

ROOD, WALTER I.—The subject of this sketch was born at Dakota, Wisconsin, June 5, 1864. He came to Valley county in the spring of 1875 and lived on the old homestead in Mira Valley till the winter of 1888, when he moved to the village of North Loup, where his home has since been. Young Walter attended the country schools but little, as he lost his father when but thirteen years of age. This forced the boy to get out and hustle for himself. By reading and studying at home evenings he prepared himself for college. In 1893 he matriculated at Milton College and studied there for two years. Then followed six years of teaching—two years in Illinois and four in Nebraska; the last two as assistant principal at North Loup. In 1897 he bought the *Loyalist*, since which time he has been its editor and publisher. He is unmarried and lives with his mother. He has been a member of the Village Board of Trustees for seven years and has been three years township clerk.

Burwell

BANK, WILLIAM—comes out of old Scotland, and is of good Scotch ancestry. He possesses many of the sturdy qualities and traits which have made Scotchmen leaders the world over. His birthplace was the city of Perth, beautifully situated on the banks of the Tay. He spent twenty-one years in the homeland, attending grammar school at Hasting, Eassa and Retrey. Full four years were then spent in apprenticeship. He became a journeyman blacksmith in 1885 and worked in this capacity for a year at Blairgowrie. Here he married Miss Susan Saunder and with his young wife came to the United States in 1886. The first stop was made in Osborn county, Kansas. The family came to Burwell in 1889, where Mr. Bank has since followed his trade. Mrs. Bank died in 1896 leaving four children living. William Bank is highly respected in his profession and outside it. He has a first class smithy, furnished with electric motor-power and other modern appurtenances. He holds high office in the local Masonic lodge, and is the chief of the fire department. He has a valuable farm a short distance from town.

BECKER, WILBER M.—may justly lay claim to be the "Pioneer Merchant" of Burwell. For his was the first store to be erected on the townsite, and with the exception of A. A. Graber, he is the only merchant who has stuck to his post continuously up to the present. Mr. Becker was born in Schoharie county, New York, in 1842, where he grew to manhood. He received his education in the common schools of his home county and at Fort Edward Collegiate Institute. The Becker family moved to Crawford county, Iowa, in 1875. Here young Wilber clerked in a store for a while and later was taken into partnership with his father, under the firm name of Wm. N. Becker & Co. The firm erected a store building at Burwell in 1883 and placed their stock of general merchandise in charge of George Hoyt. Mr. Becker did not take personal charge of the business till 1887, however, but since that time he has never for a moment let go the reins of management. It is interesting to know that the present "Pioneer Store" block has resulted from the reconstruction of two old, historical structures—the first store building erected on Burwell townsite and the C. H. Jones store building, first built at old Willow Springs and later moved to Burwell. Mr. Becker can tell of hardship and discouragement as known only to the earliest settlers. He well remembers the time that eastern wholesalers were reluctant to extend him credit on bills exceeding $50.00, and how he was forced to live on the old homestead for years after taking charge of the store, and having to drive the four miles daily, all because he was too poor to prove up on it. But those days are gone and prosperity has smiled on the Beckers. Besides doing a good business in the "Pioneer Store" he owns a thousand acres of good farm lands occupied by tenants. Mr. Becker was married to Miss Mary E. Chauncey at Amsterdam, New York, in 1866. Five children have come to bless the family. Of these the three sons assist their father in one capacity or another. Of the daughters one—Mrs. J. J. Hess—lives on a farm near Burwell.

BEYNON, DAVID S.—The present postmaster of Burwell, was born at Albia, Iowa, December 5, 1856. He was born on the farm and reared to manhood there. His early education was such as could be procured in the rural schools of those days. When twenty-one years of age he began to shift for himself and tried his hand at farming in different parts of the state. It was perhaps his marriage to Miss Christina J. Cornelia that decided him to leave Albia definitely and to seek a career in the greater, untramelled west. At any rate as soon as this event took place, in December 1883, he moved with his wife to western Iowa and there engaged in farming for two years. But Mr. Beynon was not satisfied to stop here. Accordingly the family set

David S. Beynon.

out for Nebraska and reached Willow Springs July 3, 1886. Ever since his arrival in Garfield county has Mr. Beynon been intimately connected with the progress of the county. Willow Springs was quite a town then and promised to continue the metropolis of the upper Valley. Mr. Beynon accordingly bought an interest in a drug store there, entering partnership with Dr. A. W. Hoyt. Everything went smoothly till the B. & M. commenced building to Burwell. Willow Springs was doomed and no one realized this more fully than David Beynon. In February 1888, he moved his residence across the ice of the North Loup to Burwell; the store building was torn down and rebuilt on Webster street. Within the last few years it has been moved to its present location on Grand Avenue and further remodelled. Mr. Beynon has been a careful, upright business man and has succeeded well. He operates an up-to-date drug business, being a registered pharmacist. An index to his general prosperity may be seen in the late erection of a beautiful home, costing at least $3500. In public affairs, too, has he taken a prominent part. Thus he has been a member of the school board at Burwell for ten years, chairman of the village board a number of years, and deputy sheriff two terms. While acting in the latter capacity he made an enviable record by capturing Nicholas Foley, the Antelope county murderer and desperado. He was appointed postmaster of Burwell August 7, 1897. During his term of office, Burwell postoffice has been raised from fourth to third class office, causing a raise in salary from $600 to $1100 per annum. Three rural routes and four star routes now branch out from this office. The Beynons have an interesting family. Of the four children now living Rebecca has graduated from the Burwell High School and lately from the Fremont Normal. She teaches this year at York. John, the only son, is also a graduate of the local High School.

BRAGG, CHARLES I.—county attorney of Garfield county, was born at Sanford, New York, in 1863. He was a very precocious boy as may be seen from the fact that he had already completed his course at Unadilla Academy and received a life certificate to teach school when twelve years old. After teaching for a couple of terms in his native state he came west and pursued the same occupation at Cedar Rapids, Nebraska. He spent three years in the regular army, but soon realized that in time of peace the ambitious youth may find greater avenues for advancement in civil life. He accordingly retired to private life. From 1882 onward he engaged in the insurance business. This took him to Kent, Loup county, in 1885. Next year he commenced the study of law and was admitted to the bar in 1889. Mr. Bragg has been a life-long Republican. He has been very active in public life and has taken a leading part in the councils of his party. In Loup county he held the office of county attorney one term and was county clerk for three years. He moved to Burwell in the fall of 1897 as this town seemed to offer greater possibilities for a broader usefulness.

Charles I. Bragg.

While here he became one of the founders of the American Order of Protection, though he later devoted all his time to law. He was elected county attorney of Garfield county in 1904 and fills the important position with much credit to himself and the party that elected him. Mr. Bragg married Miss Jennie M. Ginder in 1885. The happy family, including parents and six children, is now nicely located in a beautiful home lately erected in the south part of the city.

CASH MERCANTILE CO.—The Cash Mercantile Co. is one of the thriving institutions of Burwell. Being the successor of Scott Brothers' old, well established general store, it carries with its new name all the trade of the old. The store is under the management of Peter Scott who is recognized as one of the most genial and able business men of our Valley. He together with his brother George F. Scott of Taylor constitute the company. The business, which is of the nature of general merchandise, is well stocked with all that pertains to a first-class store of this kind. Dry goods, shoes, and all kinds of fresh groceries are always kept in stock. By dint of hard work and unquestionable honesty the management of the Cash Mercantile Co. has built up a trade hard to excel.

COFFIN, HARRY J.—is a Yankee bred and born. He boasts descent from the historic Tristram Coffin who settled on Nantucket Island in the middle of the seventeenth century, and whose family is scattered far and wide over the American continent today. Harry J. was born at Boston, January 16, 1860, and remained in his native town till almost 18 years old. He was educated in the excellent public schools of the old "Hub" city, and later worked in an organ factory there for several years. He left the New England states and came to Nebraska in the spring of 1878. The first pause was made at Schuyler where he farmed for four years. In 1883 he took a pre-emption near O'Neill, but after six months removed to The Forks, Wheeler county, and took a homestead. He moved to Burwell in 1902 and purchased the Garfield county branch of the Howe Lumber Co., operating the same under the title of H. J. Coffin for some time. The firm name has, however, lately been changed to Burwell Lumber and Coal Co., with Mr. Coffin as proprietor. He also operates a lumber yard and general store at Elyria under the name of Elyria Mercantile Co., with J. E. Stingley as manager. Mr. Coffin is interested in a number of other enterprises and is an extensive land owner. He has been on the board of commissioners in his home county and has served several terms on the village board. In May 1893, he married

Harry J. Coffin.

Miss Mary Halloran of Inman, Neb. They have three daughters and are nicely located in their elegantly appointed home within a block of the lumber yard.

CRAM, ALBERT I.—One of the younger business men in Burwell who is succeeding exceptionally well is Albert I. Cram. He was born at Monmouth, Illinois, November 16, 1883, and moved with his parents to Loup county, Nebraska, in 1883. He remained on his father's farm till twenty-one years old, when he decided to prepare for a business career. The Monmouth, Illinois, graded schools had given him a foundation upon which to build. Some time spent at the David City High School and the Omaha Business College then prepared him for his chosen work. He entered the First Bank of Burwell as book keeper but was soon chosen to the responsible position of cashier. Four and one-half years later he became a member of Cram Brothers, lumber dealers. When the firm was reorganized in 1900 under the name of Cram & Co., he was made manager. He married Effie V. Wilson and is the father of three children, two boys and one girl.

CRAM, WILBER I.—is proud that he comes of Irish ancestry, and one of his day-dreams for many years has been to visit the home of his fathers "across the big sea." He was born at historic Crown Point, New York, August 8, 1846, and remained there till eight years old, when he moved with his parents to Jackson county, Iowa. Here he remained for more than 27 years engaged in farming and stockraising. As a cattle judge and specialist he soon won more than local fame. He became a breeder of thoroughbred swine and one of the originators of the American Poland China Record Association. While here he married Miss Honour Filby. They have four sturdy sons who are all making their way in the world. Thus O. E. Cram manages the old home ranch in Loup county, A. I. Cram is a noted Burwell lumber dealer, Fred C. Cram manages the stockyards at Sargent, and John E. Cram is associated with his father in the Burwell stockyards. The Crams became pioneers in the unorganized territory which later became Loup county. They arrived in 1881, and homesteaded the southeast quarter of Section 3, Township 21, Range 19. By degrees they have added quarter to quarter till now the ranch, as W. J. calls it, contains 1680 acres of good land. When they first took their claim the nearest neighbors were four miles away, and water had to be hauled in barrels a distance of seven miles. This led to the sinking of a well 300 feet deep, every foot of it dug by spade.

In those days, too, the nearest freight depot was a hundred miles down the river. Mr. Cram feeds in the neighborhood of 500 steers on the ranch annually, and otherwise deals in in all kinds of livestock. He has lately completed a $4000 residence property, including a waterworks plant.

DORAN, THOMAS H.—Representative from the 49th District, is an Irishman bred and born. He came out of the picturesque county Carlow and when only six months old arrived at New York with his parents. His history in this land of his adoption has been a very honorable one. Four years saw the family and young Thomas on the trail with faces set toward the great west. The first pause in the journey came in LaSalle county, Illinois. Here the Dorans remained ten years, indeed till 1865. The next move was to Livingston county where the elder Doran died. The care of the family now devolved on the fifteen year old Thomas. The worth of the man is shown in the ability and conscientiousness with which the stripling boy took his father's onerous duties upon himself. Comparative prosperity came with hard work and in 1874 the westward march was continued to Beaver, Boone county, Iowa, where Mr. Doran engaged extensively in the grain, lumber and livestock business. His popularity and natural inclination for politics were soon rewarded by his being made postmaster of Beaver. But it is his career in Nebraska that is our particular theme here. He arrived at Burwell in 1889, and in conjunction with his brother John bought the First Bank of Burwell, then operated by the First National Bank of Ord. As an important step in strengthening their banking institution the brothers bought the Garfield County Bank and merged it with the First Bank. Mr. Doran was married at Boone, Iowa, to Miss Ettie Satterlee. Of the four children born to them only one, a son, reached maturity. The latter is now associated in business with his father. It is especially for his activity in affairs pertaining to the welfare of his own village and district that Mr. Doran has earned the thanks of his neighbors and constituents. When the county seat question came up for the last time none was more active than Thomas Doran. He has also been a prominent member of the school board for fourteen years, and one of the town board almost continually since its organization. In 1900 his brother's health failed. This led to the sale of the bank to Dann Bros. Mr. Doran and family now spent a year in restful travel in California and old Mexico. Upon returning home in 1901 he engaged in stock raising. His ranch is one of the largest in this part of the state, and is the home of many hundred head of cattle and horses. Several other enterprises in which he is interested should not be overlooked. Thus he became a member of the prominent lumber business of Cram & Co. in 1897. A few months ago he purchased A. A. Graber's hardware store and placed the same in charge of his son, and nephew. As stated above, Mr. Doran represents the 49th District in the State Legislature. He is a Republican in politics, and his popularity is shown by the fact that he carried his district, which is strongly populistic, by no less than 252 votes.

DOUGLAS, L. P.—proprietor of the Burwell House, the leading hotel in Burwell, was born in New York state in 1843. He did not come west before 1876, when he first spent six years in Iowa, after which he moved to Omaha and engaged in the mercantile business. He and his wife are practical hotel people, having managed first-class hostelries in several cities. The Douglas family came to Burwell from Bellwood where they had pursued successfully in the same business. The Burwell house caters to both transient and local trade.

FIRST NATIONAL BANK, THE—had its genesis in the First Bank of Burwell, which was for some time operated by the First National Bank of Ord. In 1889 Thomas H. and John Doran purchased this institution and merged it with the Garfield County Bank, under the name, however, of the former. In 1900 the bank was sold by the Dorans to Dann Brothers. Since that time it has been re-organized as a National Bank with a capital of $25,000, under a new management of shrewd financiers and moneyed men. The present officers and stockholders are: W. L. McMullen, president; E Bailey, vice-president; J. M. Conrad, cashier; W. I. Cram, J. A. Brownell, M. B. Goodenow, Geo. F. Scott and W. T. Barstow. This bank is doing much to promote the material progress of Garfield and Loup counties, and carries on a general banking business, receiving deposits, loaning money on approved security, discounting acceptable commercial paper, buying and selling domestic and foreign exchange, making collections, and generally exercises all the functions of a first-class banking institution. The First National is a synonym for stability and integrity. A statement of the condition of the bank at the close of business May 29, 1905, is as follows:

Resources		Liabilities	
Loans	$57,595.43	Capital	$25,000.00
U.S. Bonds and Premiums	10,437.50	Surplus	250.00
Banking house Fur. and Fix	3000.00	Undivided Profits	2329.79
Cash and Sight Exchange	72,541.26	Circulation	10,000.00
Due from U.S. Treasurer	500.00	Deposits	106,494.40
Total	$144,074.19		$144,074.19

GRABER, ALFRED A.—can rightfully boast of being one of the very first merchants in Burwell, for when he opened for business the only store on the townsite besides his own was the Becker store. He comes of good, sturdy Swiss ancestry, though born at Mount Eton, Ohio. Until he was 24 years old the young man worked out, helping his parents who were poor. But when he finally left home he drifted about considerably before settling in Garfield county. Thus we hear of him in Michigan, at Waverly, and Wahoo, Nebraska; in 1877, in western Kansas; then in 1879, toiling overland to the Black Hills with their dangers and gold. In 1880 he is back in his native state, though not to remain, for in 1883, we find him boring wells at Wahoo, Nebraska. He next formed a partnership with a Swede and engaged in the hardware business at Meade. But Loup Valley history is of more interest to us. As we have said he built the second store in Burwell. This was a small structure 10 x 22 feet large, built at the corner of Milwaukee street and Grand Avenue. The store opened the 1st of June, 1884, with a $1200 stock of hardware most of which was gotten on credit. But Mr. Graber did well in business. He took an active part in the county seat election in 1884–85 and was instrumental in securing the writ of mandamus demanding a recount of votes. Associated with him in this were Cornwell, Ferguson, Smith, Mathews and other old-timers. Down through the years the business grew substantially till Mr. Graber found himself the proprietor of quite a department store. Thus in addition to hardware he handled farm implements and furniture, and became the town undertaker. On June 27, 1903, the store was struck by lightning and partially burned, causing a net loss of $3000. Instead of rebuilding Mr. Graber bought the stock and plant of B. J. Bunnell, which he again lately disposed of to Thomas Doran. Mr. Graber is nothing if not public spirited. He has thus been a member of the village board for ten years, and a chief promoter in procuring for Burwell a system of waterworks. His wife was formerly Miss Louise Keller of Youngston, Ohio. With her bright little family of five children, three boys and two girls, she presides over the cozy Graber home situated in the northwest part of town.

HEGNER & DOWNEY—The firm of Hegner & Downey, dealers in farm and agricultural implements, though of comparatively recent origin, is doing a remarkably good business. In fact it may be said that Hegner & Downey are today the only exclusive dealers in their line in Garfield county, having recently purchased the stock carried by other concerns of the same kind. Absolute honesty and strict business principles have won for the firm public confidence and given it a very enviable name. Theodore F. W. Hegner, the senior member of the firm, is a German by birth, coming from Alstadt, Germany, where he was born March 22, 1865. He arrived at Grand Island, Neb., with his parents when just six years old. Here his boyhood was spent. The public schools in those days were rather in their infancy, so that young Theodore's schooling was not of the best. A few years in carpentry and blacksmithing closed his career in Grand Island. Now follow some years of ranching and homesteading in Rock county. His marriage to Miss Edna Akins was solemnized June 28, 1893, of which union two children are now living. Mr. Hegner seems to have preferred his early profession to farming for in 1893 he opened a blacksmith shop at Long Pine, coming to Burwell in 1895, continuing the

T. F. W. Hegner.

Mr. and Mrs. F. A. Downey.

same line here. He still owns his Burwell shop though not working it himself. The firm of Hegner & Downey was organized in March 1905, though Mr. Hegner had already been in the business a year when the change was made. Fred A. Downey was born in Buchanan county, Iowa, June 26, 1870. He lived there till he was seven years old and then came to Knox county, Nebraska. Here some nine years were spent in school and on the farm. After spending four years near Norfolk farming, he moved to Inman, where he married Miss Delia Halloran. The family arrived at Burwell in 1895 and spent ten years in farming near town. As stated above he entered the Implement business of Hegner & Downey a few months ago. Aside from carrying a full line of farm and agricultural implements, the firm handles buggies and harness of all kinds.

HOLSON, DR. JOHN CLAUDE—is one of the most successful dentists in this part of the state. He is an Iowan by birth having spent his early days in Iowa City. Here he received his early and higher education. A graduate of the city high school, he matriculated at the medical college of the state university of Iowa, pursuing the regular practitioner's course. From this he graduated in 1890. He then took a course in the Iowa State University Dental College, graduating in 1892. He opened his dental parlors in Ord in the summer of 1896 making a specialty of crown and bridge work. In September 1895, he was married to Rose I. Robbins and together they continued to make Ord their home till in 1903 they removed to Burwell where they are nicely situated in their cosy home in the south part of town. Dr. Hobson not alone takes care of the Burwell patients but has branch offices at Comstock, Taylor and Greeley Center.

JANES & SONS—One of the old-timers of the Loup doing a good business at Burwell is B. F. Janes of the successful firm of Janes & Co. He is an old Waushara county, Wisconsin, man, from the earliest date associated with the North Loup colony from that county. His father gave his life for his country during the Civil War, and thus the care of a widowed mother fell to B. F. and his brothers. He moved to North Loup in the early seventies and was for many years identified with North Loup in various business enterprises. Thus he engaged in livery and dray business and pursued carpentry for some time. Later he operated a skating rink at Ord. Then in turn he took a homestead near Kent, where he lived for some years. Becoming tired of the farm he moved to Burwell where he tried his hand at the harness trade and sale of implements. Not until the fall of 1900 did he launch upon the business which he is now pursuing—the general merchandise business. He started in with a small stock worth about $500.00, but soon built up a nice trade. Clayton McGrew now became associated with him in the business. In the spring of 1901 they bought out McMullen & Conrad; later in the year Mr. McGrew retired from the firm, whereupon William, son of B. F. Janes, came in as a junior member. During the last four years this firm has had a steadily increasing business and today carries one of the best and most complete stock of general merchandise in the city.

JOHNS & MITCHELL—Burwell is well supplied with up-to-date general merchandise stores. One of the most prominent of these is operated by the well known firm of Johns & Mitchell. The senior member of the firm has been written up elsewhere in this work and may be passed by here. The junior member, Robert J. Mitchell, was born in New York state in 1864, getting his early schooling in the old log school house there. At 13 years of age he moved to Holyoke, Mass., and remained there till 1889. In that year he came to Burwell and began farming. He took a homestead in Loup county and spent five years there. Two years were again spent in Massachusetts, after which he entered the mercantile business. This he did by purchasing the stock of J. R. Alderman & Son, which he moved to the old "Michel Store." Later he formed a partnership with Ed. M. Tunnicliffe, then county clerk. Mr. Mitchell married Miss Nannie E. Alderman, November 24, 1892, and has an interesting family of one son and three daughters. The firm remained as Mitchell & Tunnicliffe till July 5, 1904, when Mr. Mitchell sold out to Will Johns. But in February 1905, Mr. Tunnicliffe retired and Mr. Mitchell again entered the firm, now as the junior member. When Robert Mitchell launched the business six years ago he had a stock worth $600. By careful and correct business methods this stock has increased till it is now ten or twelve times as large. A full line of general merchandise, always fresh and up to-date, is kept on hand. Johns & Mitchell have succeeded because worthy of success.

KEY, FARAN M.—was born in Adair county, Iowa, on November 19, 1863. When eleven years old he left his home state and with his parents moved around considerably. Thus we find him in Cowley county, Kansas, later in Benton county, Arkansas, and then back again in Iowa. When 24 years old he married Miss Annie Wright who became the mother of two children. She died in 1893. From his second marriage Mr. Key has five children making in all seven. He came to Garfield county in 1888 and immediately pre-empted a quarter section of land, and in 1901 filed upon his homestead. Mr. Key is a popular and public spirited man. He was elected sheriff by the populist party in 1901 and re-elected two years later. He has engaged in the implement business, but at the present gives all his time to the plumbing business, and sinking of wells and erection of windmills. The deepest well in the county—325 feet—has been sunk by him. A sketch of Mr. Key would not be complete without mentioning his business with the U.S. government. The star mail routes of the upper valley have been for years in his hands. Thus he contracted to carry the mail from Burwell to Taylor and Almeria in 1894 and still controls that route. He has likewise the Blake route, and he had the prime route—from Burwell to the mouth of Gracie Creek—till it was discontinued.

LAVERTY, GUY—is practically speaking a Nebraska product. Though born in Black Hawk county, Iowa, when only two years old he came with his parents to Nebraska and Cass county. Here he spent his boyhood and attended the rural schools. The Lavertys moved to Valley county in 1884 and settled on a farm in Geranium township. Guy had no inclination to become a farmer, so came to Ord where he attended the high school. Later he taught school for some four years and in 1890 found time to attend the Fremont Normal school. In the fall of 1892 his legal career began. Then he entered the law office of Hon. Chas. A. Munn. A year later he was

The Laverty family.

admitted to the bar. He immediately thereupon moved to Burwell and was elected county attorney in 1894 and re-elected twice. He has today a very remunerative law practice, writes insurance and makes a specialty of abstracts. Mr. Laverty is a populist in politics. He was married to Miss Emma M. Glover at Ord August 31, 1892. They have two children, Cecil and Carmen. Mrs. Laverty is an expert accountant and stenographer and has been of invaluable assistance to her husband in his upward career. Mr. Laverty is very public spirited. In the M. E. church he has been for years a mainstay; on the school board he has been elected and re-elected time and again.

McGREW, I. W.—dealer in general merchandise, is one of the most prosperous merchants in the upper valley. He was born at Abbington, Illinois, February 9 1863. At eight years of age he came with his parents to Missouri. He was educated at Laclede Seminary, Lebanon, Missouri, and at the state normal located at Kirksville. The commercial world held a charm for Mr. McGrew from earliest boyhood. As soon as he felt prepared for the work he took to clerking. This was at Lineville, Iowa. Two years later he moved to North Loup and opened a small grocery store. Soon after this, however, he determined to try farm life, and accordingly spent two years on a farm in Valley county, but unfortunately lost his crops by hail. He then came to Ord and worked for some time in the Harris Clothing Store, and later for B. C. White. He finally bought the B. C. White stock of general merchandise and did a very good business. But he took the western fever about this time and selling out to Duby Brothers moved to Colorado. The western venture was not a success and Mr. McGrew was glad to get back to the Loup again. He now opened a small grocery at Burwell, investing a capital of $300. A year and a half later the stock was moved to a more commodious structure on the north side of the square, and a line of dry goods added. In 1900 boots and shoes were also put in. Through careful dealing and marked business ability the business grew steadily and warranted Mr. McGrew's removal to the brick block where he now is. The store building is one of the best in Burwell, well adapted for the display of such fancy goods as are found on the shelves here. Aside from carrying a line of general merchandise, Mr. McGrew carries an excellent stock of fine dress goods, the best of its kind in Garfield county. The business which a decade and a half ago started with $300 has now grown to an annual volume of $30,000. Mr. McGrew married Miss Ella M. Simmons at Ord in 1886. They have four children, one girl and three boys, and are nicely situated in their comfortable home in the eastern part of town.

SLY, W. J.—was born in Page county, Iowa, in September 1862, where he resided till sixteen years old. He got his education solely in the rural schools and was from boyhood inclined toward the farm. After spending three years in Ida county, Iowa, he set out for Nebraska and reached Willow Springs in 1881. His wife was formerly Miss Ida Beckwith. Mr. Sly is the proud father of eleven children who are growing up to become useful members of their home community. The Slys moved in time to the Calamus and for years farmed there. When the county seat difficulties harrowed the county Mr. Sly voted consistently with Burwell. He was elected sheriff as a Democrat with populistic tendencies in 1887 and held the office for two terms. He has also been extensively engaged in cattle raising and the purchase and sale of all kinds of stock. He has lately moved to town to give his children better school advantages than could be gotten on the farm. Mr. Sly is at present city marshal.

SMITH, ELDON J., M. D.—is a comparatively new man in Burwell, but he is already making a name for himself through his undoubted ability in his profession. He was born at Mechanicsville, Iowa, in 1879. He received a good early education there and later at South Omaha, graduating from the high school of the latter place in 1895. Like many other young men, when determined to make their own way in the world, he was for some time variously engaged. Thus he worked for some time in the large Hammond Packing Co. He next attended commercial college for a year and then became bookkeeper

for an Omaha firm. A year was
then spent in college work in the
Nebraska Wesleyan University.
But his natural bent was the
medical profession. Accordingly
he matriculated at the College
of Medicine of the University of
Nebraska. He attended the full
four years and graduated in May
1904. A month later he passed
the strict examination before
the state board and immediately
thereafter located in Burwell.
Dr. Smith makes a specialty of
diseases of the eye, nose, ear
and throat. His office adjoins
the building of the new Burwell
Drug Company, of which he is
also a member.

Eldon Smith.

STACY, EARL—now one of the most successful watchmakers and jewellers in our Valley, is an Ord product, having been born there on the 16th of September 1881. Here he grew up and was schooled. For a professional course he attended a practical school in watchmaking in the east and soon found lucrative employment in the Bell Watch Factory at Cleveland, Ohio. As a reward of thrift and ability he was soon promoted to be foreman in one of the shops, which position he held for nearly two years. Hearing the call of the west he returned to his boyhood home and was for some time engaged with E. L. Gard at Ord. December 1, 1904, he moved to Burwell and opened a first class jewelry shop and watchmaking establishment there. He carries a very fine and complete stock and has the confidence of the community in which he now moves and works.

THURSTON, EUGENE D., M. D.—was born at Richford, Wisconsin, September 3, 1859. Here he spent his boyhood and received his early education. When he was fifteen years old his parents came to Nebraska and arrived at Valley county in June 1875. The elder Thurston bought the homestead and timber claim entered by Grandpa J. C. Collins in 1873, and located just east of Ord on the Springdale road. The dwelling house on the homestead was constructed from sawed cedar logs and was covered with red cedar shingles. The two quarters were bought for $500 then. It is interesting to know that now these farms could not be bought for $20,000. Young Eugene came to the valley early enough to see antelope shot on the townsite of Ord. Thus he states that on a certain day in 1876 "Art" Stacy shot three of these delusive animals just about where the public square now is. But those days are past. In 1880 Mr. Thurston entered the Methodist Episcopal Seminary at York and remained there for some time. He later matriculated at the College of physicians and surgeons at Keokuk, only later to shift to the Medical Department of the University of Nebraska, wherefrom he graduated in 1884. He hung out his shingle at Taylor in 1886 where he remained—barring a short stay at Eugene, Oregon—till he moved to Burwell in 1900 to take the practice of the late Dr. Cameron. He married Minnie Davis in 1893. They have two children, a boy and a girl. Dr. Thurston is known far up and down the river as a careful, painstaking physician and jolly good fellow. He is a brother of "Herb" Thurston, an early-day sheriff of Valley county, who is now located at Longmont, Colorado.

TODD, WILLIAM Z.—editor of the *Burwell Tribune*, was born in Jones county, Iowa, September 28, 1866. When he was but four years old the Todd family moved to Cedar county where William remained till he was twenty years old, attending school and working in his father's law office. Mr. Todd came to Neligh, Nebraska, in 1883, and took a homestead in Wheeler county the next year. In 1888 he was induced by business men of Willow Springs to start the *Willow Springs Enterprise* in that town, to counteract the influence of growing Burwell. But when two years later the exodus to the latter town began Mr. Todd moved his printing establishment thither and founded the *Garfield Enterprise*. His public activity is from this time on chronicled in the chapter on "the Newspaper in the Valley." In August 1892, he married Mollie McKenzie. They have two children, a boy and a girl.

WICKS, ROBERT G.—the genial proprietor of the Racket Store, located at the corner of Grand Avenue and Webster Street, has had a most romantic life story. Born at Farnham, England in 1867, he took to the sea at the early age of 13. In his voyaging he soon became familiar with the ports of the Mediterranean and the Levant. He has sailed through the Suez Canal and the Red Sea to the Indian Ocean and all the Indies reached by the latter. Indeed, he can boast of having seen all the continents of our earth. Barring the distance from

Adelaide to San Francisco, he has circumnavigated the globe. But Mr. Wicks is inclined to be a little modest when talking about these, his early wanderings. Mere chance decided his coming to America and the United States. It was "heads," America and "tails" Australia. "Heads" won and the Loup added a good citizen to its population. He arrived at the small English colony on the Middle Loup, near Arcadia in 1886. But he soon tired of life there and went to Chicago and entered the employ of the Armours. But he longed for the open plains of Nebraska and again he returned to the Loup, this time to Burwell, and immediately engaged in the general merchandise business. This was June 1, 1890. His first store-building, the so-called Jerry Schuyler building, measured only 18 × 20, but readily accommodated his small first stock. In course of a few years the business grew to such an extent that a new building became necessary. Accordingly he moved into the capacious quarters now in use. He has also enjoyed a large trade from the Sargent country. So the extension of the B. & M. from Arcadia naturally worked him considerable harm. However, he has an excellent business as things are and is very prosperous. He owns some five hundred acres of farm land under rent and has just completed an elegant home which has cost him at least $4000. Mrs. Wicks was formerly Miss Addie L. Myers. They were married in 1892 and have four children, one boy and three girls.

Scotia

COOPER BROS., BLACKSMITHS AND WAGON MAKERS.—W. T. Cooper was born in Saline county, Neb., in June 1871. In 1888 his parents moved to Ord where he learned the trade under J. C. Work. In 1892 he came to Scotia and opened his shop. E. A. Cooper has been a partner with his brother from the first but left the shop in 1900. W. J Cooper is still running the shop and enjoys a big business.

DELMONT HOTEL—Jay L. Clark is a native of Illinois but his early life was mostly spent on a farm in Iowa. In the spring of 1884 he came to Nebraska and the next year he came to Scotia. For two years he engaged in the hotel business, retiring to the real estate business in 1887. The next year he engaged in the livery business on the side. This business he still retains and makes a specialty of handling fine horses. In 1900 he built the Delmont Hotel, a twenty-room house, which he is now running.

FITZSIMMONS, G. W., LUMBER, IMPLEMENTS AND FURNITURE—Mr. Fitzsimmons was born in Polk county, Iowa, in 1864. From 1885 to 1891 he engaged in the lumber business in various towns in Iowa when he moved to Scotia. At first he had only a lumber business but in 1894 added furniture and implements. From 1891 to 1901 the firm name was Fitzsimmons & Graham and was established in Ord as well as in Scotia. Since 1901 Mr. Fitzsimmons has run the business at Scotia alone, and though at first he did but a small business it has rapidly increased to its present large proportions.

HICKS, M. M., DRUG STORE—M. M. Hicks was born in Peoria, Ill., in 1860. Fourteen years later he came to Adams, Iowa. In 1889 he came to Merna, Neb., and entered the drug business. In 1896 he came to Scotia, Neb., and opened his present place of business. Mr. Hicks carries a $2500 stock and enjoys a good drug business.

McMILLAN, J. S., REAL ESTATE—Mr. McMillan was born in Portage county, Wis., May 12, 1866. However, since 1878 he has lived in Scotia. In 1893 he engaged in the real estate and loan business. He now has an extensive business in this as well as in other localities.

PICKETT, DR. J. J.—was born in eastern Indiana, February 15, 1850, and there he received his education. While yet a young man he taught school and farmed for eight years, when he began to study medicine. Receiving his degree in 1885, he came to Nebraska the following year and settled in Broken Bow. In 1900 he moved to Central City, and in 1903 again, to Scotia. Though Dr. Pickett has been here but a short time he is rapidly gaining a good practice.

SCOTIA MEAT MARKET—Fred Stanner, the proprietor, was born in Germany in 1861. When 17 years old he came to America and settled in Dubuque, Iowa, where he learned the butcher business. In 1884 he came to Scotia and has ever since been in the meat business. He has a regular meat trade and keeps fresh oysters and fish in season. Mr. Stanner also owns the ice business of the town. He is the oldest butcher in Greeley county.

SCOTIA ROLLER MILLS—Dee Vinecore, the proprietor, is purely a Loup country product, being born in Valley county and raised in Valley and Garfield counties. He married Ethel Moorman of Garfield county in December 1901. He bought the Scotia Roller Mills on August 1, 1904. At that time the mills were in bad shape but after expending several thousand dollars in repairs Mr. Vinecore has things in shape to do high grade milling. The Scotia flour and cereal products are rapidly gaining popularity.

VAN SKIKE, J. M., HARNESS SHOP—Mr. Vanskike was born in Bartholomew county, Indiana, in August 1856. Here he lived till 1877 when he came to Scotia. Here he learned the harness trade under his father, whom he succeeded in 1894. Mr. Vanskike carries a good line of harness and leather goods and enjoys a deservedly good patronage.

WEEKES, DR. CHARLES M.—was born at O'Connor, Greeley county, March 31, 1882. In 1885 his parents came to Scotia. Here he grew to manhood and graduated from the Scotia High School. In 1900 he matriculated in the Creighton Medical College at Omaha, graduating in 1904. He has since been practicing in Scotia and though a young man has had remarkable success.

WRIGHT, MRS. M. J., GENERAL MERCHANDISE AND HARDWARE—Mary Bean Wright was born in Wisconsin. Her parents came to Scotia in 1876. In 1883 she married Mr. Ed. Wright. Three years later they established their present business. In 1896 Mr. Wright died leaving Mrs. Wright and her two sons to carry on the business. Theirs is one of the largest stores in town.

Taylor

EMIG, GEORGE P.—druggist and dealer in notions, was born at Columbus, Ohio, December 25, 1849. Here he was educated and entered into business. Thus he in turn was druggist, dealer in boots and shoes, and tanner. His health failed him in 1879 and upon his physician's advice he moved west. That year he arrived at Ord with his family, consisting of wife—formerly Miss Mary Whiteside—and two children, Emma (King) and Charlie. He spent some

Geo. P. Emig, daughter and grandchild.

three years farming near Ord. A year later he established himself at Taylor, only to again return to Ord to work in the H. A. Walker drug store. In 1886 when there was talk of the Union Pacific tapping Taylor he once more located at Taylor. But disappointed in this we soon find him back at Ord in his chosen profession. Once more he returned to Taylor, carrying with him stock, building and all. Today he is the only druggist in Taylor and carries an unusually complete stock of drugs and whatever else belongs to a well appointed establishment of this kind.

KRIEGEL, JOSEPH—Taylor's successful manufacturer of harness and other leather goods, was born in 1862, at Raschen, Austria. He was sent to the excellent schools of his native country, leaving them when fourteen years old to become an apprentice in the manufacture of harness, saddles, etc. After mastering the step of journeyman he became master of trade. He now determined to immigrate to the United States. Arrived here he stopped first at Osceola, Neb., for some months working at his trade. He then operated a harness shop at Rising City for a short time and came to Ord March 15, 1885. Here he worked for Frank Misko for a few months and then moved to Taylor. Mr. Kriegel entered upon business in a small way, investing his total capital of $350 in leather and machinery. He commenced operations in a rented building. Now he owns his store building and has besides a comfortable home in the residence portion of Taylor. He has built up an excellent business, manufacturing almost all his goods at home. Mr. Kriegel was married in 1885 to Miss Mary Wolf and has two children living.

Joseph Kriegel.

MOON, ALANSON S.—county attorney of Loup county, was born in Schuyler county, New York, December 13, 1857. He spent some twenty years of his life in his native state going to school, teaching and farming. He graduated from the well-known Starkey

Academy. From New York he removed to Michigan, and in 1877 he again took up the trail and moved on to Loup county. He homesteaded near Kent where he remained till 1889. He studied law at Taylor, doing *in absentia* work, and was admitted to the bar in 1887. He is a very progressive citizen and has been engaged in several enterprises both public and private. Thus he has been in the general merchandise and lumber business, been county superintendent and for several terms county attorney. He married Miss Eva Harvey in 1886, and has three children living.

Alanson S. Moon.

MOULTON, JUDGE L. M.—was born in Woodford county, Illinois, November 19, 1839. He graduated from Eureka College in 1860 and was admitted to the bar in Nebraska June 4, 1874. He came to Franklin county, this state, in 1871, and became one of the founders of Bloomington. Later, in 1883, he moved to Loup county, where he has ever since taken an active part in public life. Mr. Moulton has seen considerable service as a soldier. In 1861 he enlisted in Co. B of the Eleventh Illinois infantry, but was discharged. In 1864 he again enlisted and served to the end of the war, taking part in the Mobile campaign. Back in Illinois he served for some time as police judge and prosecuting attorney and was judge of Franklin county, Neb., for two terms. He has also served as judge and attorney of Loup county, for two terms in each office. He is at present county judge by appointment. Mr. Moulton was married to Permeila Clingman of Woodford county, Illinois, in May 1861. The family is now pleasantly located in the north part of Taylor where the judge takes pride to show his friends one of the finest fruit orchards on the upper Loup.

RUSHO, JOSEPH—the founder of Taylor, came to Loup county in 1877, and counts himself the eleventh settler in the county. He was born in Wisconsin, May 23, 1850, and remained in his native state till thirteen years old. After living for some years in Fairbault

Joseph Rusho.

county, Minnesota, he struck out overland for Nebraska with his family and belongings. From Sioux City the course was set for Scotia, thence to Fort Hartsuff and later on up the river to the old homestead on the edge of Taylor where he now dwells. Mr. Rusho is a successful farmer and land owner. But more than this, he is a successful business man, and has for years been a leader in political and civil affairs in Loup county. He received his education in the common schools of Wisconsin and at the Milton Academy, same state. Mr. Rusho was married October 8, 1872, to Miss Josephine Murry of Delevan, Minnesota, and they are the parents of nine children, eight of whom are living. Two sons, Rusho Brothers, are engaged in the general merchandise business in Taylor and are very successful in their enterprise.

SCOTT, GEORGE F.—one of the most consistent and successful business men in the upper valley is George F. Scott of Taylor. He was born on a farm in Freeborn county, Minnesota, February 12, 1857. As he grew up his inclination for a commercial career manifested itself. He clerked in a store for a while and then attended the Mankato Normal School, rounding off his business education at the Keokuk Business College. He moved to Furnas county, Nebraska, in 1878. There at the small town of Precept, he

George F. Scott.

operated a general store till the fall of 1884. September 21st of that year he opened for business at Taylor, Loup county, under the firm name of Wheeler & Scott. He soon became sole proprietor of the business, however, and owns and operates today an as completely furnished general merchandise store as one may care to see. That Mr. Scott is enterprising, thrifty and liked by all is well demonstrated in the fact that for twenty years has he been postmaster in Taylor, change in national administration having no effect upon his incumbency of office. Mr. Scott is now a man of means. He owns 1080 acres of good farm lands and is financially interested in the Cash Mercantile Co. of Burwell and other enterprises. He was married to Della Farrand December 22, 1885. They have one daughter Aurelia and are comfortably situated in their cozy home in Taylor, set in a veritable park of shrubbery and climbing vines.

H. W. Foght.

About the Author

Born in Norway in 1869, Foght emigrated with his family from Fredrickshall, Norway, to join his father, Emil, at Fort Niobrara in the Dakota Territory in 1881. Then frightened by the Spotted Tail-Crow Dog incident, the family moved to Ord when Harold was 11 years old. After the publication of *The Trail of the Loup* in 1906, Foght went on to write articles and books on rural education as a professor of sociology at the State Normal School in Kirksville, Missouri, and as president of the Northern Normal and Industrial School at Aberdeen, South Dakota. He served seven years (1927–1933) as president of the financially troubled Municipal University of Wichita and subsequently became a director of a Navajo Agency school, a superintendent of education of the Cherokee Tribe, and in 1934 administrator of FDR's New Deal policies in the Bureau of Indian Affairs.

www.ingramcontent.com/pod-product-compliance
Lightning Source LLC
Chambersburg PA
CBHW020035120526
44588CB00031B/457